Accounting & Bookkeeping Procedures for Internal Control

The Professional's Ready-to-Use Guide to Effective and Appropriate Internal Controls

Bizmanualz, Inc.
St. Louis, MO, USA

TRADEMARKS

Bizmanualz® is a Trademark of Bizmanualz, Inc.

This publication is sold with the understanding that the publisher is not engaged in rendering legal, accounting, or other professional services. If legal advice or other expert assistance is required, the services of a competent professional should be sought. The Publisher cannot in any way guarantee the forms, agreements and statements in this manual are being used for the purpose intended and therefore assume no responsibility for their proper and correct use.

Printed in the United States of America

ISBN-13 978-1-931591-33-1

For more information about available fully editable Policy and Procedure publications visit Bizmanualz on-line at www.bizmanualz.com.

Others in the Bizmanualz Professional's Ready-to-Use Procedure Series include:

Finance & Treasury Procedures for Compliance and Performance
Computer & Network Procedures to Manage IT Systems
Sales & Marketing Procedures for Sales Pipeline Management
Business Security Procedures to Protect Assets and Employees
Disaster Recover for Business Continuity Management
Human Resources Procedures for Employee Management
ISO 9001 Standard Procedures for a Quality Management System

Cover illustration by Leo Kundas

bizmanualz®

Accounting Policies, Procedures & Forms

Section 100

Introduction

Section 100

Introduction

Introduction

This section provides an accounting primer to explain the basic concepts of accounting, its structure, standards and definitions. The need to review these concepts is greater now then ever. Please read this whole section before you begin editing your manual.

[This page intentionally left blank]

Subject Matter Expertise

JOHN MCPEEK, CPA

John McPeek is a co-author of the *Complete Guide to a Business Policy & Procedure Manual.* Mr. McPeek was also a co-author in the development the *ISO 9000 Production & Documentation Manual.* Mr. McPeek has over 18 years of operational management experience with both start-up and larger busineses.

He started as a CPA with McGladrey & Pullen, LLP, a leading CPA firm serving middle-market businesses. He then moved on to a few start-up medical and dental manufacturing companies serving in various capacities as Corporate Controller, Vice-President of Finance and Operations, and President. While in these positions, he was instrumental in establishing company wide organizational policies and procedures as well as implementing protocols for meeting Food & Drug Administration regulatory requirements for medical devices and Department of Defense contract requirements.

He is currently the President of ASI Medical, Inc. located in Englewood, Colorado and is personally responsible for the innovative design and manufacturing of their line of products. He is a graduate of Colorado State University holding a Bachelor of Science Degree in Business Administration.

BUD CARLSON, CPA

Bud Carlson brings together over 29 years of public accounting, retail and business management experience. Mr. Carlson has successfully worked both in finance, management and accounting.

As a business owner, he managed his own company for six years before selling the business. As an accountant, he has spent nine years as a CPA and computer audit specialist at KPMG Peat Marwick auditing various retail and wholesale distributors including prominent SEC clients.

He has implemented numerous management reporting systems for a various small to mid-sized businesses. Mr. Carlson holds a Bachelor of Science in Business from the University of Denver and a Bachelor of Science in Accounting from Thomas College. He is an active member of AICPA.

JAMES N. SKELTON

James Skelton has been writing policies & procedures for over twenty-five years. He has personally authored manuals on topics from administration, operations, training, to employee handbooks, personnel, policy and procedures, and accounting.

He has attended professional courses in Human Resource Management, Human Resource Management Certification (PHR), Project Management, Defense Resource Management, and National Security Planning for U.S. Global Strategic Policy. He has a background in human resource management & consulting, and has extensive background in administration, management, and technical writing. Mr. Skelton is certified as a Professional in Human Resources (PHR) through the Society for Human Resource Management and is currently an active member of the Society.

He holds a Bachelor of Science Degree in Management and Organizational Development from the University of West Florida and graduate level education in Systems Engineering and Aerospace Safety from the University of Southern California and Arizona State University respectively. He additionally has received professional education at the Naval Postgraduate School in Monterey, California and the University of Denver.

CHRISTOPHER J. ANDERSON, MBA

Chris Anderson has over 18 years of sales, marketing and business management operations experience working with small to large corporations. Over the past twelve years, he has managed, owned or worked with numerous small companies to develop profitable operations through more clearly defined processes.

He served as President of Investorsoftware.com, a catalog, Internet and mail order company specializing in finance & investment analysis books & software. He served as Vice President at Arc Tangent, a direct mail marketing software publisher where he managed all operations, sales, and administration.

Before Arc Tangent, Mr. Anderson managed North American distribution sales for Interactive Systems, a UNIX operating system developer and publisher. He has worked as a marketing analyst at Nixdorf Computer Corporation, an electrical engineer for McDonnell Douglas Corporation developing missile simulation software for the US Navy as well as developing MIL-STD documentation. He served as a Lieutenant and Aeronautical Engineering Duty Officer for the US Navy working for the Naval Air Systems Command.

He is currently the Managing Director of Bizmanualz, Inc. He holds a Master in Business Administration from Pepperdine University and a Bachelor of Science degree in Electrical Engineering from Southern Illinois University.

Table of Contents

PROCEDURES

Table of Forms

REFERENCES

1. Age Discrimination In Employment Act (ADEA)
2. Americans with Disabilities Act (ADA)
3. Bad Check Law
4. Civil Rights Act of 1964
5. Employee Polygraph Protection Act
6. Employee Retirement Income Security Act (ERISA)
7. Equal Credit Opportunity Act (ECOA)
8. Equal Pay Act
9. Executive Order 11246
10. Fair Credit Billing Act (FCBA)
11. Fair Credit Reporting Act (FCRA)
12. Fair Debt Collection Practices Act (FDCP)
13. Fair Labor Standards Act (FLSA)
14. Family and Medical Leave Act (FMLA)
15. Federal Accounting Standards Board (FASB)
16. Food and Drug Administration (FDA) Food Code
17. FRB Reg B: Equal Credit Opportunity Act
18. FRB Reg D: Reserve Requirements Of Depository Institutions
19. FRB Reg E: Electronic Fund Transfer Act
20. FRB Reg Z: Truth In Lending Act
21. Generally Accepted Accounting Principles (GAAP)
22. Guide to Record Retention Requirements
23. Health Insurance Portability Accountability Act (HIPAA)
24. Immigration Reform & Control Act (IRCA)
25. Interstate Commerce Act
26. IRS Publication 946 How To Depreciate Property
27. IRS Revenue Procedure 98-25 Records Retention
28. Occupational Safety & Health Act (OSHA)
29. Rehabilitation Act of 1973
30. Right To Financial Privacy ACT
31. Trust Fund Recovery Penalty
32. Truth In Lending Act (TILA)
33. Uniform Commercial Code (UCC)

PROCEDURES

General & Administrative

1. G&A101 Chart Of Accounts
2. G&A102 Files and Records Management
3. G&A103 Travel and Entertainment
4. G&A104 Management Reports
5. G&A105 Period-End Review & Closing
6. G&A106 Controlling Legal Costs
7. G&A107 Taxes and Insurance
8. G&A108 Property Tax Assessments
9. G&A109 Confidential Information Release
10. G&A110 Document Control

FORMS

13. G&A107 Ex1 Tax Calendar of Recurring Monthly Dates
14. G&A109 Ex1 Non-Disclosure Agreement
15. G&A110 Ex1 Request For Document Change
16. G&A110 Ex2 Document Change Control

Cash

17. CSH101 Ex1 Daily Cash Report
18. CSH102 Ex1 Deposit Log
19. CSH103 Ex1 Bad Check Notice
20. CSH104 Ex1 Bank Wire Instructions
21. CSH104 Ex2 Wire Transfer Form
22. CSH105 Ex1 Check Signing Authority Log
23. CSH106 Ex1 Check Request
24. CSH107 Ex1 Sample Bank and Book Balances Reconciliation

Inventory & Assets

25. INV101 Ex1 Inventory Requisition
26. INV102 Ex1 Inventory Count Sheet
27. INV102 Ex2 Inventory Tag
28. INV103 Ex1 Capital Asset Requisition
29. INV103 Ex2 Asset Disposition Form
30. INV103 Ex3 Bill Of Sale
31. INV104 Ex1 Material Return Notice

Revenue

32. REV101 Ex1 Sales Order
33. REV101 Ex2 Order Form
34. REV102 Ex1 Phone Confirmation Checklist
35. REV103 Ex1 Credit Application
36. REV103 Ex2 Request For Credit Approval
37. REV103 Ex3 Credit Inquiry
38. REV104 Ex1 Shipping Log
39. REV104 Ex2 Commercial Invoice
40. REV105 Ex1 Invoice
41. REV105 Ex2 Accounts Receivable Write-Off Authorization
42. REV108 Ex1 Account Collection Control Form
43. REV109 Ex1 Returned Goods Authorization

Purchasing

44. PUR101 Ex1 New Vendor Notification
45. PUR101 Ex2 Vendor Survey Form
46. PUR102 Ex1 Purchase Requisition
47. PUR102 Ex2 Purchase Order
48. PUR102 Ex3 Purchase Order Log
49. PUR102 Ex4 Purchase Order Follow-Up
50. PUR102 Ex5 Daily Sundry Payable Log
51. PUR103 Ex1 Order and Arrival Log
52. PUR104 Ex1 Receiving Log
53. PUR104 Ex2 Receiving and Inspection Report
54. PUR104 Ex3 Inventory Inspection Levels

[This page intentionally left blank]

Introduction

Who Needs Accounting Policies and Procedures?

This introduction is an accounting primer to explain the basic concepts of accounting, its structure, standards and definitions. The need to review these concepts is greater now then ever. On one hand, popular accounting programs for small and mid-sized businesses have become more widely used than ever before, and on the other hand, industry consolidation has significantly reduced the accounting program choices to just a handful.

These choices are typically inexpensive, easy to implement, and come with little support to develop appropriate policies and procedures to ensure that the data generated by these programs is accurate and complete. Entry-level software like Quickbooks® and mid-level software like MAS-90 or Great Plains share this common deficiency. The "support" documentation is long on the explanation of user features and short on policy and procedural advice for appropriate use.

The Recent Past

Only twenty years ago, small to medium sized businesses faced daunting choices for selecting an accounting system. There were only three choices: Continue to use a full manual system (a comprehensive pegboard "one-write" system, employing many journals anchored to an imposing cloth bound general ledger book that rivaled the size of the largest Webster's Dictionary), purchase or lease a computerized accounting system, or build your own.

The manual systems were not trivial. They were produced by major firms, which provided on-site implementation and training. These systems were well documented with many policies and procedures built into the regimented use of the "one-write" journals and corresponding ledgers.

An alternative decision was to purchase or lease an automated information system. But this required another decision of whether to buy a "ready made" product or build your own. To make this decision, the company would typically hire a consultant or CPA firm to perform a comprehensive "needs" analysis. The consultant would eventually select, either a commercially built multi-module accounting program (like Solomon, our Real World), or a programmer to develop the structure from custom code (RPG was a popular language used to create custom accounting programs).

Either one of these alternatives would have to run on a leased or purchased dedicated mini-computer system, (the IBM 36 was the popular mid-size business choice for many years). Both solutions required tremendous resources in time and money. Even the "ready made" solutions required plenty of additional programming to fit it into the specific company's needs. For a half a year or more, various consultants, programmers and specialists would write code, test and rewrite code.

In either case, documentation was paramount. Hence policies and procedures, as they applied to the mechanics of the accounting system were well documented as a by-product of the installation and implementation process. The total costs in the purchase or lease of the hardware and software (ready made or custom built), and in the company's own human resources, was staggering.

The Present

Imagine the months of decision making preparation, the months of development, the reams of documentation and the total costs that easily went from tens of thousands, to hundreds of thousands of dollars. Compare this to the present practice occurring throughout the country on a daily basis. The owner, or the owner's controller or other designee walks into a local retailer, picks up a copy of the most successfully marketed accounting software package, (i.e.: the one occupying the most prime and visible shelf space), drives back to the office, and loads the program on any available PC computer. There you have it: the decision making process, "needs" analysis, implementation and installation; all for the price of $299!

The future

The future begins today, with your purchase of this ***Bizmanualz™ Accounting Policies, Procedures and Forms***. This manual is needed more now than ever. Accounting systems are more accessible than ever before. Unfortunately, they come with no instructions. The user guide that comes with the accounting software only explains what the menu options do, it doesn't explain which options result in sound accounting practices.

Accounting software is looking more and more like your own internet browser home page, (no surprise since each manufacturer is competing to be your primary web portal). In the process, the actual functions of accounting are less obvious, and as a result, less understood. This introduction is a look behind the scenes of the "splash screen". Hopefully, by understanding the concepts and consistent accounting rules utilized by all accounting software programs, you will develop more confidence to rely on the information generated by the program and you will be able to use it more effectively to run your company.

Accounting Basics

Three important terms that are easily confused:

- **Bookkeeping**
- **Accounting**
- **Reporting**

What are they and how do they interrelate?

Bookkeeping

Bookkeeping and accounting share two basic goals:

- To keep track of income and expenses, thereby improving The Company's ability to achieve profitability
- To collect the necessary financial information about The Company's business to file required reports and tax returns

Bookkeeping refers to the actual transactional entering and recording of data. Examples are writing checks, processing payroll, making deposits, recording disbursements and recording receipts.

Accounting

Accounting encompasses the broader responsibilities over developing and maintaining the accounting system under which bookkeeping functions are performed. Accounting is concerned with the timely and accurate recording of transactions, providing useful management information, and properly reporting such information for various user needs. Developing and maintaining an accounting system involves setting up and maintaining an appropriate chart of accounts for the particular business. Policies and procedures are then established to provide guidance for all possible financial transactions, from source documents (checks, sales orders, etc.), to journals (payroll journal, cash disbursement journal, invoice register, etc.), to the general ledger, (based on the chart of accounts), and ultimately to a variety of reports for all internal and external needs.

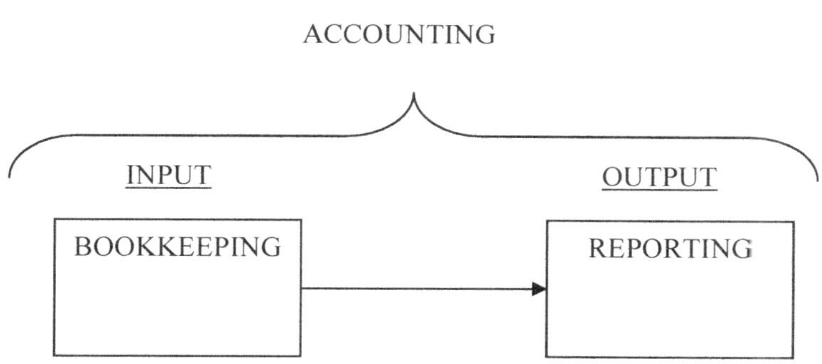

Bookkeeping and reporting can be thought of as the input and output of a complete accounting system. Accounting policies and procedures ensure

The **integrity** of the **input data**

and

The **accuracy** and **validity** of the **report output.**

Reporting

Reporting, (the output of the data generated through various bookkeeping functions), is used for both internal and external purposes.

Internal Reports are reports used within the company, by both management and other designated personnel. Internal reporting can be further divided into financial and non-financial data.

Non-financial data

Non-financial data includes a variety of measurement and productivity data, applicable to the specific business. These can be daily customer count, web page "hits", production activity per employee hour, units and total weight of product shipped, or even daily weather conditions.

Financial data

Examples of financial data reports include:

- Financial statements - Profit and loss reports (income statement), balance sheets and cash flow statements
- Daily reports with critical balances, such as, sales, cash level, inventory, accounts receivable and accounts payable
- Segmented profit and loss reports (or P/L) on specific jobs, profit centers or departments
- Register reports, listing all transactions for specific areas such as, payroll, checks, receipts, invoices, etc.
- Listings of source data files such as customer, employee, vendor and inventory lists.
- Aging reports for both Customers (accounts receivable or A/R) and Vendors (accounts payables or A/P)
- Inventory reports for costing and valuation
- Exception reports - open purchase orders, back orders, inventory stock outs.

External reports generated for the use of people or organizations outside of the business. Report data and format will vary depending on user:

- ***Banks, lending institutions.*** To observe the financial viability of a business and to determine its ability to support additional amounts and types of debt financing
- ***Employees.*** To determine the stability of the business of their employer - this may be useful in wage negotiations
- ***Suppliers.*** To assess the suitability of granting credit terms to a business
- ***Existing and Potential Investors.*** To assess the potential risk of investing in a business and to monitor the status of existing investment in a business

- ***Public.*** To gain more insight into any business, which is legally required to make certain financial information available
- ***Government.*** To fulfill the requirements of all applicable local, state and federal reporting statutes, including income, sales, insurance, property, and payroll tax returns
- ***Media / Press.*** To use available business reports in specific trade and business publications

Components of an Accounting System

The financial transactions of any accounting system can be grouped into four major transaction cycle groups: Revenue Cycle, Purchase Cycle, Payroll Cycle, and General Journal Cycle.

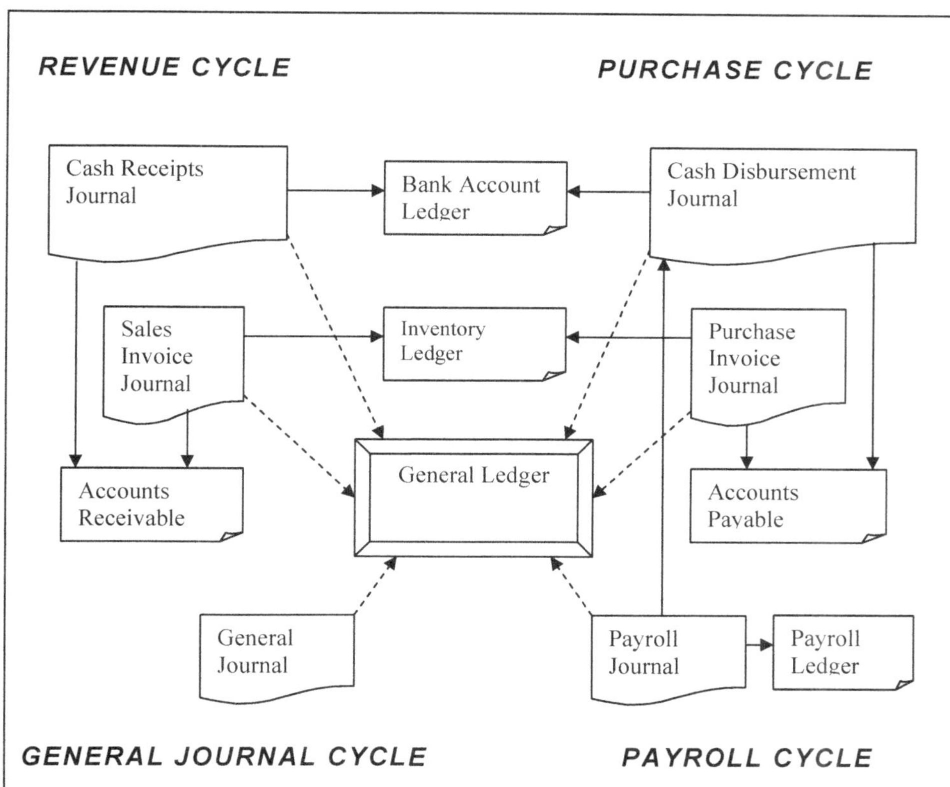

Transactions in the form of sales invoices, receipts, purchase invoices, checks and payroll entries are posted to the appropriate journals. Simultaneously, these postings are also recorded in the General Ledger. The General Ledger accumulates all transaction activity, organized by account classification. Various reports, including financial statements can then be prepared from the data collected in the General Ledger. Corrections or necessary adjustments can be made to the General Ledger by creating adjusting journal entries, posted to the general journal.

The following outline on the next two pages provides more explanatory detail on these four cycles:

1. Revenue Cycle

Order Entry

Invoices entered through direct entry, through sales orders or through a point-of-sales system, (such as a cash register) are posted to the sales journal.

These entries also accumulate on the accounts receivable ledger, organized by customer.

If the business maintains an inventory, the posting of sales also affects the inventory ledger.

Finally, all sales journal activity is also posted to the general ledger

Cash Receipts / Deposits

Receipts on sales and other bank deposits are posted to the cash receipts journal.

Sales receipts information also accumulates on the accounts receivable ledger, organized by customer.

These postings are also entered on the bank account ledger.

Finally, all cash receipts journal activity is also posted to the general ledger.

Accounts Receivable

Accounts Receivable is a separate journal that records both sales and cash receipt data by customer.

The data comes from the postings to the cash receipts journal and the sales invoice journal.

2. Purchase Cycle

Purchase Orders / Purchasing

Invoices entered through direct entry or through purchase orders are posted to the purchase journal

These entries also accumulate on the accounts payable ledger, organized by vendor.

If the business maintains an inventory, the posting of purchases also affects the inventory ledger.

Finally, all purchase journal activity is also posted to the general ledger

Cash Disbursements / Checks

Payments on account or for expenses are posted to the cash disbursement journal.

Payment on account information also accumulates on the accounts payable ledger, organized by vendor.

These postings are also entered on the bank account ledger.

Finally, all cash disbursement journal activity is also posted to the general ledger.

Accounts Payable

Accounts Payable is a separate journal that records both sales and cash receipt data by vendor.

The data comes from the postings to the cash disbursement journal and the purchase journal.

3. Payroll Cycle

Payroll data, by employee, for each payroll data is entered into the payroll journal.

These postings are also entered in the cash disbursements journal and the payroll ledger.

Finally, all payroll journal activity is also posted to the general ledger.

4. General Journal Cycle

Corrections or adjustments to the above major transaction cycles can be made through adjusting journal entries, posted directly to the General Ledger.

These are compiled in a separate journal, known as the General Journal.

How does posting work?

The specific postings, as outlined in the cycles above, do not necessarily take place as separate steps, especially in computerized environments. There are only two basic methods of posting in computerized accounting systems: real-time posting and batch posting.

In real-time posting, the source transaction, (check, bill, payment, receipt, etc.), is posted to the specific journal and any related subsidiary ledgers (accounts receivable, accounts payable, inventory, bank account, etc.), and is simultaneously posted to the general ledger.

In batch posting, the journals and subsidiary ledgers are posted, but entries are not yet posted to the general ledger. Posting these journals to the general ledger is done separately. Typically, a group of transactions is entered, a full day's worth, for example. Later, after the journals are reviewed for accuracy, this entire day's group, or "batch" is posted to the general ledger.

To understand this posting process better, it would be helpful to follow specific transactions through a sample company. First, however, we need to define various accounting terms and concepts.

Accounting Terms and Concepts

Double-Entry Accounting

We can justifiably thank the 14th century Italian merchants for developing the double-entry system of accounting that we still use today. It is widely believed that Benedetto Cotrugli was the first to document this concept of double-entry accounting. In 1458, he wrote *Delia Mercatura et del Mercante Perfetto (Of Trading and the Perfect Trader)*, which included a brief chapter describing many of the features of double entry accounting.

Years later in 1494, Luca Pacioli, from San Sepulcro in medieval Tuscany, published The *Summa*'s 36 short chapters on bookkeeping, entitled "De Computis et Scripturis" ("Of Reckonings and Writings"), so that the subjects of the Duke of Urbino could learn how to conduct business and to provide the trader with a fast method to determine his assets and liabilities.

For centuries before, commercial transactions had been recorded and journalized, whether on paper, papyrus or clay tablets. However, these journals provided only totals of transaction groupings. It was the Italians that first recognized that it is impossible for a business transaction to occur without affecting at least TWO accounts. There can never be only one effect from a transaction.

An Italian farmer sells wood to a shipbuilder for 400 ducats. To account for this transaction he would record: wood sale - 400 ducats. His "sales" account has been increased by 400 ducats. But, what else has happened? What other account was affected? His "cash" account also increased by 400 ducats. What if he sells his wood to the shipbuilder on credit, and he receives no cash? In this case it's his "accounts receivable" account, which increased by 400 ducats.

There are always, at least two sides to each transaction.

Later, when the shipbuilder pays his debt to the farmer, the farmer records an increase in his cash and a decrease in his accounts receivable by 400 ducats, respectively. You can see that an integral feature of this double entry system is that **the transactions must equal.** At the time, this new method was heralded as an astounding discovery, and was described as: "a magic mirror in which the adept sees both himself and others."

Today, double entry bookkeeping is used as a method of recording a transaction in two or more different places or ledger accounts. This practice simplifies finding errors since the totals of both ledger accounts should agree.

Debits = Credits

Bookkeeping entries are divided into DEBITS and CREDITS. The DEBIT side is typically on the left of the ledger page and the CREDITS are placed on the right. The origin of the words "Debits" and "Credits" come from the simple concept: who owes you and whom do you owe.

DEBITS record transactions relating to purchases, expenses or increases in the assets of the organization. CREDITS record transactions relating to revenues or an increase in the equity and liabilities of the organization. Recording a transaction requires both a DEBIT and a CREDIT entry. If the entries have been correctly recorded, then the totals from both sides of the ledger should agree.

This method of double-entry bookkeeping, where we list debits on one side and credits on the other is marked by the absolute requirement that those two columns sum to zero. It's the basis for tracking all our vast financial affairs today.

The following list illustrates the effect of posting either a DEBIT or CREDIT entry on each major account type:

Account Type	Debits	Credits
Assets	Increases	Decreases
Liabilities	Decreases	Increases
Owners Equity	Decreases	Increases
Income	Decreases	Increases
Expenses	Increases	Decreases

These account types are the general account classifications used in all accounting systems. They are also used to organize the general ledger, from which financial statements are developed.

An expansion of these account types is outlined below.

Basic Accounting Structure

Balance sheet

Contains accounts whose value is determined at a specific point in time

Assets - accounts with value that you own

- Cash - the amount on hand or in the bank at a specific point in time
- Accounts Receivable - how much people owe you
- Inventory - the value of business merchandise for sale
- Fixed Assets - the value of property and equipment

Liabilities - accounts with value that you owe to others

- Accounts Payable - how much you owe others for unpaid purchases
- Debt - how much you owe others for money borrowed
- Other Liabilities - services or money owed to others

Equity

- Contributed Capital - money invested in business by ownership

- Distributions - dividends and other types of money paid out to ownership
- Capital Stock - money invested in exchange for company ownership
- Retained Earnings - earnings retained in business from net profits

Income Statement

Contains accounts whose value is determined over a period of time (day, week, month, year, etc).

Income:	total sales and income recorded over a period time
Expenses:	total purchases and other expenses recorded over a period of time

Basic Accounting Formula:

All transactions are posted to one or more of these accounts. As discussed earlier, every posted transaction must balance. That is, debits must equal credits. Furthermore, the result of every posting, if done correctly, will never put the Basic Accounting Formula out of balance. All asset accounts will always equal the total of all liability and owner equity accounts. If this formula is ever out of balance, the cause will always be an incorrect transaction posting where debits did not equal credits.

Assets include those accounts, which give value to the company: cash, accounts receivable, inventory, property, etc. Liabilities are those accounts which reduce the company's value: accounts payable, debt, and other liabilities. If total assets are greater than liabilities, then this **net value** (that is, the total of all assets minus liabilities) represents the true value of the business, otherwise known as its **Equity.** Hence, the Basic Accounting Formula can be expressed and equally understood in these two ways:

Assets = Liabilities + Equity

or

Assets- Liabilities = Equity

If the company's assets are less than its liabilities, then it will necessarily show a negative equity. This makes intuitive sense to anyone following the demise of a business in bankruptcy. When a business owes more than it has in value, the resulting negative equity is an obvious warning sign.

The equity accounts include owner's contributions, distributions, and retained earnings. Retained earnings operate in a manner unique to all other accounts. It contains the net effect of postings to all income and expense accounts. It is truly the one account, which links the balance sheet accounts (assets, liabilities and owner's equity) with the income and expense accounts.

Understanding the importance of retained earnings, the Basic Accounting Equation could be expanded thus:

Investor and owner contributions, and distributions — Retained Earnings

ASSETS = LIABILITIES + (OWNER'S EQUITY ACCOUNTS + INCOME - EXPENSE)

EQUITY

The following illustrates the interrelationship of these accounts:

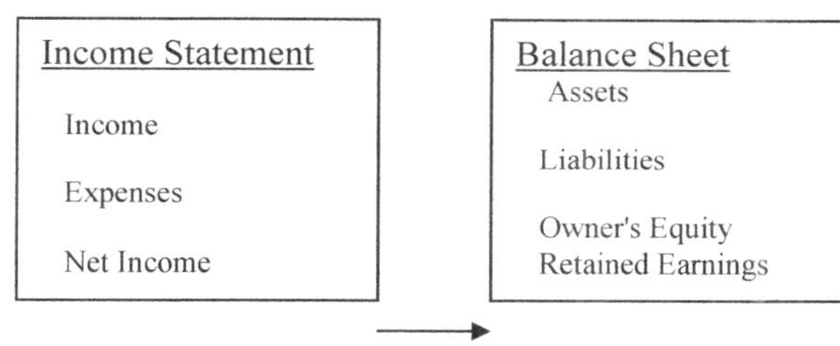

When a transaction, like writing a check or paying a bill, is executed in an accounting program, the software is designed to take this transaction event and create the proper and necessary debit and credit entries to record the effects of the transaction in the appropriate journals and general ledger accounts.

SUMMARY OF ACCOUNTING CYCLES & ACCOUNTING CONCEPTS

CASE STUDY

Slick Switch Co. - Example Company

Now that the accounting terms and concepts have been defined and explained and the accounting cycles have been presented, it's time to put it all together.

Regardless of the cycle, specific transactions are posted through journals and into the general ledger in a similar fashion.

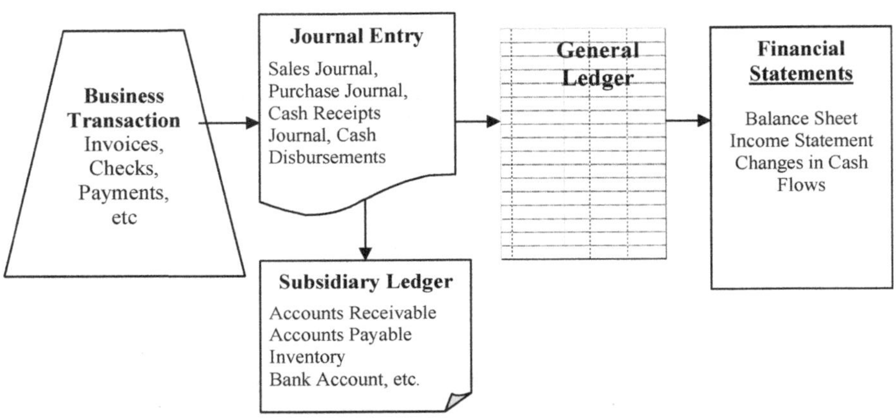

When a transaction is posted in the computer, a journal entry is automatically created along with any necessary entry to subsidiary ledgers. Subsidiary ledgers are specific lists of detail transactions. For example, the Accounts Receivable ledger organizes all invoice and cash receipt transactions by customer. Likewise, the Inventory ledger organizes all purchase and sale transactions by inventory item.

In real-time posting system, the journal entries are also, simultaneously posted to the applicable general ledger account. The general ledger contains **all** transaction postings, classified by account. The accounts are organized in the same manner as balance sheet and income statement financial statements. The order of accounts starts with the asset accounts, then the liability accounts, then the equity accounts, and finally, the income and expense accounts.

All forms of financial statements can be generated from the general ledger. Financial statements are simply a reporting component of any accounting program.

To better understand the complete process of double entry accounting through the accounting cycle process, the following pages diagram purchase and revenue cycle transactions, from purchase of merchandise to sales invoice and final collection on the sale, for the company, Slick Switch Co. We shall also assume that this business utilizes an inventory module to track inventory.

SLICK SWITCH, CO - PURCHASE CYCLE EXAMPLE

PURCHASE TRANSACTION

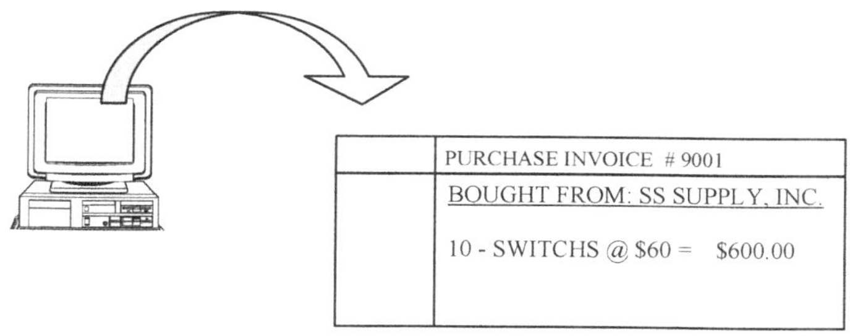

A purchase invoice is entered into the computer, when product is purchased and the bill is received from vendor.

The computer makes the following postings ***simultaneously!***:

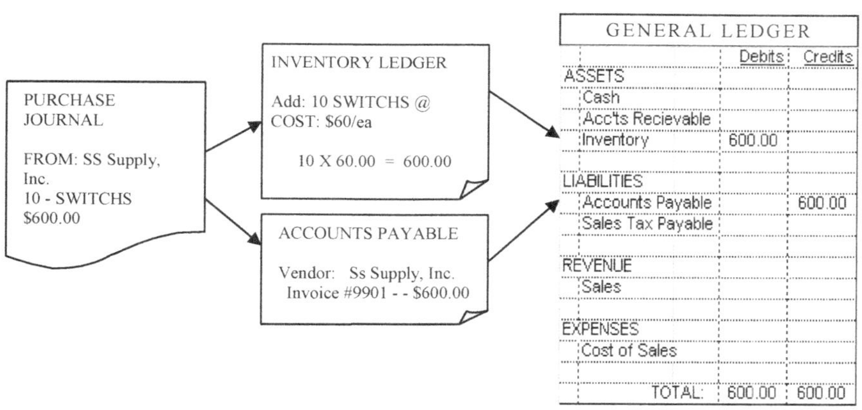

Several posting events happen automatically as a result of a single purchase entry in the computer. The purchase journal is updated to add this transaction, the inventory subsidiary ledger has an additional 10 switches added, at a cost of $60 each, and the accounts payable subsidiary ledger has an additional invoice of $600 included with Vendor: SS Supply, Inc. If this is a real-time posting system, the general ledger is also updated to reflect both the inventory and the accounts payable increase.

Notice, that there is no expense recorded at this time. The value of the inventory has increased by $600, but the company has not recorded any expense. Only when product is sold, will the cost of the product be expensed. This reflects a very important **matching** concept in accounting. The cost of the product is matched to the related sale, at the time of sale, not at the time it is purchased and added to inventory.

SLICK SWITCH, CO - REVENUE CYCLE EXAMPLE

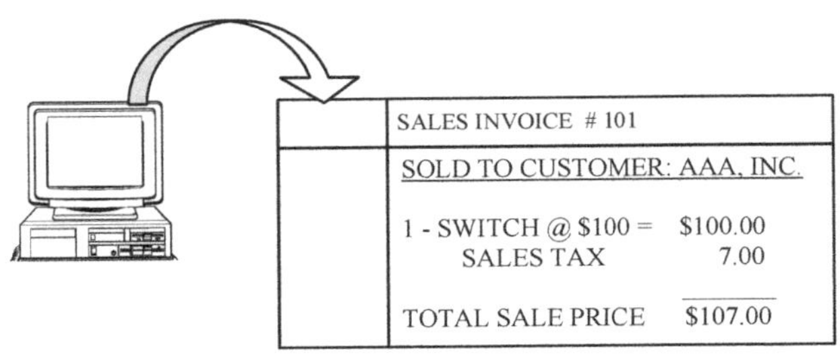

A sales order is entered into the computer, and a sales invoice is printed.

The computer makes the following postings ***simultaneously!***:

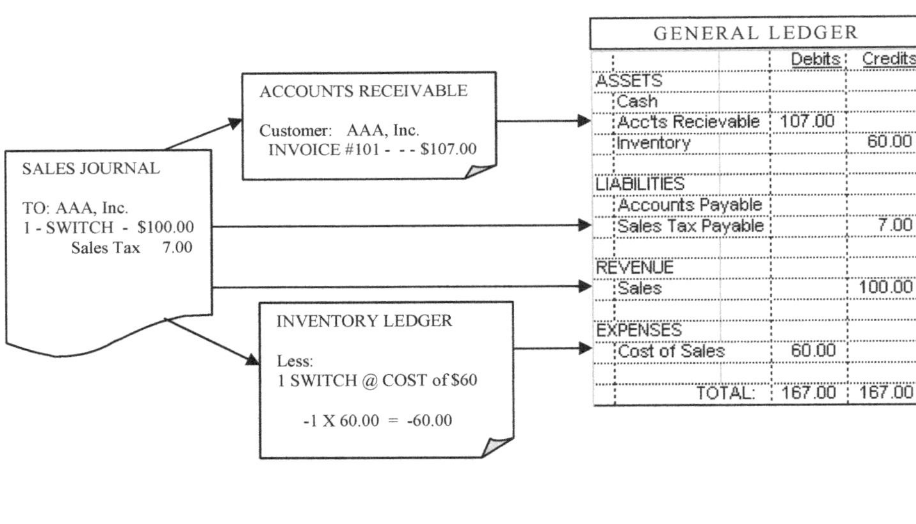

Notice how many postings are occurring from just one sales invoice. The bookkeeper enters a single invoice and the computer automatically posts journals, subsidiary ledgers and the general ledger, simultaneously. To the bookkeeper it might seem like a single entry is being made (1 switch @ $100.00). However, behind the scenes, the computer program is judiciously posting double entries for each transaction, ensuring that all debits and credits equal.

On the debit side, a receivable of $107.00 is recorded. On the credit side, a sale of $100.00 is recorded and a payable to the state for sales tax of $7.00 is recorded.

Notice that the program is now recording an expense of $60, representing the cost of the product sold . Simultaneously, it is reducing the inventory asset account by $60. In the end, all debits and credits are equal.

SLICK SWITCH, CO - FINANCIAL STATEMENT REPORT #1

Before posting any more transactions, let's produce financial statements based on the activity recorded so far. Remember that financial statements are one of many types of reports that can be prepared from the data compiled in the general ledger.

The Balance Sheet and Income Statement would look like this:

Slick Switch Company
Balance Sheet

Assets	
Cash	
Accts Rec	107
Inventory	540
Total Assets	$ 647
Liabilities & Equity	
Accts Pay	600
Sales Tax Pay	7
Retained Earn.	40
Total Liab /Equity	$ 647

Slick Switch Company
Income Statement

Income	
Sales	100
Total Income	100
Expenses	
Cost of Sales	60
Total Expenses	60
Net Income	$ 40

Slick Switch Co. shows total assets of $647 and total liabilities of $607. Using the Basic Accounting Formula, this means that Slick Switch Co. has a positive equity (or net worth) of $40. Note that the retained earnings (equity) of $40 is indeed equal to the earnings recorded on the income statement. This illustrates the relationship between these two statements.

Notice that the financial statements show a profit of $40, even though no actual cash was either spent or deposited. So far, no money has changed hands. Slick Switch bought its inventory and credit and also extended credit to its customer.

We will now add two more transactions to Slick Switch and see what the effect will be on the financial statements. The following examples will illustrate the payment of Slick Switch's bill to SS Supply, Inc. and the deposit of money received from AAA, Inc. on the open invoice.

SLICK SWITCH, CO - PURCHASE CYCLE EXAMPLE

CASH DISBURSEMENT TRANSACTION

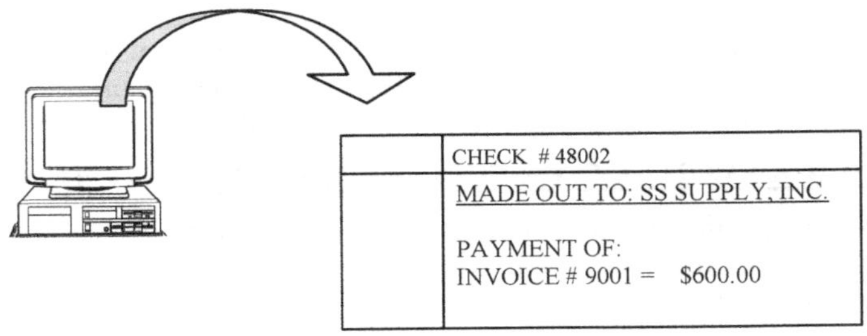

A payment is entered into the computer and a check is printed, made out to SS Supply, Inc. for $600.

The computer makes the following postings ***simultaneously!***:

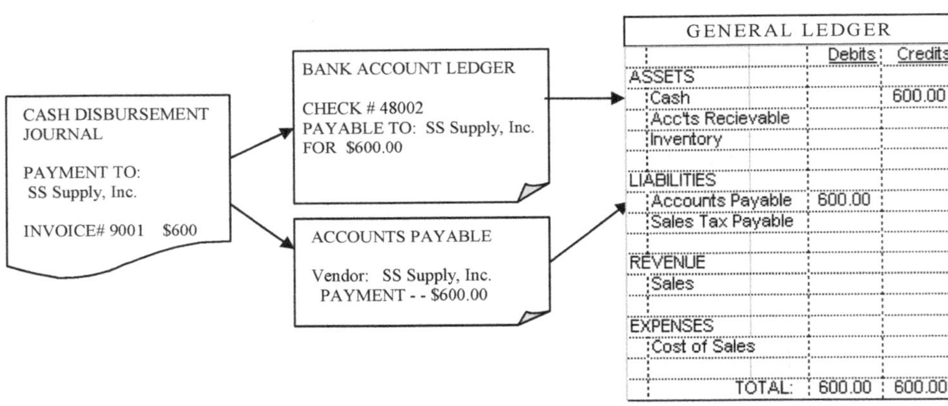

The bookkeeper simply records the payment and prints out the check. The accounting program automatically reduces cash for the check written and reduces accounts payable for the payment of the $600 bill owed to SS Supply, Inc.

SLICK SWITCH, CO - REVENUE CYCLE EXAMPLE

CASH RECEIPT TRANSACTION

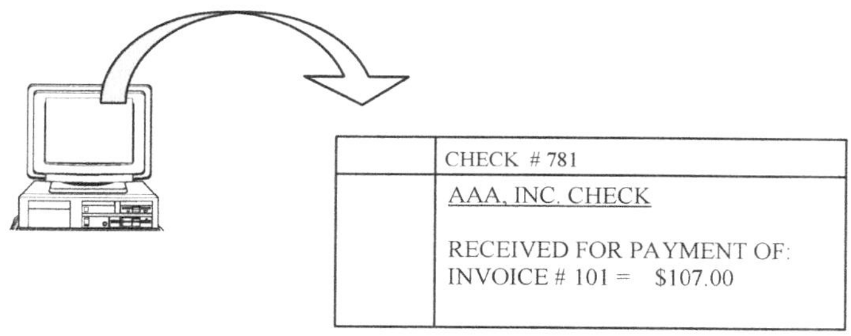

A cash receipt is entered into the computer and a deposit is made to the bank for $107 received from AAA, Inc.

The computer makes the following postings ***simultaneously!***:

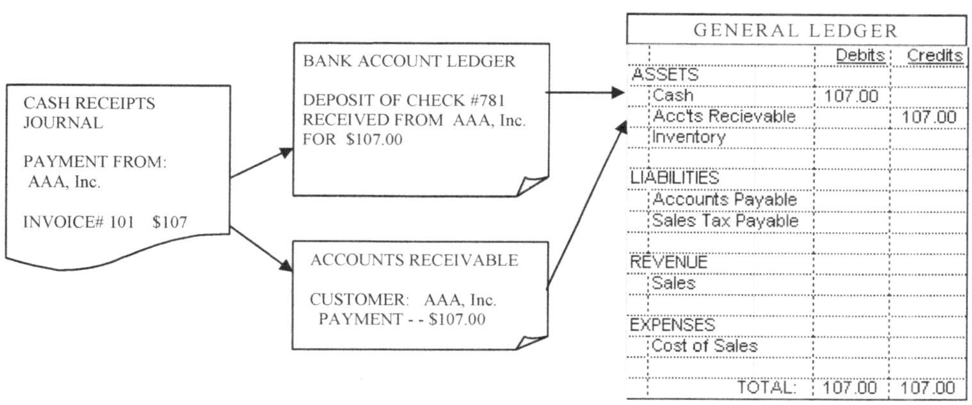

The bookkeeper simply records the payment received and deposits the money in the company's bank account. The accounting program automatically increases cash for the amount deposited and reduces accounts receivable for the payment of the $107 invoice owed from AAA, Inc.

SLICK SWITCH, CO - FINANCIAL STATEMENT REPORT #2

Now that both a payment has been made and money received, let's see what the effect is on the financial statements.

The Balance Sheet and Income Statement would now look like this:

Slick Switch Company
Balance Sheet

Assets	
Cash	(493)
Accts Rec	-
Inventory	540
Total Assets	$ 47
Liabilities & Equity	
Accts Pay	-
Sales Tax Pay	7
Retained Earn.	40
Total Liab /Equity	$ 47

Slick Switch Company
Income Statement

Income	
Sales	100
Total Income	100
Expenses	
Cost of Sales	60
Total Expenses	60
Net Income	$ 40

The most noticeable feature of these statements is the negative cash balance of $493. Naturally, it would be difficult to overdraw this amount. As a practical matter, this company would have started its business with a certain amount in its bank account, as a beginning equity contribution by the owner. Still, this example accurately illustrates the fact that a company's cash position can change significantly, even when its earnings don't change at all. Notice that the earnings are the same as in the first example.

This is a good example of the most common complaint voiced by business owners as they try to understand their own financial statements. "How can my income statement show that I'm making a profit, when I have no cash?!" Most business owners have encountered this situation, which proves the maxim:

"Cash, not profits, drives a business."

In Slick Switch's example, although a nice profit was earned on the $100 sale, the investment in inventory is consuming more cash than the company has. To remain solvent it must either borrow or inject additional working capital funds from the owner or other investors. A growing company is rarely be able to fund its growth on profits, alone. It will generally need some working capital, from either equity or debt to provide enough cash to transact business.

This dramatically demonstrates the need for a third type of financial statement: Statement of Changes in Financial Position. This is a third statement, generally included with the Balance Sheet and the Income Statement, as a necessary part of a complete financial report.

There are several ways to produce this, which are beyond the scope of this Accounting Introduction. Suffice it to say that this statement is designed to inform the reader of all the transactions that affected cash. It helps to answer the question;

"If I'm making a profit, where's my cash?"

Below is an example of an abbreviated Statement of Changes in Financial Position based on the Slick Switch, Co. example.

Slick Switch Company
Statement of Changes in Financial Position

Sources of Cash	
Net Earnings	40
Increase in Sales Tax Payable	7
Uses of Cash	
Increase in Inventory	540
Net Change in Financial Position	$ (493)

This ending number agrees with the change in cash. For many businesses, the changes that occur to cash are the most critical factors in its strategic planning. The Statement of Changes in Financial Position is helpful in this effort. However, all three financial statements should be used and referred to equally.

Accounting Structure - Accounting Software Programs

A final word concerning accounting structure is needed, here. While it is helpful to understand the accounting structure in terms of its four basic cycles (revenue, purchasing, payroll and general), and its implementation in terms of the double-entry, debit and credit system, most accounting programs are not organized in the same manner.

To navigate more easily in any accounting software it is important to understand the basic organizational structure that is common to all accounting software. In spite of all the ancillary menu options and all the different terms used by competing software products, there are really only three major components of any accounting software package: Input, Output, and Maintenance.

Input refers to all of the "bookkeeping" tasks of all four accounting cycles. This includes entering invoices, checks, bills, payments, payroll and adjusting entries. Each accounting software may "disguise" this input function under different names: "tasks" or "activities", or it may include specific input functions separately under each cycle area, or it may simply provide icon pictures of activities to be clicked on. Regardless of the specialized "look" of the program, the most important and most heavily used routine in any accounting software is data input.

Output refers to all of the reporting functions of the program. Once transactional data has been entered, the only usefulness in having it entered is the ability to retrieve it in a variety of report formats. Generally, these reporting options are found grouped together under one menu, not surprisingly labeled, "reports"! However, with some programs, they are scattered throughout the menus as appendages to each major cycle activity.

Maintenance can be broken down into two sub-categories: utility maintenance and data file maintenance. Utility maintenance refers to overall utility features like backup, restore, import and export data, fiscal year close, purge or condense data and repair data. These are all usually found on one menu and are generally placed under administrative password control to prevent unwanted casual use.

Data file maintenance does require data input, but the input is not transactional. This refers to the creation and maintenance of the chart of accounts (in support of the general ledger), the customer list, vendor list, inventory list and employee list. These are generally found in one area usually labeled "maintain" or "lists". In other programs they may be separated and found within each module (i.e.: customer list in the accounts receivable module or revenue cycle).

Understanding how your own accounting software works, (where its input, output and maintenance functions are and how the four accounting cycles are organized), is as important as understanding the actual double entry accounting that is occurring "behind the scenes". As you will discover throughout the Accounting Policies and Procedures Manual, you need to know how the numbers have developed and where they came from, in order to establish effective policies and procedures to insure their integrity, accuracy and completeness.

Accounting Methods

Accrual Method

The accounting method used in the Slick Switch Company example is called the accrual method, defined as the method of keeping accounts which shows expenses incurred and income earned for a given period, although such expenses and income may not have been actually paid or received in cash. Hence, the financial statements of Slick Switch Co. show revenues and expenses, even before any such revenues or expenses are paid.

The accrual method is the more acceptable and the more widely used because it correctly matches the earning process to the activity. In other words, revenue is recorded when services or goods are rendered or shipped, regardless of when paid.

Cash Method

The cash method of accounting is familiar to most individuals since personal income tax returns are filed on the cash basis. As the name implies, revenues and expenses are only recorded when the consideration paid actually changes hands. This could be months after the actual event occurred.

Many small business owners prefer the cash basis due to its simplicity and ease of understanding. At the end of any given period, the recorded net income will agree more closely to the change in the business's cash balance. However, when requesting financing from any bank or agency, business owners are generally asked to furnish financial statements, prepared on the accrual basis. Clearly any "stakeholders" want to see the true effect on the financial statements of activities, as they occur, as opposed to when they are paid.

Many small businesses (under $1,000,000 in sales) are allowed to use the cash basis method for filing business tax returns, even if the business keeps its books on the accrual basis. In a growing business, income taxes can be deferred for a year for revenues recorded from increases in accounts receivables.

Percentage of Completion Method

The percentage of completion method is a variant of the accrual method, used for businesses with long term contracts, primarily construction contractors. Instead of valuing revenues based on services invoiced, contractors will adjust the revenue billed to agree with the estimated percentage of the total contract that has been completed to date.

Reporting Standards

Many transactions are entered routinely through the accounting system without much concern about reporting standards. However, other transactions can be handled in different ways depending on a person's judgment over the facts and circumstances. For example, if a business decides to lease an expensive piece of machinery, how should the lease payments be recorded? Perhaps they should be simply charged to lease expense.

However, maybe the terms of the lease imply an obligation and the payments represent a pay-off of that obligation. In that case, a portion of the payment should be applied to the debt and the other portion charged to interest expense.

The resulting financial statements would look different in those two cases. The usefulness of financial statements would be severely limited if their presentation was based solely upon the preparer's judgment. Consequently, certain standards must be agreed upon and followed.

GAAP - Generally Accepted Accounting Principles

There was no commonly agreed upon standardization over accounting practices until after the great depression of 1933. In response to the vast sums lost by investors in the stock market crash, the Securities and Exchange Commission (SEC) was established and given authority to set accounting standards for publicly held corporations.

In an effort to stave off further government regulation, the accounting profession, organized under the American Institute of Certified Public Accountants (AICPA), issued its first auditing standards in 1939. This began its attempt at self-regulation, though the AICPA continues to work with the SEC and defers to the SEC on regulatory reporting requirements for publicly held companies.

Between then and 1959 the AICPA issued 51 authoritative pronouncements known as Accounting Research Bulletins (ARB) that formed the basis of what became known as generally accepted accounting principles (GAAP). From 1959 to 1973 the Accounting Principles Board (APB) issued 31 additional standards.

In 1973 a new full-time independent body, separate from the AICPA was created, called the Financial Accounting Standards Board (FASB). This board has issued over 147 Statements of Standards by the end of 2002. These standards, along with official interpretations, Accounting Research Bulletins (ARB), previously issued pronouncements, SEC rulings, industry guides, and other exposure drafts make up the current basket of generally accepted accounting principles.

The Matching Principle

Woven through all of the GAAP pronouncements are several universal principles. One is the concept of matching. Accrual and percentage of completion methods represent attempts to more properly match the financial statement presentation to the actual transactions that have occurred. Revenues are matched to services performed and product sold, and expenses are matched to activities that have incurred expenses. This is why accrual based reporting conforms to GAAP and cash based reporting does not. The matching principle is a keystone of generally accepted accounting practice.

Conformity

Conformity is another widely used concept in accounting. The method of implementing percentage of completion, for example, should be the same for all companies. Only by practicing conformity will there be comparability. Investors, lenders and business owners, could not properly evaluate the success of a particular business as compared to the rest of its industry, if all businesses used different methods for recording transactions. Conformity is another fundamental principle in GAAP.

Valuation

A common consensus in GAAP reporting is the agreement that financial statements are valued on an historical basis. This is an important concept that provides for consistent conformity. As an example, real estate is valued at its original cost, not what it might be worth on an appraised value.

Accounting board pronouncements have continued to modify this principle to make financial reports even more conservative than historical basis, by requiring a downward adjustment, if the potential selling value has fallen below the original cost.

An example is inventory, when obsolescence reduces its value below its original cost. Another example is the yearly devaluing of fixed assets through depreciation. Each year the original cost of a building or equipment is lowered by writing off a portion of its expected life and expensing it to depreciation. Other assets like accounts receivable are reviewed and written down to their expected realizable value by charging off any amount deemed uncollectible to bad debt expense.

The overall attempt is to present financial statements on the most conservative basis possible. The objective is to ensure that the net worth recorded on a company's financial statements is never more than the true value of a company, based upon the lower of historical cost or the expected realized selling price of its assets minus its liabilities.

Events in the early years of the 2000's have shown how important this objective is. In spite of all the GAAP pronouncements in place, "creative accounting" techniques that push the gray areas of accounting valuation issues have resulted in significant, previously undisclosed impairments to the financial statements of companies like Tyco, Enron, and WorldCom.

Inventory Valuation

Inventory valuation is a specially treated area that deserves specific mention. Inventory is always valued at the lower or cost or market (realizable value, net of selling costs). However, cost can be determined in three different ways.

First In - First Out (FIFO) values the cost of inventory based on the principle that the first item purchased is the first item to be sold. Visually, this method mimics a store owner's method of stocking shelves by putting its most recent purchases at the back of the shelf, so that the older product is sold first. Hence, the value of the amount of inventory on hand, always represents the cost of the very latest purchases. In a true FIFO valuation, each purchase is tracked as a separate layer with its own cost. Sales are also tracked and taken from one or more specific layers.

A variant on the FIFO method is the Average Cost FIFO method, which eliminates the need to keep track of separate purchasing layers. The cost of each new purchase is added to the "pool" which changes the overall cost of the "pool". Sales are then taken from this single "pool", leaving a value of the inventory on hand that closely resembles, but not necessarily equals, the value of inventory on a true FIFO method.

A final method of valuation is based on Last In - First Out (LIFO). This is the opposite of FIFO: the last items purchased are deemed to be the first items sold. This means that the ending inventory value is comprised of the very first items purchased. This value could be lower than the FIFO value, particularly in inflationary times.

One might ask how two opposing methods of valuation could both be allowed under GAAP, particularly, when this would seem to violate the important principle of conformity. This is one of many good examples of the challenge to create a consensus of opinion when there are several options, which have equal justification and support. Accounting principles are not static laws handed down from the mountaintop, hence the term, "generally accepted".

In this case, there is current justification and support for either method. In deference to conformity, GAAP provides that financial statements valuing inventory on LIFO are to include a footnote reference, which discloses the valuation difference between LIFO and FIFO. This is one of many compromises that provide conformity over different methods of valuation.

Materiality

A final important concept in all of GAAP is materiality. Surprisingly, coming from a group of professionals known for their penchant for chasing down pennies, every pronouncement contains a materiality clause that allows for non-compliance in any area, if the effect on the financial statement presentation is clearly immaterial. In other words, if the effect is minimal or does not represent a significant change in the financial position of the account then it might be considered immaterial.

Types of Reports

The reporting standards discussed above may not really affect many small and mid-size owners, if their reporting needs are primarily internal. However, it does help to understand the rationale for those standards. These standards trigger the most basic questions that must be answered in setting up an accounting system: cash or accrual? Or, FIFO or LIFO?

External Reports

External reports were discussed briefly in the early part of this introduction, in terms of the "audience" or specific users for company information. Generally, one of the more important users is the Internal Revenue Service (IRS) and various state and local taxing authorities. Required income tax returns can be prepared more easily from financial reports that are classified in a comparable manner. A tax practitioner is usually retained to prepare and file these returns. The report most commonly requested of the company is the general ledger and related financial statements.

The second most likely external user for a company's financial statements is a bank or other debt or equity institution. The financial institution may well dictate the report needed. Copies of tax returns and company prepared financial statements may be all that is required. On the other hand, the financial institution may require a higher level of assurance by requesting that an independent accounting firm either **compiles**, **reviews**, or **audits** the financial statements of the company.

In this case, the company might want to know what is required and the difference between these types of reports. First of all, only Certified Public Accountants (CPA) that meet a higher level peer review and other reporting standards, can issue these statements. A public accountant (PA), tax practitioner, or an accountant who is not a licensed CPA cannot issue such statements. Even a fully licensed CPA must keep their license current with continuing education and documented peer review to be able to issue opinions on these reports.

Compilation

A business owner will need to find a CPA with the necessary credentials to request a compilation, review or audit. The least expensive report, and one that should satisfy most banks for small and mid-sized business, is a compilation. Essentially, the CPA reviews the financial statements prepared by the company and attaches an accountant's report to it. No further investigation is performed.

Interestingly, the standard compilation report issued by a CPA is nothing more than a glorified disclaimer, stating that the CPA is providing no financial statement assurance. The AICPA defines a compilation as "a service where the accountant presents, in the form of financial statements, information that is the representation of the company's management and owners without undertaking to express assurance on the financial statements."

Review

A review involves essentially the same process as a compilation except that the auditor does perform certain analytical reviews: reviewing account balances for reasonableness, and questioning management about material modifications that might be made in order for the statements to be in conformity with GAAP. In a review report the CPA expresses a "limited assurance", (but not an opinion), about the reasonableness of the financial statements and their conformity to a comprehensive basis of accounting like GAAP, cash basis or income tax basis reporting.

Audit

An audit provides the highest level of financial statement assurance. An audit may take considerably more time than either a compilation or review. The audit work, itself, can fill several large binders of documentation for a small to medium size business.

Every balance sheet account is proven, within the limits of materiality. Direct confirmations of account balances are mailed from the CPA to banks, customers, vendors, and other debt holders to validate the balances of cash, accounts receivable, accounts payable, and other assets and liabilities. If inventory is material, the CPA must observe the inventory counting as of the report date. The CPA also tests the accounting procedures and internal controls, including computer controls. All transactions are subject to audit under a statistical sampling formula.

A surprisingly large amount of time is spent in non-financial areas to determine any claims, lawsuits, contingencies or other events that could harm the company. Incorporation and other organizational papers are reviewed, all leases, loan documents and other contracts are reviewed, and all minutes and other relevant correspondence is read. The CPA also sends letters to all attorneys asking for full disclosure on any relevant matter.

The AICPA defines an audit as an engagement where a CPA provides an opinion about the fairness of a financial statement presentation in accordance with a comprehensive basis of accounting such as: GAAP, cash basis or income tax basis. This is a fairly simple statement for what can easily involve weeks of work for even a relatively well-structured small business.

It's important to recognize the relative costs of these three types of reports. If the cost of an audit is $12,000, a review for the same business might average $4,000, and a compilation, $3,000. Relative to an audit, a review and compilation are considerably less expensive. However, the difference in cost between a review and compilation is not nearly as great. This is important to remember if faced with a requirement from a lender or investor. If they request anaudit, you might try to convince them that a review is adequate and certainly provides more assurance than a compilation. This could save you considerable expense.

SEC - Audit

For publicly held companies, an audit is the minimum level of assurance required. In addition to the audit, there are other SEC reporting requirements, depending on the size of the business. A full explanation of these SEC reports is beyond the scope of this introduction.

Internal Reports

Internal reports were discussed earlier in this introduction. Much emphasis has been given to financial statement reports; the balance sheet, income statement, and statement of cash flows. These three are the most important reports on the overall financial condition of the company over a given period of time. A primary objective in developing policies and procedures over the accounting function is to improve the timeliness, accuracy and completeness of these statements.

A company's accounting or information system can provide much more than those three statements, however. Management should be encouraged to use the data available in the accounting system for other uses. Financial statements are extremely useful, however, they only provide current valuation, and transactional information from the past.

A statement of cash flow, reconciling the sources and uses of cash, can be a useful starting point for extrapolating data that projects the anticipated sources and uses of cash needed into the future. By analyzing the changes in the agings of accounts receivable and accounts payable, estimates can be developed to anticipate future cash receipts and future cash payments.

The relationship between sales, inventory levels and related cost of sales can be used to determine the anticipated needs for additional inventory related to projected sales. Using the data captured by the accounting system every day, a projected cash flow report, updated daily, can be a powerful tool to alert management in enough time to properly react to anticipated additional working capital requirements.

With a powerful forward-looking cash management tool, like the described projected cash flow report, the projected activity levels in future months can be used to create budgets in the current and succeeding months.

With income statement projections, projected cash flow reports and budgets we have a truly interactive management information system. Data collected from the past is used to project the future, fed back into the budgets, which control the present and determine the future. This creates a continually updated management information loop. This provides a business with the tools to act, not just react.

SUMMARY

We hope this introduction to your Bizmanualz™ Accounting Policies and Procedures manual will increase your appreciation of the importance of establishing effective accounting procedures. Your business is a continuous flowing stream of transactions. Like a net cast across the stream, effective accounting policies and procedures will help trap all of the data; completely and accurately. Once collected, the real benefit is utilizing the data to provide the information needed to review the past, position the present and chart the future.

Accounting Policies, Procedures & Forms

Section 200

Manual Preparation

Section 200

Manual Preparation

Manual Preparation

It is vital in order for your manual to be effective that it be clearly written and easily understood by all the employees in your organization. This section provides an introduction to producing your manual. Please read this whole section before you begin editing your manual.

[This page intentionally left blank]

Manual Preparation
Table of Contents*

* The Manual Preparation Table of Contents references section page numbers (lower right corner).

[This page intentionally left blank]

SECTION 1 INTRODUCTION

This prototype *Accounting Manual* was developed to assist organizations in preparing a Company Accounting Manual. It can be custom tailored to fit one's individual company concerns and operations.

The ***Accounting Policies, Procedures and Forms*** includes eleven tabbed sections consisting of the following:

- 100 Introduction
- 200 Manual Preparation
- 300 Accounting Manual
- 400 General & Administrative Procedures
- 410 Cash Procedures
- 420 Inventory & Asset Procedures
- 430 Revenue Procedures
- 440 Purchasing Procedures
- 500 Embezzlement Prevention
- 600 Index
- 700 Notes

The *Accounting* manual provides a sample Accounting manual with associated Accounting Procedures as a guide, but it does not intend to imply these are the "best" or "recommended" text for your specific purposes. They can be used as a "minimum" documentation set for you to use to address Generally Accepted Accounting Practices.

The language style and usage is generally representative of practices in companies in the United States. In some cases information may be used which is not applicable to every business. When you edit and construct a policy it should be easy to read, to the point and convey a message that is clearly understood by both the employee and the management staff. When you have completed your Accounting Manual Procedures, have a team of managers review them and make appropriate comments.

The corrected and finished product is then ready for distribution. But remember, building an Accounting Manual is not an event; it is a continuous process so revisions will be required from time to time.

This publication is sold or distributed with the understanding that the publisher is not engaged in rendering legal, IT, or other professional services. If legal advice or other expert assistance is required, the services of a competent professional person should be sought to review the final manual.

Top Ten Management Mistakes

As a busy executive, you face some extremely difficult challenges like creating and dominating new markets or finding and keeping the best people. But then, like many executives, do you find yourself spending too much time solving everyday problems (that only you can solve, right?), which prevent you from growing your ideal business?

You may be making some of these management mistakes:

1. Do you have a compelling vision for your company, that projects a remarkable future, but few of your employees have heard of it or could explain it if asked?
2. Do you have a company mission that addresses your customer needs yet your operations fail to measure your progress towards your mission?
3. Do your objectives focus on increasing revenue and profitability while your assets are performing poorly, generating negative cash flows, or encumbered by debt to create the profit?
4. Do you talk a lot about your employees (positive or negative) without noting what your employee turnover or performance metrics are for your industry?
5. Do you spend a lot of time working IN your business on tactics yet fail to spend a greater amount of time working ON your business to define your strategy, performance metrics, and real resource needs?
6. Do you have regular interactions with employees yet fail to communicate the status of objectives, financials, or metrics?
7. Do you make money available for training yet fail to measure how that training helps your company achieve its goals?
8. Do you constantly strive to improve your company's performance yet fail to compare your performance against external benchmarks for success?
9. Do you believe that your customers, employees, and vendors all love your company yet you have no process for measuring their satisfaction on an on-going basis?
10. Do you produce forecasts and budgets yet fail to achieve the agreed upon goals or learn from the experience to improve in the future.

Daily operational issues eat up much of a manager's time. Too much for most managers. But now, with the purchase of this manual, you have the opportunity to correct all that and build a superior organization that keeps your best people, increases revenue and increases margins.

You now have an opportunity to provide your organization with the methods, tools, and training to achieve superior results. Bizmanualz has helped companies from all over the world build superior organizations with increased compliance, control, and customer satisfaction.

Manual Development Process

The manual development process consists of four phases: Discovery, Planning, Development, and Implementation. W. Edwards Deming PhD, one of the leading experts on process improvement, calls this the Plan, Do, Check, Act (PDCA) cycle. Deming's PDCA cycle identifies the four main phases of continuous process improvement. You should develop your manual in this manner to avoid mistakes that will be made later by skipping these steps.

Many people incorrectly believe that you can save a lot of money by eliminating Discovery and Planning and going directly into Development. But, if you start writing procedures without proper Discovery and Planning then you are in trouble. You can expect constant delays, cost overruns, scope creep, and a lot of rewrites once the missing elements are discovered.

This eventually leads to the feeling that nobody wants to work on this project anymore due to the lack of organization and increasing frustration. But, if you spend the time to plan it well, then the development and implementation phases run a lot smoother. What you are trying to do is anticipate the future.

Discovery

Discovery starts by clearly identifying the project vision, mission, objectives and the action plan. It is considered part of the "Plan phase" in Deming's PDCA cycle. In Discovery you are probably interpreting the results of a previous "Check" phase of some kind. You must have found the results to be dissatisfactory and therefore you are now "Acting" on those results and preparing to "Plan" for the future.

You should include clear business objectives that include how customer needs are getting satisfied with agreed upon effectiveness criteria beyond compliance. Otherwise, the procedures look like overhead and an administrative waste of time to everyone else, making it more difficult to get their buy-in and participation later on during implementation and training.

Once everyone agrees to the objectives and action plan then you can start management planning. The Discover phase takes about 2-4 weeks depending on how organized the executive management team is regarding mission, vision and objectives.

Does your project need a vision?

You bet. Every project requires a vision of the future. All the employees involved will want to know how all of this work will improve their lives. You will need to communicate a picture of "what's in it for them." If you can't explain it to them then all you have is a big wish that it turns out the way you planned. And it won't.

Planning

Planning starts with a gap analysis to determine the difference from reality to the objectives. A Gap Analysis is an audit of your current processes, capabilities, and constraints to determine the "gaps" that need to be filled.

You use the gap results, along with the objectives and action plans from Discovery to produce the management materials needed to control the project and set the budget/expectations. Other functions include creating a development team, assigning process owners for each process and deploying your effectiveness criteria to each process. This takes 2-4 weeks.

This includes producing:

- project plan (activities, resources, dates, etc.)
- project roles and responsibilities
- organization chart
- change & approval review structure
- status reports
- document control and format
- process maps identifying all process inputs & outputs
- compliance requirements
- training, implementation, testing and audit plans.

You are now 1-2 months into the project and should not have written a single procedure. But, everyone should understand the scope of the project, its relationship to the company objectives, what the future will look like, and what their roles are in development.

Development

Development starts by identifying a group of related processes and completing just that group. Follow the document control format, use the review structure, perform a walk through of the related processes, test for compliance and effectiveness, and then move on to the next group until finished. It represents the "Do phase" in Deming's PDCA cycle.

This takes 2-4 months depending on the number of processes, compliance requirements, resource constraints, and the skill and knowledge of the project managers, leaders, writers and reviewers. If you have not done this before plan on four months.

Development also includes creating all supporting documents such as job descriptions, forms, the training plan, and the collection of technical manuals, references, etc, for document & record control and later implementation.

As a rule of thumb you should plan on the Discovery, Planning and Development phases taking as much as 50% of the total project time but consuming 80% of the project cost. You should try to include the time of all personnel working on the project in your project plan so you have a real picture of the costs involved. Frequently it is a lot more than you imagine at first.

You are now 3-6 months into the project and should have completed the procedure writing. You are now ready for a complete document review. You should not implement a smaller group of processes until all process are documented and reviewed as a whole system. Otherwise, you will find yourself rewriting and re-implementing and it will take longer to complete development. You will have a chance to improve the processes later.

Focus on continuous process improvement over delayed perfection.

Implementation

Implementation includes skills assessment, training to improve competencies, and auditing of the entire system against the objectives and compliance requirements. It represents the "Check phase" in Deming's PDCA cycle. The length of time depends on number of employees, locations, and processes. It should take 3-6 months or about 50% of the project time to complete. You are working toward a stable system of processes and this takes time.

Training

Implementation starts with an assessment of employee skills and competencies to determine training gaps. Then training begins introducing the job descriptions, processes, procedures, and the relationship of people/tasks to objectives/effectiveness.

Once training is complete, you should use execute the processes as documented for 1-3 months. Procedure forms, logs, and other records should be used to collect data for measurement and analysis. All personnel should become accustomed to using the processes recently in created. In fact it is the collection of data which now becomes the most important part.

Collected data is used to:

- determine if processes are in control,
- identifying if a process can be improved, and
- demonstrating to auditors and management that the organization is progressing towards achieving the objectives.

Auditing

Auditing is one of the most important steps in building business processes. Auditing provides management visibility into the ongoing progress towards objectives and the capabilities of the organization. Without auditing, management limits its predictive knowledge of the systems potential.

Management Review

You are now 6-12 months into the project and almost finished. The last step is to analyze what's been done, review the lessons learned and look for ways to improve performance, compliance, or effectiveness. This is typically done within a Management Review meeting held after the audit cycle has been completed.

Management holds the review meeting to discuss:

- The audit report documenting the findings of the audit team.
- Progress towards objectives.
- Results of customer satisfaction processes.
- Corrective actions to be taken to resolve common cause errors.
- Preventive action to be taken to resolve special cause errors.
- Follow-up from previous meetings.

Re-Discovery

The actions from the Management Review meeting lead into Re-Discovery or the Discovery process for the next cycle. Re-Discovery starts the process of continuous improvement all over again. It represents the "Act phase" in Deming's PDCA cycle. The result is a new set of objectives and action plans for the next period and you now begin again. This phase overlaps with the discovery phase of the next year to chain together each period in a constant cause-effect cycle of improvement.

Using these four phases you should complete the project in 6-12 months. Less than six months or more than 12 months indicates problems in scope (planning). If the organization is big and complex then the problem should be broken into smaller projects and focused on core processes or, outside contractors should be used to deploy the experience and bandwidth required to meet your schedule.

Staffing for this depends on number of employees, locations, compliance requirements and processes involved. You should consider at least one full-time project leader that drives the project, manages document controls, leads the audits and reports to management on the overall effectiveness.

The project leader could be the Quality Manager. The Quality Manager should be experienced in quality control methodologies, auditing, and the compliance standard you are targeting. If your quality manager is not experienced in these areas then you should look for training. Training is available to learn how to use quality tools, auditing skills, and leading audit teams & programs.

Others are needed to create documents or perform audits. Obviously, there are a lot of variables to staffing requirements. It is difficult for one person to know everything about your business, build the system and then be responsible for auditing the processes. A solo person will lose their objectivity and they can not audit their own processes either.

SECTION 2
YOUR ACCOUNTING MANUAL

This first step in building your Accounting documentation is the creation of an "Accounting Manual". This is a separate and distinct step from developing your Accounting procedures. The purpose is to state, in a concise and brief format, the policies and objectives of your company that will be required to achieve your desired level of completeness for your organization or division.

More than likely the input for the Accounting Manual will come from your auditors, internal and external accounting staff. At a minimum, your Accounting Manual must address each one of the accounting processes of your company and or your industry specific sector requirements.

Each area that you write should cover, at a minimum, three parts: Scope, Policy and Responsibilities. These three areas are used again for each procedure.

- The Scope portion should simply state the purpose of the covered area.
- The Policy portion should state the company policy regarding the applicable Accounting practice.
- The Responsibility portion should state who, in generic titles or positions, is responsible for the policy.

A sample Accounting manual is provided in this guide for your use as a template to create your own Accounting Manual.

Style and Format:

1. Use a cover or title page.
2. Include a table of contents.
3. Put policy statements on a 8 1/2" x 11 " page and print only on one side to make revisions easier.
4. Organize material by major headings for easy reference.
5. Include an alphabetized index if your manual is lengthy.
6. Avoid a detailed paragraph identification systems of numbers and letters as this will detract from its' readability and the message will be lost.
7. Write in simple easy to understand statements to avoid confusion.

Some companies include sample administrative forms with their procedures along with instructions for their completion. This product includes forms for use at your discretion.

Considerations in writing your manual:

1. It is now common practice to use pronouns that are applicable to either sex or to use his or her, or the more personal and direct, "you". Social changes influence policies on topics concerning smoking, physical fitness, etc.
2. Have your manual reviewed by an attorney to ensure that you are in compliance with all applicable federal, state, and local laws.
3. Define terms used in your manual. Definitions should be placed in each procedure as needed.

Every organization is dynamic and in some state of change. This will lead to changes to your policies from time to time. Revisions should be completed and sent to all personnel who hold a copy of the manual. The revision should have an effective date and of course should be distributed in advance of the effective date. When making a change to your manual be cognizant that the language might have an indirect impact on other policies. And finally, make sure that there is a clear record of revisions made and that all employees have current information in a timely manner.

The Accounting Manual as well as each procedure includes a revision section at the end. It is important to keep this revision section up-to-date. It will be the only way to ensure that distributed copies of your manual are current.

Some companies, due to their size and specific business application, require expanded information. For this reason, Bizmanualz, Inc has additional business publications that include detailed, topic specific manuals.

Each manual is intended to be a simple, "top-to-bottom" guide, addressing the minimum set of statements for the administration and creation of a Management System. Most guidelines presented have immediate use and importance. However, by using the MS-WORD documents you can edit the samples and customize them to your company's individual needs.

- **Finance Policies, Procedures and Forms** - Includes instructions on creating your own business plans, capital memorandums, and sample procedures for treasury, debt and equity offerings. Answers, and step-by-step guidance for SCOR, Reg. A, Reg. D, SB-1, and SB-2 Direct Public Offerings.
- **Computer& Network Policies, Procedures and Forms** – Includes sections on Management Information Systems, Software Development and Network Security.
- **Disaster Recovery Policies, Procedures and Forms**- Includes Your Disaster Manual Preparation, Recovery Procedures and a section on Coping with Workplace Violence.

- **Production Policies, Procedures and Forms-** Includes a Manual Preparation guide and Business Procedures for Construction, Engineering, Manufacturing, and Environmental, plus associated Reports and Forms.
- **Human Resources Policies, Procedures and Forms** – Includes Employee Handbook Preparation, sample HR policies and procedures, a Human Resources Legal Guide, a sample Employee Handbook, sample Job Descriptions and sample Reports and Forms.
- **Sales and Marketing Policies, Procedures and Forms** – Includes sample procedures on Customer Service, Sales and Marketing.
- **Security Planning Policies, Procedures and Forms** – This includes sample procedures for Security Operations and a special section on Embezzlement Investigation.
- **ISO 9001 QMS Policies, Procedures and Forms -** Includes sample Quality manual as well as easily editable quality policies and procedures. Also comes with a guide to ISO 9000.

Bizmanualz, Inc is committed to providing professional publications for those business owners and managers dedicated to the development and success of their company. To this end, we will continue to publish useful business guides to assist you in your ever-demanding endeavors. To obtain the latest information on all of our products, visit our website at www.Bizmanualz.com .

Sources of additional Information

You may be able to draw on other sources of information to develop a comprehensive program that truly meets the needs of your organization.

These sources can include:

1. Industry or trade association publications (AICPA)
2. Industry or Sector Guides (GAAP)
3. The company's legal, financial and accounting counsel
4. Other related company Manuals and Procedures
5. Internal memos and records
6. Equipment User Manuals
7. Customer surveys (can be formal or informal), proposals or requirements
8. Regulatory agencies (e.g., SEC, IRS, etc.)
9. Standards Organizations (e.g. FASB,ANSI, NIST, ISO, RAB, ASQ)
10. Small Business Advisory Centers

[This page intentionally left blank]

SECTION 3 EFFECTIVE COMMUNICATION

Communication and Addressing Your Audience

It is vital in order for your manual to be effective that it be clearly written and easily understood by all the employees in your organization. Remember that the objective of your Accounting Manual is to improve the efficiency of your company, establish Accounting controls and to comply with established regulations. Therefore, the most important rule when writing an Accounting Manual is that clarity and readability are much more important than style, perfect grammar and a large vocabulary.

The writer must try to put themselves into the position of the users at all times. While developing policy and procedure statements, some general guidelines for the writer to keep in mind are:

1. Explain new or unusual terms the first time they are used or in the definitions section of the statement.
2. Avoid jargon wherever possible, especially when training new employees.
3. Avoid unneeded words.
4. Avoid complex writing. If the writer's vocabulary is unusually large or if they write using complex sentence structures, the writing may be at too high a level for many of the users. Understanding is far more important than the correctness of the language.
5. Use active verbs instead of passive phrases.
6. Write the way you speak. Use words and phrases that you would normally use in expressing the same thought orally.

Sexism in Writing

Webster's New Collegiate Dictionary defines "he" as used in the generic sense or when the sex of the person is unspecified. However, many people will not accept "he" being used when referring to people in general. There have been suggestions that the generic "he" be replaced with "he or she" and "him" with "him or her."

Another recent method that is gaining acceptance is the switch to a plural pronoun with a singular subject such as "When someone orders their supplies, they will have to complete a ..."

Often it is more practical for the writer to use generic nouns or by recasting sentences to include positions or titles (i.e., Applicant, Manager, Accountant, Driver, etc.) to eliminate the need for most sexism in writing of policy and procedure statements.

Number Usage

Writing and development of procedures may often times include the frequent usage of numbers in the writing. The following rules cover how numbers should be used in print.

1. Never begin a sentence with numbers. "Fifty states have been admitted to the union" not "50 states ..."
2. Spell numbers one through nine in words, 10 or larger in numerals.
3. Compound numbers such as fractions in numerals, for example 8 1/2" X 11."
4. When showing odds, use hyphens such as 4-to-1.
5. Decimals of less than one should be preceded by a zero, for example, 0.5 percent.
6. Dates: "the 1990s"
7. Spell % as percent.
8. Use numerals with times such as a.m. and p.m.

Organizing Your Thoughts

To help the writer formulate and organize ideas for developing and writing policy and procedure statements, it may be useful to outline the material to be covered. Outlining is a fast and effective way to show a great amount of information in a concise, efficient manner with a minimum of writing.

To achieve well-written and easily understood policy and procedure statements that flow in a cohesive and logical form, your personnel should first outline their thoughts before beginning to write a statement.

When outlining a policy and procedure statement, the following areas should be defined:

1. What is the objective that the statement is going to accomplish?
2. What is the Company's policy on this matter?
3. Who is affected?
4. When is the policy/procedure appropriate?
5. How is the objective to be accomplished? This should include outlining major areas in a step-by-step fashion in chronological order.

Outlining Technique

There are some basic standard rules for effective and consistent outlining. It may be helpful to briefly review a few of these that deal primarily with formatting. These rules concern indentation and numbering.

Standard outline formatting is as follows:

I.
    A.
        1.
        2.
            a.
            b.
    B.
II.

There should always be at least two of each type of character. For example, there should not be an I without a II, an A without a B, etc.

The four characters to mark each section level, Roman numerals, capital letters, Arabic numerals and lower case letters are followed by a period. Line up the periods vertically for each type of character. Thus, Roman numerals are shown:

 I.

II.

Arabic numerals are lined up as follows:

 5.

39.

By aligning the periods, the text is a pleasing, straight vertical line. Indentation should be uniform, usually two to five spaces for each change in type of line. The part of a single line carried to a second line should be indented the same number of spaces as the original part of the line.

Defining the Format and Organization of Your Manual

After reviewing the preliminary listing of statements to be included in the manual and discussing with the personnel assigned to each section, you should be able to determine the estimated length and usage of your manual. With the guidelines presented in this publication and from your own organization's needs determine the format of your policy and procedure statements and how you will organize the manual into sections.

The format and appearance of your policy and procedure statements are just as important as the organization and content of the manual. A manual that is appealing to the eye and that emphasizes the importance of the statements is more likely to be taken seriously and used on a regular basis by employees.

However, it is important to remember that the true objective of the manual is to disseminate information in a timely and efficient manner and <u>not</u> to "impress" the reader with intricate headings or fancy printing techniques.

The simplest format is often the best. A simple format also allows for the most time and cost effective manner for production and maintenance of the manual. Therefore, it may be best to avoid temptations such as, detailed corporate logos in headings, two sided copies, odd sized paper patterns, expensive and restrictive binding techniques, etc.

Design Features

No Accounting Manual or Procedure should ever be regarded as "complete" in the sense that it will never change. The best manual is one that is geared to continuous growth over time and incorporates design features that make this kind of growth possible.

In this regard, use of standard 8-1/2" X 11" paper housed in a three-ring binder forms an ideal employee handbook manual.

The three-ring binder provides the benefits of allowing a place for statements to be inserted while the manual is being developed and provides for easy updating through simple replacement of pages or superseded statements. Further, as the organization grows, the use of standard three-ring binders allows additional copies of the manual to be produced on an as needed basis instead of having to be concerned with minimum production runs required for hard bound versions.

Production of statements on a single-side, standard size paper medium provides for easy reproduction of the manual by high-speed copiers. Use of single-side printing also provides for easy updating of the manual with changes by allowing for one or two pages to be replaced without affecting the order or sequence of the manual.

However, if the manual becomes too voluminous for ease of handling, it may be necessary to bind the manual by different sections or utilize two-sided printing to reduce paper volume.

A window type binder should be used to describe the contents of the manual on the spine for locating sections quickly from a bookcase. If desired, the outside of the binder can be imprinted with the company's name and logo to give the manual a more professional and authoritative appearance.

Divider tabs on heavy stock should be used to separate functional areas or departmental sections for ease in finding a specific statement.

Style and Mechanics

The style and mechanics of writing include the paper, typestyle and print quality.

Paper - Some organizations use color to designate different manuals, forms, memos, etc. While color can create a pleasing appearance, it sometimes becomes too restrictive and may complicate photocopying or printing. Further, sometimes colors do not provide adequate contrast from the ink color for ease in reading. Nothing is better than black ink on white paper.

The grade of paper is usually not important since the manual is for internal purposes only and is not intended as a public relations effort. Regular 20-pound copy paper is adequate for single-sided printing. A heavier weight paper with greater opacity may be necessary if two-sided printing is used.

Typestyle - Avoid unusual artwork or type styles. These can be difficult to read and/or reproduce over a long period of time. You should strive for consistency in the overall appearance of the entire manual regardless of what area or department originates the statements by selecting a common typewriter element or word processing typestyle font. Courier 10, Elite, 12-point times roman and 12-point roman are common typestyles used by many business machines and word-processing software packages.

Print Quality - Avoid using small print, photocopy reductions, all-capital print or fancy script styles whenever possible as these are tiresome and difficult to read.

Adequate margins should be provided on the page. Recommended margins are a 1" top and bottom margin with a 1" left and right mirror margins plus a 1/2" gutter margin (for three-hole punching).

Sources of additional Information

There are a number of books on the market that provide an excellent reference for technical writers, editors, and others developing policies and procedures.

These sources can include:

1. Microsoft Manual of Style for Technical Publications; ISBN: 1572318902
2. The Handbook of Technical Writing; ISBN: 0312254962
3. Starting a Documentation Group; ISBN: 0967417902
4. Managing Your Documentation Projects; ISBN: 0471590991
5. Writing Effective Policies and Procedures; ISBN: 081447960X
6. Establishing a System of Policies and Procedures; ISBN: 1929065000
7. Achieving 100% Compliance of Policies and Procedures; ISBN: 1929065493

[This page intentionally left blank]

SECTION 4
ACCOUNTING PROCEDURES

Format

Accounting Procedures address the primary steps or tasks of an activity for a department or function and the personnel (generic titles or positions) responsible for accomplishing the procedure(s). These procedures can be organized on a departmental basis.

The Accounting Procedures in this manual start with a designation such as "REV" for Revenue or “PUR” for purchasing and may be used as a template to create your own procedures. The exact format is not required but some of the field names and/or titles are accepted as standards in the Accounting industry.

Heading Information

Many organizations use very complex headings that require space of up to one-third of a page or more and can include multiple approval signatures, distribution information, structured tabular formats and confusing retrieval numbering systems and revision levels.

The simplest approach is often the best. Heading information should be kept to the minimum necessary to accurately describe the statement, identify the revision level, demonstrate authorization and be easy to produce.

A sample heading may appear as follows:

SAMPLE COMPANY	
SOP # G1 Revision 0	Prepared by:______
Effective Date: 11/01/0X	Approved by:_____

The above heading provides the following information:

Formal Company Name or Division - Use of the company's name personalizes the statement as belonging to "our" company and not just boilerplate borrowed from another company. The company name should be located in the upper left-hand of the page.

SOP Number and Revision Level - For small manuals, no numbering system may be necessary and just the title can be used for identification purposes. With lengthy manuals, it is best to use a simple alphanumeric numbering system for identifying SOPs and for storage and retrieval purposes in data processing systems.

The first digit(s) of the number is an alphabetical character that represents the primary department or functional area covered by the SOP. For example, table5.1 shows how alpha characters could be used to describe these departments:

Code		Department
A	=	Accounting
C	=	Credit
CS	=	Customer Service
E	=	Engineering
F	=	Finance
G	=	General & Administrative
M	=	Manufacturing
MK	=	Marketing
P	=	Personnel
QP	=	Quality
S	=	Sales

Table 5.1 Alpha Department Codes

The remaining digits should be numeric and assigned sequentially as statements are developed and issued. For example, the first Accounting procedure could be A1, and the second one A2, etc. An alternative would be to designate two or three digits to a numeric assignment and begin at a starting level of 11 or 101. For instance, beginning Accounting procedures could be assigned as A101 and A102. Or beginning engineering procedures could be E101 or E102.

To allow for ease in updating and development of the manual it is best to try to avoid grouping similar SOPs together in sequential order. However, if it is desired to group similar procedures together numerically, a decimal numbering system may be used to insert a new statement between two existing SOPs. For example a new SOP could be numbered A1.1 and inserted between A1 and A2.

Once an SOP is issued, it will be subject to change and modification. A revision code should be used to identify the current one in effect and assist with purging obsolete statements. An initial SOP begins with a revision level of zero (0). If a new SOP supersedes this prior statement, the revision number will be increased by an increment of one. The SOP number and Revision level should be located underneath the company name.

Effective Date - The actual date the SOP or Revision will be implemented. Note the effective date is <u>not</u> the issue date of the original SOP. The effective date should be in the format of MM/DD/YY and is located directly beneath the SOP number and Revision level.

Page Numbering - All pages should be numbered in the form Page # of # to quickly identify the order or placement of pages within a statement. It is also useful when updating an existing SOP where only one or two pages will be replaced. The page number should be placed in the upper right corner of the page.

Subsequent pages after the title page should be identified by either the SOP # or the title along with the page number. For example, the second page of the above SOP heading would be as follows:

SOP # A1

Prepared by: - It is useful to identify the primary individual or department that has developed the statement in the event questions arise during the approval process or subsequent to the issuance of the SOP in which additional information may be needed or to be clarified. This identification can be either typed in or simply initialed by the individual. The "Prepared by" identification should be placed beneath the Page Number.

Approved by: - After the SOP has been properly reviewed and authorized, the title page should be initialed by an authorized individual. It is usually best to initial the approval section by hand rather than to type it in to clearly indicate that the SOP has been authorized and distinguish the final version from any draft versions that may still be in circulation. The "Approved by" identification should be placed directly underneath the "Prepared by" section.

Title And Introduction

The title and introduction section provides the information necessary for the reader to determine content and the reason for the SOP, whom it affects and in what situation(s), the Company policy covering this area and the definition of any new or unusual terms.

A sample Title and Introduction section can appear as follows:

Title: DEVELOPMENT AND MAINTENANCE OF STANDARD OPERATING POLICIES AND PROCEDURES

Policy: It is the policy of Sample Company that all departments will prepare and maintain standardized operating policies and procedures that cover the performance of all major functions within their department.

Purpose: This procedure outlines the steps involved in preparing, maintaining and approving standard operating policies and procedures in order to provide consistent, informative and effective procedures to the employees of Sample Company.

Scope: This procedure applies to all policies and procedures used or written by all departments and individuals of Sample Company.

Responsibilities:

All Personnel are required to understand and use this procedure.

Management is responsible for maintaining this procedure.

Definitions: Policy - A definite course or method of action to guide and determine present and future decisions. It is a guide to decision making under a given set of circumstances within the framework of corporate objectives, goals and management philosophies.

Procedure - A particular way of accomplishing something, an established way of doing things, a series of steps followed in a definite regular order. It ensures the consistent and repetitive approach to actions.

A general description of the Title and Introduction is as follows:

Title - The title of the SOP should be short but descriptive enough to allow the reader to determine the content or objective of the SOP.

Policy - The policy should clearly indicate the company's or top management's beliefs or protocol affecting this area.

Purpose - A brief description of the objective of the SOP. Similar to Policy.

Scope - Describes the areas, functions, individuals or departments affected by the SOP and in what situations.

Responsibilities - Describe who, in generic titles or positions, is responsible for implementing or maintaining the procedure or parts of the procedure.

Definitions - Describes any terms contained in the SOP that may be new or unusual to the reader.

The Body Of The Procedure Statement

The body of the SOP includes a complete description of the policy and/or the procedure, the methods to be used, form names, cross references to other SOPs related thereto, etc.

Although the narrative information in the body can vary considerably in format, it is imperative that it clearly explains to the reader in an orderly fashion exactly how to accomplish the objective of the procedure.

For lengthy statements, it may be useful to identify and segregate the steps or areas by a numbering system. For example, each procedural category would be identified with a step number, starting with 1.0 and a heading description. All the steps within the category would then be numbered sequentially (For example, 1.1, 1.2, 1.3, etc.). The step number should be located at the left margin with the related narrative indented.

A sample procedure section can appear as follows:

Procedure - Describe the main elements that make up the procedure. Include the steps or details, the methods to be used, form names, cross-references to other SOPs related thereto, etc.

Effectiveness Criteria - Describe any thresholds or standards that are used to evaluate the work product or results of the procedure. How will an employee know that the procedure was executed correctly?

References - List applicable documents, procedures, manuals, laws, regulations or other sources that were used to develop or influence the policy/procedure statement.

Records - Describe the records, minutes, reports, notes, forms, or other documents that are generated or used when implementation the procedure.

Revision History - Describe all revisions made to the procedure. Include a revision number, date of the revision, a short description of the changes made, and a source of the request for the change.

Attachments

Any forms, diagrams, illustrations or other documents referenced in the body of the statement should be attached to the SOP and referenced as exhibits in the Records section using a sequential numbering system, (For example, Exhibit 1, Exhibit 2, etc.). It may be useful to use copies of actual completed forms or documents as exhibits to illustrate to the reader how they are completed.

Once all comments have been received and a final version approved, the statement should be printed in its final form. The statement should then be authorized by the appropriate individual and released for production and distribution.

Authorization

Origination of policies and procedures usually begins at the unit level by employees or department managers. Once a draft copy of a proposed procedure is developed it should be reviewed, corrected if necessary and approved before being released as a corporate policy and procedure statement. The approval process generally consists of review for consistency and accuracy, conflict with corporate policy or with other statements and general readability.

The approval process can vary widely between companies but it is recommended to keep approvals to a minimum if possible. If too many people or managers of equal ranking are required to authorize a statement, it can turn the development of statements into a bureaucratic process, which can considerably slow the release of policies and procedures while adding little value to the final version.

A method for gaining the input of others while streamlining the process and keeping authority at the functional or departmental level is to release draft copies of proposed statements to a select number of individuals for comment. It should be made clear to these individuals that they should confine their suggestions to what they feel is really <u>essential</u> to the statement's accuracy, readability and usefulness.

The selection of who should receive a draft copy will depend primarily on the nature and content of the statement. Sensitive issues or areas that deal with corporate exposure such as in the personnel area, intellectual property or trade secrets should be reviewed by top management including the president and may also include the company's legal counsel.

Rudimentary procedures that affect only a small unit within the company and are likely to be of no interest to others should be kept to a minimal review process. However, it is still advisable to have someone familiar with the area but separate or outside of the unit or department review the proposed statement. For example, the company's finance officer may review a proposed accounting SOP. This type of review serves three purposes:

First, what makes sense to the preparer directly involved in enforcing the policy or conformance to a procedure may not be understood when read for the first time by someone not as closely involved.

Second, a review by multiple department managers may prevent a later conflict with a policy and procedure statement still in the formative or discussion stages elsewhere in the company of which the original preparer would have no knowledge.

Third, it allows the input of multiple individuals while allowing the department manager to maintain control of the integrity of the statement and to drive its completion and release in a timely manner.

Production And Distribution

Once a policy and procedure statement is authorized, it should be duplicated on standard white copy paper and three-hole punched on the left margin. Multiple page statements may be corner stapled to prevent losing pages until it is included in the manual.

The number of copies of the statement should correlate to the number of manuals that have been distributed. It is generally advisable to designate one individual in the company for the production of statements. This individual keeps track of the number of manuals issued and ensures that new or revised SOPs are distributed to the appropriate personnel.

Management of the company should decide which departments or positions will receive copies of the manual or as an alternative, sections of the manual may be distributed which pertain only to a specific function or department. However, if the manual is to serve as a communication tool, enough copies of the manual should be available to employees.

Since the manual contains many operating procedures that are vital to the company's business practices and methods, there should be some accountability for the manuals. Generally, one individual will maintain a list of the number of copies in circulation and the names of those to whom they have been assigned. When a supervisor or manager leaves the company, there should be a strong incentive to return their copy of the manual; some companies withhold final compensation until the manual has been returned.

However, one should avoid numbering each copy of a manual, unless absolutely necessary. Numbering implies confidentiality and some degree of importance, which may not be the case. Besides, the issuer must maintain a permanent record of the numbers cross-referenced to the recipients that can make personnel changes a tedious record-keeping task.

Revising And Updating Statements

As mentioned previously, the policies and procedures manual is never "complete" because it never stops changing or evolving in order to keep pace with needs of the business and business climate.

All employees should be encouraged to initiate changes or revisions to existing policy and procedure statements that affect their area of responsibility. This will assist the company greatly in keeping the manual current and up-to-date.

In addition to this continuing review process, the entire manual should undergo a complete audit as often as changing conditions both within and outside the company indicate. This may be every year or several years depending on the company's business environment.

A new SOP should be issued if an existing statement is to be modified in any way. The revised SOP should undergo the same approval process as the initial statement and should be assigned a new revision number level to indicate that it supersedes the prior statement. Superseded statements should be purged from the manual immediately and discarded.

[This page intentionally left blank]

Accounting Policies, Procedures & Forms

Section 300

Accounting Manual

Section 300

Accounting Manual

<Company Logo>

<Company Name>

ACCOUNTING MANUAL

Approved by:__________________________________ Date:____________
President/CEO

The following document contains a sample Accounting manual covering the common accounting requirements and practices.

This sample is intended only to provide an example of wording that might be used in an Accounting manual.

This sample wording can be helpful in generating ideas for developing a manual for your own company. However, accounting policies should be drafted as appropriate and as necessary to accurately reflect your company's accounting standards.

Accounting Manual

Table of Contents*

* The Accounting Manual Table of Contents references section page numbers (lower right corner).

Table of Figures

List of Referenced Procedures

Cash

1. CSH101 Cash Drawers And Credit Cards
2. CSH102 Cash Receipts And Deposits
3. CSH103 Problem Checks
4. CSH104 Wire Transfers
5. CSH105 Check Signing Authority
6. CSH106 Check Requests
7. CSH107 Bank Account Reconciliations

General & Administrative

8. G&A101 Chart Of Accounts
9. G&A102 Files And Records Management
10. G&A103 Travel And Entertainment
11. G&A104 Management Reports
12. G&A105 Period-End Review & Closing
13. G&A106 Controlling Legal Costs
14. G&A107 Taxes And Insurance
15. G&A108 Property Tax Assessments
16. G&A109 Confidential Information Release
17. G&A110 Document Control

Inventory & Assets

18. INV101 Inventory Control
19. INV102 Inventory Counts
20. INV103 Fixed Asset Control
21. INV104 Customer Property
22. INV105 Fixed Asset Capitalization & Depreciation

Purchasing

23. PUR101 Vendor Selection
24. PUR102 General Purchasing
25. PUR103 Project Purchasing
26. PUR104 Receiving And Inspection
27. PUR105 Shipping And Freight Claims
28. PUR106 Accounts Payable And Cash Disbursements

Revenue

29. REV101 Sales Order Entry
30. REV102 Point-Of-Sale Orders
31. REV103 Customer Credit Approval And Terms
32. REV104 Sales Order Acceptance
33. REV105 Shipment Of Goods
34. REV106 Invoicing And Accounts Receivable
35. REV107 Sales Tax Collection
36. REV108 Progress Billing
37. REV109 Account Collections
38. REV110 Customer Returns

1.0 PURPOSE

The purpose of this Accounting manual is to document the principles and policies governing our company's accounting practices.

The principles and policies provide:

- A foundation for a system of internal controls
- Guidance in current financial activities
- Criteria for decisions on appropriate accounting treatment.
- Accounting officers with direction and guidance in connection with those accounting transactions, procedures, and reports that should be uniform throughout the Company.

When consistently applied throughout the company, these principles and policies assure that the various financial statements issued by the company accurately reflect the results of the company's operations.

Internal controls provide a system of checks and balances intended to identify irregularities, prevent waste, fraud and abuse from occurring, and assist in resolving discrepancies that are accidentally introduced in the operations of the business.

All additional departmental or functional policies and procedures written should conform to and parallel the policies in this manual. All changes to policies and procedures are required to be reviewed to ensure that there are no conflicts with the policies stated in this Accounting Manual.

[This page intentionally left blank]

2.0 SCOPE

The Accounting Manual is an official directive of the President. It is published and maintained by the Controller as part of the general responsibility for company accounting policy assigned to the office of the Controller.

2.1 RESPONSIBILITY

The policies stated in this manual apply to all operations and activities at our company. It is the responsibility of all department managers to help implement and maintain the procedures required by this manual and to ensure all processes conform to these requirements.

It is the responsibility of all employees to follow procedures that implement these policies and to help strive for continuous improvement in all activities and processes of our company.

The goal is to make the Manual as clear and useful as possible. All users are encouraged to contact the company Controller with any suggestions for revising or improving the Manual.

2.2 EXCLUSIONS

2.2.1 Internal Auditing

Internal Auditing is not covered in this accounting manual but it is an important function required in larger companies.

2.2.2 Payroll

Payroll functions are included as part of ABR41 ***Bizmanualz™ Human Resources Policies, Procedures and Forms.***

2.2.3 Finance and Treasury

Finance and Treasury functions are included as part of ABR42 ***Bizmanualz™ Finance Policies, Procedures and Forms.***

2.2.4 Information Systems

Information Systems functions are included as part of ABR34 ***Bizmanualz™ Computer & Network Policies, Procedures and Forms.***

2.2.5 Security Planning

Security Planning functions are included as part of ABR32 ***Bizmanualz™ Security Planning Policies, Procedures and Forms.***

2.2.6 Disaster Recovery

Disaster Recovery functions are included as part of ABR33 ***Bizmanualz™ Disaster Recovery Policies, Procedures and Forms.***

[This page intentionally left blank]

3.0 MANAGEMENT RESPONSIBILITY

The accounting department is headed by the controller or Chief Financial Officer (CFO). In a smaller company this may be the same person.

3.1 ACCOUNTING ORGANIZATION

The accounting department is organized into three main responsibilities: Finance and Treasury, Accounting, and Operations staffs.

3.1.1 Accounting Department Organization Chart

The company's organizational framework provides the foundation for coordinating and administrating the accounting management system. A description of the roles and responsibilities applicable to the accounting and operations staff are provided. Responsibilities specific to certain procedures or tasks are presented in the related procedures.

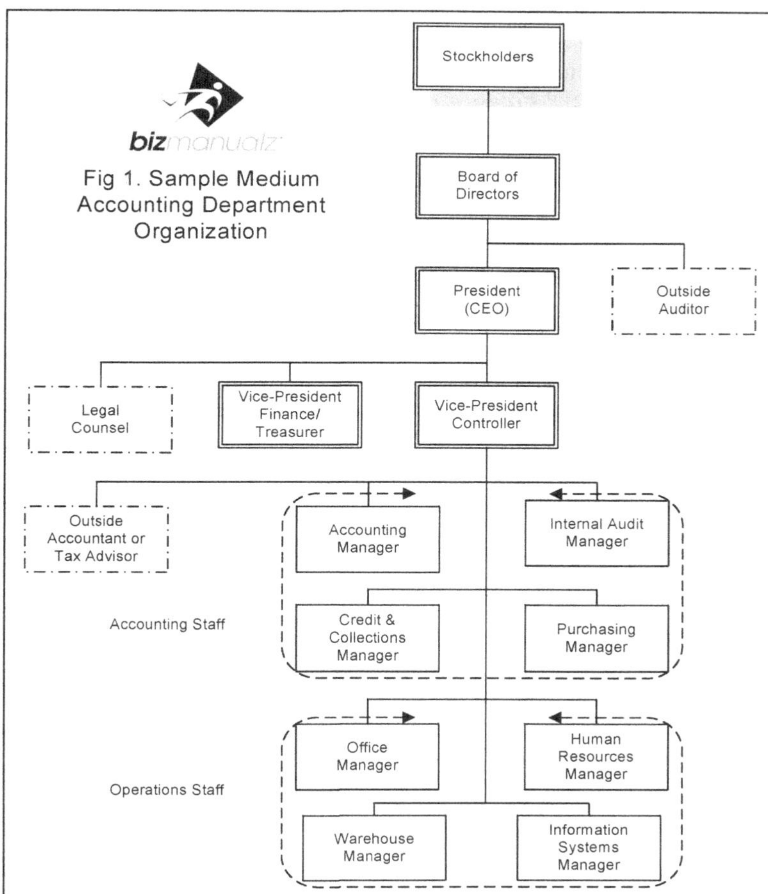

Fig 1. Sample Medium Accounting Department Organization

Figure 2 Sample Medium Accounting Department Organization shows the general organization of the company's accounting department. The actual Organization Chart may vary in detail based on the size of the department or organization involved and the type of activity performed.

[Note: in a larger company the administrative or operations staff may report to the Vice-President of Finance and Administration in order to allow the Controller to focus on the accounting operations.]

3.1.2 Finance & Treasury Responsibilities

Finance & Treasury responsibilities are focused on raising capital, debt and or equity appropriations, cash management, Treasury investments, fund balances, and management activities.

The Finance/Treasurer is responsible to the President for all long-range financial matters and to establish company-wide financial and administrative objectives, policies, programs, and practices, which insure the company of a continuously sound financial structure.

The Chief Financial Officer controls the flow of cash through the organization and maintains the integrity of funds, securities and other valuable documents. See ABR42 ***Bizmanualz™ Finance Policies, Procedures and Forms*** for a complete discussion of finance and treasury activities.

3.1.3 Controller Responsibilities

The Controller directs the accounting and control functions, reporting the results of operations and provides chronological systems. The Controller is accountable to the President and supervises the accounting and operations staff.

Major Duties and Responsibilities:

- o Develops and implements accounting policies, coordinates systems and procedures, and prepares operating data and special reports as required, including interim and year-end financial statements. Maintains the company's system of accounts and keeps books and records on all company transactions and assets.
- o Establishes, coordinates and administers, as an integral part of management, an adequate plan for the control of operations including, profit planning, programs for capital investing and financing, sales forecasts, expense budgets and cost standards, together with necessary controls and procedures to effectuate the plan.
- o In conjunction with the President and Vice President of Finance, coordinates, reviews and endorses budget proposals, discusses proposed changes and significant changes.
- o Compares performance with operating plans and standards, and reports and interprets the results of operations to all levels of management.
- o Provides for the control and editing of all company orders, to insure conformity to established policies and procedures, and to facilitate data control and retrieval of records generated by these orders.

- Establishes and administers tax policies and procedures.
- Supervises or coordinates the preparation of reports to government agencies.
- Coordinates all matters of business between the company and its stock transfer agents and registrars.
- Provides other managers and departments with information required by them to carry out their assigned responsibilities.
- Assures protection for the assets of the business through internal control, internal auditing and assuring proper insurance coverage.
- Assists Marketing in establishing and maintaining product pricing policies.
- Serves as a liaison between the company and legal counsel or outside accountant support. Recommends the appointment of independent public accountants overseeing their audit work.
- Provides advice on all matters to the Vice President of Finance and the President.

3.1.4 Accounting Staff Responsibilities

Accounting staff responsibilities are focused on accurately documenting the Company's operations, collecting all money owed to the company, and responsibly disbursing money owed to vendors.

The accounting staff consists of the following positions:

- Accounting Manager. Directs and organizes all general accounting activities and accounting staff. Prepares accounting and financial reports and ensures accurate accounting systems and record keeping. Reports directly to the Controller. Assists in supervision of Accounts Payable and Accounts Receivable Clerks.

- Credit & Collections Manager. Responsible for processing customer credit inquiries, approving credit/financing terms and collection of delinquent accounts. Reports directly to the Controller. Coordinates activities with Accounting and Sales.

- Purchasing Manager. Responsible for purchasing of all inventory, supplies and capital goods for the company including negotiating price, delivery and credit terms. Evaluates vendors and determines most cost-effective inventory and reorder levels. Reports to the Controller. Coordinates activities with all departments; works closely with Manufacturing, Accounts Payable, and Receiving.

- Internal Audit Manager. Responsible for establishing and implementing internal control mechanisms; performing audit functions on payroll, and billing; assist in developing new or refining existing accounting policies and procedures; assist in streamlining current business processes to improve the overall efficiency and effectiveness of the company.

  Note: Internal Auditing is not covered in this accounting manual but it is an important function required in larger companies.

3.1.5 Operations Staff Responsibilities

Operations staff responsibilities are focused on diligently supporting the operating transactions of the company with assistance, training, and other services, as needed.

[Note: in a larger company the administrative or operations staff may report to the Vice-President of Finance and Administration in order to allow the Controller to focus on the accounting operations.]

The operations staff consists of the following positions:

- Office Manager. Responsible for performing a variety of administrative, office and clerical functions. Reports directly to Controller. Assists and coordinates activities with the President and other managers in the company. Supervises Receptionist.
- Human Resources Manager. Develops and updates personnel policies, procedures and forms. Assists and supports department managers and employees regarding personnel issues. Maintains personnel records. Reports directly to the Controller. Coordinates activities and assists all department managers and employees.
- Information Systems Manager. Responsible for overseeing network and Internet operations; determines technical goals in consultation with top management, produces detailed plans for the accomplishment of these goals; plans and coordinates the installation and upgrading of hardware and software; analyzes the computer and information needs of the organization and determines personnel and equipment requirements.
- Warehouse Manager. Pulls orders and packs and prepares them for shipment. Supervises all shipping and receiving clerks and functions. Contracts with freight carriers for the most beneficial service of the company. Reports to Controller. Coordinates with Sales and Customer Service.

3.2 MANAGEMENT COMMITMENT

Top Management at our company shows its commitment to the accounting management system through the development and implementation of this accounting manual. Additionally, management commitment is demonstrated through the Company Accounting Policy, the specific objectives that are set and reviewed during Management Review Meetings and by providing the resources required to meet our objectives for continually improving the effectiveness of our operations and accounting system.

The management team consisting of the President and all department managers is chartered with ensuring our accounting management system meets customer as well as statutory and regulatory requirements

3.3 MANAGEMENT ACCOUNTING POLICY

Our company has established an Accounting Manual that we feel is appropriate to our organization and meets the practices set forth in GAAP. This policy is communicated throughout the company. Department managers and supervisors are responsible for ensuring all employees understand the policy. To ensure our policy remains appropriate, it is reviewed at least annually at one of our Management Review meetings.

The Company Accounting Policy:

- It is the policy of our company to design and produce financial statements in keeping with Generally Accepted Accounting Principles (GAAP), Financial Accounting Standards Board (FASB) Statements of Financial Accounting Concepts and comply with all statutory and regulatory requirements. We accomplish this by adhering to our Accounting Management System and use operational methods as documented in our Accounting Manual.
- We strive to continually improve the effectiveness of our Accounting Management System by monitoring our performance against our established objectives and through leadership that promotes employee involvement. This concept represents our company's commitment to quality accounting and the increasing need to better serve our customers, shareholders, and employees.

3.4 PLANNING

3.4.1 Accounting Objectives

Our company shall establish objectives on an annual basis. These objectives shall be measurable and consistent with the Accounting Policy, and reviewed at least annually at Management Review meetings.

3.4.2 Accounting System Planning

As part of annual strategic planning meetings, our company establishes strategic objectives and goals for revenue, profit, and expenses. These objectives are supported by specific measures that track performance against those objectives using the budgeting process. Department managers in turn set departmental objectives with specific performance measures and targets that support the company objectives.

As situations arise that demand changes to the accounting management system, either to meet objectives or because of changing business conditions, all changes will be reviewed by the management team to ensure the integrity of the accounting system is maintained.

3.5 RESPONSIBILITY, AUTHORITY, AND COMMUNICATION

3.5.1 Responsibility and Authority

Responsibilities and authorities at our company are defined in each Job Description. Job Descriptions are posted on the company intranet and are also used during annual performance reviews.

3.5.2 Management Representative

The President has appointed the Controller as the Management Representative with the responsibility and authority to:

a) Ensure that processes needed for the Accounting Management System are established, implemented and maintained.

b) Report to top management on the performance of the Accounting Management System and any need for improvement.

c) Ensure the promotion of awareness of accounting requirements throughout the organization.

d) Serve as the liaison with external parties on matters relating to the Accounting Management System.

3.5.3 Internal communication

In line with our company's policy of leadership through employee involvement, our company's personnel policies have established open communication throughout the organization.

The effectiveness of our Accounting Management System is evident through Internal Audit results, Management Reports, and the departmental performance measures. Other than confidential information, company and departmental performance measures are posted on bulletin boards throughout our company. Internal Audit results are shared at departmental meetings as appropriate.

3.5.4 Referenced Procedures:

G&A104 Management Reports

3.6 MANAGEMENT REPORTING

3.6.1 General

The President and management team shall review the company's Accounting Management System, on a semi-annual basis and more frequently if needed, to ensure its continuing suitability, adequacy and effectiveness. This review shall include assessing opportunities for improvement and the need for changes to the Accounting Management System, including the accounting policy and objectives.

The Controller is responsible for maintaining records from management reviews.

3.6.2 Review Input

The Controller and department managers provide the following information for Management Review meetings:

a) Results of audits

b) Employee feedback

c) Process performance

d) Follow-up actions from previous management reviews

e) Changes that could affect the Accounting Management System

f) Recommendations for improvement

3.6.3 Review Output

Records shall include the output from the management review and shall include any decisions and actions related to:

a) Improvement of the effectiveness of the Accounting Management System and its processes

b) Improvement of processes related to accounting requirements

c) Resource needs

3.6.4 Referenced Procedures:

G&A104 Management Reports

3.7 BUSINESS CONDUCT

Unethical business conduct, actions or even the appearance of unethical behavior is unacceptable under any conditions. The reputation of the company depends on each employee applying common sense in situations where specific rules of conduct are insufficient to provide clear direction. A strong sense of personal ethics, which should extend beyond compliance with applicable laws, is necessary to guide the behavior of all employees.

All employees should comply with the ethical standards of the company as set forth in this manual. If a situation feels awkward, then the employees should ask themselves:

- Is my action legal and ethical?
- Does my action comply with corporate policy?
- Is my action appropriate in the situation?
- Would my action be an embarrassment to the company, if known?
- Does my action agree with my personal ethics or behavior?

An employee should be able to answer "yes" to all of these questions before taking action or compromising themselves in the situation.

All Managers are responsible for the ethical business conduct and behavior of their employees. Managers should consider the appropriate courses of action in terms of both ethical and economic factors. Each decision should be based on the guidelines provided in this Accounting Manual as well as their own personal beliefs of what's right and wrong.

[This page intentionally left blank]

4.0 ACCOUNTING MANAGEMENT SYSTEM

4.1 OBJECTIVES

Through this manual and associated procedures and documents, our company has established, documented, and implemented an Accounting Management System. The system is designed to result in improving the effectiveness of our accounting operations and in our ability to satisfy auditor requirements.

4.2 REQUIREMENTS

Maintenance of the Accounting Management System is the responsibility of the Controller/CFO in conjunction with the Accounting Department.

4.2.1 Overview

The Controller maintains all documents that identify the sequence of accounting processes and, in conjunction with the appropriate department managers, defines the interactions of the processes within the procedures defining these processes.

Processes for management activities, provision of resources, and measurement reporting are included. Procedures shall include the methods needed to ensure that the accountability and control of processes are effective.

Top Management will ensure the availability of resources to support the operation and monitoring of processes through regular interaction with department managers and through review activities at Management Review meetings.

Department Managers and the Controller will monitor, measure and analyze processes and implement any actions necessary to achieve intended results and continual improvement of the processes. These results will also be monitored at Management Review meetings.

Any processes that are outsourced that may affect our company's conformity to requirements shall be controlled. The Controller and appropriate department manager(s) are responsible for defining the methods to control outsourced processes and procedures.

4.2.2 Internal Controls

Internal controls, procedures, and practices will be utilized to ensure that:

- Obligations and costs comply with applicable laws.
- All assets are safeguarded against waste, fraud, loss, unauthorized use, and misappropriation.
- Revenues and expenditures applicable to company operations are recorded and accounted for properly so that accounts and reliable financial and statistical reports may be prepared and accountability of the assets may be maintained.

- o Programs are efficiently and effectively carried out in accordance with applicable laws and management policy.

4.2.3 Audit Findings

Managers are to promptly evaluate findings and recommendations reported by auditors and then determine proper actions in response to audit findings and recommendations (e.g., develop corrective actions). Managers should complete, within established time frames, all actions that correct or otherwise resolve the matters brought to management's attention.

The audit resolution process begins when the results of an audit are reported to management, and is completed only after actions have been taken that correct identified deficiencies, produce improvements, or demonstrate the audit findings and recommendations are either invalid or do not warrant management actions.

4.3 TRANSACTIONS

All transactions recorded or posted into the Accounting Management System should be properly authorized and accurately represent the activity being documented. Both the timing and amount of the transaction should be in accordance with company accounting policies defined in this manual.

4.3.1 Authorization

Transactions and other significant events are to be authorized and executed only by persons acting within the scope of their authority. It is the principal means of assuring that only valid transactions and other events are entered into. Modification or adjustment to previously recorded transactions requires authorization.

4.3.2 Timing

All transaction dates recorded in the company accounting system should accurately reflect the date the transaction occurred. Revenues should be recognized when earned and expenses when incurred. Processing, cutoff and period-end closing schedules and procedures should be documented. Cash sales should be recorded at the time of sale and deposited.

4.3.3 Amounts

Prior or related transactions should be checked for conformity with the transaction being recorded (e.g., match invoice to purchase order). Amount of posted transactions should be checked against source documents. Balances with third parties should be verified as appropriate (i.e. debtors, creditors, or custodians of investments). Transactions should be recorded in conformity with documented policies in this manual.

4.3.4 Accuracy

Transactions should be recorded in the accounting system accurately. An approved set of general ledger and subsidiary accounts are maintained for assets, liabilities, revenues, expenses, budgetary accounts, and other accounts.

All transactions should be supported by documentary evidence, which becomes part of the accounting records. Error transactions should be reviewed, resolved, and cleared in a timely fashion. Manually determined control totals should be reconciled with recorded results.

The Accounting Management System utilizes standard forms and provides control and accountability over these forms. Supervisors should review posted accounting transactions with source documents and processing documents.

4.3.5 Referenced Procedures:

G&A101 Chart of Accounts
G&A104 Management Reports
G&A105 Period-End Review & Closing
CSH101 Cash Drawers and Credit Cards
CSH102 Cash Receipts And Deposits
REV106 Invoicing and Accounts Receivable
REV108 Progress Billing
CSH107 Bank Account Reconciliations
PUR106 Accounts Payable And Cash Disbursements

4.4 DOCUMENTATION

This Accounting Manual and the associated procedures are intended to satisfy the documentation requirements for an Accounting Management System. Department managers and supervisors are responsible for identifying any additional documents needed to ensure the effective planning, operation and control of processes.

Procedures may vary in detail based on the size of the department or organization involved and the type of activity performed. Procedure developers shall consider this as well as the complexity of the processes and interactions, and the competence of the personnel involved.

Documents may be any medium including: software programs, electronic text files, or hardcopy documents for example.

4.4.1 Accounting Manual

This Accounting Manual provides the top-level organizational document for the Accounting Management System. The Accounting Manual defines the scope, policies and processes of our company's Accounting Management system as well as Management's responsibility for the system.

4.4.2 Control of Documents

All Documents required by the Accounting Management System shall be controlled. The Document Control Procedure defines the controls needed to:

a) Approve documents for adequacy prior to issue.

b) Review and update as necessary and re-approve documents.

c) Ensure that changes and the current revision status of documents are identified.

d) Ensure that relevant versions of applicable documents are available at points of use.

e) Ensure that documents remain legible and readily identifiable.

f) Ensure that documents of external origin are identified and their distribution controlled.

g) Prevent the unintended use of obsolete documents, and apply suitable identification to them if they are retained for any purpose.

4.4.3 Control of Records

Procedures define appropriate records to be maintained for the effective operation of the Accounting Management System, including evidence of conformity to requirements. Records shall remain legible, readily identifiable and retrievable. The Files and Records Management Procedure defines the controls needed for the identification, storage, protection, retrieval, retention time and disposition of records.

4.4.4 Accounting Transactions

All transactions and other significant events should be clearly documented, properly classified and readily available for examination.

This standard applies to:

- The entire process or life cycle of a transaction or event and includes the initiation and authorization
- All aspects of the transaction while in process
- Its final classification in summary records.

4.4.5 Referenced Procedures:

G&A102 Files and Records Management
G&A110 Document Control

4.5 SECURITY

Access to resources and records should be limited to authorized personnel only. Accountability for the custody and use of resources should be assigned and maintained as well. Periodic comparisons should be made of the resources with the recorded accountability to determine whether the two agree. The frequency of the comparison shall be a function of the vulnerability of the asset. Restrictions of access to resources shall also depend upon the vulnerability of the resource as well as the perceived risk of loss, both of which shall be periodically assessed.

4.5.1 Physical Security

Physical security measures should be adopted to protect the assets and employees of the Company from abuse, fraud, theft, or damage. Security procedures for the protection of assets and employees are addressed within the company's Security Manual. See ABR32 ***Bizmanualz™ Security Planning Policies, Procedures and Forms.***

4.5.2 Disaster Security

Disaster security measures should be adopted to enable the company to continue the operations of the Accounting Management System with limited interruption. Disaster procedures for operations recovery are addressed within the company's Disaster Manual. See ABR33 ***Bizmanualz™ Disaster Recovery Policies, Procedures and Forms***.

4.5.3 Information Security

Information security measures should be adopted to protect the company's information assets from unauthorized access, abuse, tampering, theft, or use. Information security procedures for the protection and authorized use of computer and network assets are addressed within the Company's Information Systems Manual. See ABR34 ***Bizmanualz™ Computer & Network Policies, Procedures and Forms.***

4.6 COST ACCOUNTING

Cost is the financial measure of resources consumed or acquired in accomplishing a specified purpose, such as performing a service, providing a product, or carrying out a project or program regardless of when the resources were ordered, received, or paid for. Cost can be defined in a variety of ways depending on the objectives or information desired.

Cost accounting is defined as a technique or method for determining the cost of a project, process, or thing. This cost is determined by direct measurement, specific assignment, or systematic and rational allocation. Central to cost accounting is the process for tracing various input costs to the product or services of the company.

This section presents cost classifications based on the following characteristics: time incurred, reaction to changes in activity levels, and influence on decision making.

4.6.1 Costing Purposes

The Controller should accumulate, distribute, monitor, and evaluate cost information during each accounting period, when appropriate. Management will use cost information for purposes such as:

- Making decisions and planning future operations with the knowledge of the costs of projects, programs, and other activities
- Assisting in establishing standards of performance based at least partially on past cost history
- Determining the efficient and effective distribution and use of resources
- Supporting performance evaluation based on actual costs versus budgeted costs
- Recovering costs for products and services provided to entities
- Preparing reimbursable work and cooperative agreements

- o Supporting budget formulation through responses to requests for information

Cost accounting is not applicable to all activities; however, for those activities that do use cost accounting, the principles in this section are designed to assure that:

- o Cost accounting information is communicated consistently throughout the company
- o Reviews to evaluate the cost/benefit of cost information for specific programs are based on consistent criteria
- o Only the highest level of aggregated information required for management decisions

The Controller is responsible for ensuring that any cost information maintained to meet customer service requirements is minimized and that recovery of the cost to provide information to customers is maximized.

4.6.2 Cost - Time Incurred

Costs may be measured in relationship to the time the cost is incurred. In many cases, the measurement time for cost is specified in authorizing documents or contracts for a program. In other cases, the Controller is responsible for determining which cost will be used for specific purposes, and for assuring that similar activities are treated consistently within the company.

The three most common measurements are historical costs, current market costs, and budgeted costs.

- o Historical Cost is the cash equivalent price of goods and services at the date of acquisition. This cost does not change over time.
- o Current Market Cost (also referred to as replacement cost) is the current value of an asset. Depending on whether the asset is tangible or intangible and the availability of similar assets on the open market, current market cost may be measured by replacement cost, reproduction cost, sales value, net realizable value, or net present value of future cash flows.
- o Budgeted Cost (also referred to as standard cost) is the cost that should be incurred to produce a product or provide a service based on past experience producing or providing like-items. Thus, comparison of actual costs with the predetermined benchmark alerts program managers to those areas in which the actual costs appear excessive.

4.6.3 Cost - Reaction to Changes in Activity Levels

In any period, cost may or may not change in relationship to changes in levels of activity. Based on the relationship to changes in levels of activity, costs are classified as variable, fixed, or mixed costs. Activity measures can include production or service levels, machine hours, or sales in units or dollars. The way a cost reacts to changes in activity is determined by how the total cost for the period, rather than the cost of a single unit of activity, changes when activity levels change.

The Controller is responsible for developing cost projections and budgets that identify costs by variable, fixed, or mixed categories. All managers are responsible for minimizing variable and mixed costs and ensuring that fixed costs are minimized, and are fairly spread over all projects, whether or not those projects incorporate cost accounting.

- Variable Costs are costs that vary in total in direct proportion to changes in levels of activity. If total cost varies in direct proportion to activity changes, the cost per unit is constant.
- Fixed Costs represent all costs that remain constant within the Company's relevant range of activity. A relevant range is a range of activity in which costs behave in accordance with the way they have been defined, generally the normal operating range.
- Mixed Costs has both a variable and fixed component; it does not fluctuate in direct proportion with activity, nor does it remain constant with changes in levels of activity.

4.6.4 Cost - Influence on Decision Making

The Controller is responsible for classifying costs as either direct or indirect and ensuring that costs are consistently classified as either direct or indirect in similar situations.

Direct costs are all costs that can be specifically or readily identified with producing a specific product or providing a specific service. Direct costs include direct labor, equipment purchased for use on a program, and other direct costs. Direct labor is the portion of base wages and salaries, which can be identified with and charged to a particular activity. This includes:

- Fringe Benefits are those allowances and services provided to employees as compensation in addition to wages and salaries, including retirement, health insurance, and life insurance. Fringe benefits are allocated as a rate applied to direct labor costs. The Controller is responsible for determining the fringe rate based on all labor and fringe costs, regardless of where an employee works. A single fringe rate must be applied to all employees in all projects, unless the Controller has developed separate cost pools that reflect a significantly different fringe cost among groups of employees.
- Overtime and Premium Pay are charged in the same manner as the regular wage portion of an employee's earnings for hours identified with a specific activity.
- Other Personnel Costs are charged in the same manner as the related base labor charge, e.g., allowances for offsite pay, location allowances, hardship pay, hazardous duty pay, and uniform allowances.

Equipment used in an activity for which costs are accumulated can be charged in either of two manners: a) charging for the full acquisition cost, or b) recovery of a portion of depreciation. The Controller is responsible for determining whether equipment can be charged in full to a project, and if not, for determining the rate and basis for charging equipment usage to projects.

Other direct cost items that are incurred or consumed exclusively for the completion of a specific activity include the following examples:

- Miscellaneous supplies and materials
- Equipment rentals
- Travel
- Purchased services (i.e., printing, ADP services, and photographic reproduction)
- Contractual services

Indirect costs are those costs, which cannot be specifically identified with producing a specific product, or providing a specific service but which can be shown to bear some relationship to, result from, or be in support of, the product or service.

Indirect costs must be accumulated in indirect cost pools. The Controller is responsible for clearly defining identifiable cost pools. Indirect costs may include the following examples, if the item is not directly attributable to a specific activity:

- Space rental
- Utilities, including telephone expenses
- Postage
- Unemployment compensation benefit costs
- Data processing, management, and control
- Equipment rentals
- Miscellaneous supplies and materials
- Equipment costs (excluding those recovered as a direct costs)
- Training, employee development, and personnel transfers, including costs of travel and time in-transit
- Budget development and program planning
- Research and development activities
- Administrative support such as procurement, contracting, office services, property management, payroll, voucher processing, personnel services, records management, and document control
- Reports, including report preparation and distribution
- Safety management, including inspection and training
- EEO and other affirmative action programs

The indirect cost pool will generally include costs that benefit both cost recoverable and non-cost recoverable work. Although indirect costs are not required to be allocated to non-cost recoverable work, an allocation basis must be used that would, if applied to all projects or activities, fairly distribute the cost pool over the benefited activities. Cost recovery projects must not be unduly burdened with indirect costs.

The Controller is responsible for developing and documenting the allocation method, using a generally acceptable and consistently applied overhead rate based on direct costs, identifiable cost pools, and the cost elements that are charges to those pools.

4.7 BASIS OF ACCOUNTING

There are two fundamental methodologies of accounting, each with assumptions, constraints and theories, which guide all financial recording, reporting and measurement activities: Cash and Accrual.

- Cash basis accounting records financial events only when cash actually changes hands in an arms-length transaction.
- Accrual basis accounting records revenues when earned and expenses the costs associated with the revenue earned when incurred.

The company requires the use of the accrual basis of accounting for financial transactions unless otherwise stated in this manual.

[This page intentionally left blank]

5.0 PROCESSES AND CONTROLS

The company has planned and developed the processes needed to properly document, track and control transactions for revenues, expenses, assets, liabilities, and equities. The results of this planning are the processes and procedures defined in our Accounting Management System documentation.

These processes and procedures include the accounting objectives and requirements for our company, the required verification, validation, and inspection activities specific to our company and the criteria for order acceptance verification. The records needed to provide evidence that these processes meet Generally Accepted Accounting Practices (GAAP) are defined in the procedures.

Consideration is given for the need to establish processes, documents, and obtain resources specific to new orders as they are developed or during contract or order review.

bizmanualz

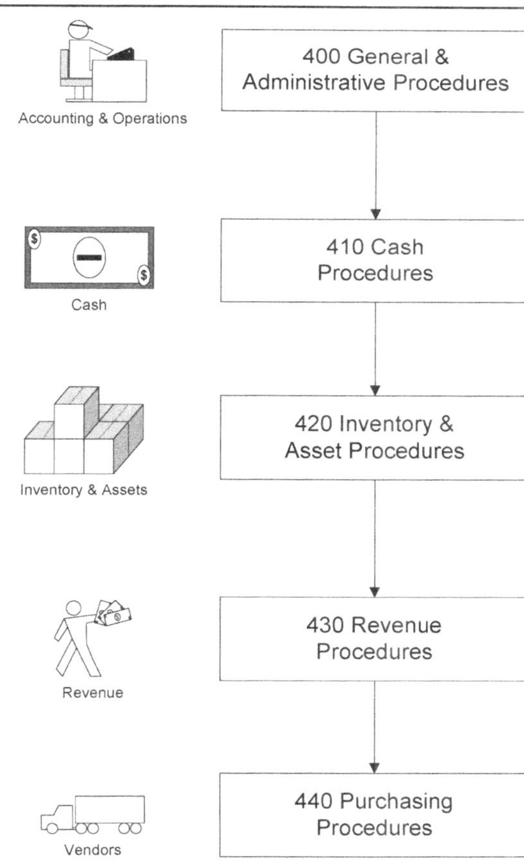

Fig 2. Accounting Management System Processes and Controls

[This page intentionally left blank]

5.1 GENERAL & ADMINISTRATIVE

The General and Administrative procedures encompass a wide range of miscellaneous activities from defining the chart of accounts, maintaining files and records, to Period-End Review & Closing, Taxes & Insurance, and producing Management Reports. The following General and Administrative Procedures should be utilized to control the company's miscellaneous accounting activities.

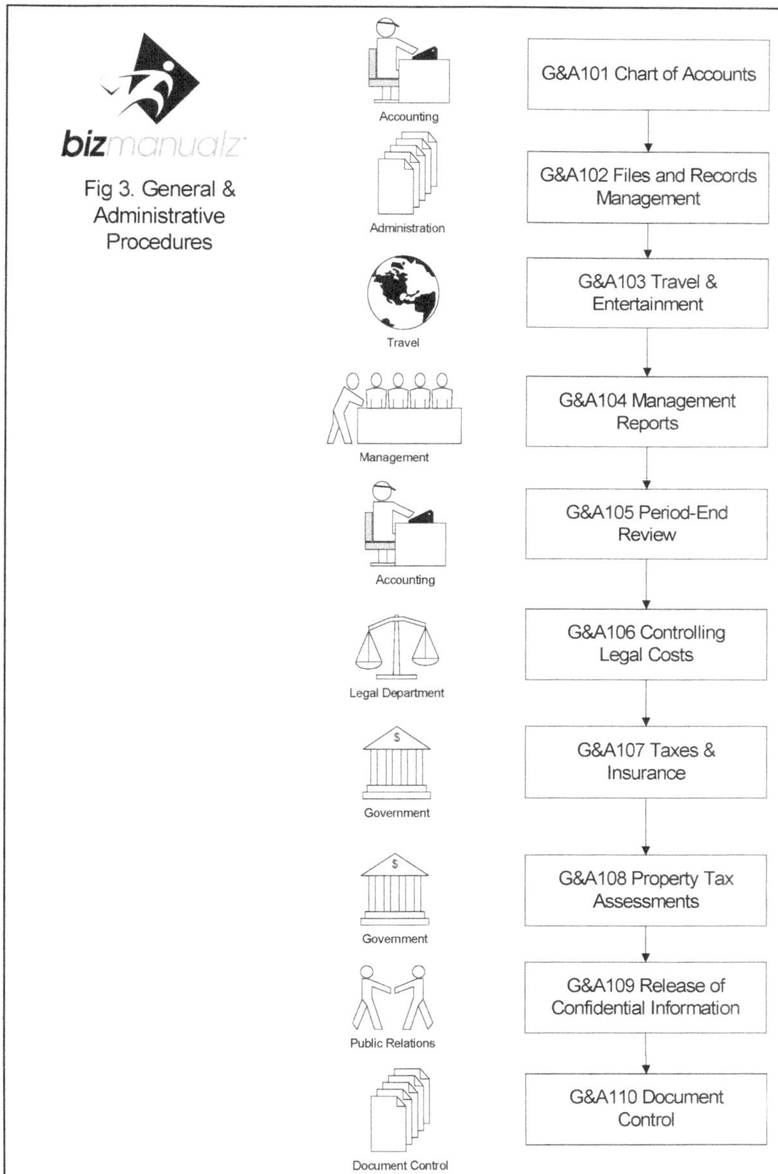

Fig 3. General & Administrative Procedures

5.1.1 Chart of Accounts

To facilitate the record keeping process for accounting, all ledger accounts should be assigned a descriptive account title and account number, also known as a Chart of Accounts. The Chart of Accounts provides the organization or method for assignment and maintenance of the company's ledger accounts, in order to produce meaningful financial data for the company.

5.1.2 Files and Records Management

The company will retain records in an orderly fashion for time periods that comply with legal and governmental requirements and as needed for general business requirements. To accomplish this policy, the company should outline the methods for filing, retaining and disposing of all business documentation generated by the company. However, this does not necessarily cover internal or certain day-to-day business correspondence.

5.1.3 Travel and Entertainment

The company should provide guidelines for travel and entertainment expenses, account for all advances promptly and accurately and to communicate the procedures for reimbursement. This applies to all departments and individuals who travel or entertain for the company.

The company recognizes that employees who travel far from home to represent the company's business interests must forego their living accommodations and may forfeit personal time. Accordingly, the company will make efforts to provide comfortable and secure accommodations for lodging, meals and travel for employees. However, these items are not intended to be perquisites and the company reserves the right to deny reimbursement of expenses that are considered lavish or extravagant.

All reservations required for business travel and entertainment should be made through the designated Travel Coordinator. Expenses are to be within established company guidelines and will be reimbursed with proper documentation. Employees are expected to spend the company's money as carefully and judiciously as they would their own.

5.1.4 Management Reports

The company should provide the format and content requirements for preparation of the Financial Reports. Department Managers will prepare summary reports of vital operating statistics for the company, including sales, current debt, operating cash, accounts receivable and projected short-term cash flows. These reports are to be prepared in brevity and are to supplement detailed monthly and quarterly financial reports and are to be used for timely "hands-on" management.

5.1.5 Period-End Review & Closing

An orderly, timely and comprehensive review of all general ledger accounts should be performed or directed by the Controller or CFO to ensure an accurate representation of the company's financial statements. These practices are aimed at proving that the financial accounts are accurate, and if not, are properly adjusted to make them accurate, prior to closing.

The company should provide a general overview of the process to be completed for reviewing the accounting records at year-end or any particular month-end prior to closing. These practices apply to all accounts. Typically, all financial accounts are reviewed and then closed out as of the company's year-end.

5.1.6 Controlling Legal Costs

All individuals with the responsibility for contracting legal services and/or approving agreements, contracts, or any other legally associated transactions should employ various methods to manage and, whenever possible, minimize legal expenses.

5.1.7 Taxes and Insurance

To ensure compliance with all Federal, state, local, and other regulatory taxation requirements, the company should outline the general areas of taxation to be used as a checklist or guide in complying with tax requirements related to each specific location and organizational structure. This statement applies to all the business activities of the company.

5.1.8 Property Tax Assessments

All property tax assessments will be reviewed for accuracy and proper assessed valuations to ensure minimum property tax costs to the company. The company should outline the areas for review in assessments and methods for appealing overstated assessments. This statement applies to the property tax assessments for all sites owned by the company.

5.1.9 Confidential Information Release

The release of financial, statistical or other information that may be of a confidential nature to the company should be controlled. Individual requests should be referred to the Chief Financial Officer, Controller, or appropriate manager for disposition.

The company should provide a means for the control of information to banks, investors, investment houses, media, credit bureaus, or other agencies and organizations. All requests by an outsider to an employee regarding financial, sales, marketing, customers, personnel, vendors, or other company confidential information. If in doubt, verify with the Chief Financial Officer or Controller.

5.1.10 Document Control

All documents used to provide work direction or set policy should be reviewed, approved, distributed and controlled by the office of the Controller. The company should define the methods and responsibilities for controlling documents used to provide work direction or set policy, and to define methods for document revision, approval, and distribution. This applies to all documents required by the Accounting Management System. Documents of internal or external origin are included.

5.1.11 Referenced Procedures:

G&A101 Chart of Accounts
G&A102 Files and Records Management
G&A103 Travel and Entertainment
G&A104 Management Reports
G&A105 Period-End Review & Closing
G&A106 Controlling Legal Costs
G&A107 Taxes and Insurance
G&A108 Property Tax Assessments
G&A109 Confidential Information Release
G&A110 Document Control

5.2 CASH

Adequate control over all cash receipts and disbursement are a vital element of the company's internal accounting controls. The following Cash Procedures should be utilized to control the flow of cash through the company.

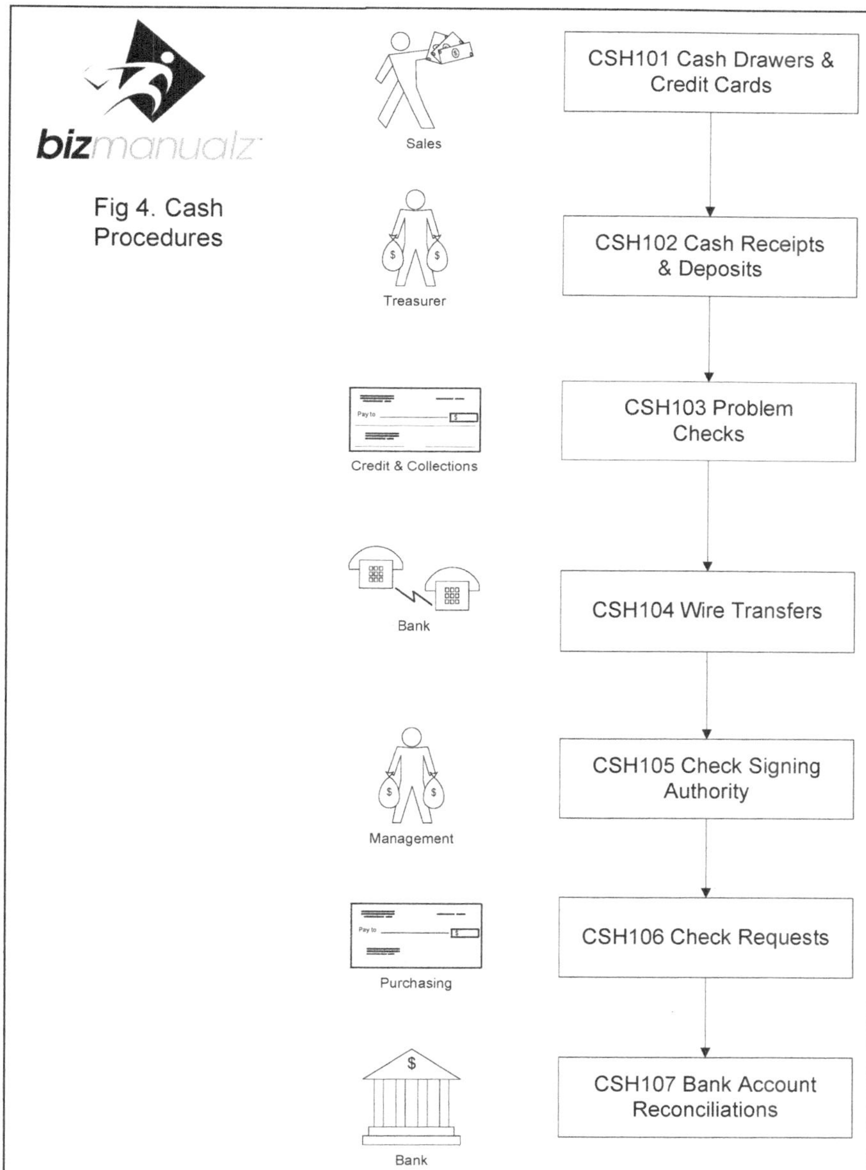

Fig 4. Cash Procedures

5.2.1 Cash Drawers and Credit Cards

Proper internal control should be maintained over funds received by cashiers or sales clerks at all times. The company should identify the practices for cash drawer control, including cash receipts, credit cards, special tender items, cash payouts and reconciliation with deposits.

5.2.2 Cash Receipts and Deposits

The company should establish the methods to be followed for receiving, applying and depositing cash receipts. This applies to all cash receipts received by the company. Accurate internal control of cash receipts and deposits should be maintained at all times. For example, Cash deposits should be made on the same day as receipt.

5.2.3 Problem Checks

The company should describe how problem checks should be handled before depositing, in order to save time in returning and following-up on unsigned checks, checks marked "payment in full", or those returned by the bank. This applies to all checks received by the company.

5.2.4 Wire Transfers

The company should provide additional payment options to customers and vendors in order to make funds immediately available to the receiving party. Wire transfers should be treated with special care and accuracy to prevent loss to the company or the customer.

The company should explain the steps necessary to ensure proper procedures are followed when processing wire transfer requests. This applies to customers who are sending or receiving wire transfers and the financial institutions, which process these requests.

5.2.5 Check Signing Authority

The company should outline "dollar limits", the check signing authority process, and limit the number of employees authorized to sign checks, while ensuring that there should be no fewer than three individuals at all times.

While a hired accountant, office manager, or accounting clerk may be responsible for entering bills, paying bills, and printing out checks, all printed checks and related documentation should be presented to a second individual for signing. No one person or employee (other than perhaps the owner) should be allowed to enter invoices, select invoices for payment, then print and sign checks. At a minimum, this process requires at least two individuals to ensure the integrity of the accounting system remains intact. This applies to all regular bank checking accounts of the company.

5.2.6 Check Requests

The company should describe the process for completing a check request form to ensure the efficient processing and record keeping of all manual check requests.

5.2.7 Bank Account Re-conciliations

The company should outline the practices for preparation of a monthly bank reconciliation and ensure the accuracy of the company's bank account records by proving the monthly balance shown in the bank's Account Register. This applies to all bank accounts maintained by the company.

5.2.8 Referenced Procedures:

CSH101 Cash Drawers and Credit Cards
CSH102 Cash Receipts and Deposits
CSH103 Problem Checks
CSH104 Wire Transfers
CSH105 Check Signing Authority
CSH106 Check Requests
CSH107 Bank Account Reconciliations

[This page intentionally left blank]

5.3 INVENTORY & ASSETS

Accurate reporting, classification and valuation of inventory are critical elements of internal controls because any changes in inventory and assets can have a dramatic and material impact on the balance sheet and income statement. The following Inventory and Asset Procedures should be utilized to account for and control all of the company's various assets.

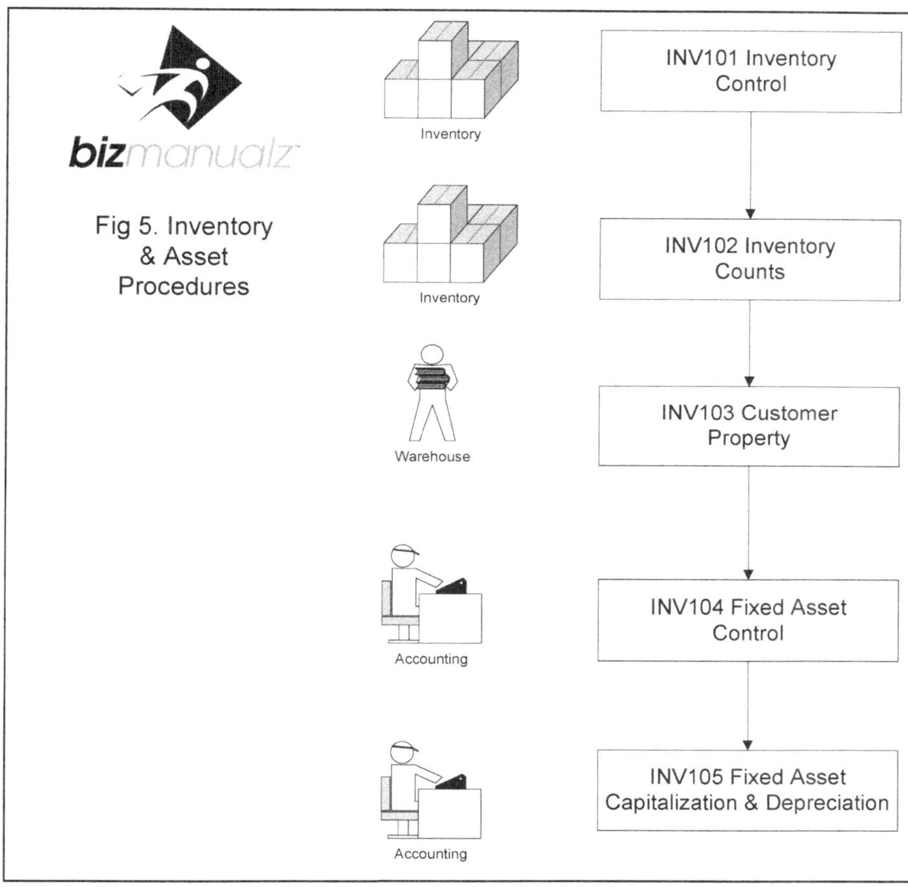

Fig 5. Inventory & Asset Procedures

5.3.1 Inventory Control

The investment in physical inventory will be maintained at the lowest effective level and supervised consistent with a common set of procedures and controls. The company should outline the actions taken for proper safekeeping and handling of all inventory to ensure it is saleable, usable, and traceable for quick selection and delivery. This applies to all inventory items including back room and warehouse storage.

5.3.2 Inventory Counts

All physical inventory will be periodically counted and reviewed on a frequent basis and under a common set of procedures and controls. The company should outline the actions to be taken to conduct an accurate physical count of all inventory items in order to verify the accuracy of the inventory ledger. This applies to all inventory items including back room, warehouse storage, off-site usage, demonstration, or customer loaner purposes.

5.3.3 Fixed Asset Control

Proper control procedures will be followed for all capital asset acquisitions, transfers and dispositions in order to provide internal control of capital equipment and to assist in reporting. The company should outline the procedures for acquiring, disposing and maintaining control of capital assets. This applies to all capital equipment with a value of $$500 or more and with a useful life greater than one year.

5.3.4 Customer Property

The company will store, as needed, a necessary level of customer property and should provide a reasonable level of protection and control for the type and value of the property. The company should define the methods to be used to identify, verify, protect and safeguard customer property while it is in possession of the company.

This applies to any items supplied by customers including: components and materials supplied for inclusion in product, tooling and fixtures used in manufacturing and inspection processes, and intellectual property for use and testing with software systems.

5.3.5 Fixed Asset Capitalization & Depreciation

Asset acquisitions with a useful life expectancy of greater than one year and with a minimum threshold amount as specified by the Controller should be capitalized by the company and depreciated.

The company should delineate the capitalization and depreciation methods for various asset groups. This applies to all acquisitions of capital assets for the company.

5.3.6 Referenced Procedures:

INV101 Inventory Control
INV102 Inventory Counts
INV103 Fixed Asset Control
INV104 Customer Property
INV105 Fixed Asset Capitalization & Depreciation

5.4 REVENUE

The proper identification and acceptance of all sales are an important element of controls for the income statement and represents the primary source of operational cash flow. The following Revenue Procedures should be utilized to account for and recognize all sales of the company.

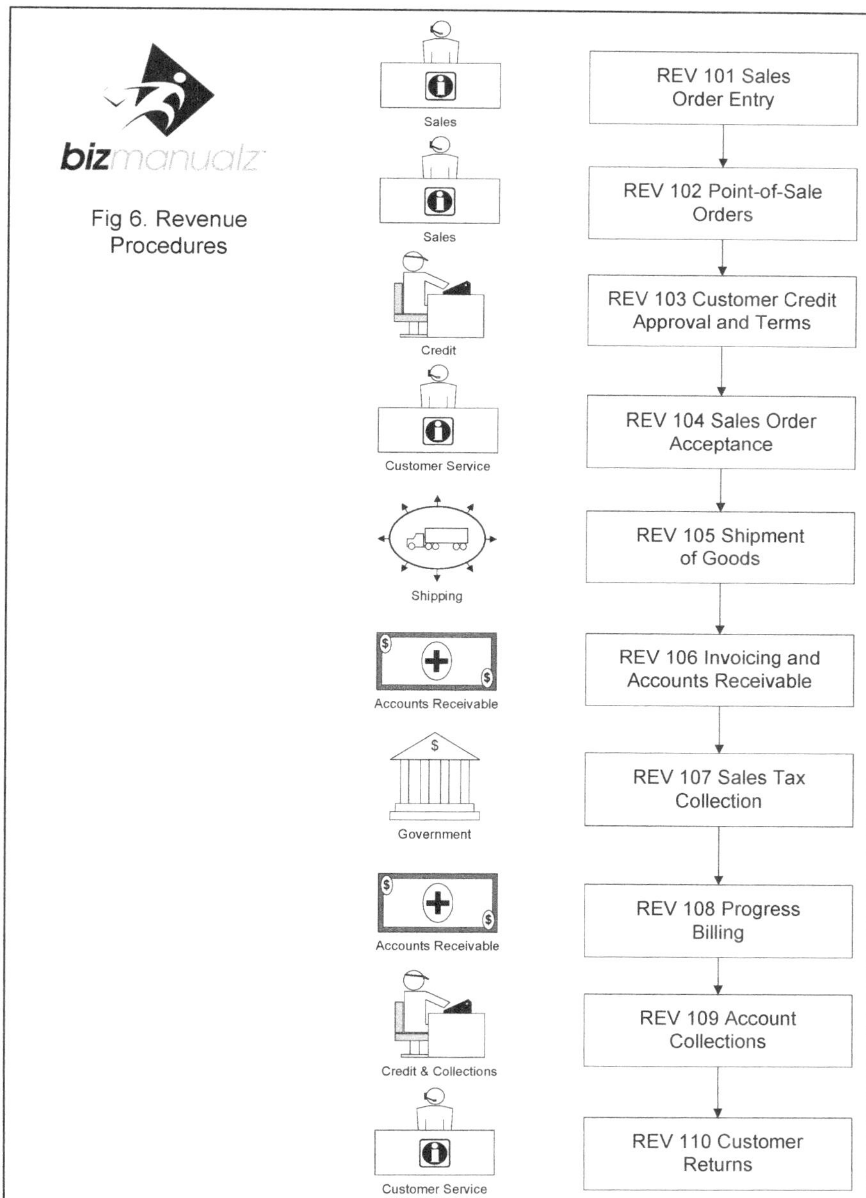

Fig 6. Revenue Procedures

5.4.1 Sales Order Entry

All customer orders will be processed in an efficient and organized manner to ensure accurate and prompt shipments. The company should summarize the preparation of documents, paperwork flow, and responsibilities by individuals and departments for obtaining a sales order from a customer through shipping and billing the customer.

Each individual involved in the sales order process should take the responsibility to determine that all required and necessary activities and documents are properly completed. This applies to all individuals and departments involved in consummation of the sales process, specifically including Sales, Customer Service, Credit, Manufacturing and Billing.

5.4.2 Point-Of-Sale Orders

The Company should provide the procedures for ensuring that all sales are proper and collectible and the effect on inventory and cash is posted correctly. There should be proper transaction controls over sales and proper reviews and authorizations by the store manager. This applies to all cashiers and cash handlers.

5.4.3 Customer Credit Approval and Terms

To reduce potential collection problems, new customer accounts or credit limit increases will be properly evaluated and approved prior to extending credit. The company should outlines the activities and responsibilities involved in obtaining credit approval for a potential customer before sales orders are consummated. These procedures are to be followed for all credit approvals requested by the Sales or Customer Service Departments for customers interested in open account, lease or rental financing.

5.4.4 Sales Order Acceptance

To ensure the highest customer services levels and reduce potential order problems, sales orders will be properly evaluated and approved prior to entry into the accounting system and fulfillment by the company.

The company should outline the activities and responsibilities involved in verifying the acceptability of all sales orders received before they are consummated. This applies all sales orders taken by the Sales or Customer Service Departments.

5.4.5 Shipment of Goods

All products and services should be delivered in an organized manner in order to maintain the highest customer service quality levels possible and to ensure compliance with all United States Customs laws and regulations when exporting goods & services.

The company should outline the steps for the packaging, safe storage, control and delivery of all products and services shipped by the company. This applies to all products and services distributed by the company, sales, customer service and shipping personnel.

5.4.6 Invoicing and Accounts Receivable

Accounting is responsible for the timely preparation and distribution of invoices to optimize cash flow and customer payments. Accounting should also maintain accurate records over Accounts Receivable and abide by proper internal controls.

The company should explain the methods for the preparation of invoices and accounts receivable records processing. This applies to all product sales and services provided by the company.

5.4.7 Sales Tax Collection

The company is liable for collecting sales tax anytime there is selling or renting of tangible personal property through a retail sale, subject to certain exemptions and conditions, within a jurisdiction in which the company is deemed to be engaged in business. The Company will at all times comply with all state and local sales tax regulations and requirements.

The Company should outline the sales tax rules, rates and exemptions for the collection of sales tax on sales and service by the company. This applies to individuals in Sales and Customer Service who are directly responsible for the sale of products.

5.4.8 Progress Billing

Progress billings will be made to clients on a timely basis throughout the life of the project. These billings will be accurate and easily understood by both parties involved.

The purpose for creating progress billings is to obtain payment for the portion of labor and materials used up to a certain point in time and before the project is fully completed. This improves the cash flow typical of long-term projects or assignments. This procedure applies to all service agreements or projects provided by the company.

5.4.9 Account Collections

All open accounts receivable with late or delinquent payment activity will be handled in a timely and effective manner to ensure maximum collections and an optimum accounts receivable turnover ratio.

The company should provide the actions and methods for processing late or delinquent payments. This applies to the Credit Department involved with collection of past due accounts receivable. The Sales and/or Shipping Departments may be involved in reference to shipping holds or special credit arrangements.

5.4.10 Customer Returns

The company should outline the steps and documents to be used for customers returning goods in order to provide adequate control of inventory and timely refunds to customers. This applies to all products and service parts sold by the company.

5.4.11 Referenced Procedures:

REV101 Sales Order Entry
REV102 Point-Of-Sale Orders
REV103 Customer Credit Approval and Terms
REV104 Sales Order Acceptance
REV105 Shipment of Goods
REV106 Invoicing and Accounts Receivable
REV107 Sales Tax Collection
REV108 Progress Billing
REV109 Account Collections
REV110 Customer Returns

5.5 PURCHASING

Proper vendor selection and utilization assist in controlling expenses and provide quailit inputs to the comapny. The following Purchasing Procedures should be utilized to account for and control all purchases and acquisitions of the company.

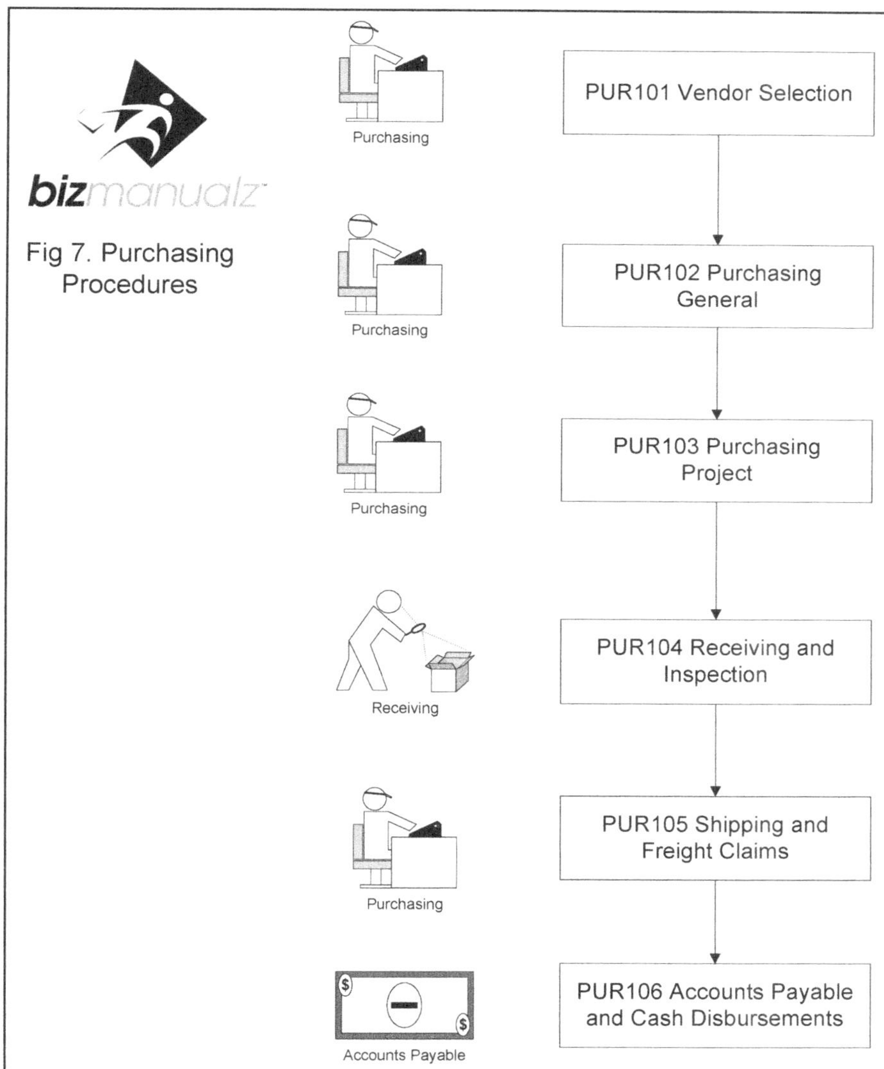

5.5.1 Vendor Selection

The company ensures purchased products and services conform to specified requirements. This starts with selection of appropriate suppliers that have the capability and systems to supply products, materials and services to the company's specified requirements.

The company should strive to validate the performance capabilities of all vendors and maintain the internal controls of the purchasing functions. Suppliers are controlled to the extent necessary based on the effect of the purchased items on the quality of the company's products and services.

The company should provide the methods for determining, documenting and, when applicable, inspecting vendors for compliance with company policies and contract purchasing requirements. This applies to all vendors of products, materials, and services that directly affect the quality of the company's products and services.

5.5.2 General Purchasing

The investment in physical inventory, supplies and capital equipment will be facilitated through the Purchasing Department, maintained at the lowest effective level and supervised consistent with a common set of procedures and controls as required by all regulatory and customer contract requirements.

To outline the actions to be taken for 1) the procurement of all inventory, supplies and capital equipment, 2) the continuous analysis of inventory usage and balances in order to minimize the investment level, 3) the completion of related documents.

This applies to the purchase of all inventory items, supplies and capital equipment for all departments within the company.

5.5.3 Project Purchasing

The company's Purchasing Department is responsible for obtaining a competitive price on materials in correct quantities in a timely fashion, so that the flow of construction is not interrupted or impeded.

The company should describe the procedures involved in maintaining the ordering, purchasing and receiving functions needed for projects in the field. This applies to the purchase of all materials, services, tools, supplies, equipment and equipment rental for all development or construction projects.

5.5.4 Receiving and Inspection

All parts, components, goods and materials should be received in an organized manner and inspected for conformance prior to stocking to provide an initial quality control inspection. Any items or shipments rejected will be properly quarantined from other inventory items until disposition.

The company should outline the steps for the receiving and inspection of materials, components, parts, finished goods, etc., and the stocking of these items or the disposition of rejected items. This applies to the receipt of all inventory items.

5.5.5 Shipping and Freight Claims

The company should strive to minimize damages to goods from shipping and to recover full amounts possible for any losses incurred by shipping damage or loss of goods as allowed by the Interstate Commerce Act.

The company should institute the methods to be followed for shipping and filing freight claims. This applies to all goods shipped and received by domestic motor and rail common carriers.

5.5.6 Accounts Payable and Cash Disbursements

Internal controls are required to ensure that only valid and authorized payables are recorded and paid. Accounting procedures should be implemented to ensure the accuracy of amounts, coding of general ledger accounts and appropriate timing of payments.

The company should explain the practices for documenting, recording and issuing payments for accounts payable transactions. This applies to all purchases including, merchandise and non-merchandise purchases.

5.5.7 Referenced Procedures:

PUR101 Vendor Selection
PUR102 General Purchasing
PUR103 Project Purchasing
PUR104 Receiving and Inspection
PUR105 Shipping and Freight Claims
PUR106 Accounts Payable and Cash Disbursements

[This page intentionally left blank]

6.0 RESOURCE MANAGEMENT

6.1 PROVISION OF RESOURCES

During planning and budgeting processes, and as needed throughout the year, the President and management team determine and ensure that the appropriate resources are available to implement and maintain the Accounting Management System and continually improve its effectiveness.

6.2 HUMAN RESOURCES

6.2.1 Accounting Staff

Managers and employees are to have personal and professional integrity and are to maintain a level of competence that allows them to accomplish their assigned duties, as well as understand the importance of developing and implementing good internal controls.

This requires managers and their staff to maintain and demonstrate at all times:

- Personal and professional integrity
- A level of skill necessary to help ensure effective performance
- An understanding of internal controls sufficient to effectively discharge their responsibilities

6.2.2 Competence, Awareness, and Training

Accounting personnel shall be competent based on appropriate education, training, skills and experience. The minimum competencies required for each position at our company are defined in each position's Job Description. Human Resources, department managers and supervisors are responsible for ensuring job descriptions are current and adequate.

Where otherwise qualified personnel require additional training or other action to meet the minimum competency requirements, these needs are identified. The department provides task-specific training. General training or education is provided or coordinated by Human Resources. The department should evaluate the effectiveness of training or other actions taken as appropriate.

The department generates records of task-specific training. Human Resources maintains records of all training and education, skills and experience in accordance with Human Resources Policies and Procedures and Computer and Network Policies and Procedures.

Department managers are responsible for ensuring their employees are aware of the relevance and importance of their activities and how they contribute to the achievement of the accounting objectives.

6.2.3 Separation and Supervision of Duties

Key duties and responsibilities should be separated among individuals. Duties and responsibilities shall be assigned systematically to a number of individuals to ensure that effective checks and balances exist. Key duties include authorizing, approving, and recording transactions; issuing and receiving assets; making payments; and reviewing or auditing transactions.

Qualified and continuous supervision is to be provided to ensure that internal control objectives are achieved. This standard requires supervisors to continuously review and approve the assigned work of their staffs as well as provide the necessary guidance and training to ensure that errors, waste, and wrongful acts are minimized and that specific management directives are followed.

6.2.4 Referenced Procedures:

See ABR41 ***Bizmanualz™ Human Resources Policies, Procedures and Forms.***
See ABR34 ***Bizmanualz™ Computer & Network Policies, Procedures and Forms.***

6.3 INFRASTRUCTURE

Our company provides the infrastructure necessary to achieve conformity to accounting standards and requirements. During the annual budgeting and strategic planning processes, buildings, workspace, and associated utilities are evaluated and provided. When new personnel are added, Human Resources coordinates activities to ensure appropriate process equipment including hardware and software, if required, and supporting services such as telephones etc., are available based on information provided on the Personnel Requisition.

6.4 WORK ENVIRONMENT

The management team, Controller and Office Manager determine and manage the work environment to ensure our company provides a safe and desirable place to work. They ensure the environment is appropriate for achieving conformity to product requirements.

Accounting Manual - Revision History

Revision	Date	Description of changes	Requested By
0	12/29/02	Initial Release	

[This page intentionally left blank]

Accounting Policies, Procedures & Forms

Section 400

General and Administrative Procedures

Section 400

General & Administrative

Procedures:

G&A101 Chart of Accounts
G&A102 Files and Records Management
G&A103 Travel and Entertainment
G&A104 Management Reports
G&A105 Period-End Review
G&A106 Controlling Legal Costs
G&A107 Taxes and Insurance
G&A108 Property Tax Assessments
G&A109 Release of Confidential Information
G&A110 Document Control

SOP # ______ Revision:______ **Prepared by:____________**
Effective Date:______________ **Approved by:____________**

Title: G&A101 CHART OF ACCOUNTS

Policy: To facilitate the record keeping process for accounting, all ledger accounts should be assigned a descriptive account title and account number.

Purpose: To provide the method for assignment and maintenance of the company's chart of accounts in order to produce meaningful financial data for the Company.

Scope: This procedure applies to all general ledger accounts.

Responsibilities: The Controller is responsible for monitoring and approving changes to the company's Chart of Accounts.

Definition: Chart of Accounts – A categorized listing of all account titles and numbers being used by an organization to track income, expenses, assets, equity, and liabilities is called a Chart of Accounts.

Procedure:

1.0 DESIGN OF ACCOUNTS

1.1 Accounts should have titles and numbers that indicate specific ledger accounts such as Cash in Checking, Furniture and Fixtures, Accounts Payable, etc.

1.2 Accounts should be arranged in the same sequence in which they appear in the financial statements. Asset accounts should be numbered first, followed by liability accounts, owner's equity accounts, revenue accounts and expense accounts.

1000 - Asset Accounts

2000 - Liability Accounts

3000 - Owner's Equity Accounts

4000 - Sales or Revenue Accounts

5000 - Cost of Sales Accounts

6000 - Administration Expense Accounts

7000 - Sales Expense Accounts

9000 - Other Accounts

1.3 Sub-divisions should be used to provide additional clarification, as needed. A sub-division among the balance sheet accounts should be designated short term to long term, (i.e. current assets should precede long term assets and current debt should precede long-term debt).

Further, accounts will be numbered so that all sales amounts are recorded by either Product or Sales Territory and so that cost of sales amounts, sales expense amounts and administration and other expense amounts are recorded according to the department that is accountable for the cost and the nature of the cost.

Unassigned number sequences should be left open within each group of accounts to provide for additional accounts, which may be added later.

1.4 Accounts may be numbered using a four-digit sequence (An automated accounting system will generally have a predetermined account numbering format). In an account number, the location and the value of each digit have a specific meaning. Below is a general description of the meaning of the numbers in a chart of accounts.

_XXX - The first digit in each account number indicates the major classification of the account in the general ledger and the value of the digit indicates whether it is an asset, liability, owner's equity, department or other kind of account. For example, the number 1000 indicates asset account.

X_XX - The second digit indicates a sub-classification of a major account and the value of the digit indicates a specific sub-classification. For example, the account number 1100 indicates Cash and Marketable Securities accounts.

XX_X - The third digit indicates a further sub-classification of each major account classification and the value of the digit indicates the specific sub-classification. For example, the account number 1110 indicates the Cash account and the account number 1120 indicates the Marketable Securities account.

XXX_ - The fourth digit is used to provide a more detailed classification of the account and the value of the digit indicates a specific classification. For example, account number 1111 indicates the Cash in Checking account and number 1112 indicates the Petty Cash account.

2.0 DESCRIPTION OF ACCOUNTS

2.1 Each account should be given a short title description that is brief but will allow the reader to quickly ascertain the purpose of the account. A sample chart of accounts is attached as G&A101 Ex1 ACCOUNT CODES.

2.2 For training and consistent transaction coding, as well as to help other non-accounting managers understand why something is recorded as it is, each account should be defined. Definitions should be concise and meaningful. One or two sentences of definition are usually sufficient.

The definition tells the user what can be recorded in a specific numbered account. However, if there is a confusing account usage, or if repetitive coding errors are being made, the definition can also inform the reader of what may <u>not</u> be recorded in this account.

Since the definitions are reference sources, they should be developed for quick and easy lookup. The account number and name should be on one line and the definition should be indented beginning on the following line in a consistent pattern. If the account is part of a group, the group title should be at the top of the group or page.

An example of definitions follows:

ASSETS

1111 - Cash in Checking

Includes all cash held in the operating bank account. All withdrawals by check and deposits are recorded here. The reported balances are supported by a bank reconciliation prepared monthly.

1112 - Petty Cash

Includes the petty cash and change fund held by the cashier. This account is used only when a new fund is initiated or an existing fund is terminated.

Revision History:

Revision	Date	Description of changes	Requested By
0	11/06/02	Initial Release	

[This page intentionally left blank]

G&A101 Ex1 ACCOUNT CODES
AS OF XX/XX/XX

ASSETS

1100 - CASH AND MARKETABLE SECURITIES ACCOUNTS

1111 - Cash in Checking

Includes all cash held in the operating bank account. All withdrawals by check and deposits are recorded here. The reported balances are supported by a bank reconciliation prepared monthly.

1112 - Petty Cash

Includes the petty cash and change fund held by the cashier. This account is used only when a new fund is initiated or an existing fund is terminated.

1120 - Marketable Securities

Includes debt securities such as government and corporate bonds and equity securities such as common and preferred stock acquired with cash that is not immediately needed in operations.

1200 – RECEIVABLES

1210 - Notes Receivable

Formal short-term receivables documented by a promissory note and a provision for interest.

1220 - Accounts Receivable

Short-term receivables generated from sales and other activities.

1230 - Interest Receivable

Accrued interest receivable generated by notes and past-due accounts receivable.

1290 - Allowance for Uncollected Accounts

The estimated accrual for bad debts result from the current period's sales.

1300 - INVENTORY ACCOUNTS

1310 - Raw Materials

The cost assigned to goods and materials on hand and not in production.

1320 - Work in Process

The cost of the raw material on which production has been started but not completed, plus the cost of direct labor applied specifically to this material and a ratable share of manufacturing overhead costs.

1330 - Finished Goods

The costs identified with completed products on hand.

1500 - PREPAID EXPENSE ACCOUNTS

1510 - Prepaid Insurance

The current portion of insurance premiums paid that cover future periods.

1520 - Prepaid Taxes

Tax payments paid by the Company that relate to a future revenue period.

1530 - Deposits

Current deposits paid by the Company for future services or acquisitions such as trade show deposits, deposits on an equipment purchase, etc.

1600 - OTHER CURRENT ASSET ACCOUNTS

1700 - FIXED ASSET ACCOUNTS

1710 - Land

Represents the company's original cost for the purchase of real estate.

1720 - Buildings

The company's original cost for the purchase of buildings and structures.

1722 - Machinery and Equipment

The company's original cost for the purchase of machinery and equipment.

1724 - Furniture and Fixtures

Represents the company's original cost for the purchase of furniture and other accessory items.

1726 - Vehicles

The company's original cost for the purchase of automobiles and trucks.

1728 - Leasehold Improvements

The company's original cost for structural additions to leased premises.

1790 - ACCUMULATED DEPRECIATION ACCOUNTS

The cumulative depreciation expense recorded to date for all assets in a class.

1790 - Accumulated Depreciation, Buildings

1792 - Accumulated Depreciation, Machinery and Equipment

1794 - Accumulated Depreciation, Furniture and Fixtures

1796 - Accumulated Depreciation, Vehicles

1798 - Accumulated Depreciation, Leasehold Improvements

1800 - INTANGIBLE ASSET ACCOUNTS

1810 – Goodwill

Represents the excess cost, over the fair market value of the identifiable assets, of a business entity purchased by the company.

1820 - Patents

The purchase price paid for the rights to a patent from an inventor. For internally developed products it also includes the cost of securing or defending a patent such as attorney's fees. Does not include research and development costs such as labor, materials, consultants, etc. which are directly expensed.

1900 - OTHER ASSET ACCOUNTS

LIABILITY ACCOUNTS

2100 - CURRENT LIABILITY ACCOUNTS

2110 - Notes Payable

Obligations (written promissory notes) that will mature within one year.

2120 - Accounts Payable

Balances owed for goods, supplies and services purchased on open account.

2130 - Wages and Salaries Payable

The amount of wages or salaries earned for time worked but not yet paid as of the period being reported.

2135 - Long-Term Debt Due Within One Year

The principal of long-term debt that will be repaid during the next year.

2140 - Interest Payable

Represents the amount of interest accrued on debt obligations but not yet paid.

2150 - Dividends Payable

Represents the amount of dividends declared or earned on stock investments but as not yet paid to the shareholder.

2160 - Payroll Taxes Payable

Represents the amount of employee's payroll taxes withheld and employer's taxes due on employees payroll that have not yet been deposited.

2170 - Property Taxes Payable

Represents the accrual amount of property taxes to be assessed to the Company but not yet paid.

2190 - INCOME TAXES PAYABLE

2191 - Federal Income Taxes Payable

Represents the estimated accrual of federal taxes due on company earnings.

2192 - State Income Taxes Payable

Represents the estimated accrual amount of state taxes due on company earnings.

2300 - LONG-TERM LIABILITY ACCOUNTS

2310 - Bank Loan

Represents the amount of debt principal that is to be repaid after the next twelve-month period.

2320 - Mortgage Payable

Represents the amount of debt principal that is to be repaid after the next twelve-month period.

OWNERS' EQUITY ACCOUNTS

3100 - Common Stock

Represents the amount of the par value for investments in common stock of the company.

3200 - Preferred Stock

Represents the amount of investments in preferred stock of the company.

3300 - Paid-in-Capital in Excess of Par Value

Represents the excess amount paid for investment in common stock of the Company over the stated par value amount.

3400 - Treasury Stock

Represents the cost amount paid by the Company to repurchase stock from shareholders.

3900 - Retained Earnings

Represents the company's cumulative net profits and losses to date.

3910 - Dividends

Represents the amount of dividends declared during the current period.

SALES ACCOUNTS

4010 - Sales Product A

Represents the amount of net sales for this product line.

4011 - Sales Returns and Allowances Product A

Represents the amount for refunds given for returned or damaged merchandise.

4020 - Sales Product B

4021 - Sales Returns and Allowances Product B

4030 - Sales Product C

4031 - Sales Returns and Allowances Product C

COST OF SALES AND DEPARTMENTAL EXPENSE ACCOUNTS

5010 - Cost of Materials Product A

Represents the costs for materials used in the product.

5020 - Cost of Materials Product B

5030 - Cost of Materials Product C

5090 - Material Price Variance

Represents the differences between actual costs paid for materials and the standard costs used by the Company for pricing these materials.

NOTE: the following accounts are set-up for each department when applicable.

5XXX - Cost of Sales Accounts

6XXX - Administration Expense Accounts

7XXX - Sales Expense Accounts

X100 - Salaries

Represents the gross amount for labor costs.

X110 - Employer Taxes

Includes the employer's matching FICA and unemployment taxes.

X120 - Employee Benefits

Includes the portion of health insurance premiums paid by the company.

X200 - Telephone

Includes the costs for monthly line fees and long-distance charges.

X210 - Utilities

Includes the costs for electricity, natural gas, water and sewer use.

X220 - Postage and Delivery

Includes the amounts for postal costs and delivery costs such as, overnight services and messenger services.

X230 - Supplies and Small Equipment

Includes the costs for office and production supplies, tools and equipment type items that fall below the company's capitalization requirements.

X240 - Dues and Subscriptions

Includes amounts paid for membership in professional organizations and amounts paid for subscriptions to publications.

X250 - Travel

Includes the amounts paid for employee's business travel, such as airfare, lodging, rental cars, etc.

X260 - Meals and Entertainment

Includes the amounts paid to reimburse employee's for meals while traveling on company business and entertainment incurred while conducting business with business prospects and customers.

X310 - Rent, Building

Includes leases payments for the company's office and manufacturing space.

X320 - Rent, Equipment

Includes amounts for lease payments for office and manufacturing equipment.

X330 - Repairs and Maintenance

Includes amounts for repairs, cleaning and general maintenance of buildings, grounds and equipment.

X340 - Depreciation

Represents the estimated amount of deterioration and depreciation of capital assets during the current period.

X350 - Amortization

Represents the scheduled amount of amortization of intangible assets during the current period.

X410 - Insurance

Represents the portion of insurance premiums paid for coverage of the current period for property, casualty and other business insurance.

X420 - Property Taxes

Represents the estimated amount of property taxes on buildings, properties and furniture and equipment for the current period.

X430 - Licenses

Includes amounts for business licenses and fees.

X510 - Consulting Services

This includes fees to non-employee individuals or firms for advisory services to the company.

X520 - Legal Fees

This includes all fees paid for attorneys, appraisers, notaries, court costs, document recording fees and witnesses.

X530 - Accounting Fees

Includes costs to outside firms for auditing services and accounting advice.

X540 - Seminars and Conferences

This includes amounts incurred by employees attending outside seminar or conference programs.

X550 - Bank Fees

This includes amounts charge by banks to the Company for processing financial transactions. This does not include interest expense items.

X610 - Advertising and Promotions

This includes costs for camera and layout work, published advertisements, brochures and trade show expenses.

X620 - Printing Costs

This includes amounts for printing, binding and padding paid to outside print shops. This does not include Advertising and Promotions.

OTHER EXPENSE ACCOUNTS

9110 - Interest Income

Includes interest income from cash and security investments.

9120 - Dividend Income

Represents dividend income from the company's security investments.

9190 - Miscellaneous Income

Includes minor income items not classified in the revenue accounts.

9210 - Interest Expense

Represents interest incurred by the Company for short-and long-term debts.

9220 - Penalties

Includes penalty items such as late payment or filing fees.

9290 - Miscellaneous Expense

Includes minor expense items not classified in the expenditure accounts.

[This page intentionally left blank]

SOP # ______ Revision:______ **Prepared by:____________**
Effective Date:_____________ **Approved by:____________**

Title: **G&A102 FILES AND RECORDS MANAGEMENT**

Policy: The Company will retain records in an orderly fashion for time periods that comply with legal and governmental requirements and as needed for general business requirements.

Purpose: To outline the methods for filing, retaining and disposing of business records.

Scope: This procedure applies to all business documentation generated by the company. However, this does not necessarily cover internal or certain day-to-day business correspondence.

Responsibilities:

The File Manager will be responsible for categorizing and maintaining a listing of records maintained and the location (i.e. by wall unit and shelf row number).

The Controller is responsible for overseeing the execution of company policy for Record Retention, Storage and Destruction of obsolete company records.

Procedure:

1.0 FILING SYSTEM

1.1 To ensure efficient access, filing centers will be established in each department. To reduce the amount of duplicate and unnecessary record retention, individual desk files should be avoided unless they are used in daily operations. All other departmental or company records should be filed in the departmental central filing areas.

1.2 Unless necessary, records should usually only be kept by the originator or sender and not by the receiver to avoid duplicate filing systems.

1.3 The following filing guidelines should be adhered to optimize filing efficiency and records access:

- All file cabinets and files should follow recognized rules of order, such as Left to Right, Top to Bottom, Front to Back and in the case of chronological records, newest to oldest.
- File markers or label headings should always be placed at the beginning or front of a file or group of files.
- Alphabetical files should always be filed under broad topical categories. Files should never be filed under individual employee names (except Human Resources records) to avoid confusion and re-filing in the event of turnover. Files should always be filed under the "proper" or company names whenever

appropriate. In the case of individuals, files should be maintained according to the persons "Last name" then First name and Middle initial.

- Alphanumeric codes should be attached to colored end tabs of all file sets to show type of file by subject area and sub-category. For instance, all files dealing with Accounting will have a green end tab on the lateral file folder with the alpha code of AC followed by a three digit numeric code to designate the sub-category (i.e. Financial Planning is AC 200, General Accounting is AC 300, Payroll is AC 340, etc.). Payroll is a function of Accounting thus the AC, payroll is a function of General Accounting (under Accounting) thus the 300 series numeric, and under General Accounting the Payroll file is series number 40, which translates to a file of AC 340. Refer to G&A102 Ex1 MASTER FILE GUIDE INDEX for a sample of the subject and sub-category file guide.
- Extra care should be used for sensitive or private information. Company financial data or personnel records that contain performance reviews, salary information, and any health related information should be kept in a secure area with limited access to only those that have a "need to know" such as the Director of Human Resources or the Controller.

2.0 RECORD RETENTION AND LONG-TERM STORAGE

2.1 Storage of archived records will be maintained in the locked storage area of the building. Access to this area will be limited to the Controller, officers of the Company and the File Manager.

2.2 Non-permanent files will be stored in cardboard file boxes. Each file box will be labeled on the front with the contents, dates covered, and destruction date if applicable. Permanent records will be maintained in metal fire-resistant file cabinets.

2.3 Files should be stored only in boxes with similar items, dates and retention periods. This will allow easier access and purging of records. A general rule to keep in mind is that it is better to only half-fill a file box than to file dissimilar types of files in the same box.

2.4 The file manager will be responsible for categorizing and maintaining a listing of records maintained and the location (i.e. by wall unit and shelf row number).

2.5 Maintain all files for as long as is necessary but only to the extent they serve a useful purpose or satisfy business or legal requirements. G&A102 Ex2 RECORDS RETENTION PERIODS, provides a guide to the typical business life of various documents. The retention periods provided are suggested with federal requirements in mind. Be sure to check with local and state authorities for specific record retention requirements.

2.6 Copies of critical records that are vital to the daily operations of the Company should be kept off site in case of possible disasters. This may include information needed to file insurance claims (assets lists, insurance contacts, policy numbers), financial data for tax purposes (wages paid, income and expenses), contacts lists to inform or restart the business (vendors, customers, investors and employees), and other data that would assist in rebuilding the business (business plans, intellectual property, or proprietary information).

3.0 RECORD DESTRUCTION

3.1 Three to six months after each year-end, the file manager will proceed with destruction of all files that have exceeded their recognized holding period.

3.2 A listing of file categories to be destroyed will be circulated to all managers thirty days prior to destruction for review and comment. The actual listing of records destroyed will be maintained permanently for future reference.

3.3 Destruction of the files will be performed by an independent, outside service for shredding and disposal. Disposal of records into the company's general trash service is not allowed.

References:

A. HEALTH INSURANCE PORTABILITY ACCOUNTABILITY ACT (HIPAA)

The Standards for Privacy of Individually Identifiable Health Information (the Privacy Rule) creates national standards to protect individuals' personal health information and gives patients increased access to their medical records. As required by the Health Insurance Portability and Accountability Act of 1996 (HIPAA), the Privacy Rule covers health plans, health care clearinghouses, and those health care providers who conduct certain financial and administrative transactions electronically. Most covered entities (certain health care providers, health plans, and health care clearinghouses) must comply with the Privacy Rule by April 14, 2003. Small health plans have until April 14, 2004 to comply with the Rule.

Note: Employment records maintained by a covered entity in its capacity as an employer are excluded from the definition of protected health information. The modifications do not change the fact that individually identifiable health information created, received, or maintained by a covered entity in its health care capacity is protected health information.

B. AGE DISCRIMINATION IN EMPLOYMENT ACT (ADEA)

ADEA applies to employers with 20 or more employees. If an EEOC charge or lawsuit is filed, keep records until final disposition of the charge or lawsuit. Otherwise, ADEA compliance suggests keeping basic employee files from one to three years as listed:

- Payrolls or other records (for temporary and permanent positions) for three years.
- Basic employee information such as employees' names, addresses, birth dates, occupations, rates of pay, and weekly compensation for three years.

- Applications and personnel records relating to promotion, demotion, transfer, selection for training, layoff, recall or discharge for one year.
- Job advertisements and postings for three years.
- Copies of employee benefit plans, seniority and merit systems must keep on file for the full period the plan or system is in effect and for at least one year after its termination

C. AMERICANS WITH DISABILITIES ACT (ADA)

ADA applies to employers with 15 or more employees. If an EEOC charge or lawsuit is filed, keep records until final disposition of the charge or lawsuit. Otherwise, ADA compliance suggests keeping employment applications and other personnel records including promotions, transfers, demotions, layoffs, and termination or requests for reasonable accommodation for at least 1 year from the making of the record or the personnel action.

D. CIVIL RIGHTS ACT OF 1964

Applies to employers with 15 or more employees. If an EEOC charge or lawsuit is filed, keep records until final disposition of the charge or lawsuit. Otherwise, basic non-discrimination compliance suggests keeping employment applications and other personnel records including promotions, transfers, demotions, layoffs, and termination or any EEO-1 Reports for at least one year from the making of the record or the personnel action. If an employee is involuntarily terminated, his/her personnel records must be retained for one year from the date of termination.

E. EMPLOYEE RETIREMENT INCOME SECURITY ACT (ERISA)

The ERISA reporting and disclosure obligations apply to all pension and welfare plans including summary plan descriptions, annual reports, reportable events, and plan termination, unless the company plan is exempt under ERISA.

ERISA suggests the company should maintain all reports, documents, information, and materials for a minimum of six years in order to disclose and or support all transactions to participants and beneficiaries (and report to certain governmental agencies), as requested or needed.

F. EMPLOYEE POLYGRAPH PROTECTION ACT

All polygraph test results and reasons for administering the test should be kept for three years.

G. EQUAL PAY ACT

Payroll records including time cards, wage rates, deductions from wages, and records explaining the difference in wage rates between men and women in similar positions should be kept for three years.

H. EXECUTIVE ORDER 11246

Applies to federal contractors and requires the preparation of affirmative action plans. Affirmative action plans must be updated annually and retained for two years along with all applications and other personnel records that form the basis of the company's employment decisions. Generally, personnel and employment records must be retained for two years.

I. FAIR LABOR STANDARDS ACT (FLSA)

FLSA applies to employers engaged in or employees who work in interstate commerce and suggests the following records are retained for three years:

- Payroll and other records containing employee's name, birth date, gender, and occupation.
- Employee's beginning of workweek and time employee begins work.
- Regular rate of pay or other basis of payment.
- Hours worked per day and for workweek.
- Daily and weekly straight time earnings.
- Deduction from wages.
- Total wages per pay period.
- Date of payment and the pay period covered.
- For exempt professional, executive and administrative employees, and those employed in outside sales, the employer must maintain records that reflect basis on which wages are paid to permit calculations of the employee's total remuneration.
- In addition, employers must keep for at least two years all records (including wage rates, job evaluations, seniority and merit systems, and collective bargaining agreements) that explain the basis for paying different wages to employees of opposite sexes in the same establishment.

J. FAMILY AND MEDICAL LEAVE ACT (FMLA)

FMLA applies to employers with 50 or more employees within a 75 mile radius and whose employee must have worked for at least one year and accumulated at least 1,250 hours of service with the employer during the previous year. FNLA suggests the following records are retained for 3 years

- Basic employee data including name, address, occupation, rate of pay, terms of compensation, daily and weekly hours worked per pay period, deductions from wages, and total compensation.
- Dates of leave taken by eligible employees.
- For intermittent leave, the hours of leave.

- A copy of employee notices and documents describing policies and practices regarding leave.
- Records of any dispute regarding the designation of leave.

K. IMMIGRATION REFORM & CONTROL ACT (IRCA)

IRCA applies to all employers and requires a signed Form I-9 is retained for three years after the date of hire and at least one year after termination.

L. OCCUPATIONAL SAFETY & HEALTH ACT (OSHA)

OSHA applies to employers with 10 or more employees and suggest that the log of occupational injuries and illnesses is retained for five years. All other records should be retained for at least 30 years after employee separation. Other records include:

- Occupational injuries and illnesses.
- The annual summary of injuries and illnesses.
- Medical records and records of exposure to toxic substances.

M. REHABILITATION ACT OF 1973

Applies to federal contractors. If a charge or lawsuit is filed, keep records until final disposition of the charge or lawsuit. Otherwise, basic compliance suggests keeping personnel and employment records including requests for accommodation, physical exams, job advertisements and postings, applications, resumes and records regarding hiring, assignments, promotions, demotions, transfers, layoffs, terminations, rates of pay and selection for training for two years (only 1 year if contractor has less than 150 employees or a federal contract of $150,000 or less). Note: Affirmative action plans also may have to be maintained by the employer

N. RIGHT TO FINANCIAL PRIVACY ACT

The act establishes specific procedures and exceptions concerning the release of customer financial records to the federal government. It provides customers of financial institutions with a right to expect that their financial activities will have a reasonable amount of privacy from federal government scrutiny.

O. GUIDE TO RECORD RETENTION REQUIREMENTS

A good source of federal retention requirements is the "Guide to Record Retention Requirements" published by the Office of the Federal Register National Archives and Records Administration. It can be purchased from the U.S. Government Printing Office in Washington DC. Additional sources of information include: IRS regulations, state and local government retention requirements or the AICPA (American Institute of Certified Public Accountants) Filing and Record Retention Procedures Guide.

P. IRS REVENUE PROCEDURE 98-25 RECORDS RETENTION

The Income Tax Regulations require that, except for farmers and wage-earners, any person subject to income tax, or any person required to file an information return with respect to income, must keep such books and records, including inventories, as are sufficient to establish the amount of gross income, deductions, credits, or other matters reported. The books or records required by must be kept available at all times for inspection by authorized internal revenue officers or employees, and must be retained so long as the contents thereof may become material in the administration of any internal revenue law.

Note: Section 6.01 requires taxpayers to maintain and make available documentation of the business processes that (1) create the retained records, (2) modify and maintain its records, (3) satisfy the requirements of section 5.01(2) of the procedure and verify the correctness of the taxpayer's return, and (4) evidence the authenticity and integrity of the taxpayer's records.

Section 6.02 sets forth four elements that the documentation required under section 6.01 must establish: (1) the flow of data through the system, (2) internal controls that ensure accurate processing, (3) internal controls that prevent unauthorized record changes, and (4) charts of account.

Section 6.03 sets forth six specific types of documentation for each retained file: (1) record formats, (2) field definitions, (3) file descriptions, (4) evidence that periodic checks are undertaken to ensure that data remains accessible, (5) evidence that the records reconcile to the taxpayer's books, and (6) evidence that the records reconcile to the taxpayer's return.

Revision History:

Revision	Date	Description of changes	Requested By
0	11/06/02	Initial Release	

G&A102 Ex1 MASTER FILE GUIDE INDEX

AC	**ACCOUNTING**
AC-100	Accounts Administration
AC-200	Financial Planning
AC-300	General Accounting
310	Checking Account Register
320	Accounts Payable
330	Accounts Receivable
340	Payroll
350	Local, State, Federal taxes {FUTA, FICA, etc.}
360	Banking Services
370	Property Inventory/Fixed Assets
380	Corporate Accountant
390	Corporate Tax Information File
AC-400	Employee Benefit Programs
AC-500	Employee Expense Accounts
AC-600	Petty Cash Management
AC-600	Corporate Loan Management
AC-700	Grants Account Management
AC-800	Purchasing
AC-900	Open
AD	**ADMINISTRATION**
AD-100	General
AD-200	Organizational Manual
AD-300	Organizational Charts
AD-400	Corporate Correspondence Manual
AD-500	Policies and Procedures
AD-600	Records Management and Retrieval
AD-700	Chief Executive Officer Administrative Memorandums
AD-800	Interoffice Staff Administrative Memorandums
AD-900	Open
BU	**BUSINESS**
BU-100	Corporate Business Plan
BU-200	Business Project Management
BU-300	Sub-Corp Business Project Management
BU-400	Business Executive Summaries
BU-500	Sub-Corp Business Executive Summaries
BU-600	Domestic Business Development
BU-700	International Business Development - Europe
BU-800	International Business Development - Asia
BU-900	International Business Development - Canada/S. America

CS	**COMPUTER INFORMATION SYSTEMS**
CS-100	General
CS-200	Equipment
CS-300	Operation and Maintenance
CS-400	Training in Systems Operation
CS-500	Open
EN	**ENGINEERING**
EN-100	General Administration
EN-200	Research and Development
EN-300	Chemical Engineering
EN-400	Graphics and Technical Drawings
EN-500	Product Information and Technical Analysis
EN-600	Product Raw Materials Data
EN-700	Engineering Safety Data
EN-800	Product Test Programs
EN-900	Industry Information
IN	**INSURANCE**
IN-100	General Administration of Insurance
IN-200	Plant and Equipment Policies
IN-300	Corporate Officer Policies
IN-400	Product Liability Policies
IN-500	Corporate Vehicles Policies
IN-600	Health Program Policies
IN-700	Life Insurance Programs for Employees
IN-800	Off Site Special Coverage
IN-900	Open
LG	**LEGAL**
LG-100	General
LG-200	Reports
LG-300	Contracts
LG-400	Litigation
LG-500	Disputes
LG-600	Legal Personnel Issues
LG-700	Agreements/Partnerships
LG-800	Product Liability
LG-900	Open

MA	**MARKETING**
MA-100	General
MA-200	Reports / Studies
MA-300	Marketing Plans
MA-400	Customer Relations
OF	**OFFICE MANAGEMENT**
OF-100	General
OF-200	Procedures
OF-300	Equipment / Furnishings / Telecommunications
OF-400	Information Processing/Communications Procedure
OF-500	Property Lease/Management Agreement
OF-600	Fax/Reproduction/Printing Procedures
OF-700	Protocol to Visitors
OF-800	Maintenance
OF-900	Open
OP	**OPERATIONS**
OP-100	General
OP-200	Daily Reports
OP-300	Weekly Reports
OP-400	Monthly Reports
OP-500	Quarterly/Annual Reports
OP-600	Performance Analysis
OP-700	Project Management Charts and Plans
OP-800	Manufacturing and Production
OP-900	Open
PE	**PERSONNEL**
PE-100	General
PE-200	Reports
PE-300	Employee Records
PE-400	Organizational Charts
PE-500	Recruiting
PE-600	Training
PE-700	Benefit Programs
PE-800	Open
PE-900	Open

PP	**PATENTS, PERMITS AND PLANS**
PP-100	General
PP-200	Reports
PP-300	Licenses/Permits/Plans
PP-400	Open
PP-500	Open
PR	**PUBLIC RELATIONS**
PR-100	General
PR-200	Reports and Studies
PR-300	Corporate Releases
PR-400	List of Clients/Industry Contacts
PR-500	Open
RG	**REGULATORY DATA**
RG-100	General
RG-200	Reports
RG-300	Correspondence
RG-400	Acts/Laws/Bills
RG-500	Regulations
RG-600	Agreements
RG-700	Guidelines/ Policies/ Resolutions
RG-800	International Regulations
RG-900	Open
SL	**SALES**
SL-100	General
SL-200	Domestic Business Development
SL-300	International Business Development
SL-400	Plans and Budgets
SL-500	Corporate Sales Procedures and Project Management

G&A102 Ex2 RECORDS RETENTION PERIODS

Record	Retention Period
Accident reports and claims (settled cases)	7 years
Accounts payable ledgers, schedules and trial balances	7 years
Accounts receivable ledgers, schedules and trial balances	7 years
Assignments	3 years
Audit reports of accountants	Permanently
Bank reconciliations	1 year
Bank statements, cancelled checks, and deposit slips	7 years
Bills of lading	3 years
Capital stock and bond records	Permanently
Cash books	Permanently
Cash receipts and disbursements	7 years
Chart of accounts	Permanently
Checks (cancelled, all other)	7 years
Checks (cancelled, for important payments, i.e. taxes, property purchases, special contracts, etc. File checks with the transaction papers)	Permanently
Construction documents	Permanently
Contracts and leases (expired)	7 years
Contracts and leases still in effect	Expiration +7 years
Corporate records and minutes	Permanently
Correspondence (legal and important matters only)	Permanently
Correspondence general	3 years
Credit Applications (Consumer)	25 Months (after notification)
Credit Applications (Business)	1 year (after notification)
Deeds, mortgages, and bills of sale	Permanently
Depreciation schedules	Permanently
Duplicate deposit slips	1 year
Electronic fund transfer documents	7 years
Employee personnel records (after termination)	7 years
Employment applications	3 years
Expense analyses and Expense distribution schedules	7 years
Expired contracts and notes receivable	7 years
Expired purchase contracts	7 years
Federal, state and local tax returns	Permanently
Financial statements (end-of-year trial balances)	Permanently
Fixed asset records and appraisals	Permanently
Forms W-4	7 years
Garnishments	3 years
General Ledgers (end-of-year trial balances)	Permanently
I-9s (after termination)	1 year
Insurance records, current accident reports, claims, policies, etc	Permanently
Interim and year-end financial statements and trial balances	Permanently
Inventories of products, materials, and supplies	7 years

Invoices ....7 years
Journals .... Permanently
Licenses .... Permanently
Loan documents, notes.. Permanently
Minute books of directors and stockholders, including bylaws and charter... Permanently
Monthly trial balances .... Permanently
Notes receivable ledgers and schedules ....7 years
OSHA logs..5 years
Paid bills and vouchers ....7 years
Payroll journals ....7 years
Payroll records and summaries ....7 years
Payroll reports (federal & state) ....7 years
Perpetual inventory records ....7 years
Petty cash vouchers ....7 years
Physical inventory records ....7 years
Physical inventory tags ....7 years
Plant cost ledgers .... Permanently
Polygraph test results and reasons for test...3 years
Property appraisals by outside appraisers .... Permanently
Property records including costs, depreciation schedules, blueprints, plans.. Permanently
Property titles and mortgages .... Permanently
Purchase journals ....7 years
Purchase orders ....7 years
Receiving sheets ....1 year
Requisitions ....7 years
Sales journals ....7 years
Sales records ....7 years
Savings bond registration records of employees ....7 years
Scrap and salvage records (inventories, sales, etc)......................................7 years
Shipping tickets ....3 years
Stock and bond certificate (cancelled) .... 1 yr
Stockroom withdrawal forms ....7 years
Subsidiary ledgers ....7 years
Tax returns and worksheets, revenue agents' reports and other documents... Permanently
Time books/cards ....7 years
Trade mark registrations .... Permanently
Uncollectible accounts and write offs ....7 years
Voucher for payments to vendors, employees, etc.
(includes all allowances and reimbursement of employees, officers) ....7 years
Voucher register and schedules ....7 years
W-4 forms ....4 years
Workman's comp documents ....11 years

SOP # ______ Revision:______ **Prepared by:____________**
Effective Date:______________ **Approved by:____________**

Title: **G&A103 TRAVEL AND ENTERTAINMENT**

Policy: All reservations required for business travel and entertainment will be made through the Travel Coordinator. Expenses are to be within established company guidelines and will be reimbursed with proper documentation. Employees are expected to spend the Company's money as carefully and judiciously as they would their own.

The Company recognizes that employees who travel far from home to represent the company's business interests must forego their living accommodations and may forfeit personal time. Accordingly, the Company will make efforts to provide comfortable and secure accommodations for lodging, meals and travel for employees. However, these items are not intended to be perquisites and the Company reserves the right to deny reimbursement of expenses that are considered lavish or extravagant.

Purpose: To provide guidelines for travel and entertainment expenses as they were actually spent, account for all advances promptly and accurately and to communicate the procedures for reimbursement.

Scope: This procedure applies to all departments and individuals who travel or entertain for the company.

Responsibilities:

Travel Coordinator is responsible for making arrangements needed for business travel.

Accounting Department will receive and review the expense report documentation and process necessary employee reimbursement.

Procedure:

1.0 TRAVEL ARRANGEMENTS

1.1 All arrangements required for business travel are to be made through the Travel Coordinator. The coordinator can solicit better corporate discounts and rates for hotels, airlines, car rental agencies and travel agencies. Employees benefit because they do not have to spend their own time comparing rates and making their own arrangements.

1.2 To arrange for travel, complete the G&A103 Ex1 TRAVEL ARRANGEMENTS FORM with all pertinent information and receive departmental approval. The form should then be forwarded to the Travel Coordinator. For maximum savings on airfares, this form should always be completed at least 15 days in advance unless an emergency trip is required.

1.3 It is preferable that all employees travel during non-working hours to maximize efficiency. The Travel Coordinator will make arrangements for the trip as required and will return a travel itinerary and any tickets or reservation forms to the employee.

1.4 **Cash Advances** - To help ensure accurate and timely expense report preparation and reduce the additional paperwork required to process and track Cash Advances, the Company generally discourages cash advances unless special circumstances apply. Employees are encouraged to use credit cards with a grace period to provide float time between incurring the expense and receiving reimbursement from the company.

If an employee requires a cash advance, the amount should be completed on the travel arrangements form with a supporting explanation for the advance. The advance request will then be forwarded to accounting for processing. Travel advances should be no less than $100 and no more than $500 (for international travel).

When a cash advance is received, the employee will reduce their expense reimbursement by the amount of the cash advance. In the case where the cash advance exceeds the expenses for the report submitted, the remaining cash must be turned into the accounting department with the expense report. Amounts owed the Company cannot be carried forward to future expense reports. Any advance outstanding will be deducted from the employee's paycheck.

1.5 **Direct Billings** - Direct billings to the Company from motels, restaurants, etc. are not permitted unless previously authorized.

2.0 EXPENSE GUIDELINES

2.1 Air Travel - The Travel Coordinator will make airline reservations based on the following criteria:

- Expediency: Getting the employee to their destination in an expedient way. (Direct flights when possible or connecting flights if necessary for faster flight schedules).
- Cost: Employees will fly coach class unless extenuating circumstances apply.
- Air Carrier: An employee's preferred airline can be utilized as long as expediency and cost factors are equal. In most cases, airfare will be directly billed to the company's travel agency account.

  On occasion, employees may have no alternative but to book their own flight. If this is the case, employees must use regularly scheduled airlines and obtain the lowest (discount) fare available. This may mean that employees will fly at times that are not always the most convenient for them.

2.2 Lodging - The travel coordinator will make lodging arrangements based on value, convenience for the traveler and according to what is usual and customary company guide lines.

Whenever multiple employees are traveling to the same location, employees will be required to share accommodations if possible (i.e. male/male or female/female). Lodging accommodations will then be made for double rooms accordingly. If an employee is accompanied by a non-employee such as family or a friend, and therefore requires separate accommodations, the employee will be responsible for payment of any excess lodging accommodations.

2.3 Meals - Employees will generally be responsible for obtaining their own meals while traveling. Meals do not include entertaining guests, which should be itemized as entertainment expenses.

Meals and miscellaneous sundry items will be reimbursed according to the lesser of actual expenses or $45.00 per day.

Occasionally, an employee may be traveling to a location with a higher than normal cost of living. For theses locations, including foreign travel, an employee can request an increase in the daily per diem rate, but should have it substantiated and authorized prior to departure.

2.4 Car Rentals - Advance arrangements should be made by the Travel Coordinator if a car is required at the destination. Vehicle selection will be based upon the most cost-effective class that satisfies requirements for the employee(s) and any demonstration equipment.

Supplemental auto insurance coverage offered by car rental agencies is to be declined as Liability and Collision coverage is provided by the company's insurance policy.

2.5 Personal Vehicles - An employee required to use their own automobile for business will be reimbursed at the prevailing rate per tax guidelines for per-mile deductions. The employee must provide on the expense report, documentation including dates, miles traveled and purpose of each trip.

The Company assumes no responsibility for personal automobiles used for business. Further, any parking or speeding violation is the sole responsibility of the employee.

2.6 Telephone - Business-related telephone charges on an itemized lodging receipt and/or telephone charge card should be itemized under telephone expense.

If an employee is out-of-town on business for several days, the employee may make personal telephone calls home, as long as the charges and length of call are reasonable.

2.7 Entertainment - In order for entertainment to be a valid deductible entertainment expenses it must be an ordinary and necessary expense directly related or associated with the active conduct of business. For tax purposes, it is very important to properly document entertainment expenses and substantiate the following elements:

- The date.
- The place (name and location).
- Description or type of entertainment.
- The business purpose and the nature of the business benefit expected to be gained by the Company.
- The business relationship to the Company of the persons entertained (name, occupation, title, etc.).

2.8 Miscellaneous Expenses - Any additional business expenses that are not categorized above should be listed under miscellaneous expenses and documented with all pertinent information to substantiate the expense.

2.9 Non-Reimbursable Expenses - Some expenses are not considered valid business expenses by the company, yet may be incurred for the convenience of the traveling individual.

Since these are not expenses for the business then they are not reimbursable. (The following can be used as a guide of expenses, which are not reimbursable)

Examples include:

- Airline or travel insurance
- Airline or travel lounge clubs
- Shoe shine or Dry-cleaning (except for extended travel beyond 5 days)
- Movies or personal entertainment
- Books, magazines or newspapers
- Theft or loss of personal property
- Doctor bills, prescriptions, or other medical services
- Parking tickets, traffic tickets or Car towing if illegally parked
- Health club memberships
- Baby sitter or Pet care fees
- Barbers and Hairdressers

3.0 EXPENSE REPORT PREPARATION AND REIMBURSEMENT

3.1 All business travel and entertainment expenditures incurred by employees of the Company are reimbursed through the use of the G&A103 Ex2 TRAVEL AND MISCELLANEOUS EXPENSE REPORT form and the G&A103 Ex3 ENTERTAINMENT AND BUSINESS GIFT EXPENSE REPORT form. Expense reports should be completed and turned in within two (2) weeks of return or incurrence of expenses.

Expense report forms must be filled out and totaled completely. Use the appropriate headings and total on a daily basis. Required receipts for items charged must be attached to the report. Any questions regarding completion of the report should be directed to the employee's supervisor or the accounting department.

3.2 Upon completion, the expense report along with all attachments should be turned into the employee's supervisor for approval. After approval, the expense report is submitted to the accounting department for processing and reimbursement. In order to expedite reimbursement, the employee should ensure that the report is completed properly, required documentation is attached, proper authorization is obtained, and any unusual items properly explained and documented.

Authorized expense reports will be reimbursed by a company check, normally within two or three weeks after receipt by the accounting department.

4.0 ADDITIONAL INFORMATION RESOURCES

More information is available from the following resources:

- VISA Corporate Card Best Practices
  http://www.visa.com/pd/comm/us/corp/best_practices.html
- American Express Corporate Services
  http://www47.americanexpress.com/corporateservices/
- MasterCard Business Programs
  http://www.mastercardbusiness.com/mcbiz/smallbusiness/index.jsp

Revision History:

Revision	Date	Description of changes	Requested By
0	11/06/02	Initial Release	

[This page intentionally left blank]

G&A103 Ex1 TRAVEL ARRANGEMENTS FORM

Name:________________________ Date:________________

Reason for Travel:____

Destination(s):____

Need to Arrive at Destination by: Date:__________ Time:________ am / ________ pm

Need to Return by: Date:__________ Time:________ am / ________ pm

Airline Preferred:________________________

Seating Preferred: (e.g. window/aisle)______________

Car Needed: ☐ Yes ☐ No Number of Days Needed:________

Hotel Needed: ☐ Yes ☐ No

If Hotel is need, # of nights at which location (if employee will be going to several areas):

Number of Nights__________ at______________________________

Signature of Supervisor or Vice-President:________________________

(Do not write below the line - for travel coordinator use only)

Travel Agency:________________________ Phone:________________

Contact:________________________

Departure:

Date:______________

Times: Departure:_______ Arrival:______

Airline:________________

Flight#:______________

Return:

Date:______________

Times: Departure:_______ Arrival:______

Airline:______________

Flight #:______________

Comments:____

____

Cost:______________ Penalties (if any):________________________

Need to Ticket by:________________________

[This page intentionally left blank]

G&A103 Ex2 TRAVEL AND MISCELLANEOUS EXPENSE REPORT

Name:____________________

Purpose of Trip:____________________

Dates and Details of Trip:____________________

TRAVEL COSTS						LODGING		MEALS			
Date	No. of miles	Mileage Reimburse	Parking	Air Travel	Ground (Car/Taxi)	Hotel	Telephone	No.	Amounts	SUPPLIES (Describe Below)	TOTALS
Totals											

Gross Amount ______
Less Advance ______

Signature:____________________ Date:______________

Approved by:____________________ Date:______________

Received by:____________________ Date:______________

Gross Amount____________________

Less Advances____________________

Net Amount Due____________________

__________ Employee
__________ Company (Attach Remittance)

[This page intentionally left blank]

G&A103 Ex3 ENTERTAINMENT AND BUSINESS GIFT EXPENSE REPORT

Name:________________________________

Department:________________________________

Date	Place (Name & Location)	Description or type of Entertainment or Gift	Business Purpose / Discussion	Individual / Company (Name, title, etc.)	Amount
Totals					

Signature:____________________ Date:______________ Gross Amount____________________

Approved by:__________________ Date:______________ Less Advances____________________

Received by:__________________ Date:______________ Net Amount Due___________________

__________ Employee

__________ Company (Attach Remittance)

[This page intentionally left blank]

SOP # ______ Revision:______ **Prepared by:____________**
Effective Date:______________ **Approved by:___________**

Title: **G&A104 MANAGEMENT REPORTS**

Policy: Department Managers will prepare summary reports of vital operating statistics for the company, including sales, current debt, operating cash, accounts receivable and projected short-term cash flows. These reports are to be prepared and are to supplement detailed monthly and quarterly financial reports and are to be used for timely "hands-on" management.

Purpose: To provide the format and content requirements for preparation of the Financial Reports.

Scope: The procedure applies to Finance and Accounting personnel required for preparation of these reports.

Responsibilities:

Department managers will be responsible for assuring effective and informative internal reporting within their departments and between departments.

Office Manager is responsible for preparing and maintaining a summary of all reports.

Procedure:

1.0 PREPARATION GUIDELINES

1.1 The logistics of preparing financial summaries will vary, depending on the accounting system used and the needs of the company. Most computerized systems offer an "executive summary" screen of critical financial information. The objective is to provide a quick recap of the financial status of the company that should lead to plans for corrective actions or adjustments.

Monthly reports should be considered "exception reports" that provide management the necessary information to understand whether the company is progressing as planned. (See ***ABR42 Bizmanualz™ Finance Policies, Procedures and Forms,*** the business planning process.)

1.2 The timing of reports is critical to the effective operation of the company. The weekly reports should be prepared and distributed by 1:00 p.m. on Monday of each week. Monthly and Quarterly reports should be prepared and distributed within five business days of the end of the month.

To improve readability, simplify preparation, and allow users to focus on the materiality of the data, all reporting should be rounded and/or plugged to the nearest $1 increments. Note: larger companies may wish to focus on $100 or more increments.

1.3 If details are not available then use control totals and note on the report any estimates. Follow up with actual results as soon as practical. The preparer should keep in mind that the objective of the report is to provide a quick recap of the financial status of the Company and not a time-consuming detailed financial analysis. Leave exhausting details in the books for later analysis as required.

1.4 Make statements easy to read. Use the following style guidelines to improve readability:

- Use 8-1/2 x 11 paper
- Use a lot of "white space" on the page
- Limit columns of figures to three columns
- Omit cents and use thousands of dollars as appropriate. Indicate on the report the units used in a legend.
- Indicate only significant expenses and group remaining items
- The preparer should date (month/day/year) and initial all reports.

1.5 The preparer should file a copy of repetitive reports in a 3-ring binder for later retrieval, auditing or trend analysis.

1.6 While current POS and accounting systems may automatically provide many types of information, it is helpful to review the manual exhibits provided to understand the mechanism for generating this type of information.

1.7 The Office Manager will prepare and maintain a summary of all reporting. An example is provided as G&A104 Ex1 DEPARTMENT REPORTING SUMMARY. The summary will include the following categories:

- Department or Functional Area
- Name of Report
- Purpose of the Report
- Frequency of Preparation
- Distribution of Copies

1.8 Updates of the summary will be issued to all company officers and department managers. Managers should use the summary to determine what information is being compiled and the format and distribution of reporting. Many times duplicate or redundant information gathering, reporting and filing can be avoided by merely changing the format or distribution of existing reports.

2.0 DAILY FLASH REPORT

2.1 The Daily Flash Report represents the summary information needed to monitor the company's current activity. The Daily Flash Report should be generated and reviewed daily by the CFO. This report supplements the Weekly Financial report as well as the detailed monthly and quarterly financial statement reports and provides an indication of real-time trends and customer behavior.

2.2 The Daily Flash Report (see G&A104 Ex2 DAILY FLASH REPORT) should include:

- Daily sales, month to date and year to date, by department as a percentage of the total.
- Cash drawer activity, reconciled to all cash received for the day and taken from the sum of all DAILY CASH REPORTS as discussed in procedure CSH101 CASH DRAWERS AND CREDIT CARDS.
- Number of customers and number of negative-on-hand items.
- Critical balance sheet levels: Inventory, A/R, A/P and cash.

3.0 WEEKLY FINANCIAL REPORT

3.1 The Weekly Financial Report represents the summary information needed to monitor the company's short-term activity. The Weekly Financial Report should be generated and reviewed each week by the CFO. This report supplements the detailed monthly and quarterly financial statement reports and provides a quick look at the overall performance of the company.

3.2 The Weekly Financial Report (see G&A104 Ex3 WEEKLY FINANCIAL REPORT) should include:

- Sales-to-date, sales orders received and current backlog.
- Operating cash receipts, disbursements and balance.
- Current receivables generated, received, balance and aging.
- Current debt incurred, paid-down, balance and aging.

4.0 SIX-WEEK CASH FLOW REPORT

4.1 The Six-Week Cash Flow Report represents a summary of the cash flowing through the company in the near term and identifies any potential shortfall that might occur in the near future before it occurs. The Six-Week Cash Flow Report should be reviewed each week by the CFO. This report supplements the detailed monthly and quarterly financial statement reports and provides a quick look at the cash performance of the company.

4.2 The Six-Week Cash Flow Report (see G&A104 Ex4 SIX-WEEK CASH FLOW REPORT) should include projected operating cash balances for each week with estimated cash receipts by major classifications and projected disbursements by major account classifications.

4.3 The controller should notify the CFO of any shortfall so that the company may determine alternative courses of action to rectify the situation. Alternatives are explored in ***ABR42 Bizmanualz™ Finance Policies, Procedures and Forms*** under options for raising capital.

5.0 BUDGET VS. ACTUAL REPORT

5.1 The Budget vs. Actual Report represents a comparison of planned operating expenses to the actual expenses incurred for the period. The objective is to highlight results against plan, percentages and variances and thus provide a basis for management decisions. The Budget vs. Actual Report is prepared and maintained by the Accounting department on a monthly basis.

Additional information is discussed in ***ABR42 Bizmanualz™ Finance Policies, Procedures and Forms*** under the business planning process. See ***ABR44 Bizmanualz™ Sales & Marketing Policies, Procedures and Forms*** for the sales forecasting process.

5.2 The Budget vs. actual report should be divided into three main components. 1) Current period budget, actual and variance totals, 2) a description of the major income and expense account classifications similar to the financial statements, and 3) the Current year-to-date budget, actual and variance totals. An example is provided as G&A104 Ex5 BUDGET VS ACTUAL REPORT. The percent column should be used to list each line as a percentage of total sales. Alternatively, it can also represent the percentage variance or change from last period.

6.0 FINANCIAL STATEMENTS

6.1 The Controller is responsible for maintaining current Financial Statements on a monthly basis. The CFO, President, and the Board of Directors should review the Financial Statements each month. This report is used for both the monthly and quarterly financial report and provides one indication of the performance of the company.

6.2 The Financial Statements (see G&A104 Ex6 FINANCIAL STATEMENTS) typically are comprised of three main parts: The Balance Sheet, Income Statement, and the Statement of Cash Flows.

The Balance Sheet lists all of the company's assets (cash, receivables, deposits, inventory, equipment, intellectual property, etc.), liabilities (debt, lease obligations, tax obligations, etc) and equity (paid in capital, stock issued, dividend paid, etc). It identifies the assets (which are "the business") and the financiers, or debt and equity holders and the relationship between the two.

The Income Statement represents the company's operational sources of cash - sales revenue - or uses - business expenses and is typically divided into operating periods that represent months, quarters or years of operations. It identifies the profitability of the company as a function of the tax and accounting decisions.

The Statement of Cash Flows is the difference between the Balance Sheet sources and uses of cash and the Income Statement sources and uses of cash. This difference assists in identifying the health of the company's operations. It identifies whether the company is producing cash or consuming cash and at what rate and from what sources.

6.3 The Financial Statements should be produced after the close of the company's period (see procedure G&A105 PERIOD-END REVIEW & CLOSING). The final Financial Statements form the basis for the company's taxes as well as formal presentations to the Board of Directors, Shareholders, or other stakeholders such as banks, or creditors in accordance with procedure G&A109 CONFIDENTIAL INFORMATION RELEASE.

7.0 DEPARTMENT REPORTS

7.1 Department managers are responsible for assuring effective and informative internal reporting within their departments and between departments.

7.2 On a quarterly basis, department managers should review all reporting generated or received by their department for usefulness and adequacy. Any appropriate changes, additions or deletions to company reporting should be implemented with notification provided to the Office Manager.

References:

A. FEDERAL ACCOUNTING STANDARDS BOARD (FASB)

Since 1973, the Financial Accounting Standards Board (FASB www.fasb.org) has been the designated organization in the private sector for establishing standards of financial accounting and reporting. Those standards govern the preparation of financial reports. They are officially recognized as authoritative by the Securities and Exchange Commission (Financial Reporting Release No. 1, Section 101) and the American Institute of Certified Public Accountants (Rule 203, Rules of Professional Conduct, as amended May 1973 and May 1979). FASB pronouncements are the primary sources of GAAP.

B. GENERALLY ACCEPTED ACCOUNTING PRINCIPLES (GAAP)

A collection of accounting principles. Typically includes the most recent developments of all generally accepted accounting principles (GAAP) as derived or collected from various technical pronouncements. Sources include FASB statements, interpretations, technical bulletins and concepts; American Institute of CPAs (AICPA); Accounting Principles Board opinions, accounting research bulletins, and position statements; and Securities and Exchange (SEC) financial reporting releases.

Revision History:

Revision	Date	Description of changes	Requested By
0	11/06/02	Initial Release	

G&A104 Ex1 DEPARTMENT REPORTING SUMMARY

As of ____________

REPORT	FREQUENCY	DISTRIBUTION	PURPOSE
Finance & Accounting			
G&A104 Ex2 Daily Flash Report	Daily	Officers	Provide recap of major financial indicators for previous day.
G&A104 Ex3 Weekly Financial Report	Weekly	Officers	Provide recap of major financial indicators for previous week.
G&A104 Ex4 Six-Week Cash Flow Report	Weekly	Officers	Projection of operating cash receipts and disbursements.
G&A104 Ex5 Budget vs. Actual Report	Monthly	Officers & Directors	Summarizes Sales, Product Development, Finance and Operations for previous month.
G&A104 Ex6 Financial Statements	Monthly	Officers, Directors, Managers, Banks, Stakeholders	Summarizes Balance sheet, Income Statement and Cash Flows for the previous month
G&A104 Ex6 Financial Statements	Quarterly	Shareholders, Employees	Summary of Sales, Product Development and Finance & Operations for previous quarter.
Sales & Marketing			
	Weekly	Sales & Managers	Listing of month-to-date bookings.
	Semi-Monthly	Managers	Projection of sales orders, backlog & anticipated delivery time frames.
	Monthly	Managers	Provide update of marketing & promotions activities for next quarter.
	Monthly	Sales Managers, Officers	Recaps sales performance.
Production			
	Semi-Monthly	Production Managers	Provide status of Inventory Level and Back-Orders
	Monthly	Officers, Manufacturing Human Resources	Provide reports of production output for the month.
	Monthly	Managers	Provide development status & projection of completion dates.
Human Resources			
	Monthly	Production Managers	Listing of month-to-date safety incidents
	Monthly	Officers, Managers	Provide hiring status with projections of job openings and recruitment.

[This page intentionally left blank]

G&A104 Ex2 DAILY FLASH REPORT

Date: ______________________

CASH ANALYSIS

Total Cash in Drawer ______________ (1)
Beginning Cash Drawer Balance ______________ (2)
Total Cash Sales (Difference line 1-2) ______________ (3)
Cash Deposit made today ______________

SALES ANALYSIS

Total Cash Sales ______________ (3)
Total Credit Card Charges ______________ (4)
Total Invoices ______________ (5)
Total Sales (Add lines 3+4+5) ______________ (6)
Cash Register Tape Totals (All Sales) ______________ (7)
Difference (line 6-7) ______________ (8)
Number of orders/customers ______________ Average order ______________
Month-to-date Sales ______________ Average Days Sales ______________
Projected Monthly Sales: (business days left in month x average days sales) = ______________

Description	Sales	Dept. One	Dept. Two	Dept. Three
Days Sales	$________	________%	________%	________%
Month to date	$________	________%	________%	________%
Year to date	$________	________%	________%	________%

BALANCE SHEET ANALYSIS

Accounts Receivable Outstanding ______________
Accounts Payable Outstanding ______________
Inventory Balance ______________
Cash Balance ______________

Product ANALYSIS

Number of negative-on-hand items ______________

[This page intentionally left blank]

G&A104 Ex3 WEEKLY FINANCIAL REPORT

Prepared by:__________________

Week Ended__________________

	AMOUNT
SALES	
Sales Orders Received:	__________________
Orders Shipped:	__________________
Sales Backlog:	__________________
Sales Month-To-Date:	__________________
OPERATING CASH	
Beginning Balance:	__________________
Cash Receipts:	__________________
Cash Disbursements:	__________________
Ending Balance:	__________________
Line of Credit Available:	__________________
ACCOUNTS RECEIVABLE	
Beginning Balance:	__________________
Invoices Issued:	__________________
Payments Received:	__________________
Ending Balance:	__________________
Aging:	
< 30 Days	__________________
30 - 60 Days	__________________
> 60 Days	__________________
ACCOUNTS PAYABLE	
Beginning Balance:	__________________
Debt Incurred:	__________________
Debt Paid:	__________________
Ending Balance:	__________________
Aging:	
< 30 Days	__________________
30 - 60 Days	__________________
> 60 Days	__________________

Distribution:

[This page intentionally left blank]

G&A104 Ex4 PROJECTED SIX WEEK CASH FLOW REPORT

Prepared by:________________

Description:	Week Ended / /	Week Ended / /	Week Ended / /	Week Ended / /	Week Ended / /	Week Ended / /
Operating Cash – Beginning						
CASH RECEIPTS:						
Accounts Receivable						
Projected Sales						
Line of Credit						
Long Term Debt						
Equity Infusion						
Other ________						
Total Cash Generated						
CASH DISBURSEMENTS:						
Trade Payables						
Loan Payments						
Rent Payments						
Deposits/Retainers						
Payroll - Net						
Payroll Tax Deposits						
Income Tax Deposits						
Other Purchases/Expenses						
Other ________						
Total Cash Requirements						
Weekly Cash Flow						
Operating Cash-Ending						

Comments:

[This page intentionally left blank]

G&A104 Ex5 BUDGET VS. ACTUAL REPORT

MONTH								YEAR TO DATE					
Current Budget	Current Actual	Current Variance	%	Last Year Actual	%	Line No.	Description	Current Budget	Current Actual	Current Variance	%	Last Year Actual	%
						1	Product-1						
						2	Product-2						
						3	Product-3						
						4	Net Sales						
						5	Cost of Sales						
						6	Gross Profit on Sales						
						7	Salaries						
						8	Rent & Utilities						
						9	Travel & Entertainment						
						10	Training						
						11	Marketing						
						12	Legal & Accounting						
						13	Research & Development						
						14	Total Expenses						
						15	Total Operating Income						
						16	Interest Expense						
						17	Depreciation Expense						
						18	Tax Expense						
						19	Other Income						
						20	Other Expenses						
						21	Net Income						

[This page intentionally left blank]

G&A104 Ex6 FINANCIAL STATEMENTS

A. BALANCE SHEET

Assets	AMOUNT	TOTAL
Current Assets		
Cash & Cash Equivalents	$________	
Accounts Receivable	$________	
Inventory	$________	
Prepaid Expenses/Other	$________	
Total Current Assets		$________
Fixed Assets		
Equipment	$________	
Accumulated Depreciation	($________)	
Total Fixed Assets		$________
Other Assets	$________	
Total Assets		$________

Liabilities & Stockholders Equity	AMOUNT	TOTAL
Current Liabilities		
Accounts Payable	$________	
Short Term Debt	$________	
Taxes Payable	$________	
LT Debt (Current Portion)	$________	
Total Current Liabilities		$________
Long Term Liabilities		
LT Lease obligations	$________	
LT Debt (less current portion)	$________	
Other non-current liabilities	$________	
Total Liabilities		$________
Stockholders Equity		
Capital Stock	$________	
Paid in capital	$________	
Retained Earnings	$________	
Period Net Income	$________	
Total Stockholders Equity		$________
Total Liabilities & Equity		$________

B. INCOME STATEMENT

Income	PERIOD	TOTAL
Revenue		
Product Sales	$________	
Services Revenue	$________	
Gross Revenue		$________
Cost of Goods		
Cost of Eq. Sold	$________	
Cost of Services. Sold	$________	
Total Cost of Goods		$________
Gross Income		$________

Expenses	PERIOD	TOTAL
Operating Expense		
Interest Expense	$________	
Depreciation Exp.	$________	
Sales, Gen. & Admin.	$________	
Total Operating Expense		$________
Net Operating Income		$________
Other Income/Expense		
Other Income/Expense	$________	
Taxes	$________	
Total Other Income/Expense		$________
Net Income		$________

C. STATEMENT OF CASH FLOWS

Cash Flows from Operating Activities		
Net income	$________	
Adj. to Reconcile net income to cash		
Depreciation & Amortization	$________	
Deferred Compensation	$________	
Changes in Accounts Receivable	$________	
Changes in inventory	$________	
Changes in prepaid expenses	$________	
Changes in Taxes Payable	$________	
Total cash provided by operating activities		$________
Cash Flows from Investing Activities		
Changes in fixed assets	$________	
Changes in other assets	$________	
Total cash used in investing activities		$________
Cash Flows from Financing Activities		
Changes in debt (liabilities)	$________	
Changes in equity	$________	
Total cash used in financing activities		$________
Total changes in cash & cash equivalents		$________
Starting cash balance		$________
Ending cash balance		$________

SOP # ______ Revision:______ **Prepared by:____________**
Effective Date:______________ **Approved by:____________**

Title: G&A105 PERIOD-END REVIEW & CLOSING

Policy: An orderly, timely and comprehensive review of all general ledger accounts should be performed or directed by the CFO to ensure an accurate representation of the company's financial statements. These practices are aimed at proving that the financial accounts are accurate, and if not, are properly adjusted to make them accurate, prior to closing.

Purpose: To provide a general overview of the process to be completed for reviewing the accounting records at year-end or any particular month-end prior to closing.

Scope: These practices apply to all accounts. Typically, all financial accounts are reviewed and then closed out as of the company's year-end. Consequently, the procedures that follow are discussed in reference to year-end review. However, a sub-set of these procedures is also applicable to month-end reviews. Month-end procedures are identified near the end of this module.

Responsibilities:

CFO is responsible for creating and reviewing all period-end activities to ensure the period-end financial statements accurately reflect the results of the Company's activities. The CFO should be familiar with the specific software procedures for keeping the prior year open until all final closing adjustments have been made and approved by the CFO.

Accounting is responsible for gathering all documentation required to complete the period-end closing and completing all ledger adjustments.

Definition: "Review" refers to the procedures involved in examining the financial statement balances at any given period to ascertain their accuracy.

"Closing" is the process of advancing from one month or period to the next or from one year to the next. In most computerized accounting systems the periods are closed by executing a menu command. Monthly closings usually involve nothing more than entering the next month and responding to the program's suggestion to print various month-end reports. Even after moving to the next month, many accounting systems allow the user to return to previous months to enter or edit transactions.

The yearly closing is more rigorous since it involves re-setting all income statement accounts to zero. Once a year is "closed", some accounting systems do not allow the user to go back or open a closed period to make changes. So be careful, once the period is closed, it is official and any adjustments that are required will need to be made in the current or next open period.

Background: The financial statement is the most important management tool for the CFO and Controller. It is comprised of the balance sheet and the income statement.

The balance sheet accounts are measured at a moment in time, like a snapshot. They reflect a total of items at any particular time: a total of cash, accounts receivable, inventory, fixed assets, accounts payable, debts, investments and earnings retained in the company.

The income statement accounts are measured over a period of time, like a movie. They represent the sum total of transactions: sales, purchases, payroll, etc. The difference in sales less all related expenses equals the net income or loss for the period of time being measured.

Accounting is a double-entry system. Thus, each business transaction has two equal sides. For example, paying an expense decreases cash on the balance sheet and increases an expense on the income statement. Getting paid for a service or sale increases cash on the balance sheet and increases revenue on the income statement. Because of this interdependency, the accuracy of the income statement is dependent upon the accuracy of the balance sheet.

It is easier to prove the accuracy of the balance sheet. Adding up how much each customer owes the store or reconciling cash to the bank statement is a much simpler process than attempting to add up each individual sales transaction on the income statement. For this reason, more time is actually spent on proving the accuracy of the balance sheet.

Once the balance sheet is proven, the income statement, in total, must be right! The only errors would be misclassifications, (i.e.: the phone bill could be incorrectly posted to the rent expense account). The accounts of the income statement are generally reviewed for reasonableness by comparing amounts to prior periods and analyzing ratios. However, the accounts of the balance sheet are compared to actual totals of items counted (cash, receivables, inventory, payables, fixed assets, etc.).

The controller or accounting manager is encouraged to understand these concepts and to take the initiative to keep the financial statements as accurate as possible, regardless of how much an outside accounting service is utilized.

Procedure:

1.0 CLOSINGS PREPARATIONS

1.1 The steps to the actual period-end are not all performed on the exact end of the period. Some accounts cannot be "settled", proved, or reconciled until all third party information is received.

Bank statements from banks usually don't arrive until a couple weeks after a month end. And, many final payroll tax payments and yearly reconciliation forms aren't due until the end of the following month. Also needed are final bills from vendors, credit card statements, month end statements from vendors and year-end loan statements from banks and other financial institutions. All of this information is needed before a business can truly "close its books".

Fortunately, most accounting systems allow a business to continue posting transactions into subsequent months of the new year, without actually "closing" the previous year-end. The CFO should be familiar with the specific software procedures for keeping the prior year open until all final closing adjustments have been made. It's not unusual for businesses to continue processing transactions for almost the entire next year before closing the prior year.

1.2 Compile all period-end documents in preparation for closing the accounting period. These documents include:

- Bank statements to all accounts
- Final payroll and tax amounts
- All final bills and month-end statements from vendors
- All credit card statements
- All year-end loan or debt statements
- All asset acquisition and disposition transactions

1.3 Fewer procedures are performed at month-end dates. For example, due to the cost involved, a complete physical inventory is rarely taken each month, although some businesses do take physical inventory every three or six months. At a minimum the following procedures would be expected for monthly closings:

- Reconcile all bank accounts
- Print and compare the aged receivables and payables to the general ledger. Make appropriate adjustments to balance the accounts.
- Review all balance sheet and income statement accounts for completeness
- Retain all above reports in a monthly summary file.

2.0 BALANCE SHEET: ASSETS

2.1 Prepare a year-end closing file to store all reconciliation documents and printed reports as described below.

2.2 **Cash accounts** - prepare the bank reconciliations for year-end balances per the bank statement to the balance per books for each account. The year-end reconciliation is especially important for preparing the final year-end financial statements to ensure that it is completely accurate.

Show origination dates and description of each reconciling item. Prepare the necessary journal entries to adjust to the reconciliations. Prepare a summary of all petty cash and change drawer funds. Totals must agree with the general ledger. File all reconciliation reports in the year-end closing file.

2.3 **Accounts Receivable** – Print a detailed aged accounts receivable report and then reconciles it to the General Ledger. This can be prepared as soon as all invoicing for products sold as of year-end is complete. Calculate possible allowances for un-collectible accounts. Adjust prior allowances to calculated amount. Write off any un-locatable differences. Retain a complete copy of the detailed accounts receivable, along with any reconciling adjustments in the year-end closing file.

2.4 **Inventory** - Once the results of the physical inventory have been compiled and entered into the accounting system, print out a full inventory valuation report showing quantities on hand and cost values, in accordance with practices described in INV102 INVENTORY COUNTS procedure. Review the inventory report for unusual variations and investigate, as appropriate.

In addition to a valuation report, (sorted by item number), the store manager should run two additional reports; one sorted by extended dollar amount and one sorted by quantity. This will facilitate a review "by exception". The top 100 items of the report, sorted by extended dollar amount, will probably constitute most of the inventory value and will warrant the most investigation.

At the other end of the sorted report there may be some negative valued items. These items should be investigated for possible recording errors. Likewise, investigate any negative quantities on the Quantity Sorted report. Finally, unusual relationships between quantity and value (like a quantity with a zero extended cost, for example) should be examined.

Once all discrepancies have been examined and adjusted, the report totals should agree with the general ledger balance. If not, post the necessary adjustments to the inventory account.

Prepare a schedule of any possibly un-returnable, damaged, spoiled, or obsolete inventory items and adjust them out of inventory. File the sorted inventory reports, of detailed inventory items, and any related adjustment sheets along with the original physical count sheets in the year-end closing file.

2.5 **Capital Assets** - Update the detailed schedule of fixed assets with any additions and deletions and reconcile to the general ledger balances. See procedure INV103 FIXED ASSET CONTROL for more detail.

2.6 **Other Assets** - Other assets include utility or real estate deposits, prepaid insurance, advances to employees or owners, and intangibles like store pre-opening costs. These should all be identified and documented. For example, a copy of the initial deposit with the utility company, or a list of the store pre-opening costs with a schedule showing how much of those costs are to be amortized each year. File copies of these documents in the year-end closing file.

3.0 BALANCE SHEET: LIABILITIES AND STOCKHOLDERS' EQUITY

3.1 Liabilities are shown as the amount to be paid in the subsequent period. If in doubt, record the liability.

3.2 **Accounts Payable** - Print a detailed aged accounts payable report and reconcile it to the general ledger. This is generally completed 2 to 4 weeks after the year-end to ensure that all vendor invoices relating to services and merchandise purchased have been received and entered.

Compare all month-end vendor statements to balances per accounts payable and investigate any differences. Consider making adjustments for any significant unrecorded liabilities such as work started prior to year-end, but not yet billed by the supplier. Retain a complete copy of the accounts payable detail, along with any reconciling adjustments, in the year-end closing file.

3.3 **Accrued Expenses** - Review accruals for sales tax, payroll, payroll tax, payroll deductions payable, interest expense on short-term borrowings and long-term debt. Determine the cost of tax and legal services through year-end and record.

3.4 **Debt** - Verify recorded accuracy of debt by ensuring the general ledger balances agree to year-end statements from lending institutions. Save all year-end statements in year-end closing file.

3.5 **Contingent Liabilities and Commitments** - Prepare a schedule of any outstanding litigation and possible losses. Prepare a schedule of all long-term rental agreements with amounts due by year for the next five years. Retain these schedules in the year-end closing file

3.6 **Stockholders' Equity** - Record any changes in the capital account, including distributions and additions to equity investments.

4.0 INCOME STATEMENT: REVENUES

4.1 **Sales** - Depending on the features of the store's point of sale system there may be a variety of detailed sales reports, including product sales, sales by department, sales by category, or period reports for daily, monthly, and yearly intervals.

4.2 Additionally, the CFO should periodically review sales trends, cost of sales, variable expenses and fixed expenses. Consider these values as a percentage of sales or compare to earlier sales periods. Look for patterns, new trends, seasonal variances, or profitable emerging products that may indicate changes in customer behavior.

4.3 The CFO should analytically review the sales reports and explain all variances. A detailed marketing/promotions journal can be used to correlate changes in sales to specific promotions. Note all expenses related to advertising, coupons, extended holiday work hours, and alike and identify their affect on sales.

5.0 INCOME STATEMENT: EXPENSES

5.1 Each expense total should be compared to expense total from the year before (and budgets if applicable). Attempt to explain any unusual variances. Some expense items are directly related to asset or liability accounts and can be reconciled in conjunction with the related balance sheet account

5.2 **Cost of Goods Sold** - A detailed report should be produced of cost of sales and analyzed in relation to sales and to prior periods. Also analyze the ratios (see 6.0 FINANCIAL RATIO ANALYSIS below) in relation to inventory levels (i.e. inventory turnover). Investigate any unusual variances.

5.3 **Payroll** - At year-end, the various payroll expense accounts should agree to total gross payroll per payroll reports. Account for all deductions for W-3 reported to the Social Security Administration, 1099s for vendors, as well as FICA and other taxes reported accordingly.

5.4 **Bad Debt Expense** - Prepare a list of all accounts written off during the year. Note specifically any addition to the allowance for uncollectible accounts.

5.5 **Interest Expense** - Prepare a schedule of interest expense by source. Reconcile amounts to short-term borrowings and long-term debt.

6.0 FINANCIAL RATIO ANALYSIS

6.1 **Inventory Turnover Ratio**. Identifies inventory productivity. Higher inventory turns can lead to higher profits and is a key indicator for any business holding significant inventory, like a retail store for example.

= Cost of Goods Sold / Average Inventories

6.2 **Accounts Receivable** (AR) Turnover Ratio. Identifies one element of cash flow productivity. Higher AR turns means more cash is available to meet expenses as a function of sales. Low AR turns in a fast growing business may require additional cash from outside sources to finance the AR or credit offered to customers.

= Sales / Average Accounts Receivable.

Where Average Accounts Receivable =
(Beginning Accounts Receivable + Ending Accounts Receivable) / 2

6.3 **Quick Ratio**. Identifies a company's ability to meet its short-term financial obligations. The quick ratio subtracts inventory from current assets because retail inventory can be difficult to liquidate quickly. Creditors will use this ratio to understand a company's ability to pay off debt quickly, under the worst possible conditions. This ratio should equal 1.0 or greater. A higher quick ratio can translate into a better credit rating. Ratios below 1.0 indicate a company in poor economic health.

= (Total Current Assets - Inventory) / Total Current Liabilities

6.4 **Earnings Before Interest Taxes Depreciation & Amortization** (EBITDA). EBITDA identifies the raw earnings power of the business. Earnings alone can be masked by interest, taxes, depreciation and amortization. To determine the raw earnings power add any interest and tax payments as well as depreciation and amortization to the net profit.

= Earnings + Interest + Taxes + Depreciation + Amortization

If the business had no debt and a lot of tax deductions or credits and no assets or fully depreciated assets, then the net profit would equal the raw earnings power of the business. EBITDA is a significant factor to valuing a business.

6.5 **Sales Averages**. A number of sales averages exist to identify the sales and marketing productivity of the business.

Average Order Size = Sales / number of orders

Average Order Margin = (Sales – Cost of Goods) / number of orders

Revision History:

Revision	Date	Description of changes	Requested By
0	11/06/02	Initial Release	

[This page intentionally left blank]

SOP # ______ Revision:______ **Prepared by:____________**
Effective Date:______________ **Approved by:____________**

Title: **G&A106 CONTROLLING LEGAL COSTS**

Policy: The Company will employ various methods to manage and whenever possible, minimize legal expenses.

Purpose: To describe the procedures for managing and controlling associated legal expenses.

Scope: This statement applies to all individuals with the responsibility for contracting legal services and/or approving agreements, contracts, or any other legally associated transactions.

Responsibilities:

Controller will resolve, negotiate, and examine all legal expenses.

Legal Counsel should provide the estimated costs of legal engagements and the most likely outcome.

Definition: Arbitration - is a private, informal process by which all parties agree, in writing, to submit their disputes to one or more impartial persons authorized to resolve the controversy by rendering a final and binding award, which is enforceable in court. It can be used for a wide variety of disputes from commercial transactions to labor grievances.

Declaratory Judgment - is a binding judgment issued by the court that defines the legal relationship between the parties and their rights with respect to the matter before the court. Commonly used in contract disputes (especially useful if no physical agreement exists and or a suit has not been filed yet) to clarify what conduct is permitted or prohibited by the contract or to clarify the contract if necessary.

A declaratory judgment provides the opposing party (defendant) with the opportunity to pick and chose the venue or jurisdiction, and the parties to the litigation. In this manner the opposing party can steal the initiative, direct the litigation, and maximize its chances of winning.

Procedure:

1.0 ARBITRATION

1.1 Whenever practical, the Company should utilize arbitration to resolve disputes. Arbitration can significantly reduce the amount of time and legal fees to resolve a dispute. The major features of arbitration are:

- A written agreement to resolve disputes by the use of impartial arbitration. Such a provision can be inserted into a contract for the resolution of possible future disputes, or can be an agreement to submit to arbitration of an existing dispute.

- Under the rules of arbitration, the procedure is relatively simple and informal. Strict rules of evidence do not apply; there is no motion practice or formal discovery; no requirements for transcripts of the proceedings or for written opinions of the arbitrators. The rules are flexible and can be varied by mutual agreement of the parties.
- Impartial and knowledgeable neutrals serve as arbitrators. Arbitrators are selected for specific cases because of their knowledge of the subject matter. Based on that experience, arbitrators can render an award grounded on thoughtful and thorough analysis.
- Final and binding awards which are enforceable in a court. Court intervention and review is limited by applicable state or federal arbitration laws, and award enforcement is facilitated by these same laws.

1.2 The following standard clause should be inserted whenever practical into contracts, agreements, etc. to provide for the arbitration of possible future disputes:

> "Any controversy or claim arising out of or relating to this contract, or the breach thereof, shall be settled by arbitration in accordance with the Commercial [or applicable] Rules of the American Arbitration Association and judgment upon the award rendered by the arbitrator may be entered in any court having jurisdiction thereof."

The arbitration of existing disputes may be accomplished by mutual agreement of parties with the use of the following terminology:

> "We, the undersigned parties, hereby agree to submit to arbitration under the Commercial [or applicable] Rules of the American Arbitration Association the following controversy.
>
> [Describe Briefly]
>
> We further agree that we will faithfully observe this agreement and the rules, and that we will abide by and perform any award rendered by the arbitrator(s) and that a judgment of the court having jurisdiction may be entered upon the award."

2.0 LEGAL SERVICES

2.1 All legal documents prepared for the company's use, such as vendor contracts, employment agreements, sales orders, etc. should be written in common language and whenever possible should avoid the use of legalese or jargon. Legalese tends to complicate even simple arrangements and often unnecessarily requires the incurrence of legal assistance for mere interpretive purposes.

2.2 Before undertaking legal disputes, the company's legal counsel should ascertain and inform the Company of the estimated costs that will be incurred for the legal engagement and the probable or most likely outcome of the case along with the probable amount of any awards or judgments. Use this information to produce a budget and clarify any matters that are increasing the budget. A budget will provide some assurance that the legal counsel has thought the matter through and it will also provide a baseline to determine the legal utility obtained from the matter.

2.3 Use legal action only as a last resort. Legal action is frequently not very effective. In fact, a threatened action — particularly with intellectual property — could result in a pre-emptive declaratory judgment lawsuit by the other party thus giving them the "home-field" advantage, which could lead to higher legal costs.

3.0 LEGAL BILLINGS

3.1 Consider negotiating a "money-back" guarantee with the right to audit any bill for up to six months. Request that all fees that are proven to be unnecessary or excessive be returned. Then examine all legal bills for any such unnecessary or excessive transactions.

3.2 Many times, legal bills are aggregated, vague and too uninformative to be useful in controlling costs. Therefore, all legal arrangements contracted by the Company should require itemized billings to include the following information:

- Start and end times and dates of each service transaction
- Detailed description of services provided or work performed
- Distinct itemization of each individual performing services

3.3 Examine all internal discussions or conferences and note exactly who is working on the case and why. Ask for a justification for all attorneys working on the case.

3.4 Consider alternatives such as contingent fees, fixed fees, and monthly retainers. All fees are negotiable.

Revision History:

Revision	Date	Description of changes	Requested By
0	11/06/02	Initial Release	

[This page intentionally left blank]

SOP # ______ Revision:______ **Prepared by:____________**
Effective Date:______________ **Approved by:____________**

Title: G&A107 TAXES AND INSURANCE

Policy: To ensure compliance with all Federal, state, local, and other regulatory taxation requirements

Purpose: To outline the general areas of taxation. To be used as a checklist or guide in complying with tax requirements related to each specific location and organizational structure.

Scope: This statement applies to the business activities of the company.

Responsibilities:

Controller is responsible for determining all tax liabilities and fees, the dates due, and for ensuring the timely payment of each.

Procedure:

1.0 ORGANIZATION FEES AND TAXES

1.1 Fees and taxes will vary depending on the legal structure of the business activity. The activities can be operated under a sole proprietorship, partnership, limited liability corporation, S-corporation, or C-corporation. Typically, if incorporated, there is a one-time **incorporation fee**, payable to the state of incorporation. Generally, the formation of any type of partnership involves a one-time fee to the applicable secretary of state. Even a sole proprietorship, in establishing a DBA, (doing business as) name may be required to pay a fee to the state when registering its name.

1.2 After the initial organizational fee is paid, some states require yearly renewal fees for S-Corporations and C-Corporations. These fees may exist in the form of an **annual registration fee** or **franchise fee**. Most states will send an annual notice of continuing registration.

1.3 The controller should check with the secretary of state to ensure all fees are paid in a timely manner. Failure to pay such fees can result in the loss of the company's legal status or structure.

2.0 BUSINESS ACTIVITY FEES AND TAXES

2.1 Most cities and some counties require businesses to be licensed. The controller should check with the city or county clerk for the requirements of doing business in the particular community and county.

2.2 Any business making retail sales must generally obtain a state **retail sales license** from the state's department of revenue. In many states, communities and counties have the option of adopting a local **sales tax**. Once a retail sales license has been obtained, the state, (and possibly communities and counties), will send information regarding the proper payment of sales taxes. These are usually remitted to the state monthly.

2.3 **Use tax** is similar to sales tax, but is imposed when tangible personal property comes into the state, and is consumed in the state by the business. Communities and counties may also impose a use tax. Use taxes are generally remitted quarterly.

2.4 Income or earnings from the business can be taxed as **income tax** or **earnings tax** at the Federal, state and local levels. If the structure of the entity is recognized as a partnership or an S-Corporation, its income is not directly taxed. When a tax return is prepared, the income shown "flows through" to the owner's personal tax return and is taxed at the owner's personal tax rate. If the entity is a sole-proprietorship, there is no separate income tax return filed. The activities of the business are reported on the owner's Schedule C of the personal tax return and income taxes are again paid at the owner's personal tax rate. Generally, only a C-Corporation pays income taxes on its own tax return.

The states usually recognize the same entity distinctions and impose similar reporting and taxing requirements. However, some states impose no corporate income tax at all. Local cities and counties have various methods for reporting income and calculating taxes. Some simply impose a tax on gross revenues, while others require a complex formula of sales, payroll levels and asset values. The owner should consult a qualified tax practitioner for advice and assistance in this area.

3.0 PAYROLL FEES AND TAXES

3.1 The Federal and state governments charge an **unemployment tax**, based on a specified minimum amount of each worker's salary level. For most states, the rate can change from business to business depending on the Company's history of claims and the economic health of the state in which the Company is located.

3.2 **Worker's compensation insurance** may be imposed by a state like a tax. It can also vary based on the amount of payroll, past history of worker's compensation claims, and the type of work in which the business is engaged. This coverage is generally arranged through an insurance company.

3.3 At the Federal level, payroll is taxed at a uniform rate for **Social Security** and **Medicare**. These two taxes are evenly shared between the company and the employee up to certain levels of income. Additionally, personal income taxes, based on the employee's compensation, must be **withheld** from the employee's earnings and remitted to the government by the company, along with the company's and employee's share of **Social Security** and **Medicare** taxes.

3.4 For those states that have income tax, a portion of the employee's compensation is also **withheld** and remitted to the state by the company.

3.5 Other payroll withholdings, mandated by Federal or state requirements, may require wage garnishments to fulfill a bankruptcy edict or childcare payment requirement.

3.6 The Treasury Department and or the Internal Revenue Service (IRS) collects all monies due the Federal Government. Technically, withholding amounts deducted from a paycheck are considered the government's money and the business owner is temporarily holding the money, in deposit, until it can be transferred to the government. Any failure to pay in a timely fashion is considered a serious matter by the IRS and will not be ignored.

The IRS will impose a penalty for failing to pay the required withholding amounts on time. In addition, interest will be charged until the amount is paid. Both interest and penalties imposed by the IRS can add up significantly. Therefore, the IRS is not a good source to "borrow" money from if cash is tight. (see ABR42 ***Bizmanualz™ Finance Policies, Procedures and Forms*** for methods of raising capital).

Note: Money due the IRS is NOT dischargeable in bankruptcy.

3.7 Certain local municipalities charge an **Earnings tax** based on payroll, income, assets, stock options granted or any combination. Check with the city clerk for details.

4.0 EXCISE TAXES

4.1 There are many different federal government taxes or fees imposed on the commerce of different types of businesses. The following represents the most common. Consult a tax advisor to determine exactly which taxes will apply and when they are due.

- Environmental taxes are imposed on the sale or use of Ozone-Depleting Chemicals (ODCs) and imported products containing or manufactured with these chemicals. In addition, a floor stocks tax is imposed on ODCs held on January 1 by any person (other than the manufacturer or importer of the ODCs) for sale or for use in further manufacture.
- Communication Taxes are imposed on amounts paid for local telephone service, toll telephone service or teletypewriter exchange communications services.
- Air Transportation Taxes are imposed on amounts paid for transportation of persons by air, use of international air travel facilities or transportation of property by air services.
- Fuel Taxes are imposed on gasoline, gasohol, diesel, kerosene, aviation, special motor fuels (including LPG), compressed natural gas, or fuels used in commercial transportation on inland waterways.

- Manufacturers Taxes applies to the tax on sport fishing equipment, bow and arrow components, coal, tires, gas-guzzler automobiles, or vaccines. Note: the term "manufacturer" includes a producer or importer.
- Retail Tax on Heavy Trucks, Trailers, & Tractors is imposed on the first retail sale of the following articles, including related parts and accessories sold on or in connection with, or with the sale of, the articles. Note: the seller is liable for the tax.
    - Truck chassis and bodies.
    - Truck trailer and semi trailer chassis and bodies.
    - Tractors of the kind chiefly used for highway transportation in combination with a trailer or semi trailer.
    - A sale of a truck, truck trailer, or semi trailer is considered a sale of a chassis and a body.
- Ship Passenger Tax is imposed on certain ship voyages, as explained later under Taxable situations. The tax is imposed only once for each passenger, either at the time of first embarkation or disembarkation in the United States.
- Foreign Insurance Taxes are imposed on insurance policies issued by foreign insurers.
- Taxes on Wagering are imposed on wagering activities either as an Occupational tax or as a Wagering tax. See IRS Form 11-C or Form 730 for more information.
- Obligations Not in Registered Form Tax is imposed on any person who issues a registration-required obligation not in registered form. A registration-required obligation is any obligation other than one that is issued by a natural person, is not of a type offered to the public, has a maturity (at issue) of not more than one year, or can only be issued to a foreign person.
- Highway Use Tax applies to highway motor vehicles with taxable gross weights of 55,000 pounds or more. Vans, pickup trucks, panel trucks, and similar trucks generally are not subject to this tax.

4.2 A number of excise taxes apply to alcoholic beverages, tobacco products, and firearms. If the company produces, sells, or imports guns, tobacco, or alcoholic products, or manufacture equipment for their production, then additional excise taxes may apply. The businesses covered include:

- Brewers and dealers of liquor, wine, or beer.
- Distillers, importers, wholesale and retail dealers of distilled spirits.
- Manufacturers who use alcohol to produce non-beverage products.
- Importers and wholesalers of imported perfumes.
- Manufacturers, importers, and dealers in firearms.

4.3 Penalties and interest may result from any of the following acts.

- Failing to collect and pay over tax as the collecting agent (see Reference A. TRUST FUND RECOVERY PENALTY).
- Failing to keep adequate records.
- Failing to file returns.
- Failing to pay taxes.
- Filing returns late.
- Filing false or fraudulent returns.
- Paying taxes late.
- Failing to make deposits.
- Depositing taxes late.
- Making false statements relating to tax.
- Failing to register.
- Misrepresenting that tax is excluded from the price of an article.

5.0 OTHER TAXES AND CREDITS

5.1 Many state, counties, and cities impose both **real estate taxes** and/or **personal property taxes**. The owner should consult with local expertise regarding personal property taxes. For real estate taxes see procedure G&A108 PROPERTY TAX ASSESSMENTS.

5.2 **Tax credits** are available for a wide range of reasons. Look for credits related to operating in a distressed community or enterprise zones, hiring or training underprivileged individuals, or maybe sales tax credits for certain merchandise. Contact your local city, county and state governments and/or consult your tax advisor on how to take advantage of some of these opportunities.

Note: credits typically only work to offset profits. If you are operating with losses carried forward and show no profit then you may not be able to take advantage of some credits.

5.3 If **Sales Taxes** are paid based on invoices (the accrual method) then a rebate may be requested for any accounts receivable that have been written off as uncollectible or for billing adjustments and allowances offered to customers.

6.0 TAX PAYMENTS

6.1 The controller should create and maintain a detailed tax calendar as a guide similar to G&A107 Ex1 TAX CALENDAR OF RECURRING MONTHLY DATES, which provides a sample guide to some of the most common taxes. The guide should serve a reminder of tax due dates.

6.2 A separate file should be created for each tax (by year). The file should contain:

- Tax return, coupon book, or required filing forms

- Instructions on completing the forms
- Copies of completed documentation along with detailed payment information.

6.3 Start work on the tax return, coupon book, or required filing forms at least seven to ten day before the forms are due. Make a copy of the completed documents and file it with the notes used to produce the figures in the tax file. Note on the Tax Calendar the date the form was mailed.

6.4 If the tax collector or field agent calls to discuss any filed paperwork then schedule a time for a conference and make sure to have a qualified tax advisor or tax attorney, and the tax preparer present. Tax laws are complex and constantly changing so it is not advisable for any controller or CFO to represent themselves.

If the tax collector wishes to speak with other employees or accounting personnel then make sure that all employees understand that the company's qualified tax advisor or tax attorney must be present for all interviews.

7.0 INSURANCE

7.1 Insurance needs for a business can be grouped in two broad categories, those that are directed at safeguarding assets and those that are furnished as employee benefits. Employee benefit insurance such as, health insurance, disability insurance and key man life insurance, should be considered in light of its importance in the entire employee compensation mix and in light of the personal needs of the company's owner(s). (See ABR41 ***Bizmanualz™ Human Resources Policies, Procedures and Forms*** for a discussion and procedures on benefits).

7.2 Insurance used for safeguarding company's assets includes: property, causality, key-man and professional liability insurance, as well as auto insurance, errors and omissions, directors' liability or business interruption insurance. The levels and terms of these policies should be determined based upon the value of the assets at risk and creditor or state and local requirements.

7.3 Small and mid-sized businesses should consider a Business Owners Policy that provides multiple protections as opposed to separate policies. A Business Owners Policy can include:

- Property insurance for buildings and contents owned by the company.
- Business interruption insurance covers the loss of income resulting from a disaster that disrupts some or all of a business' operations and may provide coverage for additional operating expenses for temporary facilities.
- Liability protection covers the company's legal responsibility for the harm it may have caused to others as a result of employee actions or inactions that then lead to bodily injury or property damage. Examples include the sale or manufacture of defective products, faulty installations or errors in services performed.
- A Business Owners Policy does NOT cover professional liability, auto insurance, worker's compensation or health and disability insurance.

7.4 Professionals that operate their own businesses, such as doctors, lawyers, or accountants, should obtain professional liability insurance to provide protection from customer lawsuit. Professional liability insurance is specialty coverage and is not provided under homeowner's endorsements, in-home business policies or Business Owners Policies.

7.5 Business with a lot of employee should consider employment practices liability insurance covers businesses against some types of employee lawsuits including:

- Sexual harassment
- Discrimination
- Wrongful termination
- Breach of employment contract
- Negligent evaluation
- Failure to employ or promote
- Wrongful discipline
- Deprivation of career opportunity
- Wrongful infliction of emotional distress
- Mismanagement of employee benefit plans

7.6 Certificates of insurance may be required to be on file or on display depending on governmental requirements. It is important to consider that the insurance policy is a contract. Each year's policy should be saved in a permanent file. A product liability suit can go back many years, and if the potential claim is significant, the protection afforded by the prior year's insurance coverage will be improved if that year's policy has been saved.

References:

A. TRUST FUND RECOVERY PENALTY

If taxable communications or air transportation services are provided then excise taxes must be collected from those persons who pay for those services. Any person that willfully fails to collect or pay over these taxes, or evades or defeats them in any way, may be subject to the trust fund recovery penalty. Willfully means voluntarily, consciously, and intentionally. The trust fund recovery penalty equals 100% of the taxes not collected or not paid over to the U.S. Government.

The trust fund recovery penalty may be imposed on any person responsible for collecting, accounting for, and paying over excise taxes. If this person knows that these required actions are not taking place for whatever reason, the person is acting willfully. Paying other expenses of the business instead of paying the taxes is willful behavior.

A responsible person can be an officer or employee of a corporation, a partner or employee of a partnership, or any other person who had responsibility for certain aspects of the business and financial affairs of the employer (or business). This may include accountants, trustees in bankruptcy, members of a board, banks, insurance companies, or sureties. The responsible person could even be another corporation--in other words, anyone who has the duty and the ability to direct, account for, or pay over the money. Having signature power on the business checking account could be a significant factor in determining responsibility.

Revision History:

Revision	Date	Description of changes	Requested By
0	11/06/02	Initial Release	

G&A107 Ex1 FEDERAL TAX CALENDAR

The 2003 due dates for filing US tax returns and reporting tax information are shown below as a guide. However, the dates are not inclusive of every tax or fee that is required for all businesses. The dates or taxes required may vary based on the specific company situation, the day (based on the year, weekends or holidays), or certain tax circumstances.

Generally, if the due date falls on a Saturday, Sunday or legal holiday, the due date should be the next business day. For **excise taxes**, there are two exceptions to this rule. (1) For deposits of regular method taxes, if the due date is a Saturday, Sunday, or legal holiday, the due date is the immediately *preceding* business day. (2) Under the special September deposit rules, if the due date falls on a Saturday, the deposit is due on the preceding Friday. If the due date falls on a Sunday, the deposit is due on the following Monday.

JAN	
10th	• Employees must report **tip income** for December of $20 or more to the company (use **Form 4070**). • **Communications and air transportation taxes** under the alternative method. Deposit the tax included in amounts billed or tickets sold during the first 15 days of December.
14th	• **Regular method taxes**. Deposit the tax for the last 16 days of December.
15th	• Pay **fourth quarter estimated tax** payment for preceding year. If you miss this deadline, you may avoid a penalty by filing your tax return for "last year" and paying the balance of your "last year" tax by January 31, "current year".
27th	• **Communications and air transportation taxes** under the alternative method. Deposit the tax included in amounts billed or tickets sold during the last 16 days of December.
31st	• Send all "last year" employees **Form W-2**. • Provide recipients with their copy of **Form 1099** if you have paid interest, dividends or reportable miscellaneous income. • If you did not pay owed estimated tax on January 15, file your **personal income tax return and pay tax due** to avoid penalties for underpaying estimated taxes (unless you are a farmer or fisherman). • Report **employee income tax withholding and FICA taxes** for the last quarter of "last year" (use **Form 941;** Employers of agricultural workers must file **Form 943)** and file annual return of **federal unemployment taxes** (use **Form 940**). If taxes are fully deposited on time, filings can be deferred to February 10. • **Form 720 taxes**. File **Form 720** for the fourth quarter of "last year". • **Wagering tax**. File **Form 730** and pay the tax on wagers accepted during December. • **Heavy highway vehicle use tax**. File **Form 2290** and pay the tax (or the first installment) for vehicles first used in December. • Trustees or issuers of **IRA**s or **SEP**s must provide participants with a statement of the account's value.

FEB	
10th	• Employees must report **tip income** for January if $20 or more, to the company (use Form 4070). • File deferred **Forms 940, 941** (See January 31)
12th	• **Communications and air transportation taxes** under the alternative method. Deposit the tax included in amounts billed or tickets sold during the first 15 days of January.
14th	• **Regular method taxes**. Deposit the tax for the last 16 days of January.
18th	• File **Form W-4** to claim exemption from withholding.
27th	• **Communications and air transportation taxes** under the alternative method. Deposit the tax included in amounts billed or tickets sold during the last 16 days of January.
28th	• File any required **Forms 1099** for interest, dividends and miscellaneous payments described under January 31 (electronic filers can defer filing **W-2**s to March 31). • File **Forms W-2** and transmittal **Form W-3** with the Social Security Administration (electronic filers can defer filing to March 31). • **Wagering tax**. File **Form 730** and pay the tax on wagers accepted during January. • **Heavy highway vehicle use tax**. File **Form 2290** and pay the tax (or the first installment) for vehicles first used in January. • File **Form 5452** to report nontaxable corporate distributions made to shareholders during the last calendar year.
MAR	
3rd	• File your **personal income tax return** to avoid penalties for underpaying estimated taxes (if you are a farmer and fisherman). • Regular method taxes. Deposit the tax for the first 15 days of February.
10th	• Employees must report **tip income** for February of $20 or more to the company (use Form 4070).
12th	• **Communications and air transportation taxes** under the alternative method. Deposit the tax included in amounts billed or tickets sold during the first 15 days of February.
14th	• **Regular method taxes.** Deposit the tax for the last 13 days of February.
17th	• File calendar year **corporate returns** (use **Form 1120, 1120-A** or **1120S**) or file for an automatic **six-month extension** (use **Form 7004**). • File returns on **Forms 1042** and **1042S** to report tax withheld at the source from nonresident aliens, foreign corporations, foreign partnerships and foreign fiduciaries of a trust or estate.
27th	• **Communications and air transportation tax** under the alternative method. Deposit the tax included in amounts billed or tickets sold during the last 13 days of February.
28th	• **Regular method taxes**. Deposit the tax for the first 15 days of March.
31st	• Electronic filers file **Forms W-2** and **1099**.

APR	
1st	• **Wagering tax**. File **Form 730** and pay the tax on wagers accepted during February. • **Heavy highway vehicle use tax**. File **Form 2290** and pay the tax (or the first installment) for vehicles first used in February. Also, pay the installments for other vehicles, if applicable.
10th	• Employees must report **tip income** for March of $20 or more to the company (use **Form 4070**). • **Communications and air transportation tax** under the alternative method. Deposit the tax included in amounts billed or tickets sold during the first 15 days of March.
11th	• **Regular method taxes.** Deposit the tax for the last 16 days of March.
15th	• File **personal tax return** (**Form 1040, Form 1040A** or **1040EZ**) or file for an automatic four-month extension (use **Form 4868**). • Household employers who paid more than $1,300 wages in "last year" file **Schedule H** (**Form 1040**). • File income tax returns for calendar-year **partnerships** (use **Form 1065**) or request an automatic **three-month extension** (use **Form 8736**). • File income tax returns for **trusts and estates** (use **Form 1041**) or file for an automatic **three-month extension for trusts** (use **Form 8736**). [Note: **Estates** seeking an **extension** must submit an application on **Form 2758** in time for it to be processed by the filing date.] • Pay the first **estimated tax** payment for individuals (use **Form 1040-ES**). • Deposit the first **estimated tax** payment for calendar year **corporations**.
25th	• **Communications and air transportation tax** under the alternative method. Deposit the tax included in amounts billed or tickets sold during the last 16 days of March.
29th	• **Regular method taxes**. Deposit the tax for the first 15 days of April.
30th	• Report **employee income tax withholding and FICA taxes** for the first quarter of "current year" (use **Form 941**). If taxes are fully deposited on time, filing **Form 941** can be deferred to May 10. • **Form 720 taxes**. File Form 720 for the first quarter of 2002. • **Wagering tax.** File **Form 730** and pay the tax on wagers accepted during March. • **Heavy highway vehicle use tax.** File **Form 2290** and pay the tax (or the first installment) for vehicles first used in March.

MAY	
12th	• Employees must report **tip income** for April of $20 or more to the company (use **Form 4070**). • File deferred **Form 941** (see April 30) • **Communications and air transportation taxes** under the alternative method. Deposit the tax included in amounts billed or tickets sold during the first 15 days of April.
14th	• **Regular method taxes**. Deposit the tax for the last 15 days of April.
15th	• Due date for information returns of calendar year **exempt organizations** (**Forms 990, 990-PF** and **990-T**). Corporations requesting an extension to file **Form 990** may file **Form 7004** for an automatic six-month extension. Other entities must file **Form 2758** in time for it to be processed by the filing deadline to request a non-automatic extension.
28th	• **Communications and air transportation taxes** under the alternative method. Deposit the tax included in amounts billed or tickets sold during the last 15 days of April.
29th	• **Regular method taxes**. Deposit the tax for the first 15 days of May. • Annual statement to IRS regarding last year account balances for an **IRA** or **SEP** (**Form 5498**). Participants and IRS must be provided with IRA plan contribution information.
JUN	
1st	• **Wagering tax.** File **Form 730** and pay the tax on wagers accepted during April. • **Heavy highway vehicle use tax.** File **Form 2290** and pay the tax for vehicles first used in April.
10th	• Employees must report **tip income** for May 0f $20 or more to the company (use **Form 4070**).
11th	• **Communications and air transportation taxes** under the alternative method. Deposit tax included in amounts billed or tickets sold during first 15 days of May.
13th	• **Regular method taxes**. Deposit the tax for the last 16 days of May.
16th	• File your **individual tax return** if you were living outside of the United States, or file for a **2-month extension** (use **Form 4868**). • Pay the second **estimated tax payment** for individuals (use **Form 1040-ES**). • Deposit the second **estimated tax payment** for calendar year **corporations**. • Foreign corporations, that do not maintain an office or place of business in U.S., file income tax return (**Form 1120F**) for last calendar year.
25th	• **Communications and air transportation taxes** under the alternative method. Deposit tax included in amounts billed or tickets sold during the last 16 days of May.
27th	• **Regular method taxes**. Deposit the tax for the first 15 days of June..
30th	• **Wagering tax.** File **Form 730** and pay tax on wagers accepted during May. • **Heavy highway vehicle use tax.** File **Form 2290** and pay the tax for vehicles first used in May. Also, pay the installments for other vehicles, if applicable. • **Floor stocks tax** for ozone-depleting chemicals (**IRS No. 20**). Deposit the tax for January 1, "current year". • **Occupational excise taxes.** File **Form 11-C** to register and pay the annual tax if you are in the business of taking wagers.

JUL	
10th	• Employees must report **tip income** for June if $20 or more, to the company (use **Form 4070**). • **Communications and air transportation taxes** under the alternative method. Deposit the tax included in amounts billed or tickets sold during the first 15 days of June.
11th	• **Regular method taxes**. Deposit the tax for the last 15 days of June.
15th	• File calendar year **partnership and trust returns** (use **Form 1065** or **Form 1041**, respectively) for which an extension was obtained.
25th	• **Communications and air transportation taxes** under the alternative method. Deposit the tax included in amounts billed or tickets sold during the last 15 days of June.
29th	• **Regular method taxes**. Deposit the tax for the first 15 days of July.
31st	• File information returns of calendar-year retirement plans such as **Keogh plans** (**Form 5500**). • Report **employee income tax withholding and FICA taxes** for the second quarter of "current year" (use **Form 941**). If taxes are fully deposited on time, filing **Form 941** can be deferred to August 10. • **Form 720 taxes.** File **Form 720** for the second quarter of 2002. • **Wagering tax.** File **Form 730** and pay tax on wagers accepted during June. • **Heavy highway vehicle use tax.** File **Form 2290** and pay the tax for vehicles first used in June.
AUG	
11th	• Employees must report **tip income** for July of $20 or more to the company (use **Form 4070**). File deferred **Form 941** (see July 31).
12th	• **Communications and air transportation taxes** under the alternative method. Deposit the tax included in amounts billed or tickets sold during the first 15 days of July.
14th	• **Regular method taxes**. Deposit the tax for the last 16 days of July.
15th	• File **individual income tax returns** (**Form 1040, 1040A** or **1040EZ**) if you have a filing extension. [Note: You may request a further **extension** until October 15. File **Form 2688**.]
27th	• **Communications and air transportation taxes** under the alternative method. Deposit the tax included in amounts billed or tickets sold during the last 16 days of July.
29th	• **Regular method taxes**. Deposit the tax for the first 15 days of August.
31st	• **Heavy highway vehicle use tax.** File **Form 2290** and pay the tax (or the first installment) for vehicles first used in July. • **Wagering tax.** File **Form 730** and pay the tax on wagers accepted during July.

SEP	
10th	• Employees must report **tip income** for August of $20 or more to the company (use **Form 4070**). • **Communications and air transportation taxes** under the alternative method. Deposit the tax included in amounts billed or tickets sold during the first 15 days of August.
12th	• **Regular method taxes**. Deposit the tax for the last 16 days of August.
15th	• Pay the third **estimated tax payment** for individuals (use **Form 1040-ES**). • Deposit the third **estimated tax payment** for calendar year **corporations**. • File extended calendar-year **corporation returns** (use **Form 1120, 1120-A** or **1120S**). • Exempt calendar-year farmers' cooperatives file last year income tax returns (**Form 990 -C**). Fiscal-year cooperatives must file by the 15th day of the 9th month following the close of the tax year. File **Form 7004** for an automatic six-month extension.
25th	• **Communications and air transportation taxes** under the alternative method. Deposit the tax included in amounts billed or tickets sold during the last 16 days of August..
26th	• **Communications and air transportation taxes** under the alternative method (special September deposit rule). Deposit the tax included in amounts billed or tickets sold during the period beginning September 1 and ending September 10. If required to make deposits using EFTPS, see September 30.
29th	• **Regular method taxes**. Deposit the tax for the first 15 days of September. • **Regular method taxes** (special September deposit rule). Deposit the tax for the period beginning September 16 and ending September 25. If required to make deposits using EFTPS, see September 30. •
30th	• **Regular method taxes** (special September deposit rule). If required to use EFTPS, deposit the tax for the period beginning September 16 and ending September 26. If not required to make deposits using EFTPS, see September 26. • **Communications and air transportation taxes** under the alternative method (special September deposit rule). If required to use EFTPS, deposit the tax included in amounts billed or tickets sold during the period beginning on September 1 and ending September 11. If not required to make deposits using EFTPS, see September 26. • **Wagering tax.** File **Form 730** and pay the tax on wagers accepted during August. • **Heavy highway vehicle use tax.** File **Form 2290** and pay the tax (or the first installment) for vehicles first used in August..

OCT	
10th	• Employees must report **tip income** for September 0f $20 or more to the company (use **Form 4070**). • **Communications and air transportation taxes** under the alternative method. Deposit the tax included in amounts billed or tickets sold during the period beginning September 11 (September 12 if required to make deposits using EFTPS) and ending September 15.
14th	• **Regular method taxes**. Deposit the tax for the last 5 days (4 days if required to make deposits using EFTPS) of September.
15th	• File **individual tax return** (use **Form 1040**) if you have a second extension. • File a calendar-year **partnership return** (use **Form 1065**) if you have a second extension.
27th	• **Communications and air transportation taxes** under the alternative method. Deposit the tax included in amounts billed or tickets sold during the last 15 days of September.
29th	• **Regular method taxes**. Deposit the tax for the first 15 days in October.
31st	• Report **employee income tax withholding and FICA taxes** for the third quarter of "current year" (use **Form 941**). If taxes are fully deposited on time, filing Form 941 can be deferred to November 10. • **Form 720 taxes.** File **Form 720** for the third quarter of 2002. • **Wagering tax.** File **Form 730** and pay the tax on wagers accepted during September. • **Heavy highway vehicle use tax.** File **Form 2290** and pay the tax (or the first installment) for vehicles first used in September.
NOV	
10th	• Employees must report tip income for October of $20 or more to the company (use **Form 4070**). • File deferred **Form 941** (see October 31)
12th	• **Communications and air transportation taxes** under the alternative method. Deposit the tax included in amounts billed or tickets sold during the first 15 days of October.
14th	• **Regular method taxes**. Deposit the tax for the last 16 days of October.
26th	• **Communications and air transportation taxes** under the alternative method. Deposit the tax included in amounts billed or tickets sold during the last 16 days of October.
27th	• Regular method taxes. Deposit the tax for the first 15 days of November.

DEC	
1st	• **Wagering tax.** File **Form 730** and pay the tax on wagers accepted during October. • **Heavy highway vehicle use tax.** File **Form 2290** and pay the tax (or the first installment) for vehicles first used in October.
10th	• Employees must report **tip income** for November of $20 or more to the company (use **Form 4070**). • **Communications and air transportation taxes** under the alternative method. Deposit the tax included in amounts billed or tickets sold during the first 15 days of November.
12th	• **Regular method taxes**. Deposit the tax for the last 15 days of November.
15th	• Pay the fourth **estimated tax payment** (for calendar-year **corporations**).
26th	• **Communications and air transportation taxes** under the alternative method. Deposit the tax included in amounts billed or tickets sold during the last 15 days of November.
29th	• **Regular method taxes**. Deposit the tax for the first 15 days of December.
31st	• **Wagering tax.** File **Form 730** and pay the tax on wagers accepted in November. • **Heavy highway vehicle use tax.** File **Form 2290** and pay the tax (or the first installment) for vehicles first used in November. Also, pay the installments for other vehicles, if applicable.

SOP # ______ Revision:______ **Prepared by:___________**
Effective Date:_____________ **Approved by:___________**

Title: **G&A108 PROPERTY TAX ASSESSMENTS**

Policy: All property tax assessments will be reviewed for accuracy and proper assessed valuations to ensure minimum property tax costs to the company.

Purpose: To outline the areas for review in assessments and methods for appealing overstated assessments.

Scope: This statement applies to the Finance Department for property tax assessments for all sites owned by the company.

Responsibilities:

The Finance Department is responsible for reviews of Assessments including the review of Property Descriptions, validating record accuracy and submitting appeals to local Assessor's Offices.

Procedures:

1.0 REVIEW OF ASSESSMENTS

1.1 All assessments are to be promptly reviewed. Many jurisdictions only allow a challenge to an assessment within 30 days after the annual notice of assessed value is sent. If the Finance Department misses the deadline, the Company loses the chance to reduce the year's property taxes. There are normally no refunds for prior years' property taxes even if successfully challenge in the future. Often, it may be advisable to begin the analysis process prior to receiving the assessment notice.

1.2 When reviewing an assessment, the first step is to find out how the property was assessed. Ask for a full explanation of how the assessed value was derived. Assessors are usually cooperative in providing this information.

1.3 Upon receipt of the basis for assessment, the following factors should be reviewed:

Note: Do not make the mistake of thinking property has received a favorable low assessment just because its assessed value is less than its market value. Many jurisdictions use "assessment ratios" that are a percentage of market value. What is important is the amount of a property's assessment compared to those of similar properties. A below market assessment may in fact be very high.

- **Research Similar Properties:** Tax assessments are part of the public record. Assessments of similar properties to the company's should be looked up to see that the company's assessment is in line. The objective is to find assessed values for similar properties that are far lower than the company's. For example, company locations within industrial parks or similar developments should be easy to find very similar properties for comparison.
- **Review Property Descriptions and Accuracy of Records:** Review records for possible clerical errors. Ensure that property descriptions are correct and the building size (total square feet) is not overstated. Make sure that all dates are correct and that all calculations are properly computed. A wrong construction date or simple mathematical error can increase tax valuations.
- **Deflate Property Valuations:** Tax assessors generally value property on the basis of historical cost and the recent sales prices of other properties in the area. Often, when figuring local property taxes, numbers reported on the federal tax return will be used. Depreciable assets are valued at cost on the federal return when figuring depreciation deductions. However, the appropriate assessment for market value for property tax purposes may very different. Further, instead of performing actual physical inspections or assessments of properties every year, local assessors use "equalization ratios" to adjust the annual assessment. The equalization ratio is a type of an inflation adjustment meant to reflect the current general trend in property values. However, the current trend in property values may not apply to the company's property.

1.4 If the Company can provide solid reasons for using different measures to value property, it may be able to receive a reduction in property taxes. Possible valuation methods can include:

- **Income Production:** Measure the current value of the cash flow stream generated by the property, which may be substantially lowered during a recession.
- **Replacement or Reproduction Cost**: How much it would cost to replace or reproduce the property should be determined. For example, if the construction industry is in a downturn, the cost to replace the property may be less than what the Company paid for the property.
- Also the Company should evaluate if it incurred any construction cost overruns due to bad weather, labor disturbances, material shortages, etc., that may have increased the cost of a new building without adding to its value. Decorative features may also add much less value than their actual cost.
- **Market Prices:** The actual recent sales of similar properties may show that the company's property is over-assessed.
- **Unique Features or Business Obsolescence:** Changes to the characteristics of the property or features specific to the company's business may reduce its value. Examples can include:

- Change in zoning restrictions that limit the use of the property.
- Changes in neighborhood logistics, such as a median divider placed in a highway that deprives a location from access to customers, rerouting of a highway, closing of a railroad line or economic decline in the area that forces the company's traditional customer base to move away.
- Obsolete design for the company's particular business needs such as a facility that has been specially designed to hold machinery that has been made obsolete by a competitor's innovation or a communications facility built with conventional wiring that is obsolete due to a switch in the industry to the use of fiber optics.
- Unique design aspects which meet company needs but would reduce the value of a property to others.
- A general downturn in the company's industry.
- Including Personal Property in Building Valuations: Property that is movable is personal property and should not be included in a valuation of the building. Many items such as piping, wiring, climate control systems, generators, special supports and foundations for equipment may look like part of the building to the assessor but should not be included in the building's assessment.

2.0 APPEALING OF ASSESSMENTS

2.1 If upon review of the assessment and all other factors, the Finance Department believes a downward adjustment to the property assessment is appropriate, an appeal should be prepared. Experience has shown that if a company presents a sound argument for challenging an assessment, the Company has an excellent chance of receiving some type of tax reducing adjustment even if it is less than the Company had requested.

2.2 The appeal case should include documentation of the above findings. It is important to keep in mind that the property tax assessor may not be familiar with the details of the company's business or industry, so the Company must prepare to explain how such factors may affect a property's value.

2.3 Once a sound case is prepared, an appeal can be sought by simply calling the local assessor's office and asking for an appointment to discuss the assessment. The meeting with the local assessor will generally be informal. It is important to not be adversarial with the assessor but to present the attitude that the Company is helping the assessor to reach a more accurate valuation for the property by presenting additional information.

2.4 If the Company does not receive any or a large enough adjustment, an appeal may be made with the local Board of Appeals. These meetings will probably be more formal and the Company may wish to provide expert testimony or obtain an independent appraisal of the property to present to the Board of Appeals.

2.5 More assistance with property tax problems may be obtained by contacting the:

Institute for Professionals in Taxation
335 Peachtree Rd STE 280
Atlanta, GA 39326
404-240-2300
www.ipt.org

Revision History:

Revision	Date	Description of changes	Requested By
0	11/06/02	Initial Release	

SOP # ______ Revision:______ **Prepared by:____________**
Effective Date:______________ **Approved by:____________**

Title: **G&A109 CONFIDENTIAL INFORMATION RELEASE**

Policy: The release of financial, statistical or other information that may be of a confidential nature to the Company should be controlled. Individual requests should be referred to the Chief Financial Officer, Controller, or appropriate manager for disposition.

Purpose: To provide a means for the control of information to banks, investors, investment houses, media, credit bureaus, or other agencies and organizations.

Scope: All requests by an outsider to an employee regarding financial, sales, marketing, customers, personnel, vendors, or other company confidential information. If in doubt, verify with the Chief Financial Officer or Controller.

Responsibilities:

Chief Financial Officer (CFO) is responsible for safeguarding all company information and determining the appropriate level of detail for release.

Controller is responsible for assuring effective control of informative requests.

Human Resources Manager shall oversee all responses to all reference requests.

Credit Manager shall oversee all responses to all credit inquires.

Procedure:

1.0 FINANCIAL INFORMATION REQUESTS

1.1 Typical written requests are for additional information concerning details of the published financial statements, litigation progress, insurance coverage, names of investors, etc. If the request is by letter or other written correspondence, the material shall be forwarded to the CFO who will decide what information may be released and who will be authorized to reply.

1.2 If the request is by telephone or a personal visit to our office, the requester should be referred to the CFO or the Controller. If either is unavailable, the requester should be asked to provide their name, company, telephone number and address, if possible. Also they should be asked the reason for the request and a brief description of the information desired. This information should be written down and forwarded to the CFO for follow-up.

1.3 The CFO should determine the appropriate response for each request. Formal Financial Statement (see G&A104 MANAGEMENT REPORTS) presentations to the Board of Directors, Shareholders, or other stakeholders such as banks, should be accompanied by an opinion or comment from the company's Certified Public Accountant (CPA) prior to any formal presentation. (If no outside CPA review is obtained then some people may consider the Financial Statements as "Pro-Forma" and then request copies of completed tax returns). The accountant will examine the Financial Statements and prepare a formal version to one of three standards: compiled, reviewed or audited. The company should use an economically appropriate CPA standard sufficient to satisfy outside requirements.

The CPA standards are as follows:

- Compiled Financial Statement. The CPA is unable to make any assurances on the data or methods used to produce the financial statements. The CPA will re-cast the financial statements into a standard format (as per Generally Accepted Accounting Principles or GAAP) with a disclaimer that the statements are un-audited and the information is solely derived from the management of the business entity.
- Reviewed Financial Statement. The CPA is able to make some limited assurances that material changes are not required in order for the Financial Statements to be in conformity with GAAP. The CPA uses limited inquiry and some analytical procedures to ascertain the reasonableness of the statements. The information is then re-cast into a standard format with appropriate footnotes and a disclaimer that the statements are un-audited and only a limited inquiry has been made into the reasonableness of the information.
- Audited Financial Statement. The CPA provides assurance, through an opinion letter, that the financial statements are a fair representation of the financial position, results of operations, and cash flows of an entity. This opinion is given after a detailed review and verification of the accounting records and processes used to produce the data. Verification steps include various analytical procedures, client surveys, third party confirmation, and detailed accounting record reviews.

Any irregularities found could lead to either a "qualified" opinion, to indicate that something is inconsistent with GAAP, or an "adverse" opinion, which calls into question the reliability of the information itself. The CPA considers an adverse opinion very serious.

1.4 Some types of confidential information may require the signing of G&A109 Ex1 NON-DISCLOSURE AGREEMENT, prior to release. This may include requests for product release schedules, development plans, elements of corporate strategy, customer lists, intellectual property, financial information, legal proceedings, or time sensitive information.

2.0 PERSONNEL INFORMATION REQUESTS

2.1 The Human Resources Manager shall oversee all responses to all reference requests. No other employee, including a former employee's immediate supervisor, shall be authorized to respond independently without first obtaining approval from the Human Resources Manager as per ABR41 ***Bizmanualz™ Human Resources Policies, Procedures and Forms*** regarding procedures for PERSONNEL BACKGROUND CHECKS.

2.2 All requests should be in writing, using company letterhead, indicating in that letter that the subject of the reference request has applied for a job. Information is not to be provided over the phone.

2.3 Each response shall be obtained only from people with first-hand knowledge of the employee's performance.

2.4 The Human Resources Manager shall review all responses to ensure that:

- Only factual information about the employee's job performance and qualifications for employment are included in the response. At no time should a response include emotions, personal feelings, rumors, non-work-related comments or exaggerations.
- If at all possible it is important that some form of documentation or solid evidence supports all information provided in the response.

2.5 Retain a copy of all responses, including the contents of any oral response, in the former employee's personnel file.

3.0 CREDIT REFERENCE INQUIRIES

3.1 All credit reference requests should be in writing, using a credit inquiry form similar to the REV103 Ex3 CREDIT INQUIRY sample form. Information requests should be directed to the Credit Manager and are not to be provided over the phone.

3.2 The Credit Manager should review the Credit Inquiry form for completeness prior to responding. Retain a copy of all responses, including the contents of any oral response, in the customer's file.

Revision History:

Revision	Date	Description of changes	Requested By
0	11/06/02	Initial Release	

[This page intentionally left blank]

G&A109 Ex1 NONDISCLOSURE AGREEMENT

This NONDISCLOSURE AGREEMENT is made and entered into as of (DATE) between (THE COMPANY NAME, STATE OF INCORPORATION AND ADDRESS), and (OTHER PARTY NAME, STATE OF INCORPORATION AND ADDRESS).

1. **Purpose.** The parties wish to explore and/or implement a business opportunity of mutual interest, and in connection with this opportunity, each party may disclose to the other certain confidential technical and business information that the disclosing party desires the receiving party to treat as confidential.

2. **"Confidential Information"** means any information disclosed by either party to the other party, either directly or indirectly, in writing, orally or by inspection of tangible objects (including, without limitation, documents, prototypes, samples, plant and equipment) that is designated as "Trade Secret", "Confidential", "Proprietary" or some similar designation, or is of such a nature or has been disclosed in such a manner that it should be obvious to the receiving party that such is claimed as confidential. Information communicated orally shall be considered Confidential Information within a reasonable time after the initial disclosure. Confidential Information may also include information disclosed to a disclosing third party by third parties. Confidential Information includes, without limitation, a disclosing party's trade secrets, know-how, intellectual property and proprietary information as well as business plans, financial data and the status and terms of any discussions between the parties regarding a potential business transaction. Confidential Information shall not, however, include any information that (i) was publicly known and made generally available in the public domain prior to the time of disclosure by the disclosing party; (ii) becomes publicly known and made generally available after disclosure by the disclosing party to the receiving party through no action or inaction of the receiving party; (iii) is already in the possession of the receiving party at the time of disclosure by the disclosing party as shown by the receiving party's files and records immediately prior to the time of disclosure; (iv) is obtained by the receiving party from a third party without a breach of such third party's obligations of confidentiality; (v) is independently developed by the receiving party without use of or reference to the disclosing party's Confidential Information, as shown by documents and other competent evidence in the receiving party's possession; or (vi) is required by law to be disclosed by the receiving party, provided that the receiving party gives the disclosing party prompt written notice of such requirement prior to such disclosure and assistance in obtaining an order protecting the information from public disclosure.

3. **Non-use and Non-disclosure.** Each party agrees not to use any Confidential Information of the other party for any purpose except to evaluate and engage in discussions concerning a potential business relationship between the parties. Each party agrees not to disclose any Confidential Information of the other party to third parties or to such party's employees or agents, except to those employees or agents of the receiving party who are required to have the information in order to evaluate or engage in discussions concerning the contemplated business relationship. A receiving party shall be responsible and liable for the action of its employees and agents with respect to a disclosing party's Confidential Information and shall fully cooperate with the disclosing party in enforcing any rights of the disclosing party against any such person in connection with a breach of this Agreement. Neither party shall reverse engineer, disassemble or de-compile any prototypes, software, or other tangible objects that embody the other party's Confidential Information and that are provided to the party hereunder. Neither party shall hire any employees of the other during the term of this Agreement and for a period of two years thereafter.

4. **Maintenance of Confidentiality.** Each party agrees that it shall take reasonable measures to protect the secrecy of and avoid disclosure and unauthorized use of the Confidential Information of the other party. Without limiting the foregoing, each party shall take at least those measures that it takes to protect its own highly confidential information and shall ensure that its employees and agents who have access to Confidential Information of the other party have signed a Non-use and Non-disclosure agreement in content similar to the provisions hereof, prior to any disclosure of Confidential Information to such employees and agents. Neither party shall make any copies of the Confidential Information of the other party unless the other party previously approves the same in writing. Each party shall reproduce the other party's proprietary rights notices on any such approved copies, in the same manner in which such notices were set forth in or on the original.

5. **Ongoing Development.** Nothing in this Agreement shall prohibit or restrict either party's right to develop, use or market products or services similar to or competitive with those of the other party disclosed in the Confidential Information as long as such shall not otherwise be a breach of this Agreement. Each party acknowledges that the other may already possess or have developed products or services similar to or competitive with those of the other party disclosed in the Confidential Information. Each party shall remain free to use in the course of its business its general knowledge skills and experience incurred before, during or after the date of this Agreement and the activities hereunder.

6. **No Obligation.** Nothing herein shall obligate either party to proceed with any transaction between them and each party reserves the right, in its sole discretion, to terminate the discussions contemplated by this Agreement concerning the business opportunity. Upon termination of such discussions the parties shall return all Confidential Information as provided in paragraph 8 and shall have no further rights to evaluate or use the Confidential Information of each other for any purpose whatsoever.

7. **No Warranty.** ALL CONFIDENTIAL INFORMATION IS PROVIDED "AS IS." THE PARTIES MAKE NO REPRESENTATIONS OR WARRANTIES, EXPRESS, IMPLIED OR OTHERWISE, REGARDING THE ACCURACY, COMPLETENESS OR PERFORMANCE OF ANY OF ITS RESPECTIVE CONFIDENTIAL INFORMATION.

8. **Return of Materials.** All documents and other tangible objects (except for any tangible objects purchased by a party) containing or representing Confidential Information that have been disclosed by either party to the other party, and all copies thereof which are in the possession of the other party, shall be and remain the property of the disclosing party and shall be promptly returned to the disclosing party upon the disclosing party's written request.

9. **No License.** Nothing in this Agreement is intended to grant any rights to either party under any patent, mask work right, trademark, trade secret or copyright of the other party, nor shall this Agreement grant any party any rights in or to the Confidential Information of the other party except as expressly set forth herein.

10. **Term.** The obligations of each receiving party hereunder shall survive until such times as all Confidential Information of the other party disclosed hereunder becomes publicly known and made generally available through no action or inaction of the receiving party. Notwithstanding the surviving obligations of a receiving party to maintain the confidentiality of a disclosing party's Confidential Information either party may at any time given written notice to the other party that it does not desire to receive any additional Confidential Information from the other party. After receipt of such notice, such party shall no longer furnish its Confidential Information to the notifying party.

11. **Remedies.** Each party agrees that any violation or threatened violation of this Agreement may cause irreparable injury to the other party, entitling the other party to seek injunctive relief in addition to all other legal and equitable remedies.

12. **General Provisions.** This Agreement shall bind and inure to the benefit of the parties hereto and their successors and assigns. This Agreement shall be governed by the laws of the State of Missouri, without reference to conflict of laws principles. This document contains the entire Agreement between the parties with respect to the subject matter hereof. Any failure to enforce any provision of the Agreement shall not constitute a waiver thereof or of any other provision. This Agreement may not be amended, nor any obligation waived, except by a writing signed by both parties hereto.

(THE COMPANY).	(THE OTHER PARTY)
By:	By: ____________________
Name:____________________	Name:____________________
Title: ____________________	Title: ____________________

SOP # ______ Revision:______
Effective Date:______________

Prepared by:____________
Approved by:____________

Title: **G&A110 DOCUMENT CONTROL**

Policy: All documents used to provide work direction or set policy should be reviewed, approved, distributed and controlled by the office of the Controller.

Purpose: To define the methods and responsibilities for controlling documents used to provide work direction or set policy, and to define methods for document revision, approval, and distribution.

Scope: This procedure applies to all documents required by the Accounting Management System. Documents of internal or external origin are included.

Responsibilities:

The Controller is responsible for controlling and reviewing, at least annually, the Accounting Manual, all procedures and instructions related to the Accounting Management System, and all External Documents that are required.

The Office Manager is responsible for maintaining and controlling the Accounting Manual, all procedures and instructions related to the Accounting Management System, and all External Documents that are required.

Department Managers and supervisors are responsible for ensuring the relevant versions of documents are available at the points of use and that they are legible.

Definitions: Controlled Document: A document that provides information or direction for performance of work is that is within the scope of this procedure. Characteristics of control include such things as Revision Number (letter), Signatures indicating review and approval, and Controlled Distribution.

Document: Information and its supporting medium. The medium can be paper, magnetic, electronic, optical computer disc, photograph, or sample.

External Document: A document of external origin that provides information or direction for the performance of activities within the scope of the quality management system. Examples include but are not limited to: customer drawings, industry standards, international standards, or equipment manuals.

Procedure:

1.0 DOCUMENT DISTRIBUTION

1.1 Engineering drawings and bills of material are distributed through the CAD system. It is up to the holder of drawings and bills of material to dispose of previous revisions as new revisions are released.

1.2 The controller will be responsible for maintaining master lists of all controlled documents. Separate lists will be maintained of documents of internal origin and external origin. Examples of external documents include National or International Standards that may be used or referenced.

The master list for internal documents will contain the following information:

- Document Number
- Document Title
- Current Revision
- Last Review Date
- Document Locations

The master list for external documents will contain the following information:

- Document Number
- Document Title
- Issue Date or Revision (both if available)
- Document Locations

1.3 The controller distributes hardcopy documents to the locations listed on the Master List, and removes and destroys any old versions of procedures or instructions. The controller distributes electronic versions of documents by moving the old revision to the OBSOLETE folder and moving the new revision to the RELEASED folder.

1.4 External documents are controlled only for distribution. All external standards should be purchased to ensure they are added to the External Document list and that new revisions are properly distributed.

2.0 DOCUMENT REVISION

2.1 The controller is responsible for coordinating with Department Managers to review all procedures and instructions at least annually and update them as required to ensure documents remain current.

2.2 Anyone may submit a new document or changes to an existing document as necessary. To submit a change, the requestor prints a copy of the document and marks the required changes on the copy. If changes are extensive, a new document may be typed and submitted.

2.3 The requestor completes G&A110 Ex1 REQUEST FOR DOCUMENT CHANGE (RDC) indicating the nature and reason for the change and submits it to the Controller for review.

2.4 The Controller reviews the request. If the request is denied, the Controller notifies the requestor the reason for the denial.

2.5 If the request is approved, the Controller indicates who else needs to review the change. Department Managers of any affected departments should be included. Only the RDC needs to be submitted for approval.

2.6 Reviewers consider the reason for the change and determine if the change is warranted. The Controller notifies the requestor if the RDC is denied.

2.7 If approved, the Controller assigns a Document Change Number (DCN) on G&A110 Ex2 DOCUMENT CHANGE CONTROL form and submits the new or changed documents along with the appropriate approvals to the Office Manager for typing and formatting. The Office Manager updates the document, indexes the revision, and updates the revision history.

2.8 The Office Manager notifies the reviewers indicated on the RDC via email when the document is available for review.

2.9 Reviewers indicate intended approval or submit comments via email. If comments are substantive, The Office Manager incorporates the comments and contacts reviewers for re-review.

2.10 When all reviewers indicate intent to approve, The Office Manager circulates the final documents to obtain signatures.

2.11 When the required approvals have been obtained, the Office Manager updates the master list with the new revision number and last review date for changed documents or with all required information for new documents.

2.12 Sufficient copies are made for distribution to all locations indicated on the master list. The Office Manager stamps "Controlled Copy" in red on each copy and distributes the controlled copies according to Section 2.1 above.

2.13 The master copy of the previous revision is pulled, marked "Obsolete" and filed in the historical files.

2.14 Because the electronic version will not show signatures, the current Master Copy is maintained as evidence of review and approval

3.0 PROCEDURE AND WORK INSTRUCTION FORMAT

3.1 Procedures and instruction should use this document as a template. If any of the headings are not applicable they may be deleted.

3.2 All procedures and instructions must have the Procedure Name, Revision and Page Number in Page X of Y format on each page of the document.

3.3 All procedures and instructions must show approval signatures on the first page or cover page. Electronic versions may show the approver names typed. The master copy must contain the signatures however.

4.0 TEMPORARY CHANGES

4.1 For many potential reasons, urgent temporary changes may need to be made to the Accounting Management System. These changes must be defined and controlled.

4.2 To ensure control of the Accounting Management System, changes that may affect accounting services must be defined in a procedure or temporary procedure and reviewed before the change is made. The temporary change may be developed in a handwritten procedure on a blank procedure template or as redlines of an existing document.

4.3 Temporary changes require review and approval by the Controller and the affected Department Manager(s) at a minimum. Review and approval are indicated by signatures on the handwritten document or by initials and date next to redlines. Even though handwritten, documents must be legible and identifiable.

4.4 Temporary change documents should include the range of dates they are valid and the scope of applicability. Use of temporary documents may not exceed two weeks without being made a permanent document.

Revision History:

Revision	Date	Description of changes	Requested By
0	12/29/02	Initial Release	

G&A110 Ex1 REQUEST FOR DOCUMENT CHANGE (RDC)

Date:______________________________ RDC No.:__________________

Originator:____

Document Title and Publication Date:____

Page and Chapter, or Paragraph Number:____

Description Of Problem, Opportunity Or Reason For Request (Define in Detail):

____

____

____

Solution Recommended (if known) Date Action Required By:______________________

____

____

____

Comments:____

____

____

____

____

Department Manager Approval:____

Recommended Solution To Problem or Postponement/Dissolution of Request
(attach all necessary documentation to support response)_________________________

____

____

____

Approved By:______________________________ Date:_____________________

PROCEDURE FOR COMPLETING FORM

1) Complete top section of this form except for RDC number
2) Obtain Department Manager's approval
3) Forward original to the Office Manager who will assign a RDC number (Note: one copy will be returned to originator with RDC number assigned.
4) The Office Manager will take action and if appropriate will proceed with an RDC.
5) The Office Manager returns a copy to Originator upon resolution of request.

Distribution: Original - RDC File Copy 1 - Originator

[This page intentionally left blank]

G&A110 Ex2 DOCUMENT CHANGE CONTROL

Date:____________________

DCN#:____________________

RDC#:____________________

Doc. or Part No.	Description of Change, Documents affected and reason(s) for change(s)	Action Code(s)	Effective Date

Change Action Required

Make/order New Document:______________________________

Current Docs:

❒ Use until depleted ❒ Return for Credit ❒ Scrap ❒ Save for spares

Other:______________________________

Comments:______________________________

Authorization(s): Controller

By:____________________

Title:____________________

Date:____________________

Authorization(s): Office Manager

By:____________________

Title:____________________

Date:____________________

[This page intentionally left blank]

Accounting Policies, Procedures & Forms

Section 410

Cash Procedures

Section 410

Cash

Procedures:

SOP # ______ Revision:______ **Prepared by:____________**

Effective Date:______________ **Approved by:____________**

Title: **CSH101 CASH DRAWERS AND CREDIT CARDS**

Policy: Proper internal control should be maintained over funds received by cashiers or sales clerks at all times.

Purpose: To identify the practices for cash drawer control, including cash receipts, credit cards, special tender items, cash payouts and reconciliation with deposits.

Scope: All personnel that deal with the cash transactions.

Responsibilities:

Cash Controller is responsible for safeguarding / verifying and controlling all cash assets.

Cashier/Sales is responsible for ensuring the completeness and accuracy of all opening, closing and intermediate transactions.

Sales Manager is responsible for overseeing all sales transactions.

Definitions: ACH. Is the acronym for the Automated Clearing House (ACH) of the Federal Reserve System, which facilitates the electronic clearing of debits and credit transactions to a merchant's bank account.

Batch All of the day's credit card transactions are collected into a "batch" of transactions. The batch is closed, usually at the end of the day, and the result is submitted to the merchant processor as a single "batch".

Chargebacks A Chargeback is the process that occurs when a customer disputes a charge that appears on their monthly credit card statement and the disputed transaction is investigated for potential reversal.

POS A Point-Of-Sale or POS system is an automated cash drawer that ties into the accounting system to record all sales transactions. The POS will typically process credit card transactions and returns, manage inventory, accounts receivable, payables or it may be web or network enabled. At its core is a computer with software that can include any number of functions.

Processor The processor is responsible for authorizing credit card transactions and settling each batch. The processor also resolves all discrepancies or "Chargebacks".

Settlement The processor clears the credit card transactions in a batch and the result is "settled" to the designated bank account via an ACH credit or debit. Settlement varies by Credit Card Company but usually occurs in 2-3 days after a batch is closed.

Tender Item Any item used to tender or pay for a transaction is considered a tender item. Tender items can include coupons, gift certificates, credits, rebates, cash, checks, barter credits, etc.

Procedure:

1.0 OPENING

1.1 Assign each cashier his or her own cash drawer. If there is only one cash drawer and there is more than one person in the store, then assign only one person to be the cashier responsible for the cash drawer. It is important to ensure that only one person has access to any one cash drawer otherwise, the integrity of the cash drawer will be compromised.

1.2 Upon beginning a shift, each cashier should count the beginning balance of their cash drawer and enter the totals onto CSH101 Ex1 DAILY CASH REPORT. The cashier should then prepare a cash change fund sufficient for operations during their shift. All change requests or questions regarding the balance of the drawer should be directed to the sales manager. Cashiers should avoid obtaining change from any other cashiers.

The cashier will then open their station, ring up sales on the cash register, collect cash, checks, process credit cards, approved "house" account charges, etc., and make change for customers. In no instance may any item be passed through a station without recording the transaction on the register.

2.0 TRANSACTIONS

2.1 Proper cash register practices should be used for all transactions. Cash drawers should only be opened when a tendered amount is entered, whether cash, check, credit card or cash is paid out.

2.2 Verify checks with two forms of ID (one with picture) and write driver's license number on the check. Checks for more than the amount of purchase should require specific approval from the sales manager. Checks should be immediately restrictively endorsed (by stamp: "for deposit only - store name".

2.3 Credit card transactions must be authorized by calling in the card numbers or swiping through authorizing hardware or software and accompanied by a signed credit card receipt.

2.4 Regardless of the specific procedures associated with the point of sale system used, proper segregation of duties should be maintained, whenever practical.

For example, voided transactions for over-rings should be approved and initialed by the sales manager; Cashiers should not ring up sales to relatives; and all returns, refunds or store credits granted should be accompanied by a signed sales receipt noting the customer's name and phone number, in accordance with REV103 CUSTOMER CREDIT APPROVAL AND TERMS.

2.5 Cash drawer payouts should be limited to selected purposes, must be accompanied by proper documentation, and have specific approval from the store manager.

3.0 SPECIAL TENDER ITEMS

3.1 Special tender items include layaway, coupons and gift certificates. The specific procedures in handling these items will depend, in large measure, on the features built into POS system.

3.2 Most POS systems incorporate a layaway feature. The item sold on layaway is entered in the register as a sales transaction. However, the tender selected is "layaway". The register tracks this layaway amount like a customer receivable. Generally, the customer pays a certain portion down immediately. This is handled similar to any customer payment received on account. When the balance is fully paid, the customer is allowed to receive the product. An important practice in layaways is to immediately pull the designated product and keep it in a secure, segregated area, identified by a copy of the initial sales receipt. The POS system immediately decreases inventory when a layaway is first recorded, so the affected merchandise should be removed from the shelf at the same time.

3.3 Coupons can take many forms. Certain vendors may promote items through coupon placement in the media or directly to potential customers. The store may promote items on its own through similar methods. Either way, when a coupon is presented to the store, the result is usually some additional discount on the promoted item, (cents off, percentage discount, one free with other purchase, etc.). Many POS systems allow for setting up these possible discount features ahead of time, and scanning the UPC code on the coupon, itself. Otherwise, the price needs to be manually overridden with a special coupon discount code. In either case, the additional discount is tracked in a separate account to provide for an accurate analysis of gross margin percentages, and control totals for end-of-day cash drawer reconciliation.

These coupons should be treated as another form of tender and should be saved in the drawer and accounted. Moreover, if vendors generated the coupons, they may want an accounting of the number of coupons redeemed. The manner in which they are saved, reconciled, and reported on, will depend upon the specific vendor requirements.

3.4 Gift certificates are different from coupons in that the store generally receives money from the sale of certificates, ahead of any specific sale. Most POS systems have separate register entries for certificates. They are "sold" like any other merchandise. They can even contain bar codes that are scanned upon issuance. Generally, the certificates are pre-numbered to provide control (over the issued certificates). As they are redeemed against purchases, they are treated by the POS system as just another form of tender.

When the cash drawer is reconciled at the end of day, the total of all redeemed certificates is included in the overall reconciliation. If the certificates are maintained manually, the serial number from the redeemed certificate should be checked off the control listing of all numbers issued. If the certificates are maintained by the POS system, then scanning the redeemed coupon will satisfy the same objective. Either way, this matching process provides a total of un-redeemed certificates, which is a liability to the store for future redemption by its customers.

4.0 CLOSING

4.1 At the end of the shift, in the presence of the sales manager, the cashier should count the cash drawer and enter the totals onto CSH101 Ex1 DAILY CASH REPORT showing the amount of the opening change fund or cash drawer, the cash receipts collected, refunds or credits granted and any cash payouts made. The settlement sheet should be compared to the cash register tape and any overage/shortage documented. The cash register "tape" will either be the tape in the register, or a printed report from the register's printer.

This type of report is always a sub-total of each day's transactions. It verifies sequential integrity and ensures that all transactions recorded through the system are accounted for. The cashier will then sign the reconciled the DAILY CASH REPORT and submit the settlement sheet and collected funds to the Cash Controller. This report should always be available and subject to review.

4.2 A summary of credit card transactions or Batch Report is also included on the DAILY CASH REPORT, since credit cards are simply another form of tender. The actual end of day closing routines for credit cards will vary, depending on the credit card merchant account and verification software.

A closing routine is executed by the computer or by entering a code into a stand-alone credit card terminal. This routine generally prints out each individual transaction and a total. Usually, Visa/MasterCard, American Express, and Discover are handled separately. Thus for all three major cards, there would be three end of day totals to add to the settlement sheet.

All of the day's credit card transactions are submitted to the merchant processor as a single batch. The processor clears the transactions in the batch and the result is "settled" to the designated bank account.

4.3 Turn in the completed DAILY CASH REPORT, credit card summary (Batch Report), and the cash drawer to Accounting for processing.

5.0 CHARGEBACKS AND DISPUTED TRANSACTIONS

5.1 A chargeback occurs when a customer disputes a charge that appears on their monthly credit card statement. Frequently this occurs when a charge is not recognized even though it may be a valid charge. This may also occur when someone, other than the cardholder, uses the credit card to make unauthorized charges. Either way, the Sales Manager is responsible for justifying the charge.

Note: without a signed credit card slip or receipt, the customer will usually win the dispute. Therefore, to protect the company, make sure a signed receipt is obtained and filed for every charge.

5.2 The merchant is notified, typically through the mail, via a chargeback notice from the merchant's processor. The notice provides the details of the transaction, a copy of the dispute description signed by the customer and instructions on how to proceed. The options include:

- Do nothing. If you agree with the dispute then nothing else is required. The processor will deduct the amount of the charge from the designated bank account.
- Justify the charge. The Sales Manager will need to write a letter to the processor explaining the situation and the reasons why the charge is valid. Provide as much documentation as is available to support the charge. The most important document is a copy of the signed credit card receipt. Other supporting documents include: proof of delivery, any form of customer correspondence, order forms, printed explanation of returns policy, or sample of marketing literature explaining the promotional offer.
- Partial Refund. Sometime special circumstances exist that warrant only a partial refund. In this case, explain the situation as above in order to justify the charge but provide a partial refund amount in the description. American Express allows for partial refunds on their chargeback form.

6.0 SECURITY PRECAUTIONS

6.1 The Sales Manager should investigate all returns or order cancellations. Creative cashiers can void valid orders or return money to themselves. Make sure all returns are authorized by the manager and/or contain the customer name, address, phone, and signature. This will help to ensure the return is valid. Consider restricting voided transactions to the manager.

6.2 Conduct periodic cash drawer audits. This can include closing the register at midday on a random basis and then re-opening it with a new drawer.

6.3 Investigate the trashcans for discarded receipts. Examine any receipts found to determine if a sale was improperly made, voided, or returned.

6.4 Spot check inventory items. The POS provides current "on-hand" levels for all items. Compare the on-hand levels with the actual inventory. Then compare these numbers with the register tape at the same time. All should match for a specific item. This does not require a complete physical inventory. Just check some popular items that are sold on a frequent basis.

Revision History:

Revision	Date	Description of changes	Requested By
0	11/06/02	Initial Release	

CSH101 Ex1 DAILY CASH REPORT

Date: ______________

Cash Drawer Assigned to: ____

CASH DRAWER

OPENING DRAWER			CLOSING DRAWER		
Dollars:	______________		Dollars:	______________	
Pennies:	______________		Pennies:	______________	
Nickels:	______________		Nickels:	______________	
Dimes:	______________		Dimes:	______________	
Quarters:	______________		Quarters:	______________	
other:	______________		Checks:	______________	
TOTAL:	______________	(1)	TOTAL:	______________	(2)
Closing Cash:	______________	(2)			
Net Days Cash:	______________	(3) = (1-2)			

Cash Register Tape Total: .... ______________ (4)

Net Days Cash: [transfer from (3) above] .... ______________ (5)

Difference: .... ______________ (4-5)

CREDIT CARD CHARGES

Visa/MasterCard: ______________

American Express: ______________

Discover: ______________

Other: ______________

TOTAL: ______________

Refunds/Credits: ______________

Voids: ______________

TOTAL Charges: ______________ (6)

Credit Card Charges Total: [transfer from (6) above] .... ______________ (7)

Total Cash Sales: .... ______________ (7+5)

INVOICES

Total Invoices: ______________

Verification and Signature

____

I agree that the totals documented above are a true and accurate recording of all sales that have occurred today through my register.

[This page intentionally left blank]

SOP # ______ Revision:______ **Prepared by:______________**
Effective Date:______________ **Approved by:______________**

Title: **CSH102 CASH RECEIPTS AND DEPOSITS**

Policy: Accurate internal control of cash receipts and deposits will be maintained at all times. Cash deposits will be made on the same day as receipt.

Purpose: To establish the procedures to be followed for receiving, applying and depositing cash receipts.

Scope: This procedure applies to all cash receipts received by the company.

Responsibilities:

Accounts Receivable is responsible for processing all cash and check transactions and depositing the results in the bank.

Cash Controller is responsible for inspecting and verifying proper signatures or endorsements on checks.

Cashier/Sales is responsible for all cash drawer transactions.

Definitions: Tender Item. Any item used to tender or pay for a transaction is considered a tender item. Tender items can include coupons, gift certificates, credits, rebates, cash, checks, barter credits, etc.

Procedure:

1.0 RECEIVING CASH DRAWERS

1.1 At the end of the day all cashiers should turn in their cash drawers along with the CSH101 Ex1 DAILY CASH REPORT as per CSH101 CASH DRAWERS AND CREDIT CARDS. Inspect the cash drawers and separate all tender items.

1.2 The accounting department should verify the totals from the DAILY CASH REPORT with the cash drawer.

1.3 Next, verify the daily summary totals from each credit card vendor with the DAILY CASH REPORT. These represent electronic deposits made to the bank, just like the cash and checks, which are physically deposited each day. Make sure to store all signed credit card charge slips in an organized manor. Signed slips will be required in case of a later dispute or chargeback.

Note: Credit card deposits will require 2-3 days to complete the settlement process before being deposited into the bank account.

1.4 Prepare the cash drawer with the starting cash required for the next business day. Prepare the remaining cash and checks for deposit (see deposit below). File all tender items and or forward to the appropriate vendor as needed.

2.0 APPLICATION OF ACCOUNTS RECEIVABLE

2.1 Inspect all incoming accounting mail for checks. New orders should be entered as per REV101 SALES ORDER ENTRY. Notification of wire transfers should be processed as a check for the purposes of this procedure and in accordance with CSH104 WIRE TRANSFERS.

2.2 Accounts Receivable should photocopy all checks. Any papers accompanying the checks should be stapled to the check photocopy and the envelopes discarded.

2.3 Accounts receivable will use the photocopy of the checks and customer remittance advices to apply the cash payments to the Accounts Receivable Ledger. Unapplied payments are to be credited against the oldest open aging column on the accounts receivable ledger. A standard letter of information and/or inquiry should be sent or faxed to the payer when there is any question as to the correct application of the check.

2.4 Checks returned once should be deposited a second time. Already re-deposited checks should be debited back to the account. See CSH103 PROBLEM CHECKS.

2.5 Prepare all checks received for deposit.

3.0 DEPOSIT

3.1 The Cash Controller will inspect all checks for proper signature or endorsement. If a check is received without a proper signature then process the check as per CSH103 PROBLEM CHECKS procedure.

3.2 All checks should be endorsed with the restrictive endorsement "For Deposit Only" along with the company's designated bank deposit account number and then prove out the numerical count made by the accounting department. No check should be withheld from daily deposit unless it is legally imperfect. The endorsed checks should then be returned to the accounting department.

3.3 Collect all cash and checks and prepare a bank deposit slip for deposit in the company's authorized bank at the end of each day. A deposit ticket should be prepared for each cashier station or a combined ticket for several funds.

3.4 Place a duplicate copy of the deposit ticket and collected cash into a cash bag for transport to the bank. Deposits should be made no less frequently than daily. If the deposit cannot be made immediately then the deposits should be stored in a secure area for later deposit. (see ABR32 ***Bizmanualz™ Security Planning Policies, Procedures and Forms***).

Extreme care should be taken to protect the safety of the person making the deposit and the deposit itself. Actions to be considered are, making deposits only during daylight hours, using random deposit times and different routes to the bank, and assigning two people to make deposits.

3.5 The deposit amount should be entered into the accounting program and then recorded on the CSH102 Ex1 DEPOSIT LOG form. The original deposit ticket should be stapled to a Daily Deposit Report generated from the Accounting program and filed accordingly.

Note: The final net cash deposit must reconcile with the taped total by territory or cash drawer and the original accounting department tape.

Revision History:

Revision	Date	Description of changes	Requested By
0	11/06/02	Initial Release	

[This page intentionally left blank]

CSH102 Ex1 DEPOSIT LOG

Control Number	Date	Deposit Amount	Comment	Initials
		$		

[This page intentionally left blank]

SOP # ______ Revision:______ **Prepared by:____________**
Effective Date:______________ **Approved by:____________**

Title: CSH103 PROBLEM CHECKS

Problem: To save time in returning and following-up on unsigned, checks marked "payment in full", or returned by the bank. These checks should be processed as follows and deposited.

Purpose: To describe how these types of checks should be handled before depositing.

Scope: This procedure applies to all checks received by the company.

Responsibilities:

Accounts Receivable is responsible for processing all check transactions.

Definitions: NSF. Non-Sufficient Funds or NSF checks are those that are returned from the bank because the balance in the checking account was not high enough to cover the check. The check is then stamped NSF or "insufficient funds", "uncollected funds", or maybe "account closed".

Procedure:

1.0 UNSIGNED CHECKS

1.1 The word "over" should be typed or written on the line where the signature would normally appear. On the back, type "Lack of Signature Guaranteed" and then add the company name, manager's name, title and signature.

Note: This indicates to the bank that the store will take back the check as a charge against its account in the event it isn't honored. In the event the check is not honored, the store manager should immediately follow-up with the issuer.

1.2 Continue processing the check as per CSH102 CASH RECEIPTS AND DEPOSITS.

2.0 PARTIAL PAYMENT CHECKS MARKED "PAYMENT IN FULL"

2.1 If there's no dispute as to the amount, a check tendered for less than the amount due and marked "payment in full" (or similar wording) can be cashed without jeopardizing the right to recover the balance. However, if there's a bona fide dispute as to the amount owing, the store runs the risk that payment will be deemed to have settled the disputed claim for the lesser amount.

2.2 To overcome any potential pitfall, the check should be endorsed with the following statement "Check is accepted without prejudice and with full reservation of all rights under section 1-207 of the UNIFORM COMMERCIAL CODE (see Reference A).

2.3 Continue processing the check as per procedure CSH102 CASH RECEIPTS AND DEPOSITS.

2.4 The credit manager should then work with the customer to resolve collection of the remaining balance due in accordance with procedure REV109 ACCOUNT COLLECTION PROCESS.

3.0 RETURNED CHECKS

3.1 A returned check for less than $100 or stamped "uncollected funds," should be re-deposited the following day as per CSH102 CASH RECEIPTS AND DEPOSITS, if the check is not already stamped, "Do Not Re-Deposit".

3.2 For returned checks in amounts greater than $100, the bank that the check is drawn against should be telephoned to determine if the check amount will clear the customer's account. If sufficient funds exist the check should be re-deposited. If the check is very large, consider taking the check directly to the issuing bank for recovery.

Note: The customer's account number should be the second number series located at the bottom center of the check.

4.0 REDEPOSITED CHECKS

4.1 In the event a re-deposited check is returned or if sufficient funds do not exist to cover the check, the credit manager should contact the issuer by phone to report the problem and discuss how the matter will be resolved. (See REV109 ACCOUNT COLLECTION PROCESS). Then issue a formal notice CSH103 Ex1 BAD CHECK NOTICE via certified mail with a return receipt requested to ensure the customer understands the seriousness of the issue.

4.2 Whenever a check is re-deposited more than once a handling fee should be considered.

References:

A. UNIFORM COMMERCAL CODE (UCC)

The "Uniform Commercial Code" or UCC began as a model for each state legislature to modify and adopt as law in that state. Therefore, the UCC is not the same in every state. Each state's court system can interpret the UCC differently thereby creating different case law in that state and producing different results. Business people cannot assume that the law will be exactly the same in each state. For more information see the Secretary of State for each State in question.

B. BAD CHECK LAW

Bad Checks are considered part of the UCC and therefore are a matter of state law enforcement. Section 3-104(2)(b) of the UCC, defines a check as "a draft drawn on a bank and payable on demand." Each state has a different "Bad Check Law" see UCC above.

Postdated check: since it is not payable on demand, most states believe that the giving of a post-dated check does not constitute a present fraud nor is it within the scope of the bad check laws.

Payments for COD or pre-existing debt: In most cases, NSF checks are not considered under the bad check law if they are used to pay a note payment or to pay an invoice that is on account. However, if the debtor provides a creditor with a NSF check for a COD order, then that act does fall within the bad check laws.

Revision History:

Revision	Date	Description of changes	Requested By
0	11/06/02	Initial Release	

[This page intentionally left blank]

CSH103 Ex1 BAD CHECK NOTICE

Date:

CUSTOMER NAME
ADDRESS
CITY, STATE, ZIP

Dear Sir:

Payment on your Check No. ______ in the amount of $___________, presented to us on, {DAY MONTH YEAR} , has been returned by your bank and marked insufficient funds. We have re-deposited your check and attempted to collect on this check twice already.

We have verified with your bank that insufficient funds remain to clear this check. Therefore, we request that you replace this check with a certified check immediately.

Unless we receive the certified funds for the amount listed above within 15 days, we shall immediately begin appropriate legal action to protect our interest. Upon receipt of replacement funds we shall return the dishonored check.

Sincerely,

Credit Manager
COMPANY NAME

Certified Mail, Return Receipt Requested.

[This page intentionally left blank]

SOP # ______ Revision:______ **Prepared by:____________**
Effective Date:______________ **Approved by:____________**

Title: **CSH104 WIRE TRANSFERS**

Policy: To provide additional payment options to customers and vendors in order to make funds immediately available to the receiving party. Wire transfers should be treated with special care and accuracy to prevent loss to the company or the customer.

Purpose: To explain the steps necessary to ensure proper procedures are followed when processing wire transfer requests.

Scope: This procedure applies to customers who are sending or receiving wire transfers and the financial institutions which process these requests.

Responsibilities:

Controller is responsible for approving and initiating all outgoing wire transfer requests.

CFO should approve all wire transfers over $10,000.

Accounts Receivable is responsible for processing all incoming wire transfers.

Definitions: ABA The American Bankers Association or ABA number is a unique routing identification code is issued to a Federal or State chartered financial institution which is eligible to maintain an account at a US Federal Reserve Bank. The ABA Routing Number (a.k.a. ABA number; Routing Transit number) is used to identify participants in automated clearinghouses, electronic funds transfer, and on-line banking.

Procedure:

1.0 INCOMING WIRES

1.1 Wire transfers are processed the same as a check in accordance with the CSH102 CASH RECEIPTS AND DEPOSITS procedure.

1.2 If a customer prefers to pay by wire transfer then send them CSH104 Ex1 BANK WIRE INSTRUCTIONS document.

1.3 Upon the banks receipt of the wire transfer the bank may create a wire transfer notification. Normally these are mailed but many banks may also provide notification via e-mail, phone, fax, or via an on-line banking interface. The bank notification serves as documentation the the money has been received.

2.0 OUTGOING WIRES

2.1 Outgoing wire transfer requesters must complete CSH104 Ex2 WIRE TRANSFER FORM in order to complete the wire transfer request. The form requires the following:

- Complete sender contact and bank information (Name, city, state, phone, account number, and ABA number of the bank that will be sending the wire).

- Complete beneficiary contact and bank information: Name, city, state, and ABA number of the bank that will be receiving the wire

2.2 The Controller must approve all wire transfers and should sign the WIRE TRANSFER FORM.

2.3 The CFO and Controller must both approve all wire transfers over $10,000, and should both sign the WIRE TRANSFER FORM.

2.4 Wire transfers should originate from a checking account. Reference A - FRB Reg D. - establishes limits on transfers from savings or money market accounts but there are no limits on transfers from checking accounts.

References:

A. FRB REG D: RESERVE REQUIREMENTS OF DEPOSITORY INSTITUTIONS

Defines consumer depository accounts (e.g., checking, savings, money market, CDs, transactions etc.) and the rules governing those accounts. This law also requires that financial institutions keep a minimum amount of reserve deposits either as vault cash or with the Federal Reserve.

The Federal Reserve Board's Regulation D limits the number of certain withdrawals and transfers from savings accounts. All financial institutions are subject to this regulation. Examples savings accounts affected by this regulation include: Regular Savings and Money Market accounts. Transactions on Checking accounts are not limited.

Regulation D, allows up to six (6) preauthorized or automatic withdrawals or transfers to another account at the same financial institutions or to a third party during a calendar month. There may be no more than three (3) of these six (6) transfers by check, debit card, or similar order, clearing an account. A "preauthorized transfer" includes arrangement the credit union make either to pay a third party, one time, on written or verbal instruction, or to pay a third party on a fixed schedule, (i.e. bill payer, ACH authorizations).

B. FRB REG E: ELECTRONIC FUND TRANSFER ACT

Establishes the rights, liabilities and responsibilities of all parties involved in electronic fund transfers and protects consumers when they use such systems. Examples of these transactions include those at automated teller machines, telephone bill-payment plans, point-of-sale purchases and pre-authorized transfers to and from a consumer's account (such as direct deposit and regular utility and mortgage payments).

Regulation E prescribes rules for the solicitation and issuance of EFT cards; governs consumers' liability for unauthorized electronic fund transfers (resulting, for example, from lost or stolen cards); requires institutions to disclose certain terms and conditions of EFT services; provides for documentation of electronic transfers (on periodic statements, for example)- sets up a resolution procedure for errors; and covers notice of crediting and stoppage of preauthorized payments from a customer's account.

Stored-value cards (also known as "smart cards") and home banking by personal computer would be subject to Regulation E because the act governs electronic fund transfers.

Revision History:

Revision	**Date**	**Description of changes**	**Requested By**
0	11/06/02	Initial Release	

[This page intentionally left blank]

CSH104 Ex1 BANK WIRE INSTRUCTIONS

BANK INFORMATION

BANK NAME Phone: ____________

ADDRESS Fax: ________________

CITY, STATE ZIP

ABA: xxx xxx xxx

Bank Wire Account # xxx xxx xxx

Account Name: COMPANY NAME

PLEASE NOTIFY US WHEN THE WIRE HAS BEEN SENT

Send us a note via e-mail, phone or fax so that we process your order as soon as possible.

Upon receipt of the wire we shall ship your order. Allow 7-10 days for shipping to international destinations.

Thank you for your order.

CONTACT

COMPANY NAME

CONTACT INFORMATION

[This page intentionally left blank]

CSH104 Ex2 WIRE TRANSFER FORM

SENDING PARTY

Last First Middle I.

Sender's Bank's Name ABA Number

Sender's Bank's Street Address City State Zip

Amount of Wire $____________ Wire Fee $____________

Form of Payment: Cash Debit Account Number:____________
Check Other (describe):____________

Comments:____________

X X

Sender's Signature

BENEFICIARY

Beneficiary Bank's Name ABA Number

Beneficiary Bank's Street Address City State Zip

Beneficiary's Company Name Beneficiary's Account Number

Comments:____________

Controller's Signature **Officer's Signature (CFO if amount is greater $10,000)**

Date **Time**

[This page intentionally left blank]

SOP # ______ **Revision:**______ **Prepared by:**____________
Effective Date:______________ **Approved by:**____________

Title: **CSH105 CHECK SIGNING AUTHORITY**

Policy: A limited number of employees will be authorized to sign checks but there shall be no fewer than three individuals at all times.

Purpose: To outline "dollar limits" and the check signing authority process.

Background: While a hired accountant, office manager, or accounting clerk may be responsible for entering bills, paying bills, and printing out checks, all printed checks and related documentation should be presented to a second individual for signing. No one person or employee (other than perhaps the owner) should be allowed to enter invoices, select invoices for payment, then print and sign checks. At a minimum, this process requires at least two individuals to ensure the integrity of the accounting system remains intact.

Scope: This procedure applies to all regular bank checking accounts of the company.

Responsibilities:

President is responsible for adding and removing check signing authority.

CFO is responsible for managing the check signing authority process and alerting all individuals and banks of any changes to authority.

Procedure:

1.0 AUTHORIZED CHECK SIGNERS

1.1 The Board of Directors and the President should approve authorized check signers in writing. All approvals should be forwarded to the CFO for processing.

1.2 The President and Chief Financial Officer should have check signing authority. Additional individuals with or without dollar limitations may be authorized as necessary.

1.3 For back-up purposes, it is advisable to have at least three check signers authorized for each checking account. One should be the owner, President or primary signer and the other should be the CFO or secondary check signer. The third should be a back-up signer. The back-up signer should be a trusted individual but not necessarily an employee. It could be a board member or another principle in the business. A back-up signer will ensure continuing operations in case both the primary and secondary signers become incapacitated for any period of time.

1.4 Maximum control is maintained if only one individual signs all checks, such as the owner or the appropriate designee, and another individual prepares the payment information.

2.0 CHANGING CHECK SIGNERS

2.1 The CFO receives all approval paperwork and should prepare and maintain a file record of all authorized check signers and CSH105 Ex1 CHECK SIGNING AUTHORITY LOG.

2.2 The CHECK SIGNING AUTHORITY LOG should be kept current of all individuals and their status to sign checks as soon as their status changes. The log should contain the following information:

- Recipient name / position or title
- Authority start date
- Authority end date
- Maximum expenditure authority level

2.2 Contact the bank that administers the checking account for details on adding, changing, or removing check signers from a checking account. Normally this is a simple process of presenting identification and singing a card to be placed on file at the bank.

Banks maintain an authorized check signers card for each checking account. Only those individuals listed on the authorized check signer's card may sign checks.

2.3 The President or the Board of Directors may revoke check signing authority. Any person who is no longer entitled to sign company checks will be notified in writing. The chief financial officer will oversee the proper notification of the company's banks whenever authorized signature changes are made.

3.0 AUTHORITY LEVELS

3.1 The following signature levels will be required according to the dollar amount of the check:

- Less than $500 - A check issued for less than $500 requires only one authorized signature.
- Greater than $500 but less than $10,000 - A check issued for an amount between $500 and $10,000 requires two different authorized signatures.
- Greater than $10,000 - A check issued for greater than $10,000 requires two signatures, one of which must be that of either the Company President or Vice President. The second signature can be that of any authorized employee.

3.2 The President or CFO may change check signing expenditure authority. All changes to authority should be recorded in the CHECK SIGNING AUTHORITY LOG.

Revision History:

Revision	Date	Description of changes	Requested By
0	11/06/02	Initial Release	

[This page intentionally left blank]

CSH105 Ex1 CHECK SIGNING AUTHORITY LOG

RECIPIENT NAME / TITLE	START DATE	END DATE	AUTHORITY LEVEL (maximum Dollar)

[This page intentionally left blank]

SOP # ______ Revision:______ **Prepared by:____________**
Effective Date:______________ **Approved by:___________**

Title: **CSH106 CHECK REQUESTS**

Policy: To ensure efficient processing and record keeping all manual check requests will be prepared on a written check request form.

Purpose: To describe the process for completing a check request form.

Scope: All manual check requests.

Responsibilities:

CFO or Controller is responsible for managing the check request process.

Procedure:

1.0 CHECK ORIGINATION

1.1 Whenever an employee requires a manual check to be issued, such as picking up items or for cash on delivery items, a CSH106 Ex1 CHECK REQUEST form should be completed with all pertinent information and required departmental approval.

If a check is to be mailed directly to the vendor, any applicable documentation such as order forms, etc., should be attached to the form.

1.2 The form should then be forwarded to the Controller for check preparation and signature by an authorized check signer.

2.0 CHECK STOP PAYMENT

2.1 It is important to place the stop payment information on the account as quickly as possible to prevent losses. The following information should be obtained and recorded on the bank's Stop Payment Form:

- Requester's name and department
- Account number
- Check number
- Date of the check
- Who the check is made payable to
- Amount of the check
- Reason for the stop payment

2.2 The stop payment information above should be forwarded to the bookkeeper or controller who will contact the bank to put a stop on the check.

2.3 An authorized check signer may need to sign the bank's Stop Payment Form, typically within ten business days. Normally, stop payments are placed on the account for approximately six months.

2.4 To release the stop payment, an authorized check signer may need to contact the bank and sign a release. Note: signing the release allows the check to be paid.

Revision History:

Revision	Date	Description of changes	Requested By
0	11/06/02	Initial Release	

CSH106 Ex1 CHECK REQUEST

Date:____________________ Requested by:____________________

Amount $____________________ Department:____________________

Required When:______________ Mail Check: Yes ☐ No ☐

Payable To:____

Address:____

City:____________________State:__________Zip:____________

Contact:____________________Phone: (   )____________

Reason for Check:____

____

____

Approved by:____________________Date:____________________

Accounting Use Only

Check No.:____________________ Account Codes Amounts

Date:____________________

Issued by:____________________

[This page intentionally left blank]

SOP # ______ **Revision:**______ **Prepared by:**____________
Effective Date:______________ **Approved by:**____________

Title: CSH107 BANK ACCOUNT RECONCILIATIONS

Policy: To ensure the accuracy of the company's bank account records by proving the monthly balance shown in the bank's Account Register.

Purpose: To outline the practices for preparation of a Monthly Bank Reconciliation

Scope: This applies to all bank accounts maintained by the company.

Responsibilities:

CFO is responsible for review and approval of all reconciliations.

Controller is responsible for reconciling all checking accounts.

Background: Errors or omissions can be made to the company's bank account records due to the many cash transactions that occur. Therefore, it is necessary to prove the monthly balance shown in the bank account register. Cash on deposit with a bank is not available for count and is therefore proved through the preparation of a reconciliation of the company's record of cash in the bank and the bank's record of the company's cash that is on deposit.

Definitions: Batch. All of the day's credit card transactions are collected into a "batch" of transactions. The batch is closed, usually at the end of the day, and the result is submitted to the merchant processor as a single "batch".

Settlement. The processor clears the credit card transactions in the batch and the result is "settled" to the designated bank account. Settlement varies by Credit Card Company but usually occurs in 2-3 days after a batch is closed.

Processor. The processor is responsible for authorizing credit card transactions and settling each batch. The processor is also the company that one must interface with on all discrepancies or "chargebacks".

Chargebacks. A chargeback occurs when a customer (cardholder) disputes a charge that appears on their monthly credit card statement. If the dispute is unable to be resolved then the transaction is charged back to the merchant. The processor charges the merchant and returns the cardholder's money.

Procedure:

1.0 BANK STATEMENT PREPARATION

1.1 After receipt of the monthly bank statement, including cleared checks, deposit slips and any other transactions; the Controller should prepare the monthly bank reconciliation and have it carefully reviewed by the CFO. The CFO review is especially important if a bookkeeper is hired to perform other cash drawer or cash posting transactions. To preserve proper segregation of duties, no single employee, other than the owner, should perform both cash transaction functions and bank account reconciliations.

1.2 Prior to preparing the bank reconciliation, the accountant should review the bank statement for any interest credits, bank charges and other fees. These should all be posted to the checking account before reconciling. Note: some accounting systems allow for the entry of interest credits, bank charges and other fees during the reconciliation process.

2.0 COMPUTERIZED FORMAT

2.1 In the computerized environment, the accounting system may provide an automated bank reconciliation task. This task is generally selected once a month in conjunction with receiving the month end bank statement. Once selected, the screen shows a list of all items that have been posted to the cash account and that have not been cleared from the previous month's account reconciliation. The screen is usually divided into two segments: one half is a list of all checks and other charges reducing cash, and the other half is a list of all deposits and other items increasing cash. This screen would also have a field for entering the proper month end date and the balance at month end, per the bank.

2.2 After the account-reconciling task is successfully completed, a report is provided which shows the reconciliation process, including outstanding checks and deposits in transit. The actual format will vary depending on the accounting system, but in general, will contain the same information as shown on the manually prepared report in CSH107 Ex1 SAMPLE BANK AND BOOK BALANCES RECONCILIATION TO CORRECTED BALANCE.

Note: Print out the full (not a summary) report, staple it to the applicable bank statement, and file the result as an important control feature. This will document that the bank statement has been successfully reconciled.

3.0 MANUAL PREPARATION AND RECONCILING ITEMS

3.1 A monthly bank reconciliation starts with the ending bank statement balance. List any deposits in transit that were made but were not yet recorded by the bank and add to the bank balance. Then, list any checks that were written on the account prior to month-end, but which have not yet cleared the bank and deducted from the bank balance. The ending balance should agree with the balance "per books", i.e.: the balance recorded in the checking account.

3.2 Now perform the same process with the monthly reconciliation of the ending balance per the company's books.

Total deposits and total disbursements should be reconciled to the bank statement, then adjustments such as any interest or any other bank credit items should be listed and added to the balance. Then, any bank charges, transfer fees, etc. should be listed and deducted from the balance.

From these steps, the "corrected" ending "book" balance is derived and should equal the "corrected" bank balance from the previous step.

3.3 Any discrepancies between the derived balance and the checkbook balance will require research to determine the cause, such as recording errors, omissions, incorrect postings, etc. In some cases, the discrepancy can be caused by not accurately entering all bank generated credits and charges; such as fees, interest, etc. If the balances still do not equal, the bank statement should be carefully reviewed for possible errors; such as, checks or deposits clearing for amounts that do not agree with those posted to the store's checking account.

4.0 COMPUTERIZED PREPARATION AND RECONCILING ITEMS

4.1 The same procedures as the manual tasks described above are followed in a computerized environment. The primary difference is in the ease of preparation. All transactions, which were not already cleared in the prior month's reconciliation, are listed.

4.2 Start by checking or clicking off with the mouse or keyboard those transactions, (mainly checks and other debit memos, and deposits and other credit memos) that agree with the bank statement. Once all bank statement items have been found and clicked off on the screen, the remaining "un-cleared" entries on the screen are, in effect, the list of outstanding checks and deposits in transit.

Furthermore, the screen typically provides a continually updating reconciled cash amount that should agree to the ending bank balance amount once all items are correctly accounted for and cleared. Usually the accounting system does the math and the screen displays both the ending bank balance and the reconciled cash amount with the remaining difference, if any.

4.3 Investigate all differences and enter any adjustments to the reconciliation or post to the cash account in order to ensure an accurate bank balance.

5.0 ADJUSTMENTS AND OTHER TROUBLESHOOTING

5.1 In spite of the best of efforts, the reconciliation result may not agree with the bank balance. The obvious first step is to make sure that all checks and deposits on the bank statement agree with the entries in the cash account. Discrepancies of this type are usually rare in computerized environments but may be caused by improperly recording manual checks or credit card deposits and fees.

Checks are generally posted and printed simultaneously so that what shows up in the accounting system will always agree to what was processed through the bank. Deposits are another matter. The bank might group deposited checks differently than they were in the accounting system. As explained in more detail in procedure CSH101 CASH DRAWERS AND CREDIT CARDS.

To simplify the month end reconciliation, receipts should be batched in a total deposit amount that agrees to both the accounting system and the bank. Make sure to print a totaled deposit report when daily receipts of checks and cash are batched for deposit. After making the bank deposit, staple the validated bank deposit slip to the deposit report. This will document the two events: 1) what was deposited per the accounting system, and 2) what was actually deposited in the bank. These two amounts must agree. This helps eliminate deposit errors for check and cash receipts.

5.2 A more difficult reconciling task is in obtaining agreement of all credit card receipts. The difficulty results from three unique situations. First, there is a time lag of several days between the time the credit card transaction occurred in the store and the time it is settled or deposited to the store's bank account. Second, depending on the type of credit card and/or the merchant provider, the fee charged (typically 1% to 4%) on each transaction may be automatically deducted from the deposit before it shows up on the bank statement. And third, "chargebacks" are usually deducted immediately by the processor and only reversed if the dispute is resolved in the company's favor. This may even occur before the chargeback notice has arrived in the mail.

Consequently, the deposit on the bank statement may not agree with the daily credit card batch (receipts). In the face of these difficulties, the CFO and Controller should thoroughly understand the particular credit card daily closing procedures. An end of day report for each credit card closing should be printed and saved as a reference for the month end reconciliation process.

Alternatively, the credit card processor will provide a month-end statement listing each credit card "batch" submitted each day. This report can be used to reconcile the credit card batches to the settlement deposits.

5.3 After reconciling checks and deposits, the next area to reconcile are bank generated Credit and Debit memos. These can result from various events including, returned checks, returned check charges, monthly bank activity charges, credit card merchant fees, charges from the use of debit cards, interest income and other service charges. The CFO may not know many of these until the bank statement is received. Each one of these entries must be entered and distributed to the proper income or expense account. Whatever the accounting system, its reconciling program usually provides a routine for entering these "end of month" bank credits and charges.

5.4 After agreeing all checks and deposits and entering all other bank credits and charges, the balance per accounting system and reconciled bank balance should agree. Any remaining difference must be investigated. If there is no other explanation, an adjustment should be made. This would be entered as a bank charge or credit and posted to a miscellaneous account.

5.5 Any outstanding checks or deposits in transit over six months old should be reviewed for disposition including write-off by a journal entry.

Revision History:

Revision	Date	Description of changes	Requested By
0	11/06/02	Initial Release	

[This page intentionally left blank]

CSH107 Ex1 SAMPLE
BANK AND BOOK BALANCES
RECONCILIATION TO CORRECTED BALANCE

Account No.________________
For Month Ended XX/XX/XX

Reconciliation of Bank Balance

Ending balance per bank statement		$10,000.00
Additions:		
Deposit in transit		2,500.00
Deductions:		
Outstanding Checks		
# 1003	150.00	
# 1232	325.00	
# 1235	1,275.00	
		1,750.00
Ending balance per checking account		$10,750.00

Reconciliation of Book Balance

Ending balance per books		$10,750.00
Additions:		
Interest		100.00
Deductions:		
Bank Charges	70.00	
Wire transfer fees	30.00	
		100.00
Corrected Balance		$10,750.00

[This page intentionally left blank]

Accounting Policies, Procedures & Forms

Section 420

Inventory & Asset Procedures

Section 420

Inventory & Assets

Procedures:

SOP # ______ Revision:______ **Prepared by:____________**
Effective Date:_______________ **Approved by:____________**

Title: **INV101 INVENTORY CONTROL**

Policy: The investment in physical inventory will be maintained at the lowest effective level and supervised consistent with a common set of procedures and controls.

Purpose: To outline the actions taken for proper safekeeping and handling of all inventory to ensure it is saleable, usable, and traceable for quick selection and delivery.

Scope: This procedure applies to all inventory items including back room and warehouse storage.

Responsibilities:

Purchasing is responsible for maintaining the investment in inventory at the lowest level, consistent with operating requirements, economy of procurement, financial plan requirements and sound business practices.

Shipping, Receiving and Warehouse Personnel are responsible for the custody and safekeeping of inventory. This includes ensuring that all items in inventory are properly accounted for, that proper procedures are followed for the movement of all inventory, and that all paperwork is forwarded to Accounting in a timely manner for the proper recording of all inventory transactions.

Accounting, is responsible for processing all paperwork received in a timely manner in order to maintain an accurate inventory status.

The Controller is responsible for revaluing certain inventory items to their Net Realizable Value and for ensuring proper inventory control.

Definitions: FIFO. First-In-First-Out or FIFO refers to the practice of using the oldest item in inventory first to ensure that the inventory is rotated on a regular basis.

Net Realizable Value The amount that can be reasonably expected or forecasted to be sold or used is considered the Net Realizable Value.

Procedure:

1.0 INVENTORY STOCKING AND STORAGE

1.1 Immediately unpack and store items upon receipt. Consider repackaging very small items (nuts, bolts, screws, etc.) in uniform, see-through plastic containers. For perishable items, use uniform, see-through, seal tight plastic containers to extend the product's life.

1.2 Mark perishable items with the date received. Use magic markers, grease pencils, or a date stamp.

1.3 Rotate inventory on a first-in, first-out (FIFO) basis, particularly food products and other perishables, when stocking shelves.

Note: It is common to put newly purchased items on the shelf in front of the older items. Instead, remove the older items from the shelf first, and then place the new items on the shelf followed by replacing the old items to the shelf but now in front of the new items. This will help keep the inventory fresh.

1.4 Check the expiration dates on the older items when they are taken off the shelf, but before they are replaced to their new position during the FIFO process. This is the best time to inspect the inventory and remove old or expired items before they are put back onto the shelf. If an items needs to be removed from inventory then put it aside (see Inventory Disposal below).

1.5 Be sure to store products in the proper places. Food items should be kept in cool, dry places. Frozen food should be kept at 0 degrees Fahrenheit or below, not 32 degrees. Refrigerated items should be stored at 41 degrees Fahrenheit or below. Some food items, such as meat, egg and cheese products, can be kept safely refrigerated for up to seven days, according to the Food and Drug Administration (FDA). Consider freezing certain perishable items such as meats if they cannot be used within seven days.

1.6 Maintain a temperature log for each refrigerator unit. The log should be posted on the front or side of the refrigerator door. Check and record refrigerator temperatures in the log at least twice a day.

1.7 Refrigeration units require circulating air to provide cold temperature to the contents. Therefore, allow sufficient space for internal air circulation between storage containers. Keep from "stuffing" the cooler and keep items away from the inside walls. Do not store foods directly on the floor of a walk-in cooler.

1.8 To deter bacteria growth, pre-cool hot items before storing them in a refrigerator by using chill blasters, cooling wands and ice baths. If hot food products must be cooled in the refrigerator, divide the food into small batches to speed up the cooling process.

2.0 INVENTORY USAGE

2.1 Review inventory requests to ensure completeness, validity and that the form has the proper approvals. Inventory requests consist of either a completed Sales Order form (see procedure REV101 SALES ORDER ENTRY) or a completed INV101 Ex1 INVENTORY REQUISITION form which is required for all internal requests.

2.2 Retrieve goods or materials as per the Inventory request and deliver to the appropriate destination indicated on the request. i.e. Sales Orders should be forwarded to Shipping. (see procedure REV105 SHIPMENT OF GOODS)

3.0 INVENTORY PROTECTION

3.1 Storage refers to protecting inventory from both damage and shrinkage or theft. Damage control includes maintaining adequate levels of insurance, keeping inventory clean and properly sheltered, and rotating inventory on a first-in, first-out (FIFO) basis, particularly food products and other perishables.

3.2 Control over shrinkage is directed at human error (data entry, POS error, receiving errors, etc) and customer or employee theft. Human error is a continual possibility. Successful business systems acknowledge this fact and incorporate preventative and detective controls to mitigate the anticipated human error. Preventative controls include written POS procedures, supervisory control, use of logs, cash-up reports and other checklists. Detective controls include cycle inventory counts, exception reports, and gross margin analyses.

3.3 Customer theft protection involves many elements from security to customer return policies. Businesses should focus on any high-dollar merchandise that can be easily hidden and carried out of the store. (see ***ABR32 Bizmanualz™ Security Policies, Procedures and Forms*** for a complete discussion of security methods).

3.4 Employee theft protection involves two important ingredients: maintaining an atmosphere of high security and eliminating the easy opportunities for theft. A climate of high-security is maintained when cycle count exceptions are followed up immediately, drivers' trucks and logs are examined immediately, merchandise is stored properly and shelved quickly, and unresolved damage claims, customer returns and returns to vendors are not allowed to build up.

Eliminating easy opportunities for theft involves structural security as well as numerous written employee procedures. Self-locking warehouse doors, restricted areas, well-lit parking lots, and installation of security cameras are examples of structural security features. Written procedures that reduce opportunities for theft include mandating that all employees exit and enter only through the front door, preventing employee from ringing up a sale for him/her or family members, monitoring customer returns, and written procedures regarding proper cash drawer and petty-cash usage. (see ***ABR32 Bizmanualz™ Security Policies, Procedures and Forms*** for a complete discussion of security methods).

4.0 INVENTORY OBSOLESCENCE

4.1 Count very perishable inventory each morning and keep a record of the remaining shelf life. If an excess amount of a particular perishable item exists, then consider creating a promotional special that uses the product before it spoils.

4.2 If the on-hand inventory exceeds the historical demand then the excess portion of the inventory should be reduced to its Net Realizable Value or expected future demand.

4.3 Review the transaction history of all items in inventory on an annual basis. If there is no usage in over 12 months (make sure the part is not a new inventory item) and there are no current open orders for the item, then consider disposing of half (50%) of the inventory on-hand (see Inventory Disposal below). If there is no usage in over 24 months and no planned usage in the near future, then consider disposing of the balance of unused inventory.

Note: The time periods for review and the amount disposed of may vary from item to item. If so, then consider producing a disposal chart with more specific requirements for specific types of inventory.

4.4 Verify the use-by or expiration date on products prior to use. Discard products if the use-by or expiration date has passed as per Inventory Disposal below.

4.5 Check all refrigeration logs twice each day (as noted above in Inventory Storage) and verify that cold foods are held at 41 degrees Fahrenheit or below. Hot foods must be maintained at or above 140 degrees Fahrenheit. The FDA Food Code allows for potentially hazardous foods including, but not limited to meat, egg and cheese products-to be between 41 degrees Fahrenheit and 140 degrees Fahrenheit for no longer than a total of four hours. After four hours, the product must be discarded.

5.0 INVENTORY DISPOSAL

5.1 Complete INV101 Ex1 INVENTORY REQUISITION form prior to disposal of any inventory item.

5.2 The purchasing agent is the most logical person to be held responsible for reclamation and salvage disposal, because of the knowledge of materials and how the company uses them. The purchasing agent is familiar with the companies that manufacture or distribute various materials and is knowledgeable about the items the Company buys and at what cost.

The four main destinations for such material for disposal are:

- reuse by some other segment of the company,
- return to original supplier for restocking,
- sale to used-material dealers or to other users, and
- storage of material yard for usage on another job at a later date.

5.3 Dispose of perishable or un-salable goods that have expired in an appropriate trash receptacle or process. For non-expired goods that retain some market value, the purchasing agent should determine which disposal methods will be utilized.

- Transfer the materials to another job or project. The Project Managers involved should negotiate the material value exchanged.
- Return the goods to the original supplier; a restocking charge may apply.
- Place the goods in long-term storage, to be used on another project at a later date. Discuss the issue with Sales and Marketing to determine if a future need may exist.

- Auction the materials or otherwise dispose of the items in the open market. The value should be determined by the Purchasing Agent from prices available on the present day in the open market.
- Recycle the goods through and appropriate organization. This may also include donating the goods to a charitable organization.
- Salvage the materials and use the parts for service, support or remanufacturing.

5.4 Under no circumstances should scrap or excess material be returned to storage without the Purchasing Department's knowledge. The Purchasing Agent should inspect the material in order to determine good's condition.

5.5 Forward all disposal requests to the Controller for approval. Upon approval, complete the disposal process. Upon disposal completion the controller will update the accounting system with a record of the inventory adjustment and file all paperwork as back-up for the period-end inventory count. (See procedure INV102 INVENTORY COUNTS).

References:

A. Food and Drug Administration (FDA) Food Code

The Food and Drug Administration publishes the *Food Code*, a reference that guides retail outlets such as restaurants and grocery stores and institutions such as nursing homes on how to prevent food borne illness.

Local, state and federal regulators use the FDA *Food Code* as a model to help develop or update their own food safety rules and to be consistent with national food regulatory policy. Also, many of the over 1 million retail food establishments apply *Food Code* provisions to their own operations.

The *Food Code* is updated every two years, to coincide with the biennial meeting of the Conference for Food Protection. The conference is a group of representatives from regulatory agencies at all levels of government, the food industry, academia, and consumer organizations that works to improve food safety at the retail level.

Obtaining the 2001 Food Code

2001 *Food Code* in HTML or PDF versions can be found at http://www.cfsan.fda.gov/~dms/fc01-toc.html and a Summary of Changes is available at http://www.cfsan.fda.gov/~dms/fc01-sum.html.

Revision History:

Revision	Date	Description of changes	Requested By
0	11/06/02	Initial Release	

INV101 Ex1 INVENTORY REQUISITION

Requested by:______________________ Date:______________

Department:______________________ Charge To:______________

Job Name: ______________________ Job No.:______________

Purpose or Use:______________________

Date Needed:______________________ Ship Via:______________

Stock Number	Product / Service Description	Qty.	Unit Price	Extended Cost

For Purchasing Department Use Only

Approvals:

Dept. Manager:______________________ Date:______________ Approved:________

Additional:______________________ Date:______________ Ordered for:______

[This page intentionally left blank]

SOP # ______ Revision:______ **Prepared by:____________**
Effective Date:______________ **Approved by:____________**

Title: **INV102 INVENTORY COUNTS**

Policy: All physical inventory will be periodically counted and reviewed on a frequent basis and under a common set of procedures and controls.

Purpose: To outline the actions to be taken to conduct an accurate physical count of all inventory items in order to verify the accuracy of the inventory ledger.

Scope: This procedure applies to all inventory items including back room, warehouse storage, off-site usage, demonstration, or customer loaner purposes.

Responsibilities:

Purchasing is responsible for forwarding all paperwork to accounting to ensure that inventory is documented and accounted for properly.

Sales & Marketing is responsible for forwarding all paperwork to accounting to ensure that inventory is documented and accounted for properly.

Shipping, Receiving and Warehouse Personnel are responsible for the custody and safekeeping of inventory. This includes ensuring that all items in inventory are properly accounted for, that proper procedures are followed for the movement of all inventory, and that all paperwork is forwarded to Accounting in a timely manner for the proper recording of all inventory transactions.

Accounting, Accounts Payable and Accounts Receivable are responsible for accounting for and processing all paperwork received in a timely manner in order to maintain an accurate inventory status.

The Controller is responsible for counting / recording procedures, cut-off procedures and for ensuring proper inventory control.

The Inventory Control Manager is responsible for the actual count. The Inventory Control Manager is appointed by the controller and should be knowledgeable about the inventory items to be counted, the counting procedures used, and the location of all inventories.

Background: It is most important for the Inventory Control Manager to fully understand the POS and accounting system as it relates to inventory, before a physical inventory is taken. This includes an understanding of how the inventory is updated by customer returns, returns to vendors, transfers from inventory to internal use, adjustments for damaged or defective product, and backorders.

The inventory General Ledger balance is affected by every purchase and sale transaction that is processed through the REV102 POINT-OF-SALE

(POS) procedure and the Accounting System. To maintain accuracy, one should periodically count the actual inventory on hand and then reconcile that count to the inventory General Ledger balance. Taking a complete physical count of all inventory items is one way to ensure that the balance is accurate.

Definitions: Cut-off refers to procedures, which ensure that all items counted are owned by the company and available for sale. In other words, an item, returned by a customer needs to be "returned" to inventory by the POS/accounting system before it is physically counted. Similarly, a defective item waiting to be sent back to the vendor needs to be taken out of the POS/accounting system and segregated from any possibility of being counted during the physical inventory.

SKU. A Stock Keeping Unit or SKU is a tracking number used by order entry system to identify stocking items in inventory. An SKU may be a manufacturer's part number.

Plan-O-Grams used to layout or plan for the display of merchandise within a retail store. Plan-o-gram analysis enables sales projections based on item-level financial data to determine product rotations. Most Plan-o-Grams are calculated on a monthly to quarterly basis and provide a tool to ensure better selling items are identified, inventoried and displayed for sale.

Procedure:

1.0 INVENTORY TYPES

1.1 There are two main categories of inventory taking:

- A complete physical inventory of all items, and
- A partial inventory of a certain locations or specific product type, (also referred to as a "cycle count").

1.2 Generally, a complete physical inventory is taken at year-end or other period-end. The ultimate objective is to arrive at a correct inventory value (correct quantity and correct cost) at a particular time. A "cycle count" is usually performed as a continuing test of the inventory system and is usually more concerned with the accuracy of the quantity than with the inventory value.

2.0 PREPARATION FOR INVENTORY COUNTING

2.1 All areas containing inventory should be organized to their optimal standard. Retail store merchandise should be displayed in its correct location prior to beginning the physical counting process. All back room and overstock merchandise should be organized with like items and clearly labeled for easy identification and accurate counting.

2.2 Any customer return items, if re-salable, should be re-entered in the computer and restocked prior to inventory. Any returns to vendors should be processed and shipped out prior to inventory. Any returns, which haven't been either restocked or shipped back, should be clearly identified and segregated from other inventory.

2.3 All loose inventory items should be removed from workstations or machines and neatly placed or stored into bins, shelves, racks, etc. Identical parts that are used in multiple locations should (if practical) be combined into one storage area to facilitate ease of record keeping.

After grouping and organizing identical parts (i.e., on shelves or bins), all inventory items should be reasonably separated and identified/labeled to avoid any confusion between similar looking or types of parts.

2.4 All non-inventory, defective or obsolete parts should be clearly segregated from inventory items to be counted. These items should also be visibly marked or indicated to their nature (i.e., "Non-Inventory - Do Not Count", "Defective", etc.).

2.5 Label all count areas (shelves, warehouse, storage, etc.) with a code to simplify identifying each location. For example, the first shelf unit would be labeled "A" with individual rows numbered from top to bottom: A1, A2, A3, etc. Alphabetical characters should be used from A to Z first, then proceed to double or Triple each Alpha character (i.e. AA, AB, AC or AAA, AAB) until all areas have been uniquely assigned a location code. Ideally, these codes can be included as another computer field along with the item's SKU number. Retail stores should label shelves with the appropriate Department/ Category designations.

3.0 PERIOD END CUT-OFF

3.1 The inventory counting procedures should be performed after the close of business to adequately control cut-off of inventory transactions for purchases (receiving) and sales. In any case, in order to maintain accuracy all operations should be completely shut down for the inventory count.

3.2 Any goods received at the end of the period, but prior to completion of physical inventory, should be kept in the receiving area and should not be unpacked, received, or entered into the computer.

3.3 To document period-end cut-off, the last five (5) sequential shipping documents and receiving reports should be copied and filed with the inventory count. Normally an internal or external auditor will request these as part of the count.

4.0 COMPLETE PHYSICAL COUNT - COST (OR"SKU") METHOD

4.1 The actual physical counting may be performed by employees or contracted out to an inventory service. Either way, proper procedures must be performed to ensure that all inventory items are correctly counted once and only once.

4.2 Pre-planning and organization is important. For example, the Inventory Control Manager should prepare a master floor plan of each area containing inventory items with individual areas established for each count team. Then, distribute to each team the counting assignments prior to the period-end count. Include with the assignments the date and approximate starting time for the physical count along with counting procedures.

4.3 Counting should be performed in teams of two. One should do the actual counting and the other should record the counts. At least one individual from each team should be knowledgeable about the inventory items to be counted.

4.4 A pre-count meeting should be held by the Inventory Control Manager and the company's Controller with all count team members to review counting procedures/instructions and answer any questions.

4.5 The Inventory Control Manager will provide to every count team pre-numbered counts sheets with pre-printed inventory items and will be responsible for keeping track of all count sheets to maintain an accurate count.

Note: Consider using a count sheet format (see INV102 Ex1 INVENTORY COUNT SHEET) with the following attributes: a Heading with the name of the Company, Date of Physical count, Sequential Page number and Description of Page (i.e., Physical Inventory Count Sheet). Individual Column Headings would be: SKU#, Description, Location, Quantity and Initials of person recording the count.

4.6 Count sheets should be organized by location number. Generally, the computer quantities should not be shown on the count sheets, however, in small environments, it may be more efficient to include the on-hand quantities, as long as the counting is performed by teams, and the person counting is not able to know the current quantities.

Note: If this latter procedure is used, the count sheets should not be produced until the close of business, thereby ensuring the latest on-hand data.

4.7 Each count team should be started by the Inventory Control Manger and should be periodically observed by the Inventory Control Manager to assure that instructions are being complied with in the counting and listing process.

4.8 If at all possible, the Inventory Control Manager should not be included in the count teams, but rather, observe the counting procedures and assist in controlling the count sheets. Provide pre-numbered blank sheets to each team to allow for the inclusion of any items not found on the count sheets. Each sheet should have a start time and the initials of the count team.

4.9 Secure all completed areas and related count sheets. Once complete, immediately enter all count sheets into the computer. Once entered, the data entry person should initial the sheets and return them to the Inventory Control Manager. Upon completion, the Inventory Control Manager should account for all count sheets (i.e., used, unused, voided).

4.10 Teams should count items in their assigned area in a logical, sequential (non-random) fashion to avoid any chance of missing or duplicating counting of items. General rules of procession should be followed (i.e., Left to Right, Top to Bottom and Front to Back)

4.11 After counting a distinguishable area (i.e., shelf unit, wall, box, etc.) attach a colored tag/label (see example INV102 Ex2 INVENTORY TAG) to both the beginning and the end of the area to indicate that the area has been counted.

Inventory comprised of small, numerous components that would involve tedious counting and also have a very low dollar value (i.e., screws, nuts, fasteners, etc.) will be reviewed with the Inventory Control Manager and if deemed appropriate will be estimated as to volume in round numbers (i.e., 250, 500, etc.).

The estimated # will be recorded on the Count Sheet but <u>must</u> be notated by the symbol "Est." before the number to indicate that the value was not obtained by a true physical count. As an alternate, these items can be weighed using a scale and counting a representative sample (i.e., 25 screws) to determine a weight/count ratio for this item and using this ratio against the total weight of the items to determine a count. If this method is utilized a "W" symbol should be noted before the number on the Count Sheet to indicate that the value was obtained through a weighed estimate and not by a true physical count.

4.12 Finished Goods and Work-In-Process will be counted and recorded on individual sheets. Finished Goods will be noted by Model # and multiplied by the respective Bill of Materials to determine the value of individual part #'s. Work-In-Process will be noted by Model # and Estimate of completion level in Percentage terms (i.e., 75%). This percentage will then be used with the respective Bill of Materials to determine the value of the inventory contained in the item.

4.13 Inventory that is out of the Company including Sales Demonstration units, Service loaners or consigned should be recorded on the INV101 Ex1 INVENTORY REQUISITION form. These forms should be copied as backup and for confirmation purposes and the inventory items counted and included with the physical count.

4.14 A final review walk-through by the Inventory Control Manager is a critical control element to ensure the accuracy and completeness of the physical count. After all counting is finished, and after all count sheets have been turned in, the Inventory Control Manager should walk through the entire area, both retail and warehouse areas, with all team members and review the area for completeness. Only after this review may the colored inventory tickets be removed.

4.15 Depending on the accounting system, all inventory counts may need to be entered before new period business is transacted. However, regardless of the system, the sooner that inventory count variances can be reviewed, the better.

4.16 Once all inventory counts have been entered, produce and examine a sorted variance report starting with the largest variances. In analyzing significant variances, look for possible misclassification of item numbers, or incorrect handling of received goods, customer returns, damaged products, or vendor returns.

4.17 Upon completion of the data entry of the physical count and the final review of variances, produce and review a detailed inventory cost and pricing report (extended by the adjusted quantity on hand). Any unusual variances in costs, prices or extended amounts should be investigated.

4.18 After all necessary corrections have been made, based on the results of the physical count and inventory valuation reviews; produce and save a final detailed inventory valuation report.

4.19 Adjust the inventory balance in the Accounting System's General Ledger, if necessary, to agree with the final inventory valuation report.

5.0 COMPLETE PHYSICAL COUNT - RETAIL METHOD

5.1 A faster method of performing a complete physical count in a retail store environment utilizes the "retail method". With this method, counts and retail prices are entered into a hand-held special purpose calculator. The operator simply enters a count, like "21", and then enters the price, like $1.29. No identification of the product is necessary, however, the counts multiplied by the retail prices are usually subtotaled within the departments, which have already been set up by the store. Inventory valuation is determined by applying the departmental gross margin percentage to the retail price subtotal by department.

5.2 With the retail method, it is imperative that all items have visible retail prices and are sufficiently organized to allow for easy counting by department or sales category. These should be clearly labeled, so that the count team knows when to execute a subtotal and when to start a new group. A store map with all department and location codes may be helpful.

5.3 All other procedures outlined in the "cost" method of inventory taking apply to the "retail" method. This includes proper sales and purchase cut-off procedures, proper organization of areas to be counted, and proper walk-through procedures after the count.

5.4 As in the "cost" method, any variances noted should be investigated as soon as possible. The report reviews will be different than the "cost" method, since there won't be any detailed inventory sheets to review. Under the retail method, only department or sales category totals are provided. However, these should be compared to prior period totals and any unusual variances explained. Some inventory systems will provide inventory valuations based on retail pricing. These valuations can also be used to compare to count valuations to identify departments or sales categories for variances that require follow-up counts and investigations.

6.0 CYCLE COUNT

6.1 A cycle count is similar to a physical count except only a portion of the entire inventory is actually counted. Cycle counting can be performed monthly, weekly, or even daily in order to test the inventory system and identify any significant inventory processing problems as soon as possible. Frequent cycle counting of expensive items will strengthen internal controls and increase your inventory accuracy.

6.2 The actual methods of cycle counting may vary depending on the company's POS or Accounting System, however, the objective should be to count all items in inventory at least once between complete physical counts. Generally a cycle count of a specific category is scheduled each week.

6.3 Preparation for the count and organization of the count area are just as important in cycle counting as they are in a complete physical count. In fact, a cycle count involves all the same concerns and procedures as a complete physical count, except that it is focused on one specific location or sales department.

6.4 The results of the cycle count should be compared to the inventory records and any variances investigated. After resolving any discrepancies, the inventory amounts carried in the computer system should be adjusted to agree with the results of the cycle count.

Revision History:

Revision	Date	Description of changes	Requested By
0	11/06/02	Initial Release	

[This page intentionally left blank]

INV102 Ex1 INVENTORY COUNT SHEET

For Period Ending:________________ Page______ of _____

Counted by:______________________ Date:_________________

Type of Inventory: □ Raw Materials □ Work in Process □ Finished Goods

PART/ MODEL #	DESCRIPTION	QTY ON HAND & LOCATION	TOTAL QTY	STD COST	EXTENDED AMOUNT

Verified by:________________________ Total this page: $______________

Date: ________________________ Carry Forward Total: $______________

[This page intentionally left blank]

INV102 Ex2 INVENTORY TAG

Tag # ____________________

Location: Area ____________________
Row ____________________
Column ____________________

Type: Finished Goods ____________________
Work In Process ____________________
Raw Materials ____________________
Resale Items ____________________
Consumables ____________________

Quantity ____________________

Unit of Measure ____________________
(Gallons, lbs., bars, pallets, bags, tanks, cars, etc.)

Description ____________________

Inventory Coding ____________________
(batch #, lot #, etc.)

Remarks ____________________

Counted by ____________________
Checked by ____________________

[This page intentionally left blank]

SOP # ______ Revision:______ **Prepared by:____________**
Effective Date:______________ **Approved by:____________**

Title: **INV103 FIXED ASSET CONTROL**

Policy: Proper control procedures will be followed for all capital asset acquisitions, transfers and dispositions in order to provide internal control of capital equipment and to assist in reporting.

Purpose: To outline the procedures for acquiring, disposing and maintaining control of capital assets.

Scope: This procedure applies to all capital equipment with a value of $500 or more and with a useful life greater than one year.

Responsibilities:

Department managers are responsible and accountable for furniture, equipment, machinery and any other capital assets in their departments and will maintain some type of control over capital assets.

Accounting will assist and evaluate any department's capital asset control procedures.

Procedure:

1.0 ACQUISITIONS

1.1 All purchases of assets costing more than $500 and less than $5,000 will be approved by the department manager and the Chief Financial Officer. Assets with a cost greater than $5,000 will also require the approval of the President.

An INV103 Ex1 CAPITAL ASSET REQUISITION form should be completed and approved for all purchases. This form is to be attached to all Purchase Orders or check requests submitted to Accounting. Department managers may source the vendor for purchase of the capital assets or can submit the request to Purchasing for procurement.

1.2 Any internally constructed or donated equipment will be reported to accounting if the item cost has a value of $500 or more. A complete description of the property, date manufactured or received, number of items, cost or estimated value and a statement that it was internally constructed or donated will be included in the report.

1.3 To maintain proper segregation and control upon termination of any employees, any employee owned tools, equipment or furniture brought on the Company premises will be reported to the department manager. The report should include the employee's name, description of items, identification numbers, if any, and reason for using the asset.

2.0 DISPOSITIONS

2.1 Capital assets may be sold or traded-in on new equipment. An INV103 Ex2 ASSET DISPOSITION form is to be completed and approved by the department manager. Any assets with an original value greater than $1,000 will also require the Chief Financial Officer's approval.

Upon approval, the department may advertise the property for sale or submit a list to purchasing for sale and disposition. After completion of the sale, an INV103 Ex3 BILL OF SALE will issued and the ASSET DISPOSITON form will be submitted to Accounting. Accounting will delete the item from the asset records and record any gain or loss on the disposition.

2.2 Worn-out or obsolete property with no cash value will be reported to Accounting on the Asset Disposition form with the description, serial number and condition. Accounting will inspect all worn-out of obsolete property before it is removed from the department and discarded. The asset will then be removed from the asset records.

2.3 Any asset that is missing or has been stolen will be reported in writing to the department manager and Accounting as soon as possible. The description, serial number, and other information about the lost item should be included in the report.

Accounting will determine the proper course of action and will notify the company's insurance carrier and any outside authorities if deemed appropriate. If un-recovered, the asset will then be removed from the asset records.

2.4 Interdepartmental transfers of assets will be reported to Accounting in writing including the description, serial number and the name of the department to receive the property.

The department manager to whom the item was assigned originally will be held accountable until accounting is notified of the transfer. After being notified, the department manager acquiring the property assumes responsibility. Accounting will then record the departmental transfer on the asset records.

3.0 ASSET RECORDS

3.1 Upon any asset acquisition, Accounting is responsible for assigning and attaching asset number tags to the property where it can be readily located.

Accounting will then maintain a detailed listing of each capital asset item along with depreciation records which will include the description, date acquired, vendor, cost basis, assigned department, depreciation method/life and accumulated depreciation and net book value.

3.2 On an annual basis, accounting will furnish each department a report showing a listing of assets assigned to that department and any acquisitions, disposals and transfers during the past year. Any discrepancies noted by the department should notify the Accounting Department as soon as possible. This report should be filed by the department manager for reference and later use.

3.3 Each department will be responsible for locating assets with its number tag attached that are recorded as assigned to their department whenever requested by Accounting, a county property tax auditor or the company's external auditors.

3.4 Whenever a change in department manager occurs, all items should be accounted for by the outgoing department manager. The incoming department manager will accept the responsibility and accountability for the departmental asset listing upon assuming the position. Accounting can assist with this audit if requested.

Revision History:

Revision	Date	Description of changes	Requested By
0	11/06/02	Initial Release	

[This page intentionally left blank]

INV103 Ex1 CAPITAL ASSET REQUISITION

Authorization for Capital Expenditure
(Must be completed for all requests greater than $1,000)

Date:______________________________

Requested by:______________________________

Department:______________________________

1) Complete item description including accessories:______________________________

____

____

____

2) Reason or justification for request, including use and capability:______________________________

____

____

____

3) Expected life in years:______________________

4) Price or Lease Quotations:

Description	New or Used	Vendor	Terms	Amount

Department Manager:______________________________

Chief Financial Officer:______________________________

President:______________________________
(required for requests $\geq$ $5,000)

[This page intentionally left blank]

INV103 Ex2 ASSET DISPOSITION FORM

Date:______________________________________

Requested By:________________________________

Department:__________________________________

Reasons for Disposition:____

____

Description	Serial Number	Date Purchased	Original Cost	Net Book Value	Expected Or Actual Proceeds	Gain or Loss

Department Manager:____________________________Date:____________________

Chief Financial Officer:__________________________Date:____________________

[This page intentionally left blank]

INV103 Ex3 BILL OF SALE

This Bill of Sale is made on (PURCHASE DATE) between (STORE or COMPANY NAME) , a (STATE) Corporation, with its principal place of business at (COMPANY ADDRESS) ("Seller") and (BUYER'S CONTACT INFORMATION) , ("Buyer").

In exchange for the payment of (DOLLAR AMOUNT) Dollars that has been received, the Seller sells, assigns and transfers all of its right title and interest in the (ASSET SOLD) (the "Goods").

The Seller warrants that it owns the Goods and that it has the Authority to sell the Goods to the Buyer. The Seller further warrants that the Goods are free and clear of all liens, indebtedness, or liabilities. The Seller also warrants that all of the Goods are in good working condition as of the date transferred.

I have carefully reviewed this Bill of Sale and agree to and accept its terms and conditions. I am executing this Bill of Sale as of the day and year first written above.

Seller:

Buyer:

____
NAME
Owner
COMPANY NAME

____
NAME

[This page intentionally left blank]

SOP # ______ Revision:______ **Prepared by:____________**
Effective Date:______________ **Approved by:____________**

Title: **INV104 CUSTOMER PROPERTY**

Policy: The Company will store as needed a necessary level of customer property and will provide a reasonable level of protection and control for the type and value of the property.

Purpose: To define the methods to be used to identify, verify, protect and safeguard customer property while it is in possession of the company.

Scope: This procedure applies to any items supplied by customers including: components and materials supplied for inclusion in product, tooling and fixtures used in manufacturing and inspection processes, and intellectual property for use and testing with software systems.

Responsibilities:

Customer Service is responsible for notifying Production and Purchasing of the customer's intent to supply materials during the quotation and contract review processes.

Purchasing is responsible for coordinating delivery of customer supplied materials.

Production is responsible for managing customer supplied tooling and fixtures.

Engineering is responsible for managing and safeguarding customer's intellectual property.

Procedure:

1.0 RECEIPT, INSPECTION AND STOCKING

1.1 Components and/or materials provided by a customer to be used in the production of their finished products should be received, inspected and marked according to the same procedures for other inventory items as per procedure PUR104 RECEIVING AND INSPECTION.

1.2 After these items have passed the appropriate inspection criteria satisfactorily, the items will be additionally tagged with customer identification and segregated in storage until required in production.

2.0 UNSUITABLE OR MISSING ITEMS

2.1 In the event of any damage, deterioration or unsuitability of customer supplied items, the procedure for Receiving and Inspection will be followed and an INV104 Ex1 MATERIAL RETURN NOTICE form will be prepared with the applicable information and returned to the customer.

2.2 If for any reason there is a shortage or loss of items that is discovered after the original receiving report was prepared, the inventory control manager will issue a written report and forward to Customer Service for follow-up with the customer.

3.0 CUSTOMER SUPPLIED TOOLING AND FIXTURES

3.1 Receiving inspects customer tooling or fixtures received and notes the condition of the items on the receiving paperwork.

3.2 Receiving delivers the items to Production and forwards the paperwork to the Production Manager.

3.3 The Production Manager arranges for the items to be marked or tagged for identification and maintains a file for customer supplied tooling and fixtures.

3.4 If the items are damaged or unsuitable for use, the condition is recorded on a nonconformance report and the Production Manger coordinates with Customer Service to obtain disposition from the customer.

4.0 INTELLECTUAL PROPERTY

4.1 Intellectual property transmittal is generally coordinated by Engineering. Transmittal may be electronic or on media.

4.2 When making arrangements for use of customer's intellectual property, Engineering will appropriately safeguard any proprietary information and determine the disposition after use (delete or return to customer).

Revision History:

Revision	Date	Description of changes	Requested By
0	11/06/02	Initial Release	

INV104 Ex1 MATERIAL RETURN NOTICE

RETURN TO (VENDOR, SUPPLIER OR SUBCONTRACTOR)	DATE	AUTHORIZED BY
	P.O. OR CONTRACT NO.	INVOICE NO.
RETURNED BY	REJECTED MATERIAL ITEMIZED MATERIAL IS RETURNED ❒ FOR CREDIT ONLY - DO NOT REPLACE ❒ FOR REWORK OR REPLACEMENT **PLEASE CREDIT OUR ACCOUNT AND REINVOICE IF MATERIAL IS REWORKED OR REPLACED.**	

QUANTITY	PART NO.	DESCRIPTION	REASON FOR REJECTION

NOTICE TO SUPPLIER:
PLEASE SEND A CORRECTIVE ACTION STATEMENT

❒ WITH NEXT SHIPMENT ❒ WITHIN _________ DAYS

[This page intentionally left blank]

SOP # ______ **Revision:**______ **Prepared by:**____________
Effective Date:______________ **Approved by:**____________

Title: **INV105 FIXED ASSET CAPITALIZATION & DEPRECIATION**

Policy: Asset acquisitions with a useful life expectancy of greater than one year and with a minimum threshold amount as specified by the Controller should be capitalized by the Company and depreciated.

Purpose: The purpose of this procedure is to delineate the capitalization and depreciation methods for various asset groups.

Scope: All acquisitions of capital assets for the company.

Definitions: Capitalization - Capitalization is the method chosen to record the purchase of a fixed asset on the Company's accounting books. If an asset is capitalized then it is not expensed in the same year the asset is purchased. Instead the asset is generally recorded on the balance sheet and individually on an asset schedule. Examples of capital expenditures are purchases of land, buildings, machinery, office equipment, leasehold improvements and vehicles. The asset is expensed each year as depreciation.

Depreciation - is an annual income tax deduction that allows the write-down or write-off of the cost of the asset over its estimated useful life to recover the cost or other basis of certain property over the time the property is used. It is an allowance expense for the wear and tear, age, deterioration, or obsolescence of the property.

As an asset ages and is used by the company, its' value declines. It, in effect, becomes worth less and less over time. The declining value or usefulness of the asset over time is represented as a discount that is applied to the original purchase price. At the end of the asset's depreciation period, (and/or useful life), its value on the balance sheet will be zero, or fully-depreciated. At the same time, the individual depreciation expenses will have all been recorded on the income statement.

Note: Land is not depreciated because land does not wear out, become obsolete, or get used up. But, the building on the land is depreciated. Land is generally viewed as an appreciating asset while all other capital assets are generally viewed as depreciating over time, with use. But, unlike depreciation, an asset's appreciation is not recorded on the books until the asset is sold, which is when the assets appreciation is realized.

Cost basis – The total amount paid for the asset, in cash or kind, is considered the "cost-basis". This should include all charges relating to the purchase, such as the purchase price, freight charges and installation, if applicable. The cost basis is not the market value or list price of the asset. It is the total amount invested in the purchase or the total amount paid.

Procedure:

1.0 CAPITALIZATION

1.1 All assets with a useful life of greater than one year and costing more than $500 will be capitalized and (except for land) will be recorded in the depreciation records. Any asset that does not meet the above criteria will be expensed such as small tools and equipment or repairs and maintenance.

1.2 The cost basis of furniture and equipment assets will include all charges relating to the purchase of the asset including the purchase price, freight charges and installation if applicable.

1.3 Leasehold improvements including painting are to be capitalized if they relate to the occupancy of a new office or a major renovation of an existing office. Expenditures incurred in connection with maintaining an existing facility in good working order should be expensed as a repair.

1.4 The cost of buildings should include all expenditures related directly to its acquisition or construction. This cost includes materials, labor and overhead incurred during construction, and fees, such as attorney's and architect's and building permits.

1.5 Maintain proper files on the details to all acquisitions, expenditures, and maintenance performed on all assets. These records are vital for proper tax preparation and are used during yearly tax reporting and planning.

2.0 DEPRECIATION

2.1 The depreciation methods/lives for assets must be selected at the time the asset is first placed into service in order to ensure consistent financial reporting and tax compliance.

The IRS requires that most business property (see exceptions below) should be depreciated using the Modified Accelerated Cost Recovery System (MACRS), which categorizes all business assets into classes and specifies the time period over which assets in each class can be written-off (see Reference A, IRS publication 946 "How To Depreciate Property").

NOTE: You ***cannot*** use MACRS to depreciate the following property.

- Property placed in service before 1987.
- Certain pre-1987-use property.
- Intangible property.
- Films, videotapes, and recordings.
- Certain corporate or partnership property acquired in a nontaxable transfer.
- Property elected to be excluded from MACRS.

The following IRS depreciation methods and useful lives should be used as a guide for the following asset classifications for financial reporting purposes:

Property or Class	Asset Description
3-year property	Computer software, Tractor units, racehorses over two years old, horses over 12 years old when placed in service, and Qualified rent-to-own property
5-year property	Automobiles, taxis, buses, trucks, computers and peripheral equipment, office machinery (faxes, copiers, calculators etc.), any property used in research and experimentation, Appliances, carpets, furniture, etc., used in a residential rental real estate activity and breeding and dairy cattle.
7-year property	Office furniture and fixtures, Agricultural machinery and equipment, and any property that does not have a class life and has not been designated by law as being in any other class.
10-year property	Vessels, barges, tugs, similar water transportation equipment, single-purpose agricultural or horticultural structures, and trees or vines bearing fruit or nuts.
15-year property	Depreciable improvements to land such as shrubbery, fences, roads, and bridges or Any retail motor fuels outlet, such as a convenience store.
20-year property	Farm buildings that are not agricultural or horticultural structures.
25-year property	Water utility property that is an integral part of the gathering, treatment, or commercial distribution of water, or any municipal sewer. And that, without regard to this provision, would be 20-year property.
27.5-year property	Residential rental property.
39-year property	Nonresidential real estate, including home offices. (Note: the value of land may not be depreciated.)

2.2 The lowest life permitted by tax regulations for asset classes should be selected to optimize depreciation deductions.

2.3 Regardless of the depreciation rate required for tax purposes, a company can elect to use a different method for financial statement purposes. Such method should be justified based on the expected useful life of the asset.

References:

A. IRS PUBLICATION 946 "HOW TO DEPRECIATE PROPERTY"

(Online at http://www.irs.gov/formspubs/page/0,,id=12895,00.html)

This publication explains how to recover the cost of business or income-producing property through deductions for depreciation. It also explains how take a section 179 deduction, instead of depreciation deductions, for certain property and the additional rules for "listed property." In addition, the publication describes how to figure depreciation and how to fill out Form 4562, Depreciation and Amortization.

The depreciation methods discussed in this publication do not generally apply to property placed in service before 1987. For information about depreciating such property, see IRS Publication 534.

Revision History:

Revision	Date	Description of changes	Requested By
0	11/06/02	Initial Release	

bizmanualz®

Accounting Policies, Procedures & Forms

Section 430

Revenue Procedures

Section 430

Revenue

Procedures:

REV101 Sales Order Entry
REV102 Point-of-Sale Orders
REV103 Customer Credit Approval and Terms
REV104 Sales Order Acceptance
REV105 Shipment of Goods
REV106 Invoicing and Accounts Receivable
REV107 Sales Tax Collection
REV108 Progress Billing
REV109 Account Collections
REV110 Customer Returns

SOP # ______ Revision:______ **Prepared by:____________**
Effective Date:______________ **Approved by:____________**

Title: **REV101 SALES ORDER ENTRY**

Policy: All customer orders will be processed in an efficient and organized manner to ensure accurate and prompt shipments.

Purpose: This procedure summarizes the preparation of documents, paperwork flow, and responsibilities by individuals and departments from obtaining a sales order from a customer through shipping and billing the customer.

This procedure is not intended to be inclusive of all steps and activities involved in the consummation of a sales transaction. Therefore, each individual involved in the sales order process will need to take the responsibility to determine that all required and necessary activities and documents are properly completed.

Scope: This procedure applies to all individuals and departments involved in consummation of the sales process, specifically including Sales, Customer Service, Credit, Manufacturing and Billing.

Responsibilities:

The Sales Representative is responsible for initiating the sales process and for obtaining/providing and reviewing all documents and information from a customer, in order to complete the sales order.

Customer service is responsible for reviewing sales orders to ensure requirements are adequately defined, that the order is consistent with the quotation if one was provided, and that Our Company has the ability to meet the defined requirements.

Sales Administration will be responsible for facilitating the sales order entry process and maintaining all sales records.

Procedure:

1.0 SALES REPRESENTATIVES

1.1 The Sales Representative will be responsible for obtaining all information from a customer in order to complete the sales order. Use REV101 Ex1 SALES ORDER. This information can include completed company Order Forms, a customer's purchase order, e-mails, request for quotes or proposals (RFQ or RFP) or credit card orders.

1.2 Payment terms for the customer must be in accordance with procedure REV103 CUSTOMER CREDIT APPROVAL AND TERMS. In the event the customer requires Lease Financing, the Sales Representative will work with the Credit Department to obtain credit pre-approval and facilitate processing of applicable paperwork. Customers may pay by credit card in accordance with procedure CSH101 CASH DRAWERS AND CREDIT CARDS.

1.3 Shipments for export outside the country of origin require extra preparation, documentation and handing. VAT, duties, or taxes may be required depending on the destination country. Indicate on the Sales Order whether the duties and taxes should be collect or prepaid.

It is often times very difficult to determine the exact amount that will be charged for these fees. Therefore, if it is possible, the simplest method is to indicate on the Bill of Lading (or waybill) to have the VAT, duties or taxes collected upon receipt. Alternatively, the Company (shipper) will pay for all fees and then Accounting must add these fees to the invoice at a later date.

The recipient must pay these fees prior to acceptance or the goods will be returned. Some countries may require that some or all of these fees be paid prior to return. Also, the carrier may require additional transportation fees for the return trip. So it is important to

Note: The Company may not physically or electronically export or re-export items or provide services to any party, whether in the United States or abroad, who is listed on the United States government export exclusion lists, including but not limited to the Treasury Department's Specially Designated Nationals List and Commerce Department's Entity and Denied Persons Lists.

Consult with the Bureau of Export Administration's Export Counseling Division and other appropriate U.S. government resources for information on embargoed countries prior to shipment (see 9.0 below for internet links).

2.0 INTERNET ORDERS

2.1 Orders from the Website require credit card transactions see procedure CSH101 CASH DRAWERS AND CREDIT CARDS.

2.2 The Website interacts directly with the inventory system to verify customer orders, generate sales orders with ship-to information, and acknowledge shipment to the customer.

2.3 If customer's run into problems with the Website or have technical questions regarding products, Customer Service can be contacted via email or phone. Customer Service either assists the customer with the Internet order or manually handles the order.

3.0 CREDIT DEPARTMENT

3.1 The Credit Department will be responsible for facilitating financing of customers and approving terms of all sales in accordance with procedure REV103 CUSTOMER CREDIT APPROVAL AND TERMS.

3.2 If the Customer is financing the order, Credit will process and forward all applicable lease documents to the third party financing source.

3.3 If Credit rejects the terms of the customer's order, Credit will notify the Sales Representative and the customer as appropriate.

3.4 Credit will review the customer's order package and if approved will authorize the Sales Order. Upon completion, the Sales Order and customer file will be forwarded to Manufacturing/Shipping.

4.0 SALES ADMINISTRATION

4.1 Upon receipt of a complete sales package with all supporting documentation from the Sale Representative, Sales Administration will validate all orders before acceptance in accordance with procedure REV104 SALES ORDER ACCEPTANCE. The validity and efficiency of the entire Sales Order Entry process is dependent on starting with accurate information. This step is vital to ensure that the terms, conditions and configuration of the order are accurate and as agreed upon.

4.2 For standard products where a quotation was not given, check the part inventories on the computer system to ensure adequate inventory is available to commit. If there is not adequate inventory, the system will estimate an availability date based on work orders in process. If there are any discrepancies or if the product is backordered, contact Sale Representative and/or the customer and resolve any issues.

4.3 When the order is accepted, enter the order information into the Sales Order Entry Screen along with any special shipping or product configuration requirements then print an Order Acknowledgement.

Note: The computer system may not print the Order Acknowledgement until approved by the credit department.

4.4 For custom products, Engineering is notified to start the design process. A copy of the Sales Order and any additional information received after the quotation process is forwarded to Engineering.

4.5 Prepare the customer file with copies of all documentation, customer correspondence, the original Order Acknowledgement along with any documentation or notes of actions taken to resolve any issues.

Create a customer file using a letter size manila type folder and label it with the organization and contact person's name (last name first) plus the state/province or country. The file should utilize a 2-hole center punch design on both sides with prongs for holding documentation.

File customer ordering information on the right side of the folder and all customer service correspondence/documentation on the left side of the folder. If the sale is to an existing customer, prepare only a temporary file for routing purposes. Upon order shipment, file the new sales order information into the pre-existing customer file.

4.6 Upon completion of all required information for the customer file, Sales Administration will forward all documents, except for any lease financing documentation, to the Credit Department for processing and approval of the Sales Order.

If applicable, lease financing documentation will be forwarded directly to Accounting/Billing where it will be held for processing upon receipt of the Accounting copy of the completed Sales Order (i.e., after shipment).

5.0 MANUFACTURING/SHIPPING

5.1 Upon receipt of the Sales Order, Manufacturing or the warehouse (reference procedure REV105 SHIPMENT OF GOODS, section 1.1) will configure and route the order to be shipped. All quality control forms should be completed and forwarded with the order.

If the order can not be completed or shipped within two to three weeks after receipt of order, Manufacturing will notify Customer Service who will be responsible for either sending the Customer a backorder notification or calling the customer to inform them of the backordered item(s) and anticipated shipment/arrival of these items.

5.2 Upon receipt of product from Manufacturing or Warehouse, Shipping will pack the items and verify that the customer's order is complete. Shipping will complete the applicable areas on the Sales Order with quantity shipped and all applicable serial numbers.

Shipping will be responsible for preparing all shipping documents (e.g., Bill of Lading, COD tags, Commercial Invoice, etc.) and determining the appropriate shipping source for delivering the product as per procedure REV105 SHIPMENT OF GOODS. If shipping determines that a customer's order will not arrive by a requested delivery date, Shipping will notify Customer Service of the delay and approximately when the order will arrive.

6.0 CUSTOMER SERVICE

6.1 Upon receipt of the customer file, Customer Service will then log the customer information into the Company's customer list database and file the customer file.

6.2 Customer Service will be responsible for maintaining all customer files. Filing will be done alphabetically and all information within the files shall be kept chronologically, front to back, with the front being the most current.

6.3 Customer Service is responsible for Post-Sale Customer Follow-Up and sending out Customer Satisfaction Surveys (see ***ABR44 Bizmanualz™ Sales and Marketing Policies, Procedures and Forms***) as per the New Order/New Customer Process.

7.0 ACCOUNTING/BILLING

7.1 Upon receipt of the completed Sales Order, Billing will prepare an invoice from the information provided on the Sales Order as per procedure REV106 INVOICING AND ACCOUNTS RECEIVABLE.

8.0 CHANGES TO ORDERS

8.1 Customer Service should process all requested changes to customer orders.

8.2 For changes in quantity or delay in due date, Customer Service reviews the status of the order on the computer system and if the order has not shipped, makes the appropriate changes as a new revision to the Sales Order. Customer Service contacts Manufacturing and Shipping to advise them of the revision.

8.3 For changes to expedite the ship date, Customer Service contacts Manufacturing and Shipping to verify the new date is acceptable, or what the earliest date may be.

8.4 If the new date is acceptable, Customer Service sends an acknowledgement to the customer. If the date is not acceptable, Customer Service contacts the customer and confirms the best possible date.

8.5 If the changes are technical changes to the product, the order should put on hold. Contact the Sales Representative to determine the appropriate action.

8.6 Records of reviews of changes to orders are maintained in the customer file.

9.0 ADDITIONAL INFORMATION RESOURCES

9.1 More information is available from the following resources:

- Commerce Department Denied Persons List http://www.bxa.doc.gov/DPL/Default.shtm
- Commerce Department Denied Entity List http://www.bxa.doc.gov/Entities/Default.htm
- Treasury Department Specially Designated Nationals List http://www.treas.gov/offices/enforcement/ofac/sdn/index.html

Revision History:

Revision	Date	Description of changes	Requested By
0	11/06/02	Initial Release	

[This page intentionally left blank]

REV101 Ex1 SALES ORDER

BILL TO: **SHIP TO:**

Phone: (   ) ______________________ Phone: (   ) ______________________

Contact: ______________________ Contact: ______________________

Sales Contact	PO #	Order Date	Date Required			Terms	Shipped Via	Ship Date
Model #	Description		Qty. Ord.	Qty. Ship	Qty. B/O	Serial #	Unit Price	Amount

No. Cartons: ________ Sub-Total ________

Total Weight: ________ Sales Tax ________

Shipping ________

Total Due ________

____

Credit/Authorization Date

Export Orders

Duties/Taxes: Collect □ Prepaid □

Value for Commercial Invoice purposes: ______________________

INSTRUCTIONS/COMMENT______________________

Distribution: White-Customer Service Yellow-Accounting Pink-Customer

[This page intentionally left blank]

REV101 Ex2 ORDER FORM

COMPANY NAME
ADDRESS
Other descriptive information

BILL TO:		SHIP TO:	
NAME	______	NAME	______
COMPANY	______	COMPANY	______
ADDRESS - 1	______ STE.____	ADDRESS - 1	______
ADDRESS - 2	______	ADDRESS - 2	______
CITY-STATE-ZIP	______	CITY-STATE-ZIP	______
>>>>>>PHONE	______ FAX ______	E-MAIL	______

PRODUCT ORDER Item #	Title	Price
(1)	______	$ ______
(2)	______	$ ______
(3)	______	$ ______
(4)	______	$ ______

o FedEx 2-day USA $24.97	o UPS Ground USA $14.97	Missouri residents add 7.325% sales tax	$ ______
o FedEx (PM) USA $34.97	o UPS Ground CANADA $19.97	Shipping Charges:	$ ______
o FedEx (AM) USA $44.97	o DHL International $call	**INVOICE TOTAL**	$ ______

PAYMENT INFORMATION

o VISA o MasterCard o American Express o Discover

Card Number ______ Expiration (MO/YR) ______

Name on Card ______ TOTAL Charged to Card $ ______

30-DAY RETURNS GUARANTEE: Our policy has always been to satisfy every customer. That's why we offer a 30-day guarantee and stand behind every sale. If you're not completely happy with your purchase, we'll gladly exchange the product or issue a credit, less shipping costs. We do ask, however, that you give us a call to receive a RMA (Return Materials Authorization) number and return all contents in their original packaging materials in new, resalable condition, within 30 days of the purchase date. These materials must be in resalable condition or we cannot accept the merchandise for return.

SHIPPING COSTS: All software orders within the U.S. are shipped UPS ground for a charge of $14.97 for up to 9 lbs. Additional shipping charges may apply for International orders. If your order is placed by 3:00PM (Central), it can ship the same day via Federal Express overnight 11AM delivery.

PAYMENT: We accept VISA, MasterCard, Discover, American Express, checks, and money orders. Orders will be shipped subject to check clearance. A $15 surcharge is added to all returned checks. NOTE: WE DO NOT CHARGE YOUR ACCOUNT until the order SHIPS!

[This page intentionally left blank]

SOP # ______ Revision:______ **Prepared by:____________**
Effective Date:_______________ **Approved by:____________**

Title: REV102 POINT-OF-SALE ORDERS

Policy: There should be proper transaction controls over sales and proper reviews and authorizations by the store manager.

Purpose: To provide the procedures for ensuring that all sales are proper and collectible and the effect on inventory and cash is posted correctly.

Scope: All cashiers

Definitions: POS. A Point-Of-Sale or POS system is an automated cash drawer that ties into the accounting system to record all sales transactions. The POS will typically process credit card transactions and returns, manage inventory, accounts receivable, payables or it may be web or network enabled. At its core is a computer with software that can include any number of functions.

UPC. A Universal Product Code or UPC is a standardized and unique product barcode used to identify packaged merchandise through the use of a barcode scanner.

Responsibilities:

CFO has authority to write off any accounts Receivable Account deemed not collectible.

Credit Manager reviews Credit Application for approval of "house accounts".

Procedure:

1.0 POINT OF SALE

1.1 The correct use of the POS/Order Entry will follow the specific guidelines of the software system. All products should have barcodes (UPC or house barcodes). Recording a transaction will involve scanning each barcode and entering the tender amount (cash, check or credit card). Specific procedures should provide for ringing up product that either has no barcode, or a barcode that is not readable. Proper procedures regarding cash register transactions are described in procedure CSH101 CASH DRAWERS and CREDIT CARDS.

1.2 Generally, the POS system automates the process of recording the proper price and cost (associated with the barcode) while determining the correct inventory amount associated with the transaction and adding the proper sales tax.

1.3 Tax-exempt transactions for customers that claim tax-exempt status should be based on proper documentation. Request a copy of a state approved tax-exempt certificate to be kept on file to support all tax-exempt sales. The company may be required to produce proper tax-exempt sales documentation during a state sales-tax audit.

1.4 The manager should periodically review the end of day gross margin reports for reasonableness in margins and sales tax charged. The manager should also periodically spot check specific transactions. Exceptions should be promptly followed-up.

2.0 SALES ORDERS AND INVOICES

2.1 Most POS systems include the ability to produce both sales orders and sales invoices. Depending on the level of customer service offered, the sales manager may process sales orders for large telephone orders that can be pre-assembled by the company prior to customer pickup. By transcribing the order into the POS sales order system, the affected inventory is put on a "committed" status. This inventory should be pulled from the shelves, grouped in a customer holding area, and a copy of the sales order should be placed with this merchandise.

When the customer arrives for the order, the POS system generally allows for an automatic conversion from sales order to sales invoice, without needing to re-enter all data. It is important to note that an entered sales order does not record a sale or decrease inventory in the accounting system. It simply creates a memo pending sale and a committed status for the affected inventory. Only when the sales order is converted to a sales invoice, does the accounting system record a sale and a decrease to the affected inventory quantities.

2.2 For POS registers that do not provide sales orders, a manual sales order book can provide the same memo ability. The information will have to be entered into the system once the sale has occurred. If a sales order book is used, (for phone in orders, deliveries, etc.), it should contain pre-numbered forms in duplicate. The second copy should remain in the book at all times. The original should be torn out and placed with the order, but the second copy remains as the control.

2.3 If the company offers deliveries, a sales order system should generally be used to provide organization and control over selection and delivery of merchandise. After the order is pulled and grouped, but before loading in the vehicle, the actual sales invoice should be generated. This should be compared to the original sales order, and double-checked with the actual merchandise as it is loaded in the vehicle. This helps detect any possible inventory selection errors.

The original sales order and the customer copy of the Invoice should go with the delivery. Upon delivery, the customer should be encouraged to check off all items as they are unloaded, and the driver should obtain the customer's signature on the original Sales Order as documentation that the order was complete and satisfactorily received. A second copy of the invoice can also be used for this purpose.

Depending on the terms (credit, COD, etc.) the driver returns with the proper tender and the signed sales order, and/or signed invoice copy. Upon return to the company, these documents should be taken immediately to the register in which the original invoice was entered. Every delivered sale should be documented by a customer signed sales order or invoice and the correct tendered amount.

2.4 If the delivery service is significant, with a long route and multiple deliveries, a driver route log should be developed. This worksheet provides a place for each customer's name, location, and the amount tendered. Upon return, the sales manager or designee should perform a driver check-in. The driver's vehicle should be inspected, the log sheet reviewed and the various forms of receipts should be totaled and compared to the invoiced amounts. In effect, the driver's "cash pouch" becomes an additional store cash drawer for the day, and should be appropriately reconciled at the end of the day.

2.5 For all other shipments see procedure REV105 SHIPMENT OF GOODS.

3.0 SALES INVOICES AND ACCOUNTS RECEIVABLE

3.1 POS systems can produce and print an invoice in the same manner as a cash register receipt. These systems also maintain accounts receivable. Cash or checks presented for payment on account can be processed through the cash drawer and settled just like all other cash/check/credit card transactions.

3.2 Monthly statements should be produced for mailing. An aged accounts receivable report should be run and reviewed by the manager as often as needed, but not less than once a month. The Accounts Receivable balance in the month-end financial statements should agree with the total aged Accounts Receivable from the POS system. Only the CFO should have the authority to write off any Accounts Receivable account deemed not collectible.

3.3 Credit sales will generally only be allowed for pre-approved "house accounts". Approval should be made by the credit manager, based on a review of a credit application, maintained in a customer file. These practices are explained in procedure REV103 CUSTOMER CREDIT APPROVAL AND TERMS. The credit manager should implement a "hold" of further credit for any delinquent account, and the system should prevent a cashier from issuing additional sales on credit to that customer.

Revision History:

Revision	Date	Description of changes	Requested By
0	11/06/02	Initial Release	

SOP # ______ Revision:______ **Prepared by:____________**
Effective Date:______________ **Approved by:____________**

Title: **REV103 CUSTOMER CREDIT APPROVAL AND TERMS**

Policy: To reduce potential collection problems, new customer accounts or credit limit increases will be properly evaluated and approved prior to extending credit.

Purpose: This procedure outlines the activities and responsibilities involved in obtaining a credit approval for a potential customer before sales orders are consummated.

Scope: These procedures are to be followed for all credit approvals requested by the Sales or Customer Service Departments for customers interested in open account, lease or rental financing.

Definition: Credit scoring is the process of assigning values to various elements of a customer's credit history and payment performance to quantify its creditworthiness. It is popular because it creates a common, unbiased approach to evaluating credit requests.

Responsibilities:

Sales person is responsible for reviewing Credit Application for completeness and accuracy.

Credit Manager is responsible for application review and investigation of the applicant's credit history.

Procedure:

1.0 CREDIT APPLICATION

1.1 Upon determining the intent of a customer to purchase products from the company, the salesperson should have the customer complete a REV103 Ex1 CREDIT APPLICATION and return it by mail or fax.

The salesperson should review the application for completeness and accuracy. Missing or erroneous information may result in delays or rejection of the application.

1.2 The salesperson should then prepare a REV103 Ex2 REQUEST FOR CREDIT APPROVAL and submit this form along with the customer's credit application to the Credit Department for processing.

2.0 CREDIT INVESTIGATIONS

2.1 The Credit Department will review the application for the following key categories of information:

- **Legal name** of business.
- **Trade name** or "Doing Business As" (DBA) name.

- **Type of Business** - Sole proprietorship, partnership, corporation, subsidiary or division, or nonprofit organization.
- **Complete address** - street, city, state/province, zip code/postal code and telephone number(s). A post office box is not acceptable.
- **Years in business** - Credit risks increase for businesses in existence for less than five years.
- **Primary bank** and the name of the applicant's commercial loan officer. Since money can be moved around easily, a reference does not mean much if an account has had significant balances for less than six months. A year is much better. If an applicant switched primary banks within the past year, find out why.
- **Trade References** - Five references are better than the standard three references. References will be contacted but should be expected to be favorable as people seldom give out "bad" references. Also some references could be friends or relatives.

2.2 After careful review of the application for completeness, the investigation for credit amounts less than $20,000 will proceed as follows:

1) Start the investigation by finding out whether the Company is in good legal standing. Should a customer default, creditors must have the legal name to file a valid claim. To obtain this information for corporations, call the secretary of state's office in the customer's state to determine if a corporation is in good legal standing. If the customer is a proprietorship or partnership, call the county clerk to verify that a DBA has been filed with that office.

   These calls should also yield and/or verify the firm's legal street address, the names and addresses of the chief executive officer, chief financial officer and corporate secretary, plus the name and address of the firm's legal agent for service of process.

2) Find out whether credit is being sought for a parent company or a subsidiary. Many companies apply for credit in the name of a subsidiary, yet bank and trade references are for the parent company. The parent company could have a very favorable credit history compared to the subsidiary. Also, the parent company can remove assets from a subsidiary. In the event the subsidiary is given credit and files for bankruptcy, creditors cannot sue the parent company unless the subsidiary had previously given a cross-company guarantee from the parent company.

3) Contact the Better Business Bureau for a "Reliability Report". Contact Directory Assistance for the phone number of the local office serving the customer's area.

4) The customer's bank(s) should be contacted to determine how the customer handles their finances.

5) Contact each credit reference provided by telephone, fax or mail. Each reference should complete a REV103 Ex3 CREDIT INQUIRY form. The Credit Manager should evaluate the completed form upon its return.

6) If additional information is deemed necessary, a Credit Bureau Report on the customer should be obtained. Note: written authorization is required for most inquiries.

2.3 The data collected above can be used to assign customer credit scores or ratings that can be used to segmenting that customer base by risk category. Segmenting the customer base by risk -- high, medium, and low -- allows the company to achieve collection efficiencies by better prioritizing accounts and identifying customer trends. There are two types of scores consumer and business.

1) A consumer credit score is made up of the following components:

- Payment History
- Number of Accounts and Total Outstanding Balances
- Length of Credit History
- Number of New or Recent Accounts
- Types of Credit in Use

2) A business credit score is made up of the following components:

- Business Sales Size
- Industry Type
- Number of Years in Business
- Assets of the Company
- Checking Account Balances
- Total Cash on Hand
- Net Income and Liabilities

2.4 Look for warning signs consisting of high levels of debt, low cash on hand or income to service debt, increasing number of debt accounts or balances, frequent late payments, few years in business or little credit history.

2.5 Customers requiring a credit line of $20,000 or more should provide their last two years of financial statements. Audited, compiled or reviewed statements, signed by their auditor or accountant, are preferred over ones prepared by the customer.

3.0 CREDIT APPROVAL/REJECTION

3.1 The Credit Manager will review the credit application and the results of the credit investigation to determine approval or rejection of credit for the customer, and the credit line and terms authorized if approved. Credit terms will be in accordance with the company's credit policies as follows:

Organization Type	Acceptable Terms
a. Individuals and Proprietorships	Prepay, COD, Credit Card or Net 30 with Personal Guarantee.
b. Corporations and Partnerships	Prepay, COD or Net 30.
c. Nonprofits and government agencies	Prepay, COD or 2%-10,N30.
d. International companies or agencies	prepay in U.S. Dollars drawn from a U.S. bank. No foreign checks including cashiers accepted unless the shipment is held until funds clear the company's bank. Irrevocable Letter of Credit in U.S. Dollars drawn against a U.S. bank.

3.2 Upon determination of the credit status of the customer, the Credit Department will complete the approval/denial section of the REV103 Ex2 REQUEST FOR CREDIT APPROVAL form and forward it and the original REV103 Ex1 CREDIT APPLICATION back to the originating salesperson for follow-up with the customer.

3.3 If the application is rejected, the Credit Department will send out a standard credit denial letter to the customer and/or work with the sales contact to arrange possible alternate financing. Common reasons for credit denial include:

- Incomplete information
- Unable to verify credit data
- Insufficient or unacceptable credit references
- Insufficient income or revenues
- Recent bankruptcy
- Limited credit experience or history
- Excessive obligations or high credit balances
- Current collections actions in process
- Outstanding judgments or liens
- Poor credit performance
- Adverse credit reports (list addresses of credit reporting agency used)
- Other

4.0 ADDITIONAL INFORMATION RESOURCES

4.1 Credit Reporting Agencies (CRA):

- Equifax 800-685-1111 www.equifax.com
- Experian 888-EXPERIAN (888-397-3742) www.experian.com
- Trans Union 800-916-8800 www.transunion.com

References:

A. EQUAL CREDIT OPPORTUNITY ACT (ECOA)

ECOA prohibits creditors from discriminating against credit applicants on the basis of race, color, religion, national origin, sex, marital status, age, or because an applicant receives income from a public assistance program.

The types of credit transactions that are protected by the ECOA include, but are not limited to, business loans, consumer leases, consumer loans, auto loans, credit cards, agricultural loans and loans to purchase, improve, refinance or construct residential or commercial real estate. If the credit transaction provides for the deferral of payment of the debt, it is also covered by ECOA and Regulation B even though it may not be defined as a credit transaction by the Truth in Lending Act.

B. TRUTH IN LENDING ACT (TILA)

TILA refers to Title I of the Consumer Credit Protection Act (see Reference E. FRB Reg B). In the TILA, creditors and lenders are required to furnish a clear description of all the important terms and requirements relating to any credit transaction. Creditors and lenders must furnish detailed information to consumers **before** extending credit.

This requirement extends to **all** credit transactions covered by *TILA*, including installment loans, credit cards, and home equity lines of credit. In addition, there are several special rules governing credit card transactions regarding initial disclosures, periodic disclosures, and rules concerning disputed charges.

The following information must be given to the consumer prior to entering into a credit transaction:

- **Total sales price** of the goods purchased including interest, down payment or trade-in value, or any other charges.
- **Finance charge** or dollar cost of the credit transaction, which includes the dollar cost of all the interest to be paid over the term of the loan and the cost of all other charges imposed by the creditor as a condition of extending credit to the consumer. "Other charges" may include points (prepaid interest), service charges, appraisal fees, credit report fees, and/or charges for any credit insurance purchased. Application fees are not part of the finance charge for any consumer credit transaction.

  Note: Special rules apply to mortgage transactions which exclude many of these "other charges," such as title examination fees, credit report fees, escrow payments for taxes and insurance, and reasonable attorneys' fees, from the finance charge.
- **Annual Percentage Rate or APR**. Installment credit contract or closed-ended credit transactions assume that the total finance charge is paid in equal installments over the term of the loan and then calculates the amount paid

each year as a percentage of the amount financed. Open-ended transactions such as credit cards are computed by multiplying the periodic interest rate by the number of periods in a year to arrive at an annual rate.

- **Total of all payments** the consumer must make under the agreement, which equals the amount financed plus the finance charge. Credit cards offer a continuous form of credit, therefore some special pieces of information must be clearly described
- **Schedule of monthly or periodic payments** must be clearly set out in the contract. This includes the due date for each payment, the number of payments required and the size of each payment. If any payment is for a different amount, this must also be clearly indicated. Credit card issuers must provide consumers with statements at the end of each billing period.

The *Truth-in-Lending Act (TILA)*, a federal law, has several special rules governing credit card transactions. These special rules fall into three categories: initial disclosures, periodic disclosures, and rules concerning disputed charges.

Initial Disclosures: Credit cards offer a continuous form of credit, therefore when one applies for a credit card some special pieces of information must be clearly described:

- The conditions under which a **finance charge** (including interest and late fees) may be imposed on the consumer's account, including the extent of any "grace period" before finance charges accrue;
- The method by which the creditor will determine the **balance** on which a finance charge is imposed.
- The method of determining the amount of any **finance charge**, including interest, late fees and any minimum or fixed charge;
- The **periodic rate of interest** (such as 1½% per month);
- The so-called **nominal Annual Percentage Rate (APR)**, which is computed by multiplying the periodic interest rate by the number of periods in a year to arrive at an annual rate;
- Disclosure of whether the agreement gives the creditor a **security interest** in any merchandise purchased with the credit card (or any other property); and,
- A statement of the consumer's **right to dispute charges** (this statement must also be provided every six months).

Periodic Disclosures: Credit card issuers also must provide consumers with statements at the end of each billing period which include the following additional disclosures (these should be familiar to you from your monthly credit card bills):

- The date of the bill and the beginning date of the billing cycle;

- The outstanding balance owed at the beginning of the billing cycle;
- The date and amount of each extension of credit during the billing cycle, with a description of the transaction sufficient to identify it;
- Any credits to the account (such as payments received);
- All finance charges for the billing cycle, itemized as interest, late fees, minimum fees, annual fees, etc.;
- The balance on which the finance charge was computed and a statement as to how the balance was arrived at;
- The APR;
- The final balance;
- The date by which payments must be made to avoid any finance charge;
- The address of the creditor for purposes of disputing charges or other inquiries.

Dealing with Errors: In addition to disclosure requirements, TILA establishes a three-step procedure by which consumers can **dispute errors** in their credit card periodic statements:

1. If the consumer notices an error in their statement, or questions the validity of a charge, they must notify the credit card company in writing (at the address listed on the periodic statement) of the error within 60 days of the date of the billing statement. They will need to identify themselves, using the same name as on the credit card, give the account number, and describe the nature of the claimed billing error. If the problem is an unidentified charge, the merchant must provide "documentary evidence" such as a copy of the sales slip for that charge.
2. The credit card company must send an acknowledgment of the complaint within 30 days of receiving the notice of error.
3. The credit card company must, within two billing cycles or 90 days (whichever is shorter), either correct the error or provide an explanation for the charge, if requested. The company must also provide documentary evidence (such as a copy of the receipt) of the validity of the disputed charge.

C. FAIR CREDIT BILLING ACT (FCBA)

The FCBA applies to "open end" credit accounts, such as credit cards and revolving charge accounts - such as department store accounts. It does not cover installment contracts - loans or extensions of credit on a fixed schedule. Consumers often buy cars, furniture and major appliances on an installment basis and repay personal loans in installments.

D. FAIR CREDIT REPORTING ACT (FCRA)

The FCRA is designed to promote accuracy and ensure the privacy of the information used in consumer reports and to guarantee that the information supplied by consumer reporting agencies is as accurate as possible. Amendments, which went into effect September 30, 1997, expanded employer responsibilities to ensure (1) that individuals are aware that consumer reports may be used for employment purposes and agree to such use, and (2) that individuals are notified promptly if information in a consumer report may result in a negative employment or credit granting decision.

E. FRB REG B: EQUAL CREDIT OPPORTUNITY ACT

Regulation B prohibits creditors from discriminating against credit applicants, establishes guidelines for gathering and evaluating credit information, and requires written notification when credit is denied. The regulation prohibits creditors from discrimination against applicants on the basis of age, race, color, religion, national origin, sex, marital status, or receipt of income from public assistance programs.

Model credit application forms are provided in the regulation to facilitate compliance. By properly using these forms, creditors can be assured of being in compliance with the application requirements.

The regulation also requires creditors to give applicants a written notification of rejection of an application, a statement of the applicant's rights under the Equal Credit Opportunity Act, and a statement either of the reasons for the rejection or of the applicant's right to request the reasons. Creditors, who furnish credit information, when reporting information on married borrowers, must report information in the names of each spouse.

The regulation establishes a special residential mortgage credit monitoring system for regulatory agencies by requiring that lenders ask for and note the race, national origin, sex, marital status, and age of residential mortgage applicants.

The regulation covers all credit transactions (unlike other regulations that may cover only consumer credit), with some modifications applicable to certain classes of transactions.

F. FRB REG M: CONSUMER LEASING ACT

Requires that institutions disclose the cost and terms of consumer leases (e.g. vehicle leases). Regulation M applies to leases of personal property for more than 4 months for personal, family, or household use. It requires leasing companies to disclose in writing the cost of a lease, including a security deposit, monthly payments, license, registration, taxes and maintenance fees and, in the case of an open-end lease, whether a 'balloon payment' may be applied. It also requires written disclosure of the terms of a lease, including insurance, guarantees, responsibility for servicing the property, standards for wear and tear, and any option to buy.

G. FRB REG Z: TRUTH IN LENDING ACT

Regulation Z prescribes uniform methods of computing the cost of credit, disclosure of credit terms, and procedures for resolving errors on certain credit accounts.

The credit provisions of the regulation apply to all persons who extend consumer credit more than 25 times a year or, in the case of consumer credit secured by real estate, more than 5 times a year. Consumer credit is generally defined as credit offered or extended to individuals for personal, family, or household purposes, where the credit is repayable in more than four installments or for which a finance charge is imposed.

The major provisions of the regulation require lenders to:

- Provide borrowers with meaningful, written information on essential credit terms, including the cost of credit expressed as an annual percentage rate (APR).
- Respond to consumer complaints of billing errors on certain credit accounts within a specific period.
- Identify credit transactions on periodic statements of open-end credit accounts.
- Provide certain rights regarding credit cards.
- Provide good faith estimations of disclosure information before consummation of certain residential mortgage transactions.
- Provide "early" disclosure of credit terms to consumers interested in adjustable rate mortgages (ARMs) and home equity lines of credit.
- Comply with special requirements when advertising credit.

Revision History:

Revision	Date	Description of changes	Requested By
0	11/06/02	Initial Release	

[This page intentionally left blank]

REV103 Ex1 CREDIT APPLICATION

Credit Line Requested:______________________ Date:______________

BUSINESS INFORMATION:

Legal Business Name:______________________________

Contact:________________Title:__________ Phone:(   )________

Street Address:__________________City, State, Zip:______________

Type of Business: Corporation: □ Partnership: □ Sole Proprietorship: □ Non/Profit: □ Years in Business:_

Status of Practice/Business: New: □ Established: □ Number of Years:________

Owner/Principal Name:________________Social Security Number:____________

Street (home address):________________City, State, Zip:____________

Owner/Principal Name:________________Social Security Number:____________

Street (home address):________________City, State, Zip:____________

Do any unsatisfied judgments exist? Yes □ No □ If yes, please explain:____________

____

Have you ever filed Bankruptcy? Yes □ No □ If yes, please explain:____________

____

BANK AND TRADE RELATIONSHIPS:

Primary Bank:__________Branch:__________ Phone:( )__________

Bank Officer:__________________ Account #:________________

Other Bank/s:______________________Phone:( )__________

Bank Officer:__________________ Account #:________________

TRADE REFERENCES:

Name:____________________Phone:(   )__________Contact:__________

Name:____________________Phone:(   )__________Contact:__________

Name:____________________Phone:(   )__________Contact:__________

In consideration for credit being extended, I or we acknowledge and agree to the following: (1) Payment is jointly, severally and unconditionally guaranteed within 30 days of date of delivery; (2) any charges unpaid after the above 30 days are to be increased by 1½% per month; (3) any charges still outstanding after 90 days from date of delivery are subject to collection, and all collection or arbitration expenses, attorney's fees, and court costs will be borne by the purchaser; (4) title to all work shall remain with the creditor until all invoices and additional charges have been paid in full; (5) all claims, requests for adjustments, or notification of errors must be made within thirty days, or charges are considered accepted; (6) this agreement shall apply to all current and future charges unless revocation is received by registered mail; (7) credit privileges may be withdrawn at any time without invalidating the terms of this agreement.

CREDIT CANNOT BE EXTENDED UNTIL THIS FORM IS COMPLETED AND VERIFIED

______________________________ ______________________________

Authorized Signature Date Title

[This page intentionally left blank]

REV103 Ex2 REQUEST FOR CREDIT APPROVAL

Customer Name: ______________________ Date: ____________

Salesperson: ______________________

Information about Customer including type of business, products or services and projected monthly sales to customer:

____

____

____

____

____

Credit Use Only

APPROVED:

Credit Line______________ Terms:______________

Special Conditions if applicable:______________________

By:______________ Date:______________

DENIED:

By:______________ Date:____________

Reason for Denial:______________________

____

____

____

Rejection Letter Sent:__________ Date: ____________

Other Possible Financing Arrangements:______________________

____

____

____

[This page intentionally left blank]

REV103 Ex3 CREDIT INQUIRY

Contact:____________________________ Date:__________________

Company:___________________________ Phone:_________________

Address:____

City, State, Zip:____

In order that we might process a Credit Application that we have received on the above account, we would appreciate your providing us with the information requested below. Please know we will treat your response with confidentiality.

Date Account Opened:________________________

Average Yearly Sales:________________________

Terms:________________________ Special Terms:__________________

Largest Amount Owed:______________ When:______________________

Total Amount Now Owed:____________ Current ☐ Yes ☐ No Amt. Past Due:___

Recent Trends: ☐ Promptness ☐ Full Term ☐ Slightly Slow ☐ Very Slow

Makes Unjust Claims (explain):__________________________________

____

Credit ☐ Honored ☐ Refused (explain):____________________________

____

Check Manner of Payment:

☐ Prompt and Takes Discounts
☐ Prompt and Satisfactory
☐ Prompt to__________ Slow
☐ Makes Partial Payments
☐ Asks for Additional Time
☐ Slow but Collectible
☐ Slow and Unsatisfactory
☐ Accepts C.O.D.'s Promptly
☐ Collected by an Attorney
☐ In Hands of Attorney
☐ An Excellent Account- Best Recommendation
☐ We Do Not Recommend Extending Credit to This Account

Special Comments:

We will be pleased to share any information we have that will assist you in your credit decisions. Thank you for your assistance.

____
Name

____
Title

[This page intentionally left blank]

SOP # ______ Revision:______ **Prepared by:____________**
Effective Date:_______________ **Approved by:____________**

Title: **REV104 SALES ORDER ACCEPTANCE**

Policy: To ensure the highest customer services levels and reduce potential order problems, sales orders will be properly evaluated and approved prior to entry into the accounting system and fulfillment by the company.

Purpose: This procedure outlines the activities and responsibilities involved in verifying the acceptability of all sales orders received before they are consummated.

Scope: These procedures are to be followed for all sales orders taken by the Sales or Customer Service Departments.

Responsibilities:

Credit Manager approves credit application and confirms order amount is within the approved credit line granted.

Definitions: Sales Tax Exemption Certificate. A document typically used by a non-profit organization to certify an exemption from paying tax on a purchase. This is presented at the time of purchase.

Procedure:

1.0 DOCUMENT VERIFICATION

1.1 Sales Orders may arrive from a variety of sources and utilize a variety of payment methods. Verify that all of the correct documents have been used and are present to support the order. The following documents are required to complete the Sales Order:

Invoice Orders:

- Sales Order (see procedure: REV101 SALES ORDER ENTRY)
- Approved Credit Application (see procedure: REV103 CUSTOMER CREDIT APPROVAL AND TERMS)
- Customer Purchase Order
- Sales Tax Exemption Certificate (required for tax exempt sales)
- Customer correspondence, support documentation, coupons, new vendor applications, etc

Cash/Check/Credit Card Orders:

- Sales Order (see procedure: REV101 SALES ORDER ENTRY)
- Approved Cash/Check/Credit Card transaction (see procedure: CSH101 CASH DRAWERS AND CREDIT CARDS)
- Sale Tax Exemption Certificate (required for tax exempt sales)

- Customer correspondence, support documentation, etc

1.2 Verify that all required information is available to complete the order prior to billing.

Customer correspondence: Note any special terms, comments or shipping instructions and verify they are correctly indicated on the Sales Order.

Sales Order: Verify billing and shipping addresses are correctly indicated, that product and quantity are clearly defined, PO number is correct, and that any special terms or shipping instructions are indicated.

Credit Application: Verify the Credit Manager has approved the application and confirm the order amount is within the approved credit line granted.

Purchase Order: Verify the Purchase Order is valid and complete, that the PO number is on the sales order and that the contact information for billing and shipping addresses are legible and correctly indicated.

Note: A Purchase Order is a legally enforceable promise to purchase goods or services. As such, in order for it to be valid it should contain the following:

- Complete contact information (on the customers letter head or standard purchase order form with a purchase order number)
- Date
- Description of goods (by title or part number)
- Purchase price
- Authorized signature (i.e. CEO, CFO, Controller, Purchasing Manager, etc.)

Cash/Check/Credit Card transaction: Verify the check/credit card receipt is signed, or wire has been received, and/or the credit card transaction has a valid approval code.

Sale Tax Exemption Certificate: Review the exemption to ensure it is appropriate to the items being purchased.

1.3 Review the customer's Accounts Receivable aging and determine that the customer is current with their payments and that the new order will not increase their balance above their credit limit.

1.4 Review that products ordered are available in inventory, and that delivery or installation schedules of appropriate personnel are acceptable in order to ensure that the order can be processed correctly.

2.0 TELEPHONE CONFIRMATION

2.1 Phone calls serve to confirm all information collected is accurate, that orders placed are valid, and that the customer agrees to all terms and conditions of the sale. Calls should be made only after all documents and data have been verified.

This will ensure that any discrepancies found can be addressed during the first call made.

2.2 Ask to speak to the person that issued the Purchase Order or the one that signed the check/credit card receipt. Explain the reason for the call is to confirm the order details. Proceed to confirm the order details as indicated on REV104 Ex1 PHONE CONFIRMATION CHECKLIST.

2.3 Record the date and time, the name of the person talked to, answers to all questions, and note any comments or discrepancies. Sign and date the PHONE CONFIRMATION CHECKLIST. Attach the completed form to the Sales Order.

2.4 If any information discussed is contrary to the sales order documentation, then advise the customer you will have to get further information. Place the order on Hold and contact the Salesperson for clarification or, if needed, discuss the discrepancy with the Sales Manager. Upon clarification or correction, complete the confirmation process.

3.0 ORDER ACCEPTANCE

3.1 Once the order documentation has been verified and confirmed, then the order is ready for order entry and processing. See procedure REV101 SALES ORDER ENTRY.

3.2 If documentation, data accuracy or their credit line is found to be an issue then the order should be returned to Sales for correction. Explain on the Sales Order the reasons the order is being returned. If the correction is minor, consider calling the customer to discuss the issue and then make the corrections.

Revision History:

Revision	Date	Description of changes	Requested By
0	11/06/02	Initial Release	

[This page intentionally left blank]

REV104 Ex1 PHONE CONFIRMATION CHECKLIST

1. Ask to speak to the person that issued the purchase order or the one that signed the check/credit card receipt. Explain the reason for the call is to confirm the order details.
2. Confirm the following points:
   - Purchase Order Number: ______________________
   - Products and Quantity Ordered______________________
   - Prices and Credit Terms ______________________
   - Shipping Terms and Delivery Dates______________________
   - Authority and Billing Contacts______________________
   - Special considerations: (coupons, discounts, trade-ins, etc.) ____________

     ____

     ____
   - Additional marketing questions (see separate sheet as needed).
3. Collect any further customer comments.______________________

   ____

   ____

   ____
4. Party Spoken To: ______________________
5. Sign form

   ______________________ ______________________

   Signed Date/Time Call Made
6. File with customer documentation.

[This page intentionally left blank]

SOP # ______ Revision:______ **Prepared by:____________**
Effective Date:______________ **Approved by:____________**

Title: **REV105 SHIPMENT OF GOODS**

Policy: Insure all products and services are delivered in an organized manner in order to maintain the highest customer service quality levels possible and to ensure compliance with all United States Customs laws and regulations when exporting goods & services.

Purpose: To outline the steps for the packaging, safe storage, control and delivery of all products and services shipped by the company.

Scope: This statement applies to all products and services distributed by the company, sales, customer service and shipping personnel.

Responsibilities:

Shipping and Warehouse Personnel are responsible for ensuring that the items ordered by the customer are safely packed, that they arrive at their destination in a timely fashion, and that all paperwork is forwarded to Accounting for proper invoicing.

Accounting and Accounts Receivable are responsible for processing invoices only after satisfactory delivery of goods or services has been made.

Sales and Sales Administration are responsible for ensuring that all delivery information is accurate and complete to ensure the customer receives their items as expected.

Definitions: Bill of Lading. The documents made out by or on behalf of the shipper that constitute the contract between the shipper and the carrier for the carriage of freight. It may also be known as a waybill or airway bill. The Bill of Lading is a written acknowledgement by the carrier of the receipt of goods to be transported to a designated place and delivery to a named person or to his or her order. Before accepting goods for transport, the carrier is required to issue a Bill of Lading.

Carriage. It is equivalent to the term transportation. Refers to the process or movement of shipments, including all services and operations of the carrier, provided by the carrier.

Carrier. It is the carriage (transportation) company taking responsibility (through the Bill of Lading) for transporting and delivering the consignment (goods) from the consignor (shipper) to the consignee (destination).

Consignment. It is similar to the term "shipment." It refers to one or more pieces tendered by one shipper at one time, at one address, and receipted for in one lot, and moving on one Bill of Lading to one consignee at one destination address.

Consignee. The ultimate person or company, whose name appears on the Bill of Lading, to whom the shipment is to be delivered to by the carrier.

Consignor. It is also known as the shipper. It is the person or company that is originating or shipping the goods.

Harmonized Code. The Harmonized Tariff System (HTS) is a universal classification system that is used to provide duty rates for virtually every item that exists. Every item that is exported is assigned a unique 10-digit identification code. Every 10-digit item is part of a series of progressively broader product categories.

For example, the harmonized system number for concentrated frozen apple juice is: 2009.70.0010. The concentrated frozen apple juice is assigned a 10-digit identifier that is aggregated into a broader category assigned a 6-digit identifier described as apple juice (2009.70.) The 6-digit identifier described as apple juice is aggregated into a broader category assigned a 4-digit identifier (2009) described as fruit juices and vegetable juices, etc. The 4-digit identifier is further aggregated into a broader category assigned a 2-digit identifier (20) described as Preparations of Vegetables, Fruit, Nuts etc. The first 6-digits of the classification number are universal, the last four may vary from country to country.

Incoterms. A collection of 13 internationally used terms of sale or terminology used in international trade to identify who is responsible for different activities in the delivery process. Incoterms define each element of the delivery process for both the seller and the buyer.

- EXW: Ex Works (named place; usually seller's place)
- FCA: Free Carrier (named place; usually seller's place or main carrier's terminal)
- FAS: Free Alongside Ship (named port of shipment)
- FOB: Free on Board (named port of shipment)
- CFR: Cost and Freight (named port of destination)
- CIF: Cost, Insurance and Freight (named port of destination)
- CPT: Carriage Paid to (named place of destination)
- CIP: Carriage and Insurance Paid to (named place of destination)
- DAF: Delivered at Frontier (named place; usually a border location)
- DES: Delivered ex Ship (named port of destination)
- DEO: Delivered ex Quay (named port of destination)

- DDU: Delivered Duty Unpaid (named place of destination)
- DDP: Delivered Duty Paid (named place of destination)

The scope of Incoterms is limited to matters relating to the rights and obligations of the parties to the contract of sale with respect to the delivery of goods sold, but excluding "intangibles" like computer software.

The International Chamber of Commerce maintains the Incoterms. Further information on Incoterms can be found on the International Chamber of Commerce website: http://www.iccwbo.org/index.asp.

Manifest. A document that lists all outbound (or inbound) packages picked-up by a specific carrier on a specific day.

Procedure:

1.0 SHIPPING INSPECTION AND PACKAGING

1.1 Upon receipt of goods from manufacturing (refer to ABR43 ***Bizmanualz™ Production Policies, Procedures and Forms*** for the manufacturing process) or from inventory, see procedure INV101 INVENTORY CONTROL, and receipt of the Sales Order, see procedure REV101 SALES ORDER ENTRY) the Shipping Clerk will arrange for appropriate shipping methods for products and ensure that protection and quality is maintained during shipping and through delivery to the destination (or to recipient's carrier). If it is determined that a customer's order will not arrive by a requested delivery date, then immediately notify Customer Service and/or the Sales Representative on the SALES ORDER of the delay and approximately when the order will arrive.

1.2 Pack the items and verify that the customer's order is complete. Ensure that the product is properly packaged and loaded. Proper packaging materials such as bubble wrap, foam peanuts or similar such material will be used to protect the goods in transit.

For high dollar items, obtain the originating carrier's inspection and approval of these processes if possible. Document accurate records of the condition of the product when tendered to the originating carrier.

Note: the Bill of Lading acknowledgement, that the carrier received the shipment in good condition, only applies to products that are open to inspection by the carrier.

1.3 Prepare all shipping documents or labels (e.g., Bill of Lading, COD tags, etc.). Attach them to the package and prepare for pick-up. Make sure to print an extra copy of the manifest for the customer file. Utilize special care when entering the address onto the label. Most shippers charge an extra address correction fee for undeliverable packages and the package will be delayed if the address has a problem. The most common errors consist of transposing numbers or hitting the wrong key, so check all entries for accuracy before printing.

Note: Most carriers today maintain an automated system on the Internet for producing all required documentation for both domestic and international shipments (see 5.2 below for some of the common shipping carrier internet links). Enter the appropriate information on-line and print the needed documents.

1.4 Complete the applicable areas on the REV101 Ex1 SALES ORDER with quantity shipped and all applicable serial numbers. Attach the Packing list (copy 3) of the REV101 Ex1 SALES ORDER to the packing boxes.

1.5 Inspect all shipping documentation, noting any provisions serving to limit the carrier's liability.

Note: whether the freight rate is dependent on the value of the shipment to be transported or whether a value will be imputed if no declaration is made, a value sufficient to cover any potential loss should be declared.

2.0 EXPORT SHIPPING

2.1 Shipments for export outside the country of origin require extra preparation, documentation and handing. Value Added Tax (VAT), duties, or taxes may be required depending on the destination country. Examine REV101 Ex1 SALES ORDER and determine whether the duties and taxes should be collect or prepaid.

It is often times very difficult to determine the exact amount that will be charged for these fees. Therefore, if it is possible, the simplest method is to indicate on the Bill of Lading (or waybill) to have the VAT, duties or taxes collected upon receipt. Alternatively, the Company (shipper) will pay for all fees and then accounting must add these fees to the invoice at a later date when they become known.

The recipient must pay these fees prior to acceptance, or the goods will be returned. Some countries may require that some or all of these fees be paid prior to return. Also, the carrier may require additional transportation fees for the return trip. So it is important to make sure that all international shipping information is accurate prior to shipment.

2.2 Determine the harmonized code for the goods being shipped. The code is used to determine the duty rates for each individual country. Most carriers will require the Schedule B or complete harmonized code number on the airway bill or the commercial invoice.

To obtain a Schedule B/Harmonized System number, visit the U.S. Census web site http://www.census.gov/foreign-trade/schedules/b/index.html#download . Look for the keyword search to produce the Schedule B number. Enter a keyword that describes the goods being shipped. Select the appropriate number and find the Harmonized System number that correctly describes the goods being shipped. For product classification assistance, call the Bureau of the Census Foreign Trade Division at (301) 457- 1084. At the recorded voice prompt, choose the appropriate option for product classification assistance.

2.3 A completed REV105 Ex2 COMMERCIAL INVOICE is required for all International shipments. Make 5 copies of the final document. Attach one copy to the customer packet as a record for the customer files. Insert the original and 4 remaining copies into a plastic pouch attached to the outside of the package.

2.4 Incoterms should be listed on your commercial invoice and in your contract. Every Incoterm has its own unique three-character abbreviation. Every Incoterm must be accompanied by the name of a geographic place or range of places.

2.5 The Company may not physically or electronically export or re-export items or provide services to any party, whether in the United States or abroad, who is listed on the United States government export exclusion lists, including but not limited to the Treasury Department's Specially Designated Nationals List and Commerce Department's Entity and Denied Persons Lists.

Consult with the Bureau of Export Administration's Export Counseling Division and other appropriate U.S. government resources for information on embargoed countries prior to shipment (see 5.1 below for government internet links).

2.5 Shipper's Export Declaration (SED). No Shipper's Export Declaration is required when shipping electronically. The Automated Export System (AES) is the electronic filing of the Shipper's Export Declaration (SED). AES can be used by U.S. Principal Parties in Interest (USPPIs), forwarders, or anyone else responsible for export reporting. For information on the Automated Export Service and other items visit: http://www.aesdirect.gov.

The Shippers Export Declaration (SED or Form 7525-V) is used to compile trade statistics and help in interdicting illegal exports. The SED must be filled out for any shipment valued at $2,500 or above (If the shipment is valued at over $2,500 but is made up of various commodities falling under several Schedule B numbers none of which is valued at $2,500 or higher, no SED is required.) Anytime an ECCN number is required, a SED must be filled out.

Shipments valued at less than $2,500 do not require an SED. However, the exporter must include one of the following statements on the bill of lading, air waybill, or other loading document he/she provides to the carrier: "No SED Required--Section 30.55 (h) FTSR." or, "No SED Required--Valued $2,500 or Less."

If the shipment is valued at over $2,500 but is made up of various commodities falling under several Schedule B numbers none of which is valued at $2,500 or higher, no SED is required. However, the exporter must include the following statement on the bill of lading, air waybill, or other loading document the exporter provides to the carrier: "No SED Required-No Individual Schedule B Number Valued $2,500 or Higher."

For merchandise after importation for repairs or alterations where the value of such repairs is $2,500 or less, no SED is required. However, the exporter must include the following statement on the bill of lading, air waybill, or other loading document: "No SED Required--Value of Repairs $2,500 or Less."

Shipper's Export Declaration (SED) forms may be downloaded from the Internet at: http://www.census.gov/foreign-trade/regulations/forms/index.html. Generally a freight forwarder has the SED forms or can tell the exporter where to get one. Copies of this form may be purchased from the Superintendent of Documents, Government Printing Office, Washington D.C. 20402 or from a local U.S. Customs office. The SED and instructions on how to fill it out are available from the U.S. Census Bureau's home page (http://www.census.gov/foreign-trade/www).

The complete document MUST be printed on standard weight 8 1/2" by 11" paper. All information on the form must be included on the printed copy in the exact location and must be readable. The document should be printed on buff or goldenrod colored paper.

3.0 MANIFEST SYSTEMS

3.1 Most carriers today maintain an automated system on the Internet for producing all required documentation for both domestic and international shipments (see 5.2 below for some of the common shipping carrier internet links). Enter the appropriate information on-line and print the needed documents. Make sure to print an extra copy of the shipping label or a manifest of the shipment for the customer file.

3.2 Attach the printed documents to the package and prepare for pick-up.

4.0 SHIPMENT PICK-UP

4.1 If daily pick-up has been arranged place the package into the designated location for pick-up. If there is no daily pick-up then call the carrier and arrange the pick-up. Note: calls should be placed before 2PM to provide the carrier with enough time to schedule a pick-up.

4.2 Prepare and maintain distribution records for shipments of all products. The REV105 Ex1 SHIPPING LOG should be maintained and must contain the following information:

- Date Shipped
- Recipient Name / Address
- Carrier or Method of Shipment
- Number of Packages Shipped
- Tracking Number

4.3 Forward Copy 1 of the Sales Order along with the customer file to Customer Service and Copy 2 to Accounting/Billing.

5.0 Additional Information Resources

5.1 Government resources:

- Commerce Department Denied Persons List
  http://www.bxa.doc.gov/DPL/Default.shtm
- Commerce Department Denied Entity List
  http://www.bxa.doc.gov/Entities/Default.htm
- Treasury Department Specially Designated Nationals List
  http://www.treas.gov/offices/enforcement/ofac/sdn/index.html
- U.S. Census Bureau foreign trade page
  http://www.census.gov/foreign-trade/www
- U.S. Census Bureau Schedule B/Harmonized System number keyword search
  http://www.census.gov/foreign-trade/schedules/b/index.html#download
- Customs offices http://www.customs.gov/location/service1.htm
- US International Trade Commission http://www.usitc.gov/taffairs.htm)

5.2 Shipping Carriers resource:

- Federal Express - http://www.FedEx.com
- United Parcel Service - http://www.UPS.com
- DHL International - http://www.DHL.com
- United States Postal Service - http://www.USPS.com
- Emory Worldwide - http://www.emeryworld.com
- TNT - http://www.tnt.com
- BAX Global - http://www.baxworld.com
- US Freightways - http://www.usfc.com
- J.B. Hunt - http://www.jbhunt.com

Revision History:

Revision	Date	Description of changes	Requested By
0	11/06/02	Initial Release	

REV105 Ex1 SHIPPING LOG

DATE	RECIPIENT NAME / ADDRESS	CARRIER	PKGS	TRACKING NO.

[This page intentionally left blank]

COMPANY NAME

REV105 Ex2 COMMERCIAL INVOICE

Company Name
Street address
City, State, Zip
Country phone email website etc.

MAY BE OPENED OFFICIALLY
PEUTETRE OUVERT D'OFFICE

INTERNATIONAL AIR WAYBILL NO.	
DATE OF EXPORTATION	EXPORT REFERENCE / INVOICE NO.
SHIPPER NAME AND ADDRESS	CONSIGNEE NAME AND ADDRESS
COUNTRY OF EXPORT	IMPORTER – IF OTHER THAN CONSIGNEE
COUNTRY OF MANUFACTURE	
COUNTRY OF DESTINATION	

MARKS	NO. PKGS	TYPE OF PACKAGING	DESCRIPTION OF GOODS	QTY	WEIGHT	VALUE	TOTAL
	1	Box	Software / Manuals / Equipment Shipping Charges *** US DOLLAR AMOUNTS **		.		000.00

TOTAL NO. OF PKGS. [ ] TOTAL WEIGHT [ ] TOTAL INVOICE VALUE [ ]

THESE COMMODITIES ARE LICENSED FOR THE ULTIMATE DESTINATION SHOWN. DIVERSION CONTRARY TO UNITED STATES LAW IS PROHIBITED. **(CFR: Cost and Freight)**

I DECLARE ALL THE INFORMATION CONTAINED IN THIS INVOICE TO BE TRUE AND CORRECT.

SIGNITURE OF SHIPPER/EXPORTER ______________________ DATE ______________

[This page intentionally left blank]

SOP # ______ Revision:______ **Prepared by:____________**
Effective Date:______________ **Approved by:____________**

Title: **REV106 INVOICING AND ACCOUNTS RECEIVABLE**

Policy: Accounting is responsible for the timely preparation and distribution of invoices to optimize cash flow and customer payments. Accounting will also maintain accurate records over Accounts Receivable and abide by proper internal controls.

Purpose: To explain the methods for the preparation of invoices and accounts receivable records processing.

Scope: This procedure applies to all product sales and services provided by the company.

Procedure:

1.0 SALES ORDER ROUTING AND REVIEW

1.1 Shipping will immediately forward to Billing completed Sales Orders as per procedure REV105 SHIPMENT OF GOODS along with shipping documentation and the customer's Purchase Order. All Sales Orders will be routed on a daily basis to ensure prompt billing. Accounts Receivable will then prepare invoices to be mailed by the next business day.

1.2 The SALES ORDER should already contain all pertinent billing information as part of the company's REV104 SALES ORDER ACCEPTANCE procedure. However, as part of proper internal control, Billing will verify the information contained on the customer's purchase order or company order form with the sales order and completed shipping documentation.

As part of this review process, the propriety and accuracy of contact information, prices, credit terms, transportation charges, extensions and footings will be determined.

2.0 INVOICE PREPARATION AND POSTING

2.1 The next sequentially numbered Invoice (see REV106 Ex1 INVOICE) will be prepared from the information from the Sales Order (see REV101 Ex1 SALES ORDER) and will include the invoice date, date of shipment, description of items shipped with model Nos., quantity, selling price and extended amounts and the customer's shipping and billing addresses.

2.2 Add additional fees as needed. Calculate Sales tax and add to the invoice as per procedure REV107 SALES TAX COLLECTION. Add shipping, handling, and any other final costs to the invoice.

2.3 Any additional fees resulting from the order but received after the order has been billed, such as VAT, duties and Taxes, should be entered onto a new invoice and processed as they are received. Make sure to note on the new invoice the original purchase order number and invoice number from the original order.

2.4 Post the invoice to the Sales Journal and the Accounts Receivable ledger.

Note: In some systems this may occur automatically when the invoice is printed.

3.0 DISTRIBUTION

3.1 A sequentially numbered, four part invoice is utilized by the Company and is distributed as follows:

First and Second Copy:	Mail to the Customer the first two copies. The Second copy is to be returned by the customer along with the payment to assist in properly applying cash receipts.
Third Copy:	File in the Customer File (Customer Service).

3.2 In the event of backorders, the customer should only be charged for items shipped, unless otherwise instructed.

4.0 ACCOUNTS RECEIVABLE

4.1 Accounts Receivable will receive and process payments from customers in accordance with the CASH RECEIPTS procedure.

4.2 On a monthly basis, Accounts Receivable will generate an aged trial balance of customers' accounts with individual invoice information and days outstanding and will forward to Credit for timely collection activities, as per the REV109 ACCOUNT COLLECTIONS procedure.

4.3 Accounts Receivable will generate monthly statements of outstanding customers' accounts and issue them to customers no later than 10 days after each month end.

4.4 Accounts Receivable will issue Credit Memos to customers upon receipt of approved returns in accordance with the REV110 CUSTOMER RETURNS procedure.

4.5 A Write-Off Authorization, see REV106 Ex2 ACCOUNTS RECEIVABLE WRITE-OFF AUTHORIZATION, will be issued for un-collectible accounts as determined by the Credit Manager. Accounts written off will be transferred from the Accounts Receivable ledger to a separate write-off ledger and control account for internal control purposes.

Revision History:

Revision	Date	Description of changes	Requested By
0	11/06/02	Initial Release	

[This page intentionally left blank]

REV106 Ex1 INVOICE

INVOICE NO. ____________

SOLD TO: SHIP TO:

SALESPERSON NUMBER	PURCHASE ORDER NO.	SHIP VIA	DATE SHIPPED	TERMS	INVOICE DATE

QTY ORD	QTY SHIP	QTY B/O	ITEM OR MODEL #	DESCRIPTION	UNIT PRICE	EXTENDED PRICE

COMMENTS		
	SUB TOTAL	
	DEPOSITS/OTHER	
	SALE AMOUNT	
	MISC. CHARGES SALES TAX FREIGHT	
	TOTAL	

[This page intentionally left blank]

REV106 Ex 2 ACCOUNTS RECEIVABLE WRITE-OFF AUTHORIZATION

Customer: Date:

Invoice No's: **Amount of Write-Off**

TOTAL $

JUSTIFICATION

Summary of Collection Actions To Date:
(Include brief description of collection actions taken by accounting, other Company departments and outside collection agency or legal, if applicable)

Approvals:

Credit Manager:______________________________ Date:______________

Controller:___________________________________ Date:______________

[This page intentionally left blank]

SOP # ______ Revision:______ **Prepared by:____________**
Effective Date:______________ **Approved by:____________**

Title: **REV107 SALES TAX COLLECTION**

Policy: The Company is liable for collecting sales tax anytime there is selling or renting of tangible personal property through a retail sale, subject to certain exemptions and conditions, within a jurisdiction in which the Company is deemed to be engaged in business. The Company will at all times comply with all state and local sales tax regulations and requirements.

Purpose: To outline the sales tax rules, rates and exemptions for the collection of sales tax on sales and service by the company.

Scope: This procedure applies to individuals in Sales and Customer Service who are directly responsible for the sale of products.

Responsibilities:

The Sales Representative is responsible for computing and adding sales tax to all sales quotes, or customer order forms.

The Accounting department is responsible for preparing all invoices showing all sales tax amounts collected.

Procedure:

1.0 BASIS OF TAX

The sales tax must be computed on the gross sales price less discounts to customers except for the nontaxable portions mentioned below. Note: Cash or trade discounts (i.e., 2% net 10) cannot be excluded from the tax base.

1.1 Labor Charges for Repairs - Labor charges are not taxable if separately stated on customer billings. Parts and accessories used in repairs are taxable.

1.2 Installation Services - The amount charged the customer for labor or services rendered in installing equipment is not taxable if separately stated in the customers' billings.

1.3 Transportation Charges - If the customer pays for shipping costs directly to a common carrier (e.g. UPS), these costs usually do not have to be included in the tax base. Check with the Sales Tax authority for details.

2.0 APPLICABLE SALES TAX RATES

2.1 State Sales Tax rates are specific to each state. The following briefly illustrates the potential for processing customer sales taxes in different states or with additional taxable authorities.

- State (#1) X.XX %
- State (#2) X.XX %

- County X.XX%
- Municipal X.XX%

2.2 Any applicable sales tax to customers must be separately detailed on customer billings. However, this does not necessarily apply to sales proposals to customers. Further, it is unallowable to directly or indirectly offer discounts or refunds to customers as an offset or in lieu of the customer incurring the sales tax. Any price negotiations can only be on the selling price.

3.0 NONTAXABLE SALES

3.1 Sales tax must be charged to any person, company or concern within our jurisdiction unless they meet one of the following exemptions:

- Sales to other licensed dealers for resale.
- Service Sales (i.e., seminars, training and support contracts). However, equipment maintenance agreements are still taxable.
- Sales to Governmental agencies, and religious, charitable or not-for-profit organizations.

3.2 If a purchase order is submitted by an organization, their tax-exempt status should be indicated on the purchase order; otherwise taxes should be collected. Normally, tax-exempt organizations will provide a disclaimer known as a Sales Tax Exempt Certificate. Examples of this certificate can be found on the Internet on the state government's website for the state the customer does business in.

3.3 Sales Tax Exempt Certificate disclaimers must be kept in the customer's file along with the other sales documentation.

4.0 SALES OUTSIDE OF STATE JURISDICTION

4.1 The Company does not generally collect sales taxes outside its state jurisdiction if it is not deemed to be actively engaged in business in any other area. (i.e., the Company does not have any employees, locations, field sales personnel or delivery trucks operating in any other state).

4.2 The Company is, therefore, exempt from collecting tax on sales outside of its taxing area according to the following restrictions:

- Consummation of the sale must occur outside the state jurisdiction (i.e., out-of-state customers should not sign contracts while in the state).
- Actual delivery of the product(s) must be outside the state jurisdiction by mail or common carrier (i.e., out-of-state customers should not return to their state with company product(s) while they are in company's state for demos, training, etc.).

5.0 SALES TAX BILLING

5.1 The Sales Representative is responsible for computing and adding sales tax (if applicable) to all sales quotes, or customer order forms, prior to submitting the paperwork to sales administration for preparation of a sales order. The Sales Representative is responsible for informing the customer on prepaid or COD orders of the amount of tax so that the proper remittance is paid to the Company.

5.2 The Accounting/Billing Department will prepare all invoices showing all sales tax amounts collected. The Accounting Department will be responsible for remitting and filing all applicable sales tax returns.

Revision History:

Revision	Date	Description of changes	Requested By
0	11/06/02	Initial Release	

[This page intentionally left blank]

Prepared by:_______________ **SOP # _____ Revision:___**
Approved by:_______________ **Effective Date:__________**

Title: **REV108 PROJECT REVENUE: PROGRESS BILLING**

Policy: Progress billings will be made to clients on a timely basis throughout the life of the project. These billings will be accurate and easily understood by both parties involved.

Purpose: The purpose for creating progress billings is to obtain payment for the portion of labor and materials used up to a certain point in time and before the project is fully completed. This improves the cash flow typical of long term projects or assignments.

Scope: This procedure applies to all service agreements or projects provided by the company.

Definitions: Statutory Declarations. A statutory declaration is a sworn statement. For official purposes, it is signed by a person who is legally authorized to administer an oath (i.e. a lawyer, judge, or notary public).

Holdback Requirement. A condition in an agreement where money is withheld or "heldback" until a specific event or milestone occurs.

Responsibilities:

Project Manager is responsible for the confirmation of all final quantities; the Division Administration Manager is responsible for knowing the correct procedures to be followed for each contract.

The Division Administration Manager is responsible for knowing the correct procedures to be followed for each contract.

Procedure:

1.0 CONTRACT TYPES

1.1 Unit price contract. Progress claims for many Unit Price Contracts CTS involve use of "pay quantities" prepared by the supervising Engineer, and it is also common to employ a progress claim format supplied by the Engineer. Timing and preparation of claims of this type are usually dictated by the contract terms. The Project Manager is responsible for the confirmation of all final quantities; the Division Administration Manager is responsible for knowing the correct procedures to be followed for each contract.

1.2 Cost Plus Contracts. Cost Plus contracts often require that satisfactory evidence of payment for labor, materials and service accompany each progress claim. The terms of the contract will dictate the timing and documentation necessary in support of the progress claim. The Division Administration Manager will be responsible for knowing the correct procedures to be followed for each contract.

2.0 BREAKDOWN OF CONTRACT AMOUNT

2.1 The Project Manager is responsible for preparing the breakdown of contract amount and for obtaining its approval. The breakdown of contract amount by the cost of each major work item provides the basis for progress claims during the life of the project. The form of the breakdown will vary with different types of contracts. Normally, the contractual agreement will specify the procedures for payment and may also specify the form of the breakdown of contract amount that is required. Care should be taken to be sure that the front-end items, such as bond and insurance premiums or move-in and set-up costs are properly reflected in initial billings.

2.2 The breakdown of contract amount may need to be prepared on a special form or document specified in the contract documents. It will normally show the costs of the major work items by specification division. It should be prepared so that it is readily understood, in order to obtain an early approval by all parties, and to preclude disagreement in subsequent applications for progress payment.

2.3 The breakdown of contract amount, listing the major work items, forms the basis for the Progress Claims. The information normally furnished is as follows:

- item number
- description
- dollar value
- percent completed to date
- dollar amount previously claimed
- dollar amount this request

2.4 The standard procedure for preparation of a breakdown of contract amount is as follows:

- Secure each subcontractor's progress claims, including a listing and value of all stored materials and all change orders. Also, each subcontractor should submit a properly executed Statutory Declaration with each payment request. Subcontractors should have previously been advised when this information is due and the general format to follow.
- Determine the percent and value of work completed to date for each progress claim item, including change orders.
- Determine the value of all stored materials.
- Determine the total value of work completed (including stored materials if appropriate).
- Determine the holdback and deduct from accumulated total.
- Compute the monthly amount due by deducting previous payments.

- Appropriate correspondence should be directed to the individual specified to receive the progress claim, usually the Architect and Engineer.

3.0 PROGRESS CLAIMS

3.1 The Project Manager is responsible for preparing the draft progress claim and obtaining approval from the customer. The Division Administration Manager is responsible for having the progress claim typed and checked, for supplying supporting Statutory Declarations (where required) and for expediting payment of the progress claim.

3.2 The contract documents should be studied to determine the procedure and requirements for preparing and processing the progress claim. Some important items to be reviewed are holdback requirements and payment for stored materials. Payments for stored items can be held up or paid depending on where the materials are stored. The provisions in the contract for payment of stored materials should be reviewed carefully, because this is such a large cost.

3.3 To ensure accuracy in billing, the Project Manager should verify that each subcontractor's request is correct. A detailed breakdown is required from each subcontractor. The Project Manager must check the reasonableness of the entire progress claim, including the subcontractor's portion before submitting it for administration.

4.0 RELEASE OF HOLDBACK

4.1 Progress claims for release of holdback moneys must be timely and accurately reflect the contract amount, retention for deficiencies, if any, and be supported where possible by the supervising Engineer's certificate of substantial completion and performance.

4.2 Care must be taken to ensure that the date of the Engineer's certification of substantial completion performance is properly reflected. Review the contract status with the Division Administration Manager prior to requesting the certificate of substantial completion and performance.

Revision History:

Revision	Date	Description of changes	Requested By
0	11/06/02	Initial Release	

SOP # ______ Revision:______
Effective Date:______________

Prepared by:____________
Approved by:____________

Title: **REV109 ACCOUNT COLLECTIONS**

Policy: All open accounts receivable with late or delinquent payment activity will be handled in a timely and effective manner to ensure maximum collections and an optimum accounts receivable turnover ratio.

Purpose: To provide the actions and methods for processing late or delinquent payments.

Scope: This procedure applies to the Credit Department involved with collection of past due accounts receivable. The Sales and/or Shipping Departments may be involved in reference to shipping holds or special credit arrangements.

Responsibilities:

The Credit Department reviews all records for a customer to determine a possible explanation for non-payment prior to commencing the collection process.

Definition: Bad Debt consists of unpaid accounts receivable invoices that are considered to be uncollectible.

Debt collector is any person who regularly collects debts owed to others. This includes attorneys who collect debts on a regular basis.

Procedure:

1.0 COLLECTION PROCESS

1.1 No matter how careful customers are screened prior to credit approval, slow pay or delinquent accounts will occur from time to time. Once an account becomes past due by even a few days, the collection process should commence immediately. Studies have shown that the sooner the collection process starts then the more likely that the debt will be collected.

1.2 Prior to commencing the collection process, the following should be reviewed by the assigned Credit Department Representative:

- Verify that after the sale the Invoice was immediately sent out, along with a copy of the Purchase Order, to the correct billing address. Sometime Purchase Orders will be sent by one contact, for delivery to a second contact, with bills to be sent for payment to originate from a third contact. Therefore, make sure the billing contact noted on the Purchase Order correctly receives a copy of the invoice along with a copy of the Purchase Order. This is frequently the cause for the delay of payment for many Invoices.
- Make certain that the Company has not received the customer's payment or applied it to the wrong account. Verify that a Returned Goods Authorization

has not been issued. These seem obvious, but it can avoid an uncomfortable situation in wrongly accusing the customer of delinquent payments.

- Verify with the Customer Service Department that the customer has received the product(s) and that they are satisfied.
- Review the customer's past payment activity. Determine if they are chronically late and what their response has been to any other overdue notices to determine payment patterns or trends.

1.3 Upon review of the above, the Credit Department Representative should then proceed with the collection process by completing an REV109 Ex1 ACCOUNT COLLECTION CONTROL Form. This form will assist in planning and tracking the collection effort. Depending on the amount and the customer situation, the representative can choose to follow-up with collection letters, telephone calls or both.

Record all actions taken (late payment notice, telephone call, etc.) with a date on an ACCOUNT COLLECTION CONTROL Form filed in the customer folder. All customer agreements and explanations should be noted. If payment has not reached the Company by the expected date, immediate follow-up action should be taken with another collection call or letter. The longer an overdue account is ignored, the longer the customer will ignore it, too.

1.4 Telephone communication will often speed up the collection process. Credit representatives, when speaking with a delinquent account, should observe a few tips or principles.

- Identify yourself and the Company and state the reason for calling. Be direct and use a controlled, confident voice. Concentrate on listening to the customer and don't rush through the call.
- Get the Facts - The most powerful tool is knowledge. During the phone conversation, try to gain as much insight into the situation as possible. Remember, the goals and objectives are to:
  - ❑ Collect the money!
  - ❑ Identify reasons for non-payment
  - ❑ Settle on an agreement for clearing the debt, including special payment plans and exact dates when a check will be sent.
- Never argue, accuse or be condescending - Verbally fighting or talking down to the customer will only serve to produce negative feelings and may hamper the collection effort. The ultimate purpose is to secure payment, and this is best accomplished without becoming defensive or irritated.
- There are several common objections, complaints and excuses used to elude payment. Study the following examples to learn the most effective responses to the most frequently used ploys.

"I didn't get the invoice." - Respond by verifying the debtor's name and address, and then review the account information with them.

"The check is in the mail." - Extend your thanks, then ask for a check number, amount, date posted and address to which it was mailed.

"Your payment is being processed." - Ask when the payment will be ready for the mail. Determine the process that the payment undergoes after it leaves your contact's desk.

"I need proof of delivery." - Give the customer the name of the person who signed the delivery slip.

"The computer is down." - When do you expect it to be up? Can we get a manual payment?

"I'll pay you when we get paid." - Respond calmly, but make a direct request for payment, such as When can I expect payment?"

"I have no money" - Create a payment plan. Be flexible and consider alternatives offered by the customer. Work toward making the plan acceptable to both of you.

1.5 Many people find it difficult to confront customers regarding delinquent payments. Just keep in mind that it is the customer, who should feel uncomfortable in this situation.

1.6 If customers stop paying, their phone has been disconnected, and you cannot find them, consider using these resources to locate these debtors and their assets:

- City directories
- Post office (for a forwarding address)
- A customer's employer
- Department of motor vehicle license and registration records
- "In case of emergency" contact, references or closest relatives listed on a credit application
- Old files and correspondence
- The Internet (i.e. http://www.isleuth.com/peop.html)
- Skip-tracing services or private investigator
- Credit bureau reports
- Neighbors
- Directory assistance

2.0 SERIOUSLY DELINQUENT OR UNRESPONSIVE ACCOUNTS

2.1 When an account becomes more than 60 days past due, the immediate target of securing prompt payment should take on a greater sense of urgency. The Credit Manager should review the account with sales to determine if the customer's business is valued.

If their business is valued, the following strategies may be used to collect payment:

- Restrict any further credit until the past due amount is paid in full.
- Withhold delivery of products or services already ordered. The harsh reality of having inventory/supplies curtailed often can spur a delinquent account into action.
- Invoke a "COD-plus" system. Deliver merchandise on a COD basis with an additional amount added to the cost of the order to cover past unpaid balances

2.2 If all other avenues for collection of the account have been exhausted, the Credit Manager should determine and authorize the use of an outside collection agency.

2.3 All uncollectible accounts will be reviewed by the Credit Manager for disposition. Reference procedure REV106 INVOICING AND ACCOUNTS RECEIVABLE.

3.0 WORKING WITH COLLECTION AGENCIES

3.1 Collect all material records for the debt in question and send them to the collection agency. The agency will require a copy of the invoice, credit application (if available), proof of delivery, and/or any other correspondence that may help them collect the debt.

3.2 Record the date the debt was sent to collections in the accounts receivable file.

3.3 If payments are received after the debt has been sent to collections, then notify the collection agency immediately in order to stop any further collection efforts. The agency will take their fee for any debt that has been collected once it has been registered by the agency.

3.4 If all other avenues for collection of the account have been exhausted, the owner and/or store manager should consider further legal action.

4.0 WRITING OFF UNCOLLECTED DEBT

4.1 Write-off any debts remaining uncollected or that are returned from the collection agency and record as a bad debt expense and deduct from accounts receivable.

4.2 If any payments are received after being written-off from accounts receivable, then receive them in as income and recovery of bad debt.

4.3 If bad debt is a recurring problem then consider setting up a reserve account or allowance for bad debt at the beginning of the year. Also, look into tightening up the credit process and restrict credit granted to customers as outlined in REV103 CUSTOMER CREDIT APPROVAL AND TERMS.

References:

A. FAIR DEBT COLLECTION PRACTICES ACT (FDCP)

The FDCP requires that debt collectors treat consumers fairly and prohibits certain methods of debt collection. Personal, family, and household debts are covered under the Act. This includes money owed for the purchase of an automobile, for medical care, or for charge accounts. Business debt is not included.

Debt collectors may not 1) harass, oppress, or abuse the debtor or any third parties they contact. 2) Use any false or misleading statements when collecting a debt. For example, debt collectors may not:

- Use threats of violence or harm;
- Publish a list of consumers who refuse to pay their debts (except to a credit bureau);
- Use obscene or profane language; or
- Repeatedly use the telephone to annoy someone.
- Falsely imply that they are attorneys or government representatives;
- Falsely imply that the debtor may have committed a crime;
- Falsely represent that they operate or work for a credit bureau;
- Misrepresent the amount of the debtor's debt;
- Indicate that papers being sent to the debtor are legal forms when they are not
- Indicate that papers being sent to the debtor are not legal forms when they are.
- Give false credit information about the debtor to anyone, including a credit bureau;
- Send the debtor anything that looks like an official document from a court or government agency when it is not.
- Use a false name.
- Collect any amount greater than the debtor's debt, unless the debtor's state law permits such a charge;
- Deposit a post-dated check prematurely;
- Use deception to make the debtor accept collect calls or pay for telegrams;
- Take or threaten to take the debtor's property unless this can be done legally.
- Contact the debtor by postcard.
- Say the debtor will be arrested if they do not pay the debt;

- Say they will seize, garnish, attach, or sell the debtor's property or wages, unless the collection agency or creditor intends to do so, and it is legal to do so.
- Say they will take actions, such as a lawsuit against the debtor, when such action legally may not be taken, or when they do not intend to take such action.

Revision History:

Revision	Date	Description of changes	Requested By
0	11/06/02	Initial Release	

REV109 Ex1 ACCOUNT COLLECTION CONTROL FORM

Account Name:______________________________

Address:______________________________

____

____

Contact(s):______________________________

Telephone #'s:____________________________

____

Payment Terms:____________________________

Comments:_______________________________

____

____

Invoice	Date Due	Amount	Date Paid	Running Total Due

Date	Customer Reply or Action Taken

[This page intentionally left blank]

SOP # ______ Revision:______ **Prepared by:____________**
Effective Date:______________ **Approved by:____________**

Title: **REV110 CUSTOMER RETURNS**

Policy: All sales of products returned must be in accordance with the following return procedures in order to provide adequate control of inventory and timely refunds to customers,

Purpose: The procedure outlines the steps and documents to be used for customers returning goods. In order to provide adequate control of inventory and timely refunds to customers, all products returned for any reason must be in accordance with the following return procedures.

Scope: All products and service parts sold by the company. Affects the following departments: Sales, Customer Service, Inventory Control, Quality Assurance, and Accounting.

Responsibilities:

Sales, Customer Service or Service Departments will prepare a Returned Goods Authorization and resolve damages and discrepancies.

Credit Manager approves refunds requested after a 30 day period.

Accounting prepares the customer refund for returned goods.

Procedures:

1.0 ORIGINATION

1.1 Customer Service should process returns per the company's return policy (see REV110 Ex1 30 DAY SATISFACTION GUARANTEE). Any return under the company's 30-day money back guarantee program will be refunded in full to the customer. Any returns after 30 days are not allowed without sufficient justification. These returns are subject to a 15% restocking charge and cannot be returned for credit without the additional approval of the Credit Manager.

1.2 Upon notification by the customer of the intent to return goods, the Sales or Service Department will prepare a Returned Goods Authorization (RGA) reference REV110 Ex2 RETURNED GOODS AUTHORIZATION form, and provide the RGA Number to the customer to identify the product upon return.

1.3 If the RGA is for defective product, a Customer Complaint Survey should also be completed (see ***ABR44 Bizmanualz™ Sales and Marketing Policies, Procedures and Forms***) as per the Customer Complaint Process.

2.0 RECEIVING GOODS AND PROCESSING

2.1 The RGA will be used as a receiving report for the return. All items received should be inspected, counted and recorded on this report. See procedure PUR104 RECEIVING AND INSPECTION The individual responsible for receiving the items will sign and date the report. Any damage and discrepancies are to be noted on this report and resolved by Customer Service.

2.2 If any goods are returned by the customer without a proper RGA or other notification, the goods should not be restocked but should be held in receiving until either Sales or Customer Service completes a RGA or otherwise informs Receiving of the appropriate disposition.

3.0 RETURNED GOODS DISPOSITION

3.1 Sales/Service Department Manager should inspect and approve RGA returns from receiving.

3.2 If the RGA is complete and satisfies the Company Return Policy then forward the RGA to Accounting for return processing.

3.3 Customer Service should resolve any further discrepancies. If the returned goods do not comply with the company's refund policy then notify the Customer of the discrepancy.

3.4 Notify Quality Control to inspect returns before disposal. (See ABR211 ***Bizmanualz™ ISO9000 QMS Policies, Procedures and Forms***) for a complete discussion of the quality process.) For Invalid Returns, Customer Service resolves disposition with the customer including the possibility of a return to the customer.

Revision History:

Revision	Date	Description of changes	Requested By
0	11/06/02	Initial Release	

REV110 Ex1 30 DAY SATISFACTION GUARANTEE

All of the Company's products are covered by a 30-day Money Back Guarantee. When we say "Satisfaction Guaranteed", we mean just that! Every product that you purchase from the Company must meet your expectations. If you're not satisfied that it's practical, reliable, and authoritative and that it's an essential resource for increasing the productivity of your organization, then return it to us within 30 days, postage prepaid, along with a copy of your invoice. You'll owe nothing. No strings attached. If you've prepaid, you'll receive a prompt refund of your money.

Our 30-day return policy is offered to all customers and we are happy to offer that. All that we ask is that you return the product within 30 days of receipt. However, beyond 30 days, and/or if the product purchased is damaged, we cannot accept the return.

For a return or replacement of your product please contact our customer service department or send an e-mail for a Return Authorization number (RA). Please return the product in original condition, shipping prepaid, and include all packaging, documentation and, if applicable, its' blank warranty card, and you are entitled to a refund of the original purchase price of the item, excluding shipping and handling charges.

How To Receive An RA Number

For a return or replacement of your product please contact our customer service department at [PHONE NUMBER] or send an e-mail to [E-MAIL] for a Return Authorization number (RA). Please provide the following information to customer service in order to receive a Return Authorization, (RA) number.

1. Order conformation number, or customer PO number from the packing slip.
2. The name of the product for return.
3. Customer name.
4. Reason for return (defective, DOA, non-defective)
5. Note: refund or a replacement?
6. Customer e-mail address.

Return Authorization Policy

1. Any defective products must be returned within 30 days of invoice date.
2. Remember to include your packing slip or invoice from the original order so we know who the return is from.
3. Return the product with shipping prepaid. Shipping and insurance charges are not refundable
4. All items must be in "as-new" condition, in original packaging, and with all warranty cards, manuals and accessories. Any discrepancies could result in a delay or partial forfeiture of your refund.
5. The RA is valid for 30 days from date of issuance. The RA number must appear on your return packing label on the outside of the box. Returns will not be accepted without an RA.
6. Returns must be sent via UPS, Federal Express, DHL or any courier that issues a tracking number.
7. Please allow 2-4 weeks for the credit.

Please contact customer service before you make a return. No returns will be accepted without an accompanying Return Authorization (RA) number and a copy of the original invoice.

[This page intentionally left blank]

REV110 Ex2 RETURNED GOODS AUTHORIZATION

Step 1: CUSTOMER SERVICE

Date:______________________ RGA Number:______________________

Customer: ______________________ Reason for Return:______________________

Address: ____

____

____

Contact: ______________________ Telephone: ______________________

Step 2: RECEIVING AND INSPECTION

Part / Model #	Description	Qty. Returned	Qty. Returned	Inspected Pass/Fail

Comments:____

____

____

Received by:______________________ Date:______________

Step 3: APPROVALS

Sales/Service Manager	Date	Credit Manager	Date

Step 4: ACCOUNTING

Credit Memo to be issued: ❒ Yes ❒ No $____________

Amount to be refunded to Customer $____________

Remarks:____

____

[This page intentionally left blank]

Accounting Policies, Procedures & Forms

Section 440

Purchasing Procedures

Section 440

Purchasing

Procedures:

PUR101 Vendor Selection
PUR102 Purchasing General
PUR103 Purchasing Project
PUR104 Receiving and Inspection
PUR105 Shipping and Freight Claims
PUR106 Accounts Payable and Cash Disbursement

SOP # ______ Revision:______ **Prepared by:____________**
Effective Date:______________ **Approved by:____________**

Title: **PUR101 VENDOR SELECTION**

Policy: To ensure the performance capabilities of all vendors and maintain the internal controls of the purchasing functions, appropriate vendor selection and inspection procedures will be followed.

Purpose: To provide the methods for determining, documenting and, when applicable, inspecting vendors for compliance with company policies and contract purchasing requirements.

Purchased products and services should conform to specified requirements. This starts with selection of appropriate suppliers that have the capability and systems to supply products, materials and services to satisfy Company requirements. Suppliers are controlled to the extent necessary based on the effect of the purchased items on the quality of the Company's products and services.

Scope: This procedure applies to all vendors of products, materials, and services that directly affect the quality of the Company's products and services.

Responsibilities:

Purchasing is responsible for initial supplier identification and for collection of business information related to the potential supplier. Purchasing is also responsible for maintaining supplier performance data for ongoing suppler evaluation.

Finance is responsible for evaluation of the potential supplier's financial information.

Quality Assurance is responsible for evaluating the supplier's quality systems as appropriate and for reporting supplier quality performance on a continuous basis.

Procedure:

1.0 VENDOR SELECTION

1.1 New vendors are to be evaluated using the following criteria:

- Pricing: competitive pricing is one component of the evaluation and may be out weighed by other factors. Pricing alone will not be a deciding factor unless all else is equal.
- Parts availability and shipping time frame.
- Performance capability (i.e., financial status, sufficient facilities, capability of equipment and employees).
- Internal Quality Assurance program: Companies certified to ISO 9001 or equivalent are given preference.

- Reference checks.

1.2 Ongoing evaluation of suppliers:

- On-Time Delivery, 100% on time expected (0 days early, 0 days late)
- Quality: (Items (or lots) rejected/Total items (or lots) received) X 100. Ratings less than 95% require corrective action. Exceptions to the 95% Corrective Action requirement may be given where the total quantity of items or lots received is small and at the Quality Manger's discretion.

1.3 Qualified vendors will be maintained on an Approved Vendor List for purchasing.

1.4 Complete PUR101 Ex1 NEW VENDOR NOTIFICATION form for approval of all first time purchases from a vendor. Make sure to document any related party transactions or vendors the Company or employees could have a potential conflict of interest with on this form.

1.5 Disqualification: Suppliers not responsive to Corrective Action Requests or unable to correct problems with delivery or quality may be disqualified. Disqualification is generally a consensus decision between the Quality Assurance Manager and the Operations Manager.

2.0 VENDOR INSPECTIONS

2,1 For critical components or for inventory purchases that the Company desires to rely on the quality assurance of the vendor to reduce receiving inspection or testing requirements, an on-sight vendor inspection must be performed and approved.

2.2 The Director of Quality Assurance will coordinate with Purchasing to plan, arrange and designate staff for all vendor inspections. Complete PUR101 Ex2 VENDOR SURVEY form and note applicable approval or disapproval of the vendor's performance capability and quality assurance program.

3.0 VENDOR FILES

3.1 A vendor file will be prepared and maintained for all vendors on the Approved Vendor List, which will be used for significant or on-going purchasing. The vendor files will be kept alphabetically and should include the following:

- PUR101 Ex1 NEW VENDOR NOTIFICATION form
- PUR101 Ex2 VENDOR SURVEY form
- Completed REV103 Ex1 CREDIT APPLICATION form
- IRS W-9 Taxpayer Identification Certificate (a PDF download is available at: http://www.irs.gov/pub/irs-pdf/fw9.pdf)
- Resale certificates (only required for those that resell their purchases)
- Legal contracts, dealer or marketing agreements, etc.

- Long-term blanket purchase order commitments
- Any other relevant correspondence or documentation

3.2 Form 1099 must be filed at year-end for the proper reporting of income to certain vendors. To determine whether or not one needs to be filed, all non-merchandise vendors should complete an IRS W-9 Request for Taxpayer Identification Number Certificate. A copy can be obtained via the IRS website (www.IRS.gov) or by contacting the local IRS office. The vendor indicates on the form the reporting status. Note: Incorporated vendors do not receive 1099s.

This applies to all contractors for service (repair person, accountant, consultant, etc) who are NOT incorporated, and to all lawyers, regardless of incorporation. It is important to make this determination before engaging the contractor so that all payments can be properly tracked for 1099 reporting purposes at the inception.

Revision History:

Revision	Date	Description of changes	Requested By
0	11/06/02	Initial Release	

[This page intentionally left blank]

PUR101 Ex1 NEW VENDOR NOTIFICATION

Date:______________________________

Anticipated Usage:
- ☐ One Time Only__________
- ☐ Intermittent__________
- ☐ Ongoing__________

Prepared by (source):______________________________

Contact Information:

Vendor Name:______________________________

Address:______________________________

Phone :(   )______________________ Fax:(   )______________________

Contact Person:______________________________

Products to be provided:______________________________

____

____

____

____

____

____

Payment Terms:______________________________

Estimated Annual Dollar Volume Expected with this Vendor:______________________

Has the Vendor completed an IRS W-9 Request for Taxpayer Identification Number Certificate and is it on file with the company? ☐ Yes ☐ No

Related Party Transactions:

Is the Vendor a relative or close friend of any employee of the company?
☐ No ☐ Yes

If yes, please describe relationship: ______________________________

____

____

____

____

Distribution: Purchasing (Vendor File), Accounts Payable

[This page intentionally left blank]

PUR101 Ex2 VENDOR SURVEY FORM

Date:____________________

Vendor Name: ____

Address: ____

____

____

Phone : (_______)_______ Fax: (_______)____________________

NOTICE: I (We) certify that the information contained in the attached survey form is accurate and complete as of the date indicated. Where trade secret or other proprietary information is involved, the person interviewed has initialed those responses not verified by the interviewer. All information obtained will be kept confidential. A corporate officer of the Company surveyed will review all responses made at the time of survey. This survey has been made with the permission of the Company surveyed

Signature	Title	Location
Signature	Title	Location

PART I - GENERAL INFORMATION

Annual Sales:	Years in Business:	Privately Owned:	Subsidiary Division:

Other Plant Locations

____

____

Major Customers ____________________ Type of Contract ____________________

____________________ ____________________

____________________ ____________________

____________________ ____________________

☐ Not Available ☐ Not Available

List Company Management

Name	Title	Interviewed

Product for which survey was performed (**Attach Labeling**):____________________

____

Total Employees__________Number of Supervisors__________Number of Production__________

Work Schedule Hours__________Number Shifts__________Days Per Week__________

Are Training Programs for Personnel Utilized ☐ Yes ☐ No

FACILITY

Buildings On Site____________________

Type:

- ☐ Single ☐ Multistory ☐ Wood
- ☐ Brick ☐ Block ☐ Steel

Location In:

- ☐ Industrial Park ☐ Suburban
- ☐ Urban ☐ Rural
- ☐ Eq. Owned ☐ Leased

Square Footage In:

Manufacturing____________________

Administration____________________

Storage____________________

Engineering/R&D____________________

List Process Capabilities And Special Manufacturing Equipment Essential To Materials Being Procured.

1)____________________

2)____________________

3)____________________

4)____________________

5)____________________

Is There A Document/Process Flow Manual Outlining All Manufacturing Step, Records, And Controls From Raw Materials To Finished Product? (As Required For Some Government Contracts.)

☐ Yes ☐ No

Does The Manufacturer Have Liability Insurance?

☐ Yes ☐ No

Insured By____________________

List Manufacturing Done By Outside Sources (Subassembly, Packaging, Kit Assembly, Etc.)

1)____________________

2)____________________

3)____________________

4)____________________

5)____________________

Has The Manufacturer Been Inspected By Any State Or Federal Agencies Within The Last Two Years?

☐ Yes ☐ No

Name Of Agencies:____________________

Were Recalls Involved?

☐ Yes ☐ No

Comments____________________

____

PART II - RAW MATERIALS

PURCHASING

Is Qualification Based On Written Specifications And Approval Of Vendor Sources?

☐ Yes ☐ No

Are Reject/Accept Limits Shown?

☐ Yes ☐ No

Is Approval Based On:

- ☐ Quality History ☐ Supplier ☐ On-Site
- ☐ Own QC ☐ Cards ☐ Survey
- ☐ Certificate ☐ Testing
- ☐ Other____________________

Are Specification Changes Reviewed And Signed Off By QC Personnel?

☐ Yes ☐ No

TESTING

Are Written Test Procedures In Use?

☐ Yes ☐ No

Are Test Results On File?

☐ Yes ☐ No

Is a Sampling Plan Used?

- ☐ 100% ☐ Mil Spec ☐ AQL ☐ Random
- ☐ Other____________________

Do Test Results Indicate

- ☐ Quantity Sampled
- ☐ Method Of Analysis
- ☐ Date/Signature Of Analyst
- ☐ Sample Traceability

Is There A Retention Sample System For Raw Materials/Components?

☐ Yes ☐ No

IN PLANT CONTROL

Is Material Assigned Alpha-Numeric Or Identifying Mark For Each Incoming Lot?

☐ Yes ☐ No

Is Material Visibly Marked As

- ☐ Sampled ☐ Approved
- ☐ Rejected ☐ Not Marked

Is an Inventory Log Or Record Kept?

☐ Yes ☐ No

Is Storage Area Separate?

☐ Yes ☐ No

Is Storage Area Segregated?

☐ Yes ☐ No

Is a Stock Rotation (FIFO) System Used?

☐ Yes ☐ No

Is There Authorized Custodian Control?

☐ Yes ☐ No

Is General Housekeeping Neat And Orderly?

☐ Yes ☐ No

Rejected Materials Are:

Clearly Identified ☐ Yes ☐ No

Physically Segregated ☐ Yes ☐ No

PART III - MANUFACTURING

MASTER PRODUCTION RECORDS

Is There A Single Controlled File Of Master Records For Each Product?

☐ Yes ☐ No

Are These Master Records Signed And Dated?

☐ Yes ☐ No

Double Signature ☐ Yes ☐ No

Revision Dates ☐ Yes ☐ No

Are The Process, Assembly, Or Manufacturing Steps Fully Described:

In The Master Production Record?

☐ Yes ☐ No

In A Separate Document Or Record?

☐ Yes ☐ No

Does The Master Document Indicate:

QC Points For In-Process Manufacturing?

☐ Yes ☐ No

Type Of Test Or Inspection To Be Made?

☐ Yes ☐ No

Method Of Measurement?

☐ Yes ☐ No

Who Performs Test Or Inspection?

☐ Yes ☐ No

Level Of Accept/Reject (Limits)?

☐ Yes ☐ No

For Manufacturing, Processing, Subassembly, Or Packaging Done By Outside Sources, Are There:

Master Production Records?

☐ Yes ☐ No

QC Specifications And Methods Records?

☐ Yes ☐ No

Outside Sources Not Used?

☐ Yes ☐ No

PRODUCTION AREA

Is The Work Flow Organized?

☐ Yes ☐ No

Distinct Staging Area For Raw Materials Or Components Used In Manufacturing?

☐ Yes ☐ No

Production Or Assembly Lines Segregated?

☐ Yes ☐ No

Are General Housekeeping And Environmental Factors Adequate?

☐ Yes ☐ No

Are Written Procedures For Plant Sanitation Available?

☐ Yes ☐ No

PRODUCTION EQUIPMENT

Are Maintenance Or Service Records Available?

☐ Yes ☐ No

Are Calibration Records Kept On Periodic Basis?

☐ Yes ☐ No

Are There Means Of Readily Identifying Type, And Stage Of Processing Being Done, On The Equipment?

☐ Yes ☐ No

PRODUCTION RECORDS

Are Production Documents Collected And Filed?

☐ Yes ☐ No

Production Documents Kept ______(Years)

☐ Complete History

☐ Labeling Samples Included

☐ Partial History

☐ Traceability By Lot Or Serial#

PACKAGING

Are Finished Goods Packaging Operations Segregated?

☐ Yes ☐ No

Finished Goods Under Supervised Control?

☐ Yes ☐ No

Label Records Kept?

☐ Yes ☐ No

Pre-Label:

☐Count ☐ Reconciliation

Are Finished Goods Properly Identified, Labeled, And Stored?

☐ Yes ☐ No

☐ Prior To Release ☐ After Release

REJECTED MATERIALS

Are There Written Procedures For Disposing Of Or Reworking Rejected Items?

☐ Yes ☐ No

Are Rejected Products Held In Quarantine Pending Final Disposal?

☐ Yes ☐ No

☐ Held In Segregated Area

☐ With Special Markings

RETENTION SAMPLES

Are Samples Of Finished Goods Retained?

☐ Yes ☐ No

☐ From Each Production Run

☐ In A Separate Controlled Area

☐ In The Same Container/Closure System In Which They Are Sold

☐ In Containers Different From Unit As Sold

☐ Kept For A Period Of ______(Years)

☐ Written Log Or File

STERILE COMPONENTS (If Applicable)

Are There Procedures For Establishing And Maintaining Aseptic Conditions?

☐ Yes ☐ No

Are There Methods For Routine Auditing Of Sterile Areas Used?

☐ Yes ☐ No

Are There Procedures For Working In Sterile Areas?

☐ Yes ☐ No

For Cleaning And Sterilization Of Equipment?

☐ Yes ☐ No

For Bulk And Final Product Sterility Testing?

☐ Yes ☐ No

Is Process Sterility For Each Run Documented In The Production Records?

☐ Yes ☐ No

Are Sterile Processes Used?

☐ Radiation ☐ Steam ☐ ETO

☐ Filtration ☐ Chemical

Other:______________________________

____

____

____

____

____

____

____

PART IV - QUALITY CONTROL / ASSURANCE

ORGANIZATION AND FUNCTION

Does The Quality Control-Inspection Group Report Directly To The Top, Independent Of Production, Marketing, Or Other Organization Groups Within The Manufacturing Company?

☐ Yes ☐ No

Does The Quality Control-Inspection Group Have Full Authority To Withhold Shipment Or Further Production Of Rejected Items?

☐ Yes ☐ No

Are The Quality Control Procedures:

Revised On A Periodic Basis?

☐ Yes ☐ No

Does The Quality Control/Assurance-Inspection Group Have:

Education, Training Or Experience

☐ Yes ☐ No

Understanding Of Their Function

☐ Yes ☐ No

OPERATIONS

Are Stamps, Tags, Markers, Etc. Used To Verify Inspection Activity?

☐ Yes ☐ No

Are The Markings Used Traceable To An Individual Inspector?

☐ Yes ☐ No

PART V - CUSTOMER COMPLAINTS AND RECALL CAPABILITIES

Is There An Organized Complaint File System?

☐ Yes ☐ No

Does Each Complaint State:

☐ Nature Of Complaint

☐ Response To Customer (Repair, Refund, Replace)

☐ Further Corrective/Preventive Action By Manufacturer

Complaint Files Kept For __________ (Years)

Is There A Periodic Review Of Complaint Files For Trends? ☐ Yes ☐ No

Is The Review File As A Written Summary?

☐ Yes ☐ No

Is There A Group Or Individual Assigned To Handle Customer Inquiries And Follow Up On Complaints?

☐ Yes ☐ No

Are Product Defects Verified By Manufacturer Through Testing?

☐ Yes ☐ No]

Was Review Of Complaint Files For Survey Product Made?

☐ Yes ☐ No

Are Production Samples For QC Testing:

Adequately Identified As To Source

☐ Yes ☐ No

Recorded Somewhere At Time Of Sampling

☐ Yes ☐ No

Entered On Filed Test Report

☐ Yes ☐ No

Written Sampling Plan Based On:

☐ 100% ☐ Mil. Spec ☐ AQL ☐ Random

Other_______________

Is The Product Used Tested Prior To Final Release?

☐ Yes ☐ No

Are Outside Sources Used For Production Testing?

☐ Yes ☐ No

☐ Under Formal Contract

☐ Used Test Protocols

☐ Written Procedures

☐ Copies In The Manufacturing File

☐ Facility Registered Or Licensed By Any Federal, State Or Professional Agency

☐ Outside Test Results Filed By Manufacturer

Is There A Formal Quality Assurance Program Involving Performance Testing Of The Product(S) After Release?

☐ Yes ☐ No

RECALL CAPABILITIES

Is There A Company Recall Plan?

☐ Yes ☐ No

☐ Shows How Decisions Are Made And By Whom

☐ How Recall Will Be Accomplished

☐ Instructions For Recovery And Accountability Of Recalled Product

Do Shipping Or Distribution Records On File Show:

Customer/Distributor Name And Address?

☐ Yes ☐ No

Date Of Shipments And Quantity Shipped?

☐ Yes ☐ No

Lot Or Serial Number Of Product Shipped

☐ Yes ☐ No

Distribution Records Are Maintained ______ (Years)

Distribution Records Are Stored As:

☐ Computer Listing

☐ Microfilm/Microfiche

☐ Manual Card/Paper Files

PART VI - REGULATORY COMPLIANCE

☐ Yes ☐ No

Are The Survey Product(S) Listed With Bureau Of Medical Devices?

☐ Yes ☐ No

Are All Necessary Approvals For Marketing Products Available?

☐ Yes ☐ No

Is There A File With Past And Current Labeling For Each Survey Product?

☐ Yes ☐ No

Is There A Formal Auditing Program Of The QC Operation. If So, Done By Whom

☐ Yes ☐ No

List Of Attachments And Comments

____

____

____

____

____

____

____

____

____

____

____

____

____

____

____

____

[This page intentionally left blank]

SOP # ______ Revision:______ **Prepared by:____________**

Effective Date:______________ **Approved by:____________**

Title: **PUR102 GENERAL PURCHASING**

Policy: The investment in physical inventory, supplies and capital equipment will be facilitated through the Purchasing Department, maintained at the lowest effective level and supervised consistent with a common set of procedures and controls as required by all regulatory and customer contract requirements.

Purpose: To outline the actions to be taken for 1) the procurement of all inventory, supplies and capital equipment, 2) the continuous analysis of inventory usage and balances in order to minimize the investment level, 3) the completion of related documents.

Scope: This procedure applies to the purchase of all inventory items, supplies and capital equipment for all departments within the company.

Responsibilities:

All personnel that require a product or service must complete purchase requisitions specifying items for purchase and obtain required approvals.

Purchasing is responsible for using good purchasing methods, optimizing price savings, quality or value of products, vendor working relationships, assuring proper inventory control and inspections, maintaining raw material inventories, placing orders with approved suppliers, negotiating pricing with suppliers, and forwarding all paperwork to accounting for payment.

Accounting and Accounts Payable are responsible for payment of invoices only after satisfactory completion or delivery of goods or services has been made.

Receiving and Warehouse Personnel are responsible for receiving, inspecting materials, and forwarding all paperwork to Purchasing.

Definitions: Average Monthly Usage (AMU) - For the purpose of this procedure, is the normal demand averaged over a moving twelve-month period. The average monthly usage is obtained by adding the last twelve months and dividing the sum by twelve.

Economic Order Quantity - The calculated reorder quantity that results in the lowest total cost for procurement and possession. Procurement costs are comprised of administrative and handling costs such as solicitation, requisition, purchase, receipt, handling and storage and payment. Possession costs are stated as a percentage of the quantity purchased based on obsolescence, interest, storage costs and other overhead items.

Just-in-Time. A method of timing scheduled deliveries to occur at or around the same time as the item is required for production or sale in order to reduce inventory carrying costs.

Reorder Point - The point at which an item will be reported for review and calculation of the reorder quantity.

Safety Stock - The calculated minimum quantity considered necessary to satisfy demand during the requisition, purchase and receipt cycle for replenishing the item. The suggested safety stock should be a 30-day supply, based on the average monthly usage, but should be adjusted according to market conditions.

Procedure:

1.0 ORDER DETERMINATION AND REQUISITION

1.1 Purchasing should obtain the optimal price for all inventory purchased. Consider using the following purchasing techniques:

- Long term purchase agreements
- Volume purchase commitments
- "Just-in-Time" scheduled deliveries
- Daily requisitions

1.2 Vendor selection for inventory and non-inventory items will be in accordance with procedure PUR101 VENDOR SELECTION.

1.3 The reorder quantity of standard inventory items will be determined per available stock on hand in conjunction with the requirements to satisfy the monthly sales plan (see ***ABR44 Bizmanualz™ Sales and Marketing Policies, Procedures and Forms*** for sales forecasting).

1.4 Each day the inventory file should be reviewed on a line-by-line basis to determine the items that have reached a reorder point. Note items for review for possible action if:

- Quantity on-hand is equal to or less than the calculated minimum or safety stock amount.
- Quantity on back order is 50% of the quantity on order.
- Changes are required as per the monthly production plan.

1.5 The quantity requirement under review should be compared to the vendor pricing schedules and the economic order quantity. Purchase Orders are then prepared and placed accordingly (see Order Placement below).

1.6 For non-inventory production items, including supplies and engineering components, a PUR102 Ex1 PURCHASE REQUISITION form will be prepared by the originating individual or department. Requisitions should be completed and approved with the following items and any additional supporting documentation:

- Complete description with part or model numbers if available
- Engineering drawings and specifications
- Type, Class, Grade required
- Quantity required
- Date required
- Requesting department and accounting code
- Recommended vendor or source if applicable
- Quality Management System requirements
- Special shipping requirements
- Special inspection requirements upon receipt

1.7 If the requisition is for subcontracted services:

- A complete description of the service to be performed
- Engineering drawings and specifications if appropriate
- Requirements for qualification of personnel
- Quality standards to be applied
- Quality Management System requirements

1.8 Purchasing will analyze terms, vendor, pricing, quantity breaks, etc., and will order accordingly in the company's best interest. Purchasing will notify the requester of any material variances prior to placement of the order.

1.9 The U.S. Customs Service is responsible for administering tariffs and for processing import entries. Contact the nearest Customs office with questions about how potential imports should be classified.

2.0 ORDER PLACEMENT

2.1 Purchasing is responsible for completing a PUR102 Ex2 PURCHASE ORDER form for all orders. The Purchase Order should be completed, with all applicable information, authorized and entered into the PUR102 Ex3 PURCHASE ORDER LOG.

Note: computerized accounting systems may generate the Purchase Order and then post to the Purchase Order Journal (log).

2.2 Purchase Orders for standard inventory items may print directly from the computer system using data from the Master Item List. Inspection requirements identified by QA should show up as comments on the Purchase Order.

2.3 If there are any requirements for items to be inspected at the supplier's or the Company's premises by the Company or our customer, the arrangements and method of product release shall be included in the purchasing information.

2.4 Buyers must review their purchase orders for accuracy. The buyer signs the Purchase Order indicating the review was performed.

2.5 Orders can be placed with the vendor either by telephone, fax, internet or mail. When placing orders by telephone, the vendor contact and date of order should be noted and a confirming copy of the order sent to the vendor.

2.6 Purchasing is responsible for communicating with receiving, following-up on shipping, delivery, expediting and partial shipments of ordered items, and to assist manufacturing with consistent production flow and other department's operational requirements. Purchasing can either telephone vendors or use a PUR102 Ex4 PURCHASE ORDER FOLLOW-UP form to verify, trace or expedite orders.

3.0 RECORDKEEPING AND MATCHING

3.1 When Purchase Orders are issued, the Purchasing and Accounting copies will be placed in an Open Purchase Order File until the items are received.

3.2 Items will be received in accordance with procedure PUR103 RECEIVING AND INSPECTION. The completed vendor's packing list and/or Receiving Report will be forwarded to Purchasing.

3.3 Purchasing will match the receiving paperwork to the open purchase order and forward the accounting copy, with the receiving paperwork and supporting requisition paperwork, to Accounts Payable. The Purchasing copy will be filed in the Closed Purchase Order File.

3.4 For partial shipments, a photocopy of the Purchase Order and the receiving paperwork will be forwarded to Accounts Payable. The original Purchase Order will be kept in the open file until all items are received.

4.0 SUNDRY PURCHASES

4.1 The Purchasing Department will be responsible for issuing and controlling the books of Field Purchase Orders. By means of a periodic review, Purchasing will be able to determine whether the Field Purchase Order system is functioning as planned within the guidelines established. The Project Manager and Project Superintendent will issue the Field Purchase Order for small or short-term rental as specified above. (See procedure PUR103 PROJECT PURCHASING)

4.2 The field representative will give the original and one copy to the supplier, who in turn will attach the original and one copy to his invoice and forward to the Division Office for payment.

4.3 Upon receipt of the invoice and Field Purchase Order, review all paperwork to ensure that all necessary data is shown and the purchase is within allowable established limits.

If the authorized amount has been exceeded, then forward the invoice to the Purchasing Manager for appropriate action.

4.4 As supplier invoices are received, sort the invoices according to the Project Manager approval required.

4.5 Record the invoices on a PUR102 Ex5 DAILY SUNDRY PAYABLE LOG and send the sorted originals to each Project Manager for approval. Once such approval is obtained, normal processing for the Daily Sundry Payables will be followed.

Revision History:

Revision	Date	Description of changes	Requested By
0	11/06/02	Initial Release	

[This page intentionally left blank]

PUR102 Ex1 PURCHASE REQUISITION

Requested by:______________________ Date:______________

Department:______________________ Charge To:______________

Purpose or Use:______________________________________

Vendor Name:______________________________________

Vendor Address:______________________________________

Vendor Address 2:______________________________________

Vendor Contact:______________________ Phone:______________

Date Needed:______________________ Ship Via:______________

Stock Number	Product / Service Description	Qty.	Unit Price	Extended Cost

For Purchasing Department Use Only

Approvals:

Dept. Manager:______________________ Date:______________ Approved:________

Additional:______________________ Date:______________ Ordered for:______

P.O. No.:________

Vendor EIN or SS on file? ❒ Yes ❒ No Date:____________

[This page intentionally left blank]

PUR102 Ex2 PURCHASE ORDER

SAMPLE COMPANY

PO No.: ___________

Order Date:

Page:

VENDOR:

SHIP TO:

Ship Via:		Freight Charges:	Terms:			Sales Taxable:
Item No.	**Part or Reference No.**	**Description**	**Qty**	**Unit**	**Unit Price**	**Extension**
					Total:	

NOTE: THE ABOVE PURCHASE ORDER NUMBER MUST APPEAR ON ALL PAPERS, PACKAGES, AND CORRESPONDANCE RELATIVE TO THIS ORDER.

Authorized Signature:______________________________

[This page intentionally left blank]

PUR102 Ex3 PURCHASE ORDER LOG

PO Number	Date Rqd	Requesting Department	Engineering drawings and specs	Qty Rqd	Recommended Vendor	Special Shipping Requirements

[This page intentionally left blank]

PUR102 Ex4 PURCHASE ORDER FOLLOW-UP

To:

Date:______________________________

Please rush a reply to us by fax or telephone on the information requested below. Thank you.

Our Purchase Order #:____________

From:

Dated:______________________________

Please Respond To Our Request As Indicated Below

- ☐ Please rush shipment. Advise delivery date:______________________________
- ☐ Has shipment been made? Advise carrier/date:____________________________
- ☐ Partial shipment received. Balance to ship when?__________________________
- ☐ Can you ship in accordance with our requested date?_______________________
- ☐ This shipment will be shipped via what?__________________________________
- ☐ Price on Terms do not match quotation:__________________________________
- ☐ Please review attached and confirm accuracy of all information and prices. Acknowledge below.
- ☐ These items are not taxable. Our Tax Exempt No. is _______________. Please revise invoice.
- ☐ Incorrect calculations on invoice noted. See attached and verify.
- ☐ Other____

____

____

____

Comments or Reply:____

____

____

____

____

[This page intentionally left blank]

PUR102 Ex5 DAILY SUNDRY PAYABLE LOG

Field PO Number	Date Ordered	Supplier/Vendor Name	Description of Items Ordered or Equipment Rented	Authorized Amount	Job Number	Cost Code	Cost Class	Authorized By

[This page intentionally left blank]

Prepared by:_______________ **SOP #** ______ **Revision:**___
Approved by:_______________ **Effective Date:**___________

Title: **PUR103 PROJECT PURCHASING**

Policy: The Company Purchasing Department is responsible for obtaining a competitive price on materials in correct quantities in a timely fashion so that the flow of construction is not interrupted or impeded.

Purpose: To describe the procedures involved in maintaining a seprate but parallel ordering, purchasing and receiving functions needed for construction projects in the field.

Scope: This procedure applies to the purchase of all materials, services, tools, supplies, equipment and equipment rental for all development or construction projects.

Responsibilities:

Construction personnel that require a products or services to complete a project must complete purchase requisitions specifying items for purchase and obtain required approval from the Project Manager.

Purchasing is responsible for maintaining raw material inventories, placing orders with approved suppliers, negotiating pricing with suppliers, and forwarding all paperwork to accounting for payment.

Project Management is responsible for identifying, approving, tracking and the proper disposition of all materials, equipment, tools, goods or services required to complete the project.

Accounting and Accounts Payable are responsible for payment of invoices only after satisfactory completion or delivery of goods or services has been made.

Receiving Personnel are responsible for receiving, inspecting materials, and forwarding all paperwork to Purchasing.

Procedure:

1.0 PURCHASING OVERVIEW

1.1 The Purchasing and Equipment Department has the responsibility for the purchasing of the materials, services and tools and equipment required to complete the project. Purchasing will be performed by one central group in each Division office to maintain the most economical and efficient method of obtaining the required materials and services.

1.2 The purchasing function requires adequate time for performance to realize the maximum possible benefits from the system. It is important that the Project Manager provide the Purchasing Department with as much lead time as possible. Rushed purchases invariably result in paying premium prices for the materials and higher delivery charges.

1.3 Purchasing is also responsible for obtaining and maintaining the Company's library of product information including:

- library index
- details of products
- applications
- technical data
- limitations
- alternatives
- delivery information
- current pricing

This library of information is available to assist the Project Manager. All descriptive literature and pamphlets received by the Project Manager may be routed to the Purchasing Department for listing and inclusion in this library.

2.0 REQUISITION FOR MATERIAL ORDER

2.1 The first step in the procurement cycle is the preparation of PUR102 Ex1 PURCHASE REQUISITION, which must contain all pertinent information. The Project Manager is responsible for preparing this document for all of the materials that are permanently built into the project.

2.2 The Project Manager is responsible for preparing the requisition covering major equipment rentals, services and major formwork material items. The Project Manager may elect to delegate to the Project Superintendent the task of preparing requisitions for minor purchases. In this event, it is important that the Project Manager retains control over all purchases initiated by the Project Superintendent.

2.3 The Purchasing Department must immediately notify the Project Manager if the requirements of PUR102 Ex1 PURCHASE REQUISITION cannot be fulfilled. In this event, the Project Manager will be responsible for determining the alternative course of action to be taken.

3.0 ORDERS AND ARRIVALS

3.1 A PUR103 Ex1 ORDER AND ARRIVAL LOG should be created and used to record the purchase from request to arrival. The following steps should be recorded:

- the order placed for materials or services, including:
    - quantity
    - description
    - price
    - cost code

- the receipt of the goods ordered
- the approval of the purchase and the approval of the payment for the materials or services

3.2 To reduce the volume of paper required to process repetitive orders, a Blanket Order and Arrival Log should be created and used. This is an "open" order to supply materials or services for a fixed price and for a specified period of time and to a specified maximum quantity or amount. The Blanket Order and Arrival form can be used for such items as:

- concrete
- sand and gravel
- gas, oil and propane
- rental of portable toilets
- concrete testing services

4.0 FOLLOW-UP

4.1 It is the responsibility of the purchasing agent or buyer to ensure that the vendor fulfills the delivery agreements made and recorded on the purchase order. The Project Manager may use the services of the Purchasing Department to obtain the current delivery status of critical materials.

4.2 The Project Manager should request a copy of PUR102 Ex4 PURCHASE ORDER FOLLOW-UP to confirm the status of the purchase order.

4.3 Expediting may be required to improve the original delivery date promised by the supplier. This is also the responsibility of the purchasing agent or buyer. The Project Manager should advise the Purchasing Department if the delivery date must be improved for a purchase.

5.0 RECEIVING PROCEDURES

5.1 The Project Manager is responsible for ensuring that satisfactory receiving procedures are established for the project in accordance with procedure PUR104 RECEIVING AND INSPECTION. These procedures should be customized to the size, location and spread of the project, to the complexity of the material control function and to the nature of the project (industrial or commercial).

5.2 The receiving procedures should ensure that a particular individual or individuals are given responsibility for:

- receiving all materials
- ensuring that the materials are in good condition
- ensuring that the quantities are correct and in agreement with the delivery slip
- ensuring that the materials are as specified
- documenting the receipt of the materials

6.0 MATERIAL TRANSFERS

6.1 The purchasing agent is the most logical person to be held responsible for reclamation and salvage disposal, because of the knowledge of materials and how the company uses them. The purchasing agent is familiar with the companies which manufacture or distribute various materials and is knowledgeable about the items the Company buys and at what cost. The four main destinations for such material for disposal are: reuse by some other segment of the company, return to original supplier for restocking, sale to used-material dealers or to other users, and storage of material yard for usage on another job at a later date.

6.2 The purchasing agent, at the completion of a job or large project, will have an inventory taken on remaining material. Disposal of material will be carried out by one of four methods.

- Where possible, material should be transferred to another job or division. The Value of material should be negotiated by the Project Managers involved.
- Prime material that can be restocked with original supplier; a restocking charge may apply.
- Material returned to the yard for storage, to be used on another job at a later date. Value to be determined by Purchasing Agent from prices available on the present day in the open market.
- Surplus materials to be sold or otherwise disposed of by the Project Manager.

6.3 Under no circumstances should scrap material be returned to the Division yards without the Purchasing Department's knowledge. The Purchasing Agent should visit the site first to inspect the material in order to determine if the material in fact should be returned to the yard or taken immediately to the dump.

7.0 SUNDRY PURCHASES

7.1 The Purchasing Department will be responsible for issuing and controlling books of Field Purchase Orders. By means of a periodic review, Purchasing will be able to determine whether the Field Purchase Order system is functioning as planned within the guidelines established. The Project Manager and Project Superintendent will issue the Field Purchase Order for small or short term rental as specified above.

7.2 The Field Purchase Order form should be a small, three-part, pre-numbered form bound in books of 25 to 50. The form should provide for the following information for completion in the field:

- supplier name and date of order
- brief description of items ordered or equipment rented
- authorized amount
- job number
- cost code and cost class

- unit number when applicable
- authorized signature

The field representative will give the original and one copy to the supplier, who in turn will attach the original and one copy to his invoice and forward to the Division Office for payment.

7.3 The Accounting Department, upon receipt of invoice and Field Purchase Order, will review to ensure that all necessary data is shown and purchase is within limitations established. If the authorized amount has been exceeded, Accounting will forward the invoice to Purchasing Department for appropriate action. As supplier invoices are received, Accounting will sort the invoices according to the Project Manager approval required. The invoices will be recorded on the PUR102 Ex5 DAILY SUNDRY PAYABLE LOG and the originals will be sent to each Project Manager for approval. Once such approval is obtained, normal processing for the Daily Sundry Payables will be followed.

Revision History:

Revision	Date	Description of changes	Requested By
0	11/06/02	Initial Release	

[This page intentionally left blank]

PUR103 Ex1 ORDER AND ARRIVAL LOG

PO Number	Request Date	Request Quantity	Requested Material Descritpion	Request Price	Cost Code	Recommended Vendor	Date Approved	Date Received	Date Paid

[This page intentionally left blank]

SOP # ______ Revision:______
Effective Date:______________

Prepared by:____________
Approved by:____________

TITLE: **PUR104 RECEIVING AND INSPECTION**

Policy: All parts, components, goods and materials will be received in an organized manner and inspected for conformance prior to stocking to provide an initial quality control inspection. Any items or shipments rejected will be properly quarantined from other inventory items until disposition.

Purpose: This procedure outlines the steps for the receiving and inspection of materials, components, parts, finished goods, etc., and the stocking of these items or the disposition of rejected items.

Scope: This procedure applies to the receipt of all inventory items.

Responsibilities:

Receiving and Warehouse Personnel are responsible for receiving, inspecting materials, and forwarding all paperwork to Purchasing.

Purchasing is responsible for accepting or rejecting damaged goods.

Accounting and Accounts Payable are responsible for payment of invoices only after satisfactory completion or delivery of goods or services has been made.

Quality Control will review and authorize all rejections.

Definitions: FIFO. First-In-First-Out or FIFO refers to the practice of using the oldest item in inventory first to ensure that the inventory is rotated on a regular basis.

Bill of Lading. The documents made out by or on behalf of the shipper that constitute the contract between the shipper and the carrier for the carriage of freight. It may also be known as a waybill or airway bill. The Bill of Lading is a written acknowledgement by the carrier of the receipt of goods to be transported to a designated place and delivery to a named person or to his or her order. Before accepting goods for transport, the carrier is required to issue a bill of lading.

Procedure:

1.0 RECEIVING

1.1 A "receiver" is any form used to record the specific types and counts of product received. With computerization these "receivers" are rarely standard blank forms. Occasionally, the accounting system will provide a receiver for each purchase order. It looks much like a purchase order, but without the prices. The quantities ordered are generally visible, making it possible to immediately detect discrepancies. There is usually a blank column for the recording of actual counts next to the purchase order quantity. Sometimes the receiver is the purchase order, and sometimes it is actually provided by the vendor and is not part of the company's system at all.

An example of this would be a detailed packing slip, furnished by the vendor with the shipment. Regardless of the format, all incoming product is to be counted and reconciled with what was originally. Discrepancies must be recorded. Related shipping documentation, like Bill of Ladings, are generally for the shipping carrier to control case or pallet counts and are not as detailed.

1.2 All incoming shipments must be examined for apparent package damage. If the shipment has apparent damage, notify Purchasing immediately. Purchasing will decide to either accept or reject the shipment from the carrier and/or file a freight claim in accordance with procedure PUR105 SHIPPING AND FREIGHT CLAIMS.

1.3 If the shipment shows no signs of damage or Purchasing has decided to accept a damaged shipment, count the shipping pieces (i.e., packages, skids, barrels, boxes but not the contents; see Inspection below) and confirm with the bill of lading and note any exceptions (i.e., package damage or shortages).

1.4 Obtain the packing list from the shipment and record the date, sender, carrier, number of packages and who received the goods in PUR104 Ex1 RECEIVING LOG. Record date and receiving log number on the vendor's packing list. Match up shipment with the Receivers on file. If there is no packing list with the shipment, fill in the first line of the PUR104 Ex2 RECEIVING AND INSPECTION REPORT form.

1.5 Transport the shipment and documentation (and or PUR104 Ex2 RECEIVING AND INSPECTION REPORT) to the receiving holding area for internal inspection.

Note: any non-production shipments (i.e., office supplies) will be logged in the Receiving log and delivered to the proper department.

2.0 INSPECTION

2.1 At the receiving holding area, each shipment should be unpacked and all items piece counted and matched to the packing list. If a packing list is not available, complete Part I of PUR104 Ex1 RECEIVING AND INSPECTION REPORT.

2.2 The shipment will then be inspected for conformance according to the inspection level required for each part number (see PUR104 Ex3 INVENTORY INSPECTION LEVELS). If multiple part number classes are included in the shipment, each class will be segregated and inspected accordingly.

2.3 Any previously undiscovered damage to individual inventory items should be noted on the inspection report and immediately followed up with the vendor.

3.0 REJECTION, DISCREPANCIES AND DISPOSITION

3.1 Any count discrepancies will be noted on the packing list or PUR104 Ex2 RECEIVING AND INSPECTION REPORT, signed and forwarded to Purchasing. Purchasing will then follow-up with the vendor to resolve the shipping discrepancy.

3.2 If there is a non-conformance discrepancy, the suspect goods will be red-tagged and separated (quarantined) from other inventory and immediately taken to the quality control hold area for disposition.

3.3 If only partial goods in the shipment are of non-conformance, the accepted goods should be noted on the paperwork and stocked per above procedure.

3.4 Complete PUR104 Ex2 RECEIVING AND INSPECTION REPORT for any rejected parts. Quality Control will review and authorize all rejections and complete Part II of the report.

3.5 Goods found to be in conformance or suitable for their intended use and accepted by Quality Control will have the red tag removed and be returned to the receiving area for stocking. Quality Control will note on the report the justification for any accepted parts and forward the report along with the packing list to Purchasing.

Goods rejected by Quality Control will continue to be quarantined and red tagged until disposed. Purchasing will determine and arrange for the appropriate disposition of rejected items (i.e., return to vendor for credit, scrap, etc.).

3.6 Unidentified shipments should be resolved by Purchasing. Contact Security to resolve any suspicious looking packages.

4.0 STOCKING

4.1 If the shipment has no discrepancies or rejected items, then sign off and forward the packing list, Receiver, and the Receiving and Inspection Report, to Purchasing.

4.2 Accepted parts will then be taken to their appropriate areas and stocked (i.e., shelf, bin, rack, etc.) according to the INV101 INVENTORY CONTROL procedure.

5.0 PRODUCT RETURNS

- Refused Shipments.
- RGA See procedure REV110 CUSTOMER RETURNS.

Revision History:

Revision	Date	Description of changes	Requested By
0	11/06/02	Initial Release	

PUR104 Ex1 RECEIVING LOG

Date	Sender	Carrier	# Pkgs.	Received By

[This page intentionally left blank]

PUR104 Ex2 RECEIVING AND INSPECTION REPORT

PART I RECEIVING Date: ______________

Vendor/Supplier/Subcontractor: ______________________________

P.O. Or Contract No.: ______________________________

Item No.	Description	INSPECTION Criteria	QUANTITIES Ordered	Received	Inspected	Accepted	Rejected

Received By: ______________________________

PART II INSPECTION

Inspected By: ______________________________

Sample Lot

Conformance/Discrepancies to Specifications

Lot Size: ____________

Sample Qty: __________

	YES	NO		YES	NO
Shipping Damage	❐	❐	Functional	❐	❐
Markings/Finish	❐	❐	Dimensions	❐	❐
Attributes	❐	❐	Other	❐	❐

Accepted: ______________ Date: ___________ Rejected: _________ Date: ______

❐ Place in Stock

❐ Forward to Next Operation

Cause for Rejection: ______________________________

____

______________________________ ______________________________

______________________________ ______________________________

PART III REJECTED PARTS DISPOSITION

Return to Vendor

Conditional Acceptance Approvals

______________________________ ______________________________

Signature Signature

Remarks: ____

____

Further comments may be noted on back of report or additional sheets if necessary.

[This page intentionally left blank]

PUR104 Ex3 INVENTORY INSPECTION LEVELS

The following are generic descriptions of the type of inspections that should be performed for various classes of inventory items. These descriptions are not completely comprehensive for all the possible types of inventory that can be received and therefore, the inspector should use appropriate judgment to determine any special inspection procedures that may be necessary for unique items.

The inspection levels are intended to be cumulative in that higher level inspections will also include all lower level inspection procedures.

The percentage of the total parts inspected will be according to the part number specifications. For example, an inspection level indication of "Level II, 25" would require that 25% of the parts received in the shipment will be examined at a Level II inspection.

If defects or rejected items are discovered within a shipment and less than a 100% inspection has been performed, the receiving inspector will consult with the Quality Control Manager to determine the appropriate action for assurance of the remainder of the shipment.

Level I: Visual inspection of the shipment or lot. Items appear reasonably to match packing list description(s). Nothing comes to the attention of the inspector as noticeable defects or as unusual and unordinary.

Level II: Actual hands-on visual inspection of individual parts. Each part inspected will be analyzed for the quality of workmanship and construction and the appearance of any defects.

Level III: A functional test of the part will be performed as appropriate for the item. For example, pneumatic parts should indicate function when attached to compressed air source; moving parts should rotate, slide etc.; electrical components should operate, light, etc.

Level IV: The part will be inspected against a set performance or measurement standard as indicated in the part file. For example, structural items will be measured for compliance to drawings within specified tolerances; electrical and mechanical devices will function according to specified performance standards.

[This page intentionally left blank]

SOP # ______ Revision:______ **Prepared by:____________**
Effective Date:_______________ **Approved by:____________**

Title: **PUR105 SHIPPING AND FREIGHT CLAIMS**

Policy: The Company will always strive to minimize damages to goods from shipping and to recover full amounts possible for any losses incurred by shipping damage or loss of goods as allowed by the Interstate Commerce Act.

Purpose: To institute the methods to be followed for shipping and filing freight claims.

Scope: This procedure applies to all goods shipped and received by domestic motor and rail common carriers.

Responsibilities:

Receiving and Warehouse Personnel are responsible for receiving, inspecting materials, and forwarding all paperwork to Purchasing.

Purchasing is responsible for accepting or rejecting damaged goods and the filing of all freight claims.

Definitions: Bill of Lading. The documents made out by or on behalf of the shipper that constitute the contract between the shipper and the carrier for the carriage of freight. It may also be known as a waybill or airway bill. The Bill of Lading is a written acknowledgement by the carrier of the receipt of goods to be transported to a designated place and delivery to a named person or to his or her order. Before accepting goods for transport, the carrier is required to issue a bill of lading.

This document contains important provisions governing the carrier's liability for damage and for the processing of damage claims. For example, the bill of lading can contain a released valuation provision, which limits a carrier's liability on the basis of the value of the shipment as released to the carrier. Many carrier tariffs also provide that a shipper's failure to declare a value for the shipment will be deemed to limit the carrier's liability to the lowest released value contained in the tariff.

Carriage. It is equivalent to the term transportation. Refers to the process or movement of shipments, including all services and operations of the carrier, provided by the carrier.

Carrier. It is the carriage (transportation) company taking responsibility (through the Bill of Lading) for transporting and delivering the consignment (goods) from the consignor (shipper) to the consignee (destination).

Consignment. It is similar to the term "shipment." It refers to one or more pieces tendered by one shipper at one time, at one address, and receipted for in one lot, and moving on one Bill of Lading to one consignee at one destination address.

Consignee. The ultimate person or company, whose name appears on the Bill of Lading, to whom the shipment is to be delivered to by the carrier.

Consignor. It is also known as the shipper. It is the person or company that is originating or shipping the goods.

Procedures:

1.0 SHIPPING

1.1 Prior to shipment, the shipping department will ensure that the product is properly packaged and loaded in accordance with procedure REV105 SHIPMENT OF GOODS. For high dollar items, obtain the originating carrier's inspection and approval of these processes if possible.

1.2 Document accurate records of the condition of the product when tendered to the originating carrier since the bill of lading acknowledgement that the shipment was received by the carrier in good condition only applies to products which are open to inspection by the carrier.

1.3 Inspect all shipping documentation, noting any provisions serving to limit the carrier's liability. Specifically inquire as to whether the freight rate is dependent on the value of the shipment to be transported or whether a value will be imputed if no declaration is made. If so, a value sufficient to cover our potential loss should be declared.

2.0 RECEIVING

2.1 Inspect all shipments received immediately. Require the delivering carrier to describe and note any damage on the delivery receipt. Take photographs of the damage. If the damage is extensive, consider rejecting the shipment or hiring an independent inspector to evaluate the extent and cause of the damage.

2.2 Inspect the contents as per procedure PUR104 RECEIVING AND INSPECTION, paragraph 2.0.

3.0 CLAIMS PROCEDURES

3.1 Contact the carrier to obtain a claim form. If no claim form is available then send a written claim to the delivering carrier as soon as possible. Most carriers provide proof of delivery and claims processing at their website, so check online for details first.

3.2 The carrier may require a physical inspection so maintain all packaging/goods, as received, in their original condition until the inspection status has been verified.

3.3 For concealed damage claims (damage not apparent on delivery), claims should be filed within 15 days after the shipment is received.

3.4 For non-delivery or shortage of goods, contact the carrier and request proof of pick-up and delivery. File a claim after thirty days if no answer or notification of loss is received from the carrier. Also check with the vendor to ensure the products were shipped correctly

4.0 ADDITIONAL INFORMATION RESOURCES

4.1 Government resources:

- Interstate Commerce Act explanation in PDF http://ostpxweb.dot.gov/policy/carmack/cgolia.pdf
- U.S. Department of Transportation (DOT) http://www.dot.gov

4.2 Shipping carriers resource:

- Federal Express - http://www.FedEx.com
- United Parcel Service - http://www.UPS.com
- DHL International - http://www.DHL.com
- Untied States Postal Service - http://www.USPS.com
- Emory Worldwide - http://www.emeryworld.com
- TNT - http://www.tnt.com
- BAX Global - http://www.baxworld.com
- US Freightways - http://www.usfc.com
- J.B. Hunt - http://www.jbhunt.com

References:

A. INTERSTATE COMMERCE ACT

The liability of domestic motor and rail common carriers for freight loss or damage to interstate shipments of regulated commodities are governed by the Interstate Commerce Act. The act provides that such a carrier may be liable for the full, actual loss of shipments tendered to it for transport if the claimant can establish the following:

1. That the shipment was tendered to the carrier at origin in good condition.
2. That the shipment was delivered at destination in damaged condition.
3. The amount of damage can be substantiated.

Since many times a shipment can be moved from origin to destination by a number of connecting carriers, it can be virtually impossible for a claimant to establish where in the chain of transport the damage occurred. Therefore, a claimant can assert its claim against either the originating or delivering carrier.

A carrier may avoid liability for lost or damaged freight if the claimant does not file a written claim within nine months after the shipment is delivered. Further, if the carrier denies a claim, the claimant must initiate legal action within two years after declination of the claim.

Transportation by express or package carriage, such as United Parcel Service or Federal Express, are subject to a standard liability limitation based on weight or on the package. The shipper who chooses such carriage is put on notice of the limitation by clear language on the bill of lading. The shipper can declare higher value and pay an excess valuation charge.

Transportation of most goods is performed under contract to provide specified services under specified rates and conditions. The carrier and shipper, negotiating for contract carriage, may make any reasonable contractual stipulations, except that they may not waive provisions governing the carrier's registration, insurance, or safety fitness.

Revision History:

Revision	Date	Description of changes	Requested By
0	11/06/02	Initial Release	

SOP # ______ Revision:______ **Prepared by:____________**
Effective Date:______________ **Approved by:____________**

Title: **PUR106 ACCOUNTS PAYABLE AND CASH DISBURSEMENTS**

Policy: Internal controls are required to ensure that only valid and authorized payables are recorded and paid. Accounting procedures should be implemented to ensure the accuracy of amounts, coding of General Ledger accounts and appropriate timing of payments.

Purpose: To explain the practices for documenting, recording and issuing payments for accounts payable transactions.

Scope: This procedure applies to all purchases including, merchandise and non-merchandise purchases.

Responsibilities:

The CFO is responsible for reviewing Accounts Payable material and adding his signature.

Purchasing is responsible for forwarding all paperwork to accounting for payment.

Accounting and Accounts Payable are responsible for payment of invoices, but only after satisfactory completion or delivery of goods or services has been made.

Background: Properly recording liabilities is generally a three-step process, particularly, for merchandise purchases.

The first step is recording the liability upon receipt of merchandise, using the purchase order estimates as a guideline. For accuracy and timeliness of data, a liability should be recorded as soon as the company receives the purchased items. By necessity, this initial recording is usually an estimate and can be finalized when the actual invoice arrives. This is why a Purchase Order is so important for merchandise purchases. It documents the company's understanding of how much each item will cost, per the vendor's terms. This includes estimates for freight and any other charges.

The second step takes place when the vendor's invoice is received. At this point the actual liability is finalized, with any necessary adjustments to the item costs, freight, or other charges.

The third step involves the preparation, issuance of payment for the goods received, and subsequent filing of all paperwork for easy retrieval.

Procedure:

1.0 DOCUMENTING ACCOUNTS PAYABLE

1.1 The following documents will be forwarded to accounts payable for temporary filing and subsequent matching to form an accounts payable voucher package:

- Purchase Order with purchase requisition if applicable
- Packing Slip with receiving report if applicable
- Vendor invoice

1.2 Once the accounts payable department has received all of the above documents, the following steps will be performed to ensure proper authorization, validity of purchase, receipt of purchased items or services and accuracy of amounts.

- The vendor invoice will be stapled on top of the packing slip and receiving report followed by the purchase order and requisition.
- The purchase order should be evaluated for proper authorization and the nature of the purchase and pricing as shown on the invoice reviewed for validity.
- The quantities shown shipped or delivered on the invoice will be compared to the packing slip and/or receiving reports. Any discrepancies must be followed-up and resolved prior to commencing with the voucher process.
- Calculations on the invoice will be recomputed such as quantities received multiplied by unit price and totals.

2.0 RECORDING MERCHANDISE PAYABLES

2.1 As described in section 3.0 RECORD KEEPING AND MATCHING of procedure PUR102 PURCHASING, once merchandise has been physically received, and all documentation has been reconciled with any discrepancies resolved, the accounting system must now be updated to record the received goods. The matched documentation required consists of the original purchase order, receiving report and packing slips.

2.2 If the purchase orders for merchandise purchases originated in the accounting system, then the original purchase order is brought up on screen and the specific items and related quantities received are clicked off or recorded, based on the actual receiving report.

The immediate effect is that inventory is increased for the items received as the payable to the vendor is recorded.

Note that this is accomplished prior to receiving the vendor's invoice. But at this stage, most accounting systems record a "waiting for bill" invoice. This is a pro-forma invoice created by the accounting system, using the costs from the purchase order, including any estimated freight costs.

If the Purchase Orders were prepared manually, then record on PUR102 Ex3 PURCHASE ORDER LOG the received status and then enter the purchase details in the accounting system.

2.3 Upon receipt, compare the actual vendor's invoice to the "waiting for bill" invoice already recorded in the accounting system. This is the final comparison for Accounts Payable accuracy. The vendor's prices or discounts may vary from the Purchase Order, or the vendor's quantities may vary from the actual quantity received per the receiving report, or other variances may exist in freight and other charges. Resolve all discrepancies immediately, if possible, and record the correct amount owed in the Accounting System.

3.0 RECORDING NON-MERCHANDISE PAYABLES

3.1 Non-merchandise expenditures like utilities, rent, insurance, taxes, repairs, professional fees, etc., are generally not recorded through the purchase order routine. However, there may be other documentation, like contracts, requisitions, and other agreements. These should be filed in the applicable vendor file as documentary support. Upon receipt of the invoice, the charges should be entered into the payable system and coded to the appropriate expense account.

3.2 Generally, once invoices (both merchandise and non-merchandise) have been entered, they can be filed in the respective vendor files, ordered by date. To guard against misfiling an un-entered invoice, consider stamping "entered" on each invoice when it's recorded in accounts payable. It is also helpful to note the entered date and initial the entry.

4.0 PAYMENT OF ACCOUNTS PAYABLE

4.1 Accounts payable systems generally provide an aged report and a "bills to pay" report. Examine the "bills to pay report" on a weekly basis. The controller should select the current week's bills to be paid based on the funds available and a projection of cash flow or receipts over the coming week. Once complete, process or print the checks for the selected bills to be paid.

Note: Accounts payable should normally be paid within seven days of their payment term unless otherwise determined by the Chief Financial Officer.

4.2 Any vendor credits which are amounts owed to the company for returns, marketing co-op, or price adjustments, should be applied to amounts currently owed to the vendor when determining payment. These are normally received in the form of a credit memo or adjusting invoice. These should be entered into the system like any other invoice and applied to the next payment being made. There is no reason to "age" a credit memo.

4.3 Pull all Invoices to be paid from the files and match them with the printed checks. Present the materials to the CFO for review and signing.

4.4 Immediately ensure that all checks signed and approved are correctly recorded in the accounting system. Stamp the invoices "paid" to document they've been paid. Consider using checks that incorporate a two stub plus check form in order to attach one stub to the paid invoice and the other to the remittance copy of the Invoice.

If one check pays several Invoices then either photocopy the stub and attach a copy to each paid Invoice or consider attaching all paid Invoices to the one check stub. File all resulting documentation in the applicable vendor payables file.

4.5 Mail the checks as soon as possible once checks have been posted and "paid" by the system. It is not advisable to "hold" checks for additional days after posting. This practice usually occurs when there are insufficient cash flows. However holding checks increases the difficulty of projecting cash flow, reduces cash balance accuracy, and causes confusion when trying to reconcile accounts payable vendor balances. None of these balances will be accurate if printed checks are held back from mailing. If cash flow is insufficient to mail the checks, then it is advisable not to post and print checks in the first place.

5.0 MANUAL CHECKS

5.1 The first element of control begins by using pre-numbered blank checks and storing them in a secured area.

5.2 Occasionally, it may be necessary to take a blank check and fill it out manually. (This should be strongly discouraged.) Special care must be used to maintain control over blank and manually prepared checks. Make sure to enter all manual checks into the check register and or into the accounting system immediately after use.

5.3 Most accounting systems utilize a check form that often has the check and a perforated remittance section. When a check is used manually, it should be taken in sequence with the remittance section (which should contain the preprinted check number) left in the secured area. The controller should write today's date, the payee and purpose, and if known, the amount on the blank remittance area.

5.4 After the check is written, the receipt or invoice should be brought back as soon as possible, stapled to the original remittance that was left with the checks, and entered into the accounting system. This stapled documentation should then be filed in the applicable vendor file.

Revision History:

Revision	Date	Description of changes	Requested By
0	11/06/02	Initial Release	

[This page intentionally left blank]

bizmanualz®

Accounting Policies, Procedures & Forms

Section 500

Embezzlement Prevention

Section 500

Embezzlement Prevention

EMBEZZLEMENT PREVENTION

[This page intentionally left blank]

CONTRIBUTING EDITOR DANA L. TURNER

Dana Turner is a security practitioner with Security Education Systems -- a research, consulting and training firm located near San Antonio, Texas.

Combining the knowledge gained in a successful law enforcement career with tactical business operations procedures, Dana has created unique security and loss prevention programs for governmental agencies, and the retail, service and financial industries. These programs consist of loss prevention techniques, security policy and procedures, and disaster recovery and business resumption strategies designed for use as training tools, planning mechanisms and reference guides.

Dana has served as a law enforcement officer in several capacities, including the investigation of business and banking crimes; as a community college instructor and administrator in both the law enforcement and business management fields; and as a program development specialist and trainer for private businesses, governmental agencies and professional associations. Dana is celebrating his 30th year in crime prevention.

As a speaker...

Dana has delivered more than 3,000 presentations. He has acquired an outstanding reputation as a dynamic, knowledgeable and entertaining instructor. In addition to his work with state banking and credit union associations, he designs and participates in continuing education programs offered by:

- Law firms;
- State examining agencies;
- CU Conferences;
- America's Community Bankers;
- American Bankers Association;
- American Society for Industrial Security;
- Association of Certified Fraud Examiners;
- Association of Financial Crime Investigators;
- Bank Administration Institute;
- Bankers' Hotline;
- Conference of State Bank Supervisors;
- Credit Union Executives Society;
- Drug Enforcement Administration;
- Federal Financial Institutions Examination Council;
- Independent Community Bankers of America;
- Institute of Internal Auditors.

AS A CONSULTANT...

Dana has completed more than 1,000 projects and assisted in the development and delivery of components of several seminars, schools and conferences, including:

- ABA's National School for Bank Security;
- BAI's Advanced Bank Security Officer School;
- BAI's Audit & Compliance Conference;
- BAI's Basic Bank Security Officer School;
- BAI's Disaster Recovery & Business Resumption Seminar;
- BAI's Graduate Schools of Banking;
- BAI's Internal Crime Prevention & Investigation Seminar;
- BAI's Loan Fraud Prevention Conference;
- BAI's Security & Risk Management Conference;
- Bankers' Hotline Security Officer's Workshop;
- CSBS's Banking School of Hard Knocks Conference;
- CSBS's Deputy Conference;
- CSBS's Emerging Issues Conference;
- FFIEC's Payment Systems Risk Conference;
- FFIEC's White Collar Crime School;
- ICBA's CEO Excellence Seminar;
- ICBA's Security & Risk Management Seminar;
- M&I Data Services' Annual Conferences;
- National Conference on Credit Union Fraud & Loss Prevention;
- National Credit Union Supervisory Committee Conference.

AS A WRITER...

Dana has written many manuals and books, and numerous newspaper, trade publication and magazine articles published and distributed both nationally and internationally. His written works published since 1984 include:

- Business Crime Prevention Handbook
- Conducting Investigations Manual For Financial Institutions;
- Coping With Crimes Of Violence Manual For Businesses
- Disaster Management Planning Manual For Corporations
- Disaster Recovery Manual For Financial Institutions;
- Internal Crime Prevention & Investigation Manual For Businesses
- Loss Prevention Techniques & Training Manual For Financial Institutions;
- Security & Operations Manual For Corporations
- Security & Operations Manual For International Corporations
- Security Program Manual For Financial Institutions;
- Violent Crime Manual For Financial Institutions; and
- More than 250 newspaper, trade publication and magazine articles published and distributed both nationally and internationally.

AS AN INDUSTRY AUTHORITY MEDIA REPRESENTATIVE AND TALENT

Dana has worked in several capacities, including:

- Local, on-screen television interviews concerning police investigations;
- Local, on-air radio personality for a weekly business crime radio show;
- Local and national on-screen and on-air, radio and television interviews concerning crime and disaster recovery topics;
- Local and national news publication interviews concerning crime and disaster recovery topics;
- Developer and on-screen narrator of the *Career$kill$* series of work experience seminars for the Santa Rosa Junior College;
- Assistant Editor of Banker's Hotline;
- Moderator for BankersOnline.com; and
- Developer, writer and on-screen narrator of the *It Can Happen To You* workplace violence videotape training program for the Bankers' Video Library.

[This page intentionally left blank]

EMBEZZLEMENT PREVENTION

Table of Contents*

*The Embezzlement Prevention Guide Table of Contents references section page numbers (lower right corner).

Table of Forms

1.0 ORGANIZATIONAL STRUCTURE AND FUNCTIONS

A company's structure, and the manner in which various functions are assigned, may contribute significantly to the development of "windows of opportunity" for embezzlers to act.

One of your first tasks will be to examine every facet of your company using Section 7, "Loss Prevention Audit and Examination Guidelines" as a risk assessment device, and locate the company's windows of opportunity. One of your next tasks will be to close those windows.

Because embezzlements are generally "habit" crimes, and are made up of a series of rhythmic, predictable and cyclic events, it becomes a simple matter to answer the question of just why certain types of companies are so susceptible to this type of activity. Besides the fact that many companies store money, property and data, remember that most companies function in a traditional way.

For our purposes "traditional" is defined as:

Traditional. An activity that is conducted in a conventional, established, predictable, common and habitual manner.

If an employee wants to embezzle, he/she does not want to work within an industry whose unpredictable operations may expose the crime. The embezzler must plan the crime to take advantage of the opportunities presented by the rhythmic, cyclical and predictable pattern of tasks and events.

1.1 WHERE EMBEZZLERS LOOK FOR OPPORTUNITIES

Opportunities for embezzlement are generally available within each of the following categories:

- Policies and procedures;
- Personnel;
- Documents;
- Computers and records; and
- Facilities.

1.2 CORPORATE CULTURE

A company's "corporate culture" is a significant factor when determining the company's vulnerability to misuse and misappropriation.

For our purposes "Corporate culture" is defined as:

Corporate culture. An environment influenced by the prevalent morals, ethics, ideals, and standards for behavior as developed, implemented and demonstrated by management: the company's conscience.

1.3 CODE OF CONDUCT

Many company auditors and other risk managers recommend that a company's board of directors require the company to adopt ethical codes. This "Code of Conduct" is an excellent method to communicate with employees and to describe acceptable standards of behavior. This communication should deal with the solicitation and receipt of things of value; conflicts of interest; use of confidential information; and cooperation with internal investigations.

The company's Code of Conduct should clearly state that an employee's failure to cooperate with an internal investigation will subject the employee to discipline, up to and including termination. The Code of Conduct may also explain the right of the company to suspend an employee, with or without pay, during the conduct of an investigation.

Terms in the company's Code of Conduct are often enforceable as contractual rights. Companies should be careful not to include exaggerated statements concerning standards of conduct that they are not willing to enforce in a universal manner. The selective enforcement of a Code of Conduct could result in the company not being allowed to enforce it against an employee suspected of unlawful activities.

Employees need to be shown where they fit into the company; need to know what the company stands for and what it won't allow; and need to be led by example. If the company fails to communicate effectively its response to any of these needs, it is preparing the means for its own destruction. Embezzlers themselves cite these reasons for the discontentment that led them to commit their crimes.

1.4 SUMMARY

The company's Code of Conduct statement is also an excellent device to describe an employee's rights and obligations. Employees who believe that they are treated fairly, and treated as every other employee, are less likely to become discontented. This section addresses the basic areas of concern that provide embezzlers the means and the motivation to commit the crime. The next section examines the rights granted to all employees.

2.0 EMPLOYEES' RIGHTS

Every investigator must remember that employees have certain legally protected rights that are inherent in any employment relationship. In our society, a person is believed to be innocent (not responsible) until proven guilty (responsible). We'll learn later that, as investigators, we suspect everyone.

For our purposes a "right" is defined as:

> **A right. A power or a privilege granted to either the employer or employee. A right includes both duties and obligations relevant to all parties in the relationship, and it may extend beyond the term of the relationship.**

2.1 ESTABLISHING THE COMPANY'S AND EMPLOYEES' RIGHTS

An employee may also have additional rights that arise from the contractual relationship between the employer and the employee. However, the investigator is not a sworn law enforcement officer, so federal constitutional limitations that apply to the actions of the police do not apply to the investigator who is a private citizen.

The term of the contract between a company and an employee may be as formal as a written employment agreement, or as informal as an unwritten practice of doing things in a certain manner. Most companies have written policies and procedures for at least part of their operations. Every investigator should consider these informal but commonly-accepted practices, employment agreements, or policies and procedures to be part of the contract between the company and its employees.

Many courts have held that the parties to any contract owe each other a duty of good faith and fair dealing. In the context of an investigation, this duty extends to the methods used in the investigation, and the discipline, if any, imposed after the investigation is completed.

The company's failure to follow established and reasonable procedures can be used as the basis for a legal action by an employee.

Regardless of the reason for discipline or discharge, the company's failure to follow established and reasonable procedures can be used as the basis for a legal action by an employee, charging a breach of the company's duty of good faith and fair dealing.

2.2 EMPLOYEE RIGHTS TO PRIVACY AND RELATED ISSUES

Many states have extended the right of privacy to the employer/employee relationship. This right of privacy may limit the investigator's ability to inquire into the private life of the employee; to search an employee's work area; or to examine an employee's checking or savings accounts. Many states also have statutes that prohibit the monitoring or recording of telephone calls, conversations and interviews without the express consent (sometimes, written consent) of the employee.

In addition to privacy issues, an improperly conducted interview may expose a company to possible civil or criminal liability under state law, for false arrest, false imprisonment or intentional infliction of emotional distress.

Some privacy rights cease to exist if the employee does not have a "reasonable expectation" of privacy. For example, an employee handbook or Code of Conduct can disclose that a financial institution employee's checking or savings accounts are subject to review by the institution's audit department or internal investigators. The handbook or Code of Conduct can state that all lockers, desks, cabinets, and similar places where things can be stored, belong to the company and may be searched by its representatives at any time.

A non-union employee does not have the right to have a union or other representative, including an attorney, present during an investigative interview. An employee also does not have the right to confront witnesses. However, the duty of good faith and fair dealing requires that an employee should be given the opportunity to respond to charges made against him or her.

2.3 THE EMPLOYEE POLYGRAPH PROTECTION ACT

Federal law prohibits most private employers from using any lie detector test, either for pre-employment screening or during the course of employment. The *Employee Polygraph Protection Act of 1988* contains several limited exemptions that authorize polygraph tests under certain conditions, including the testing of employees who are reasonably suspected of involvement in a work place incident that results in economic loss or injury to the employer's business.

Subject to numerous conditions and restrictions, an employer may request an employee to submit to a polygraph test, but no other type of lie detector test, and only if:

1. The test is administered in connection with an on-going investigation involving economic loss or injury to the employer's business, such as theft, embezzlement, misappropriation, or an act of unlawful industrial espionage or sabotage;
2. The employee had access to the property that is the subject of the investigation;
3. The employer has a reasonable suspicion that the employee was involved in the incident or activity under investigation;
4. The employer provides the examinee with a statement, in a language understood by the examinee prior to the test, which fully explains with particularity the specific incident or activity being investigated, and the basis for testing particular employees which contains, at a minimum:

(i) An identification with particularity of the specific economic loss or injury to the business of the employer;

(ii) A description of the employee's access to the property that is the subject of the investigation;

(iii) A description in detail of the basis of the employer's reasonable suspicion that the employee was involved in the incident or activity under investigation; and

(iv) The signature of a person (other than the polygraph examiner) authorized to legally bind the employer; and

5. The employer retains a copy of the statement described above for at least three (3) years and makes it available for inspection by the Department of Labor.

2.4 ADMONISHMENT TO SUSPECT EMPLOYEES

As a private person acting as the investigator, you do not have the legal obligation to inform a person suspected of a crime of his/her rights against self-incrimination, as does a sworn law enforcement officer. Don't overlook the significant advantage of stating a similar admonition to a suspect employee, however.

If you will be acting as the investigator, draft your own suspect admonition to create an emotional impact and establish your authority, as long as similar statements are included in your company's employee handbook or other distributed materials.

The following admonition is a suggestion only:

- You are an employee of this company, and subject to the same policies, procedures and standards of behavior and performance as all other employees;
- The company is conducting an investigation in connection with an event(s) involving economic loss or injury to the company's business, such as theft, embezzlement, misappropriation, or an act of unlawful industrial espionage or sabotage;
- The company believes that you, as an employee, had access to the property, goods, title or money that is the subject of the investigation;
- The company maintains a reasonable suspicion that you, as an employee, were involved in or had knowledge of the incident or activity under investigation;
- You have previously acknowledged, in writing, that you have read, understood and are prepared to abide by the same policies, procedures and standards of behavior and performance as all other employees;
- You may be disciplined according to the terms of the company's policy if you remain silent, purposely withhold information which may be pertinent to this investigation or otherwise fail to cooperate with this investigation;

- You do not have the right to have an attorney or a witness present with you during questioning;
- Do you understand your rights as an employee of this company, as I have explained them to you?
- If so, will you cooperate in this investigation to the best of your ability?

Document the statement using the **Report of Investigation: Statement S**.

A sample form is located on the next page.

2.5 SUMMARY

We'll return to this topic again when we present additional information about conducting interviews and interrogations. This section addresses the basic rights possessed by both employees and the company. The next section examines the development of an effective loss prevention program, with a specific emphasis upon embezzlement prevention.

REPORT OF INVESTIGATION: STATEMENTS

Report # ____________________

Day: ______________	Time started: __________
Date: ______________	Time ended: __________
Name	
Address	
City/State/Zip	
Phone	
DDL #	
SSN #	
Location	
Investigator	
Witness	

Admonition:

1. You are an employee of this company and subject to the same policies, procedures and standards of behavior and performance as all other employees;
2. The company is conducting an investigation in connection with an event(s) involving economic loss or injury to the company's business, such as theft, embezzlement, misappropriation, or an act of unlawful industrial espionage or sabotage;
3. The company believes that you, as an employee, had access to the property, goods, title or money that is the subject of the investigation;
4. The company maintains a reasonable suspicion that you, as an employee, were involved in or had knowledge of the incident or activity under investigation;
5. You have previously acknowledged, in writing, that you have read, understood and are prepared to abide by the same policies, procedures and standards of behavior and performance as all other employees;
6. You may be disciplined according to the terms of the company's policy if you remain silent, purposely withhold information which may be pertinent to this investigation or otherwise fail to cooperate with this investigation;

7. You do not have the right to have an attorney or a witness present with you during questioning;
8. Do you understand your rights as an employee of this company, as I have explained them to you?

Yes:	No:	Initials:

9. If so, will you cooperate in this investigation to the best of your ability?

Yes:	No:	Initials:

Statement::
Statement (cont.)

I declare that I have written this statement voluntarily, without threats or promises of any kind, to the best of my ability and recollection. I declare under penalty of perjury that this information is true and correct. This declaration was executed in:

City and state:	
Date	Time
Signature:	
Investigator:	
Witness:	

Record of interview:
Your position title is:
You have worked in this position since:
Other positions you have held at this company are:
From:_____ To: ______
From:_____ To: ______
From:_____ To: ______
Other companies you have worked for and position titles:
Employer: From: To:

Position:
Employer: From: To:
Position:

Employer:
Position:
A brief description of your current duties, responsibilities and level of authority, or duties as of the date of the incident is:
Your supervisor is:
Your salary scale is:
Your employee benefits are:
Do you receive any additional benefits (e.g., expense account, vehicle allowance, mileage repayment, schooling?)
If you do receive additional benefits, describe them:
Your employee identification number is:

Do you have checking or savings accounts? If you do have checking or savings accounts, describe them:

Account #1:

Institution/branch:

Account #2:

Institution/branch:

Account #3:

Institution/branch:

Do you own your own home?

Do you have any other sources of income?

If you have other sources of income, describe them:

Source #1:

Amount: Monthly / yearly?

Source # 2:

Amount: Monthly / yearly?

Source # 3:

Amount: Monthly / yearly?

Do you consume alcoholic beverages?

If you consume alcoholic beverages, how much and how often?

Do you consume drugs, either prescribed or illegal?

If you consume drugs, describe the drugs and how frequently do you use them?

Do you gamble using money or other valuables?

If you gamble, describe what type of gambling you prefer and how much you generally win or lose?

Do you have any problems at home or at work?

If you have problems at home or at work, describe them:

Describe your financial situation – past, present and future:

Why did you leave your last job?

May I institute a credit check to examine your current financial status?

Your signature:

May I contact the institutions where you maintain accounts and examine the activity in those accounts?

Your signature:

Other questions:

Other questions (cont.):

[This page intentionally left blank]

3.0 EXAMPLES OF EMBEZZLEMENT SCHEMES

3.1 MISUSE OR MISAPPROPRIATE FUNDS

Employees may misuse or misappropriate funds or property in a variety of ways. For our purposes:

- Misuse is abuse of privilege or position without a specific intent to steal; and
- Misappropriation is the taking of funds or property with a specific intent to steal.

3.2 THE MOST POPULAR EMBEZZLEMENT SCHEMES

The most popular examples of misuse and misappropriation are, in order:

- Using the company's telephones, copy machines, and mail services for personal business;
- Using the company's equipment, machinery, vehicles, supplies, and computer programs for personal business;
- Using the company's expense accounts and credit cards to pay for personal expenses;
- Creating "cash loans" from one's own area of control to pay personal expenses on a "temporary" basis;
- Operating credit, interest and check kites;
- Establishing fictitious accounts, phony loans, lines of credit, and other related types of credit frauds;
- Covering or withholding deposit of one's own, or other employees' checks, from the daily work until payday;
- Misrouting personal checks issued for cash or merchandise to take advantage of "float time" until personal deposits can post;
- Wiring funds from the company's or customers' accounts to secret personal accounts;
- Stealing cash or negotiable documents from another employee's area of control;
- Forging or altering the company's documents, particularly signature cards at financial institutions, powers of attorney, money orders, travelers and cashier's checks made payable to the company;
- Manipulating account balances through on-line computer terminals, and making "adjustments" to accounts, particularly dormant accounts;
- Creating "ghost" or non-existent employees for the company's accounting system for payroll purposes;

- Hiding merchandise, cash, computer data and account information in the company's garbage container for retrieval by a confederate;
- Converting titles to "double-ordered", abandoned or stored company property, then selling the property;
- Accepting and holding "favorite customers'" and employees' post-dated checks, until they can make a corresponding deposit to the paying financial institution, for a fee;
- Assisting a customer or another employee in operating credit, interest and check kites, and "bustout" schemes, for a fee;
- Short-changing customers during any transaction;
- Secret unsecured, personal loans from "favorite customers"; and
- Burglarizing the company's premises, dual-custody containers, and safety deposit boxes.

3.3 Summary

Although the number of methods used to commit the crime of embezzlement is only limited by the embezzler's imagination, this listing highlights the techniques most frequently used. This section addresses the most common schemes used by embezzlers. The next section examines those operational areas most vulnerable to embezzlement.

4.0 CRITICAL AREAS OF RISK TO EMBEZZLEMENT

4.1 AREAS OF RISK

There are six areas of risk frequently capitalized upon by embezzlers. While these areas of risk are not the only ones containing "windows of opportunity", these are the areas that offer the most significant sources of exposure to the company:

(1) **Cash**:

Crimes involving cash are most often committed by line personnel (both new and experienced), and by their immediate supervisors. The most effective methods for preventing these crimes are by:

- Developing and enforcing written policies governing cash handling and cash station security procedures;
- Requiring strict dual control over cash drawers and keys;
- Secure all containers used to store or transfer cash;
- Require that all refunds be approved by a supervisor and that the refund of more than a small dollar amount be accomplished by a company check instead of cash;
- Conducting frequent, unannounced cash counts;
- Rotating tasks among personnel at unpredictable intervals; and
- Requiring all employees to remain off the company's premises for at least five (5) uninterrupted business days annually.

The most frequently-identified examples of crimes involving cash are:

- Holding cash from a transaction instead of placing the cash in a cash container (e.g., register, vault or safe);
- Taking cash from an unsecured "petty cash" container;
- Taking cash from unsecured personal items left on the premises (e.g., wallet, purse, briefcase, backpack);
- "Short-changing" customers at the time of the transaction;
- Refunding stolen items for cash;
- Cashing stolen and forged documents for a confederate; and
- Theft of cash from another employee's work area.

(2) **Negotiable documents issued or sold by the company**.

These crimes are committed by all levels of employees, often using documents that are often stolen and forged; negotiated after reported void;

or negotiated after payee and/or amounts are altered. The most effective methods for preventing these crimes are by:

- Developing and enforcing written policies governing document storage, inventory and handling, and cash station security procedures;
- Requiring strict dual control over negotiable documents, including checks, refund authorizations and credit and debit memos;
- Requiring that all negotiable documents be ordered from a single printer by one person, with a supervisor's approval, and received by a person other than the person who placed the order;
- Conducting frequent, unannounced audits;
- Rotating tasks among personnel at unpredictable intervals; and
- Requiring all employees to remain off the company's premises for at least five (5) uninterrupted business days annually.

The most frequently-identified examples of negotiable document crimes are the negotiation of;

- Refund authorizations;
- Unauthorized use of credit and debit memos to manipulate accounts;
- Money orders;
- Forgeries;
- Travelers checks; and
- The company's official checks.

(3) **Credits to accounts**:

These crimes are committed by all levels of employees, and require the manipulation of account information; generation of phony accounts; or the use of fictitious identities. These crimes may also require the co-operation of personnel working at other companies. The most effective methods for preventing these crimes are by:

- Developing and enforcing written policies governing the opening and handling of all types of accounts;
- Requiring strict dual control procedures, including the involvement of a supervisor in every account adjustment request;
- Develop a triggering device to alert management when a dormant account (90 days or older) has been accessed for any type of activity;
- Rotating tasks among personnel at unpredictable intervals; and
- Having all credit and other account activity independently reviewed frequently by selected individuals or by a committee.

The most frequently-identified examples of these types of crimes involve the manipulation or creation of:

- Inactive or dormant accounts, particularly senior citizen, foreign customer and conservator ship accounts;
- Unauthorized transfers between general ledger accounts;
- "Ghost" employees for payroll fraud;
- Loans and lines of credit for fictitious borrowers;
- Deposit accounts for fictitious persons or entities to receive stolen or forged checks; and
- Deposit accounts for check kiting.

(4) Items delivered or received

These crimes are committed by all levels of employees and involve the taking or misapplication of instruments or other property delivered to the company. In addition to product inventory, these items are often intended to be used as collateral or to be held for safekeeping. The most effective methods for preventing these crimes are by:

- Developing and enforcing written policies governing the shipping, receiving and storing of all instruments or other property;
- Developing and enforcing written policies governing the shipping, receiving and storing of items held for safekeeping or as collateral;
- Requiring strict dual control procedures for all property transfers from one department/facility to another;;
- Insuring that the company's garbage is inaccessible to non-employees and that periodic inspections are conducted prior to employees leaving the premises;
- Requiring that items purchased by employees are opened and inspected before the employee leaves the premises;
- Establishing and monitoring a comprehensive receipt system;
- Designating and equipping a secure storage facility;
- Rotating tasks among personnel at unpredictable intervals;
- Conducting frequent and unannounced audits of instruments and other property received by the company;
- Requiring all employees to remain off the company's premises for at least five (5) uninterrupted business days annually.

The most frequently-identified examples of crimes involving items delivered or received include the conversion of:

- Money paid against a "layaway" purchase;

- Property by placing items in the company's garbage for retrieval by a confederate;
- Property by misusing an "employee discount privilege" to benefit friends and others;
- Raw materials and scrap used in the production process;
- Stocks and bonds;
- Items held in trust;
- Negotiable instruments; and
- Equipment and supplies.

(5) Wire transfers

These crimes are committed by employees who are either assigned to the wire transfer function, or who coordinate the theft with another employee who is assigned to the wire transfer function. Theft by wire transfer may also be committed by an external source, often based on information made available by an internal source. The most effective methods for preventing these crimes are by:

- Developing and enforcing written policies governing all wire transfer operations;
- Requiring strict dual control procedures, including the involvement of employees designated as "receiver", "sender" and "validator";
- Establishing, monitoring and frequently changing a comprehensive password system, with each employee accessing the system being assigned a separate and confidential personal identification number (PIN) to be used for all transactions;
- Rotating tasks among personnel at unpredictable intervals;
- Conducting periodic, unannounced reviews of transfer documents by an independent person or group;
- Frequently auditing the person(s) responsible for assigning passwords;
- Establishing a reasonable security procedure agreeable to both the sender and recipient; and
- Requiring all employees to remain off the company's premises for at least five (5) uninterrupted business days annually.

The most frequently-identified examples of wire transfer crimes involve the manipulation or alteration of:

- The company's own accounts or transfer instructions; and
- Faxed transfer instructions received from an unauthorized source; and
- Customer accounts or transfer instructions falsified by an employee.

(6) Computer crimes: These crimes are committed by employees who are either assigned to the data processing function, or who coordinate the theft with another employee who is assigned to the data processing function. Computer frauds are committed by means of unauthorized access to, or manipulation of, a computer system by either internal or external sources. The criminal's goal is to transfer or credit funds to his/her accounts, to transfer title to property, or to impair the ability of the company to conduct business. The most effective methods for preventing these crimes are by:

- Developing and enforcing written computer system security policies that require the company to:
- Properly identify and document persons accessing any system, either by direct access or by modem;
- Control access to information by assigning passwords to every person authorized to access the system, even if the system is only a personal computer;
- Routinely monitor employees' work and levels of access;
- Notify appropriate persons of unauthorized activities; and
- Routinely audit and document system controls and integrity.
- Requiring strict dual control procedures;
- Rotating accounting, inventory and backup tasks among personnel at unpredictable intervals;
- Conducting periodic, unannounced reviews of activity logs by an independent person or committee;
- Frequently auditing the person(s) responsible for assigning the passwords and maintaining the system; and
- Requiring all employees to remain off the company's premises for at least five (5) uninterrupted business days annually.

The most frequently-identified examples of computer crimes involve the manipulation or employment of:

- Customer account information to "skim" the account for re-sale, or other criminal use;
- "Salami" or "trap door" techniques, to "skim" a small amount of money from each transaction processed, electronically transferring the amount to another account;
- "Data diddling" schemes to alter the manner in which a computer program works, or to neutralize control mechanisms;
- "Trojan horse" programs, to insert extra commands into a computer program, causing the computer to perform authorized and unauthorized functions simultaneously; and
- "Logic bomb" commands, or a set of instructions programmed to perform various functions at appropriate or periodic times. This

technique is used to shift funds, erase data, or shut down the entire system at a given time.

4.2 SUMMARY

This section addresses what resources the company offers that the embezzler may use to commit the crime. The next section examines the universal symptoms that embezzlers display.

5.0 UNIVERSAL SYMPTOMS OF EMBEZZLEMENT ACTIVITY

All people have reasons for behaving as they do. All people have developed behavior patterns. No person changes an established behavior pattern without a significant reason. The principle of cause and effect applies to the relationship between a change in some aspect of a person's life, and an accompanying change in that person's behavior.

5.1 EMBEZZLEMENTS ARE PREDICTABLE

Embezzlements are rhythmic, cyclic and predictable crimes. As an employee embezzles, his /her behavior also becomes rhythmic, cyclic and predictable. Further, embezzlers generally suffer from low self-esteem, which has been repeatedly linked as a contributory factor to criminal behavior. Guilt and anxiety will cause a marked and predictable change in both the embezzler's behavior and appearance. The embezzler's own behavior often signals the investigator to narrow the investigative focus.

5.2 MOTIVES FOR COMMITTING EMBEZZLEMENT

The investigator is always seeking a motive – the reason for the person's behavior. Understanding a motive allows the investigator to also understand why an event occurs, and where to seek additional information. There are three (3) primary motives for a person to embezzle:

- Need for money;
- Revenge; and
- Excitement.

While there is no such person as an “average” embezzler, most employees who embezzle consistently display universal crisis “symptoms”. These symptoms are also known as “crisis signals”, and serve as a warning that an employee is unbalanced mentally, physically, emotionally, spiritually or financially. These symptoms are clues that are often apparent to supervisors and coworkers, who are in daily contact with the employee.

For our purposes:

> **A symptom is defined as a characteristic, feature, indication or manifestation demonstrated by a person's behavior, or by means of associated lifestyle events.**

.Demonstrating any one of these symptoms does not mean that an employee is embezzling. It simply means that the employee is “at risk” of a breakdown of his/her morals, values, and ethics, and that intervention may prevent an escalation of the imbalance. As you review these symptoms, recognize that most people have demonstrated at least one such behavior or lifestyle event at some point in their lives.

The true value of these symptoms becomes readily apparent to the investigator who is trained to recognize them for their true significance. These symptoms serve as guideposts, eliminating many employees from suspicion, and directing the investigator's attention towards other employees who may be responsible for the crime.

The listed symptoms all involve a significant change in behavior, attitude, lifestyle or job performance. Active embezzlers generally display addictive behavior, and simultaneously demonstrate three (3) or more of these symptoms:

- A suddenly enriched, extravagant lifestyle, unsubstantiated by normal wages: Embezzlements are generally "ego" crimes. The embezzler often feels compelled to flaunt the proceeds of the crime, in effect daring someone to call attention to his/her behavior.
- Frequent requests for cash advances, or delayed repayment of prior loans: This indicates that the employee has expenses exceeding income, a cycle that generally will continue until it is interrupted. The employee must embezzle an ever-greater amount of money to cover past thefts that remain unpaid.
- Telephone calls at work from creditors: This is generally a collection agency's last resort, and indicates that the agency has been unsuccessful in past collection efforts. The agency will eventually initiate court proceedings against the employee, applying greater pressure to pay off past-due amounts.
- Wage garnishment: A court order served by a Sheriff or Marshal that requires the company to withhold all or a part of the employee's wages, and puts the employee's finances under the control of the court. Embarrassment results, and the employee may escalate any existing embezzlement activity.
- Borrowing constantly from fellow employees, and seldom repaying these loans: If the employee has expenses exceeding income, and the company is unaware of the discrepancy, he/she will use other employees as an alternative source of funds. Embezzlers often maintain outside business interests that create a constant cash drain and require frequent cash injections.
- Careless or sloppy work habits; failure to follow instructions or giving conflicting instructions; unusual errors in judgment; frequent absences from the work area; repeated or unreasonable accidents on or off the job; or significant change in behavior, attitude or performance: To be successful and avoid detection, embezzlement must be a full time and time-consuming "job". Attention given to the tasks related to embezzlement must logically be diverted from other daily activities, and preoccupation, confusion and mistakes become conspicuous.
- Unexplained or poorly explained absences from work; chronic tardiness and early departure; or excessive use of sick time: An embezzler needs time to recover from guilt, stress and anxiety frequently and generally uses excessive amounts of sick and vacation time to do so. Unexplained absences may mean that the embezzler simply cannot face other employees and supervisors.

- Refusing to take time off, or passing vacation options: Embezzlements are "rhythm" crimes, and must accommodate the company's schedule of events and routine business operations. The embezzler must be present on the premises to track transactions, and to prepare explanations for suspicious activities that may be discovered during an audit.
- Constantly working overtime without sufficient reason, and often without pay: Again, the embezzler must be present on the premises to track transactions, and may not have the opportunity to do so during the normal business day. "Volunteering" to work without pay also enhances the employee's image, and appears to demonstrate dedication and a commitment to the company's success.
- Gambling at the workplace, or excessive references to gambling activity: Often social gambling leads to compulsive gambling, an extremely expensive habit. Paralleling the attitude of embezzlers, gamblers believe they can't lose. Compulsive gambling also invites association with persons willing to lend money at exorbitant repayment rates. Once the gambler fails to meet repayment obligations and the cycle of missed payments begins, the "lender" will begin the "collection process", using threats, extortion, and physical violence.
- References to current excessive consumption of alcoholic beverages; consumption of alcoholic beverages during the work day; or evidence of frequent hangovers: Embezzlers often abuse alcoholic beverages and other mind and mood-altering drugs. People under the influence of alcoholic beverages generally make grossly inappropriate decisions, and references to or evidence of over-consumption may indicate a significant reaction to stress, anxiety, and guilt.
- References to substance abuse of a drug other than alcohol, either the overuse of prescription medication, or consumption of illegal drugs; substance abuse in any form during the work day; or evidence of the cumulative effects associated with substance abuse: Generally, people who abuse alcoholic beverages also abuse other substances for the same reasons. Often substance abuse leads to compulsive consumption, another extremely expensive habit that initiates the same unsavory relationships as found among compulsive gamblers.
- References to significant domestic problems; telephone calls received at work from family members regarding domestic problems; or evidence of physical, mental or emotional spousal abuse and accompanying signals of distress: If an employee is unhappy and unfulfilled at home, he/she may resort to embezzlement as a means of self-expression and self-fulfillment, and to obtain the means to escape an intolerable lifestyle.
- Meeting with questionable associates at the work place. Drug dealers and loan sharks ("lenders") often "visit" their "clients" at the workplace: These visits are intended to be interpreted as a means of subtle intimidation to

stimulate repayment of debts, or as a follow up to an extortion demand. The employee may also be cooperating with the associate in planning a crime against the company.

- Disruptive or erratic behavior; withdrawn or preoccupied manner; inappropriate displays of anger and frustration; extreme mood swings; and a visible deterioration of physical appearance, and mental and emotional stability: Living an increasingly complex lifestyle often requires the use of escape mechanisms to cope with the cumulative effects of distress. The creation of diversions and distractions to shift attention away from the embezzler, and hiding, are the most common escape mechanisms used by embezzlers. It is often a person's change in physical appearance that signals distress to an alert observer.

5.3 SUMMARY

One of the investigator's best tools for both prevention and investigation is the continuing awareness of people, and understanding the significance of the behaviors those people display.

This section addresses common behavioral symptoms displayed by "at risk" employees. The next section examines how to use the understanding of behavior and other statistical information to develop psychological profiles of those employees most likely to become embezzlers.

6.0 PROFILE OF AN EMBEZZLER

We know that there is no such person as an "average" embezzler. There is no exact description to tell us how an embezzler looks, acts, thinks or feels. We can draw upon experience and available statistical information, however, to develop an embezzler "model", or "profile". For our purposes:

A profile is a characterization, outline, representation or portrait depicting certain attributes or anticipated behaviors.

6.1 COMMON CHARACTERISTICS SHARED BY MOST EMBEZZLERS

Statistically, embezzlers share many common characteristics. Combining these characteristics with an understanding of behaviors and their symptoms, we can develop two (2) important tools:

- The ability to identify potential embezzlers before they become significant risks; and
- The ability to use this information to create numerous investigative devices if an embezzlement occurs.

Embezzlers are generally profiled in one of two categories: chronic/compulsive, and needy. Both categories share some common profile information.

Each type of embezzler generally:

- Is a high school graduate;
- Is a staff employee, if female; is an officer, if male;
- Is a bright, very competent, and superior employee;
- Is neat, precise and attentive to detail;
- Leads an increasingly complex lifestyle;
- Has worked, and continues to work, in the same industry and job category;
- Embezzles to repay increasing debts, not to accumulate wealth;
- Believes that he/she will never be discovered;
- Does not see him/herself as a criminal;
- Incorporates lying, cheating and stealing into every facet of his/her lifestyle;
- Has embezzled from his/her last four (4) employers prior to discovery;
- Is rarely criminally prosecuted;
- Does not receive a jail sentence upon conviction; and
- Does not repay the victim or court costs.

Common Characteristics Shared By Needy Embezzlers

In addition to the common characteristics shared by most embezzlers, needy embezzlers may:

- Have an acute, short-term need for money for a legitimate purpose;
- Have knowledge of other employees' embezzlement activity, and ask to become temporarily involved;
- Retaliate for perceived promotion discrimination, or sexual harassment;
- Feel cheated, unrecognized, or unrewarded for their efforts on behalf of the company;
- Feel there is a lack of promotional opportunity in general;
- Be suffering minor personality conflicts and related problems;
- Be occasional substance abusers, and possess altered mental and emotional states caused by a dependency upon drugs or alcohol;
- Be facing what appears to them to be overwhelming debts, and fear the loss of reputation and esteem of coworkers; and
- Feel unprepared or uncomfortable in the jobs in which they work, accompanied by an apparent lack of interest and attention by the company.

Common Characteristics Shared By Chronic/Compulsive Embezzlers

In addition to the common characteristics shared by most embezzlers, and the more specific characteristics shared by needy embezzlers, chronic/compulsive embezzlers generally:

- Feel "superior" to management and other employees in intellect or ability;
- Think of embezzlement as a "game" they believe they can win;
- Lie, cheat, and steal as a lifestyle to either receive a reward or to avoid punishment;
- Have a driving desire to prove how "smart" they are;
- Discover an area of potential exposure within the company that appears too good to leave alone, and feel challenged to take advantage of the opportunity;
- Need to support a failing outside business interest;
- Feel there is a lack of promotional opportunity, in relation to their skill levels;
- Be suffering acute personality conflicts and related problems; and
- Be chronic substance abusers, who possess altered mental and emotional states caused by a dependency upon drugs or alcohol.

6.2 SUMMARY

You now have most of the information necessary to develop an effective loss prevention program, with a specific emphasis upon embezzlement. This section addresses common characteristics shared by most embezzlers. The next section provides you with a comprehensive risk-assessment device designed to help you conduct a thorough evaluation of your company's operations.

7.0 LOSS PREVENTION AND AUDIT EXAMINATION GUIDELINES

7.1 CONDUCTING THE LOSS POTENTIAL RISK ASSESSMENT

An appropriate risk assessment device is essential for security officers, auditors and examiners to use in determining a company's vulnerability to acts of embezzlement. These are important issues to address during any operational review or examination. If the company has not adequately addressed these issues, it is particularly vulnerable to each of the three types of crimes:

- Crimes committed by document (e.g., forgery, check and credit kite, loan fraud, theft of inventory, embezzlement);
- Crimes committed by trickery, deceit and device (e.g., pigeon drop, "bait and switch" scheme, phony billing and collection call, inventory and real estate swindle, embezzlement); and
- Crimes committed by fear, force or violence (e.g., robbery, bomb threat, kidnapping, hostage event).

Although the guidelines contained in this segment specifically emphasize embezzlement issues, use of the same guidelines will reduce the likelihood of and potential loss from, all types of crimes.

The guidelines contain both questions that should be asked and the rationale for asking the questions. They are not designed to serve as a replacement for a comprehensive audit manual, but to place special emphasis upon those factors contributing to internal and external crimes. While a reviewer may not specifically search for them, the issues addressed may surface during any review or examination.

A "no" answer to any of these questions, taken alone, does not indicate that the company is crime-prone. A negative response to a single issue is simply a "window of opportunity" for the commission of a crime.

Experience indicates, however, that several common denominators, or clues, existed in companies that were victims of an embezzlements. Multiple "no" answers to the questions should create a serious concern for the reviewer to address, because the company's safety and soundness is at risk.

7.2 THE EMBEZZLER'S STRATEGIC PLAN

Professional embezzlers generally develop a "strategic plan" for their activities, much the same way as do the companies they work for. This strategic plan is designed to identify available windows of opportunity and to determine the best method to take advantage of those windows.

The "strategic plan" most frequently used by embezzlers resembles an auditor's review worksheet, and tests these areas of opportunity in order of priority:

- Policy and procedures;
- Personnel;

- Documents, computers and records; and
- Facilities.

7.3 THE COMPANY'S LOSS PREVENTION STRATEGIC PLAN

The guidelines follow the same plan, and addresses both conventional issues to be resolved within a company, and unconventional but effective methods for taking advantage of windows of opportunity by embezzlers. Many of these unconventional crime methods are also used to commit "street crimes" by external professional criminals. Resolving these unconventional issues, therefore, also reduces the risk to external crime.

7.3.1 Policies and Procedures

Answers to the following questions will provide the basis for the Loss Prevention Stretegic Plan:

Has the company developed, implemented and provided a means to monitor and update comprehensive written policy and procedure statements governing the activities of all departments, cash-handling facilities, functions and personnel?

Lack of a comprehensive policy manual may indicate ineffective leadership and direction from management. It may also promote arbitrary and capricious decisions by personnel at all levels within the company, allowing for an individual's interpretation of a policy that is commonly accepted, but not committed to writing.

Lack of a comprehensive operations and procedural manual ("desktop procedures") may indicate ineffective planning and preparation for the accomplishment of tasks. It may also promote arbitrary and capricious decisions by personnel at all levels within the company, allowing for an individual's interpretation of a procedure that is commonly accepted, but not committed to writing.

Functional responsibilities for both departments and cash-handling facilities that are informal and unwritten, poorly defined or nonexistent, may lead to confusion, ineffective prioritization of tasks, and misinterpretation of directions. It also makes assessing the responsibility for results difficult, if not impossible.

Position (job) descriptions that are informal and unwritten, poorly defined or nonexistent, make assessing the responsibility for results difficult, if not impossible.

Policy and procedure manuals, position descriptions and the company's description of functional duties and responsibilities may be introduced into court proceedings to demonstrate the elements of an embezzlement. Lack of attention to these areas may cause law enforcement and prosecuting agencies to refuse to prosecute, and may open the company to costly civil actions.

Summary:

Embezzlers prefer to commit crimes within companies whose business facilities are geographically dispersed; where management decisions are decentralized; where duties and responsibilities conflict or overlap; and where an ineffective internal reporting system exists.

Comprehensive written internal control techniques?

Both internal and external crimes rely upon the lack or ineffective use of internal control techniques. They depend upon the variety of mistakes and misunderstandings generated by such failure to be effective. Effective written internal controls should govern:

- Authorization and approval levels for all employees;
- Recording of all transactions, incidents, suspicions, and dispositions of inquiries;
- Safeguarding all facilities, assets and records; and
- Accountability for results at all levels.

Effective internal control techniques are designed to perform three (3) functions:

1. Detect mistakes as they occur, preventing costly losses;
2. Protect honest employees from the dishonest activities of other employees; and
3. Gather evidence necessary to identify, apprehend and prosecute dishonest employees.

The most common breaches of internal controls occur because employees feel it is often inconvenient, time-consuming and unnecessary to practice effective controls. Creating and enforcing methods to limit access to control codes by employees for facilities, departments, documents, computers, computer programs, delivery and receiving of inventory, equipment and supplies, dual custody containers, night drops, ATM cards, wire transfers, and safety deposit boxes, eliminates the majority of potential areas subject to use in an embezzlement.

Summary:

Embezzlers prefer to commit crimes within companies whose internal controls are lax, arbitrary or non-existent; where physical evidence is routinely compromised; where mistakes and misunderstandings are common and tolerated; where the responsibility for results is not clearly defined; and where the responsibility for results is not accompanied by the authority to act.

Comprehensive safeguards against abuses by officers and directors, or other "insiders"?

Significant insider abuse has been identified as a proximate cause for the failure of the nation's businesses. Insider abuse also accounts for more than half of all financial fraud and embezzlement cases investigated by law enforcement agencies, as indicated by crime statistics compiled and maintained by the FBI.

In addition to addressing loan and other forms of credit abuse, these safeguards should contain provisions prohibiting or restricting the diversion of assets and income for personal use; approvals of questionable transactions involving relatives; sales or purchases of assets at preferential prices or quantities; and the acceptance of bribes or gratuities.

Summary:

Embezzlers prefer to commit crimes within companies whose internal controls allow, and often encourage, abuse; where management and others are exempt from policy and procedures; where nepotism is allowed but not acknowledged; and where gratuities are commonly accepted.

A program for the rotation of employees' schedules and work assignments at unpredictable intervals?

Embezzlements are rhythmic, cyclical, habitual and predictable, and are built upon the company's operating routines. The employee must depend upon an established routine to avoid detection.

Summary:

Embezzlers prefer to commit crimes within companies where employees' movements and schedules are not tracked effectively; where "important and special" positions require a particular employee's daily presence; and where each position is expected to be filled by the same person daily.

A program for documenting suspicious incidents; a mechanism for notifying the Security Officer and Auditor of suspicious incidents without fear of reprisal; and included this information in the employee orientation training program and employee handbook?

Employees, who are unsure of approved methods of handling suspicious incidents, or to whom to report their suspicions, often will not place themselves at risk by reporting unusual incidents.

In the majority of embezzlements, at least one other employee is aware of the crime, and chooses not to report it. Fear of loss of reputation, or reprisals from the suspect employee or a peer group, are often cited as the primary reasons employees fail to report unusual circumstances.

Summary:

Embezzlers prefer to commit crimes within companies where the Auditor and Security Officer rarely appear at the work site; where previous "whistleblowers" have been criticized or subjected to disciplinary action; and where suspicious activity reporting policy and procedures are unclear or non-existent.

7.3.2 Personnel

Has the company developed, implemented and provided a means to monitor and update:

The fulfillment of key positions at all levels with qualified personnel who create the security-conscious atmosphere critical to embezzlement prevention?

- Management's development and promotion of a moral, legal and ethical working environment (corporate conscience) is one of the key elements of a company's total security program. A company tends to employ personnel whose personal values are similar to the company's corporate values.
- Embezzlers recognize special opportunities for theft when working within a company where one person is responsible for many unrelated functions. Companies that assign functional responsibilities based upon an employee's availability rather that qualifications, are particularly at risk.

Summary:

Embezzlers prefer to commit crimes within companies where management is not involved in daily operations; where key employees are untrained or ineffective, or are responsible for a functional area by default; where discrimination is allowed; and where there is no written statement of the company's values and purpose.

A policy for a formal Audit Committee composed solely of independent directors, and provided with the necessary guidance, resources, authority and training to effectively oversee the company's affairs?

The Audit Committee should be assigned specific duties and responsibilities which are set forth in a charter approved by the Board of Directors.

Summary:

Embezzlers prefer to commit crimes within companies where the Audit Committee is ineffective, untrained or non-existent.

A policy requiring that the Security Officer and Auditor positions are filled by more than one person; have written position descriptions, duties and authority; and that the persons fulfilling each role may report directly to the Board of Directors or the Audit Committee?

- Both the Auditor and Security Officer have the special responsibility to investigate suspicious incidents and crimes committed against, and within, the company. Too often those investigations involve senior managers and executives who may attempt to inhibit or stop such investigations.
- Both auditors and security officers are often terminated or transferred to another assignment when they refuse to cooperate with management's unsound or illegal tactics.

Summary:

Embezzlers prefer to commit crimes within companies where the Auditor and Security Officer rarely appear at the work site; where the Auditor and Security Officer are also responsible for other duties and responsibilities; where the Auditor and Security Officer positions are treated as "informal" positions, and where the Security Manual is ineffective or non-existent.

The performance of a new executive officer, particularly a chief executive officer, who immediately begins making significant changes within the company's structure?

Examples are:

- Terminating or reassigning existing officers, particularly auditors and others skilled in operational functions, replacing them with highly-paid, personally-selected personnel:
- Existing officers with historical knowledge of the company and operational backgrounds are dangerous to an embezzler. These officers will immediately become aware of the drastic operational changes that accompany an officer embezzlement, and will be replaced or reassigned.
- Imposing limits on the monetary and personnel resources dedicated to periodic audits of the company's financial condition, and the scope of those audits:
- An executive officer who embezzles must initially restrict and control the resources allocated to the audit function; distract the auditor from the functional area(s) used to commit the embezzlement; and re-focus the auditor's attention upon a non-suspicious functional area.
- Relocating his/her office from a visible and accessible location, to a remote and secure area of the building, or erecting physical barriers designed to isolate him/her from other personnel.
- All embezzlements are "secret" crimes, and persons who embezzle become secretive, withdrawn, non-communicative and paranoid. Officer embezzlers are not monitored in the same manner as other personnel, and they recognize that isolation decreases the risk of exposure of these behavioral aberrations.
- Involving him/her in the loan and line of credit approval process.
- All embezzlers must have a working knowledge of the company's policies and procedures, to accommodate its rhythm and routines. This knowledge then allows the officer embezzler to create loans and lines of credit for associates.
- Purchasing an expensive new vehicle as his/her "company car" and authorizing similar purchases for other executives.

This is consistent with the behavior habits of chief executives of all types of businesses who seek to flaunt the proceeds of their crimes. Gathering a loyal team depends upon the distribution of a share of the proceeds ("perks").

Summary:

Embezzlers prefer to commit crimes within companies where leadership is ineffective or non-existent; where the Board of Directors is inattentive to events; where the company is relatively new and experiencing natural growth and frequent personnel modifications; where the Auditor and Security Officer positions report directly to him/her; and where individual achievement is more valued than teamwork.

Written position descriptions, levels of authority and reporting routines for all personnel?

Employees frequently exceed the scope of their position descriptions and levels of authority, and assume by default more responsibilities than they are authorized to exercise. If such an employee causes a loss, or embezzles, it is difficult to assess responsibility for results.

Summary:

Embezzlers prefer to commit crimes within companies that offer theft opportunities based upon the company's indifference to, or treat poorly, employees; that use ineffective screening and hiring procedures; that exercise ineffective operational controls; that fail to monitor the decisions and actions of their employees at all levels; and where training programs and opportunities for advancement are minimal or non-existent.

A policy requiring that all new employees provide handwriting and fingerprint samples, and a photograph; that the company provide notice that it will conduct credit checks on all applicants and that it may conduct credit checks on employees at unspecified intervals during any employee's term of employment?

- Most embezzlers have worked for similar companies, often within the same role or assignment. If handwriting samples and fingerprints have never been collected, identification, investigation and subsequent prosecution efforts may be seriously impaired.
- Photos are useful in the event an employee is reported missing, or is the victim of an extortion attempt. A series of annual facial photos also demonstrates the aging process, as well as the stress accompanying embezzlement activity.

- A poor credit history may demonstrate lack of regard or attention to detail, and generally indicates financial need. Other credit history information may reveal multiple names, Social Security numbers and driver's license numbers.

Summary:

Embezzlers prefer to commit crimes within companies that do not share information with other companies; that do not effectively identify potential job applicants; that either do not require or know how to appropriately interpret a credit report; or that will not recognize symptomatic evidence of embezzlement during routine record searches.

A written Employee Handbook?

The handbook should include policy statements:

- Referring to the company's Code of Conduct,
- Requiring all employees to cooperate with an investigation, and that failure to cooperate may result in disciplinary action;
- Informing employees that the company will report, and will prosecute, any employee or Board member for embezzlement-related activity;
- Advising all employees that they may be held personally liable for acts of willful misconduct or gross negligence;
- Advising that employees' accounts at the company are subject to review by the company's auditors or investigators;
- Advising that all lockers, desks, cabinets and similar places where things may be stored belong to the company, and may be searched by the company's representatives at any time;
- Governing employees' access to work areas during mandatory time off or enforced leave, and addressing the removal of documents, computer files and work papers from the company's premises, for work to be conducted at another site; and
- A section for written acknowledgment of the terms and conditions of employment by the employee, at the time of hiring, position change, and again at the conclusion of the annual performance review.

Summary:

Embezzlers prefer to commit crimes within companies that do not comply with current personnel laws and regulations; that will not hold employees personally liable for specific types of losses; or that do not maintain written performance standards.

A written Security Training Program for employees at all levels within the company?

Employees may become dissatisfied, confused and reluctant to make decisions when they are uncertain where they fit in the company. Lack of an effective orientation program promotes distrust, fear and anxiety, and may lead to costly mistakes, theft, and acts of sabotage. While monetary gain is the primary motive for embezzlement, revenge is another dominant factor.

An effective orientation program has three (3) elements:

- Orientation: All new employees, regardless of position description, should be oriented regarding the company's philosophy, organizational and reporting structure, goals, priorities and other appropriate information;
- Transfer/Promotion: Any employee who has been transferred to a new department, or has received a promotion, should be thoroughly trained regarding his/her new duties and responsibilities, and the policies, procedures and control mechanisms used in this new capacity; and
- Updating: Any change in management, business philosophy, technology, legal requirements, policy or procedure should require re-training of all involved employees.

Having employees who are knowledgeable about the company's security procedures, the risks associated with each employee's role within the company, and appropriate loss prevention techniques, reduces the potential for operational losses. Experiential training promotes comfort and confidence on the part of employees, which negates two of the most significant factors contributing to an employee's desire to embezzle.

Standardized training for all employees results in a teamwork effort for loss prevention, and promotes reasonable behavioral expectations.

Summary:

Embezzlers prefer to commit crimes within companies that do not practice effective security techniques; that do not assign to them a competent employee as an orientation trainer; or that do not train all employees in loss prevention and security techniques.

A policy prohibiting employees from accepting service of legal process directed at the company but covering wages, accounts or other property of the employee (e.g., levies, attachments, garnishments)? Also, a policy requiring any employee subpoenaed to testify on behalf of the company to notify his/her supervisor?

The company's Security Officer should be made aware if an employee is experiencing a desperate need for money as a result of a civil judgment. Wage garnishments are usually served on the Personnel Department. Subpoenas and Complaints may be served on the employee. Other legal process is likely to be served on the office that houses an employee's account.

Court proceedings may be an intimidating experience for an employee receiving a subpoena to testify on the part of the company. The company should consider assigning a supervisor to accompany the employee, to ensure the employee's participation and to protect the company's interests.

Summary:

Embezzlers prefer to commit crimes within companies that do not practice effective document control techniques; where the company is ignorant about their private lives; and that fail to supervise adequately their representation in company matters.

Employees' acceptance of gifts from customers?

- Employees are often offered gifts by customers or suppliers in appreciation of some special effort or at holidays. A written policy governing what gifts may be accepted, and in what manner, should be included in the company's employee handbook. Gifts of cash, or items convertible to cash, by employees from customers and suppliers should be forbidden.
- Gifts are also given to employees by criminals, to distract the employee's attention from transactions, or to cause the employee to feel guilty if the crime is discovered later.

Summary:

Embezzlers prefer to commit crimes within companies where gratuities are offered and accepted freely; where casual observation would not reveal the size, type or amount of "reward for service" and where a transfer of money or documents would not be suspect.

7.3.3 Documents, Computers and Records

Has the company developed, implemented and provided a means to monitor and periodically update:

The process used to prepare and submit audit work papers, compliance reports and any regulatory documents, to insure that all information is accurate?

Multiple corrections and additions to these documents may indicate undue influence is being exerted upon the preparer to alter the documents to hide irregularities.

Summary:

Embezzlers prefer to commit crimes within companies where documents are altered easily and frequently without leaving an adequate audit trail.

The process used to reconcile official checks and wire and property transfer records?

Embezzlers often use official checks to operate kites and loan and credit frauds, using wire transfers to shift the stolen funds to another location. This is particularly common in companies where the same employee generating the disbursement order or wire or property transfer is also responsible for reconciling the documents.

Summary:

Embezzlers prefer to commit crimes within companies where negotiable documents are unsecured; where improper segregation of duties exists; and where personal identification numbers are shared freely as a matter of convenience.

A policy requiring that all customer documents must be signed in an employee's presence, including financial records, payable instruments, credit applications and loan documents?

- Witnessed documents may be introduced in court more easily that un-witnessed ones. It may be necessary to submit un-witnessed documents to costly and time-consuming document examination, to determine authorship.
- Blank financial documents, payable instruments, credit applications and loan documents are readily available to employees. These may be removed from the premises and new ones created or altered.

Summary:

Embezzlers prefer to commit crimes within companies where identification procedures are ineffective or non-existent; where documents requiring signatures are unsecured; where empty spaces on documents requiring signatures are left empty; and where policy and procedures prohibiting adding, deleting or altering signatures are ineffective or non-existent.

A policy prohibiting the removal of original company documents and computer files from the workplace, and mandating creating copies of critical original documents?

If the embezzlement involves the alteration of records, the embezzler frequently must remove those records to a private location, to make necessary adjustments or destroy the originals. The policy should limit the removal of documents and computer files to copies of originals only, using a sign-in, sign-out form.

Summary:

Embezzlers prefer to commit crimes within companies where document control procedures are ineffective or non-existent; where critical original documents are not inventoried, copied or secured; and where employees have unrestricted access to computer files.

A policy prohibiting financial records, loan papers and similar documents from leaving the premises?

Maintaining absolute control over financial records, loan papers and related documents makes it more difficult to create fictitious accounts; convert, add or delete signature information; or create fictitious persons to ultimately blame if a crime is discovered.

Summary:

Embezzlers prefer to commit crimes within companies where document control procedures are ineffective or non-existent; and where original documents may contain un-witnessed signatures.

A policy prohibiting disbursements as a result of the presentation of an "authorization letter" rather than the presentation of a check, draft, or an official, controlled company document?

Companies routinely negotiate transactions based upon information contained in customer correspondence, and these items of correspondence are subject to interpretation. Honoring only a check, draft or controlled company document leaves no room for interpretation, and indicates that the company is exercising reasonable and prudent care.

Summary:

Embezzlers prefer to commit crimes within companies where original documents may contain un-witnessed signatures; and where transactions are conducted based upon non-uniform or faxed documents and "verification" of the written instructions by phone.

A policy restricting the negotiation of payable instruments bearing facsimile signatures (rubber stamp or computer-generated), or stamped markings, such as PAID, CANCELLED, FOR DEPOSIT ONLY, ORIGINAL, INVOICE, CERTIFIED or similar markings, where the facsimile signature or stamped markings are printed with what appears to be black ink?

- Any business or individual signing or endorsing documents using a facsimile signature should only be permitted to do so with the company's written authorization.
- Copy machines are often used to forge actual documents, and these forgeries are then passed in place of the actual item. Insisting that all facsimile and rubber stamp images be printed with a colored ink makes the passing of forgeries more difficult.

Summary:

Embezzlers prefer to commit crimes within companies where original documents may contain stamped instructions and facsimile signatures; and where those instructions and facsimile signatures are printed with black ink.

A policy restricting a power of attorney used to open new accounts and to direct disbursements?

Companies routinely allow staff level employees to conduct transactions based upon the unverified information contained in a power of attorney. The exclusive use of witnessed or notarized powers of attorney, in the company's own format, reduces the opportunity for fraud and misrepresentation.

Summary:

Embezzlers prefer to commit crimes within companies where a power of attorney may be used to open accounts and to direct disbursements; where several power of attorney formats are in use; and where signatures are un-witnessed.

A policy requiring employees to photocopy identification and related documents furnished to open a new account (driver's license, Social Security card, etc.), and securely storing the photocopies with the account file?

Internal and external criminals depend upon an employee's inability to identify persons and documents at time of trial. Routinely photocopying and marking documents, and retaining them for possible use in court, positively identifies persons and documents; reduces confusion; and enhances successful prosecution and recovery of funds.

Summary:

Embezzlers prefer to commit crimes within companies where controls governing the opening of new accounts are ineffective or non-existent; where new account applicants are improperly identified; and where inadequate account records are maintained.

A policy requiring customers to furnish copies of appropriate sole proprietorship, partnership or corporate papers when opening a commercial account, and securely storing the photocopies with the account file?

The manner in which a customer company operates its business directly affects how the company conducts its own. Businesses tend to de-emphasize effective internal controls, reporting requirements, documentation and document handling procedures. This may be as a result of poor training, ignorance, convenience or design.

Requiring that a prospective commercial accountholder furnish appropriate documentation, indicates that the company has taken reasonable care to identify a legitimate customer.

Summary:

Embezzlers prefer to commit crimes within companies where controls governing the opening of new accounts, particularly commercial accounts, are ineffective or non-existent; where new account applicants are improperly identified; where inadequate account records are maintained; and where commercial account holders do not practice effective dual control techniques.

A program to review closely sole proprietorship accounts, particularly cash-intensive businesses such as general contractors, restaurants and bars, and senior citizen accounts?

General contractors, restaurants and bars are examples of those types of businesses most likely to practice ineffective accounting controls; declare bankruptcy; practice kiting; and become involved in "cash flow" crimes. These types of businesses are also used frequently as money laundering vehicles.

Senior citizen accounts are often linked to significant funds and are often poorly monitored by the accountholder. These accounts are particularly vulnerable to theft by family members, and may be used by employees for embezzlement and bunco schemes.

Summary:

Embezzlers prefer to commit crimes within companies that maintain a significant sole proprietorship client base, particularly cash-based businesses; and that actively solicits and maintains a significant number of senior citizen accounts.

A program to monitor closely all new account activity, particularly employees' accounts, for at least ninety (90) days, and document and follow up on all unusual activity?

The majority of credit and checking account frauds are committed by two distinctly different types of account holders: criminals and the company's best customers.

Employees, who may also be professional check kiters, will operate their schemes for 45 - 90 days, and then close the scheme down and withdraw funds. These accounts are subject to a predictable cycle of activity:

- **1 - 30 days**: Minimum activity to test the company's posting and statement routines.
- **31 - 60 days**: Moderate activity to develop the rhythm of transactions necessary to establish a busy, honest and predictable appearance to a casual observer. Each transaction will be of a greater dollar amount than the previous transaction. Deposits will be made in relation to the number of days' float available.

- **61 - 90 days:** Excessive activity necessary to keep the kite afloat, with the kiter making several deposits a day. Each transaction will be of a greater dollar amount than the previous transaction. Deposits will be made in relation to the number of days' float available.

The company's "best customers" will use a kite to provide necessary cash flow, and will repay the kite when the actual cash flow is sufficient to satisfy immediate needs. The company finds these persons frequently but, because they are "best customers" the company will allow them to deliver funds to cover the overdrafts.

Summary:

Embezzlers prefer to commit crimes within companies that do not routinely monitor new account activity; and which condone overdraft activity.

A policy to prohibit "less cash" deposits to any commercial account?

Businesses often consolidate several areas of responsibility into one position description (e.g., accounts payable, accounts receivable, delivery inventory control, mail opening, check depositing, check preparation, checkbook reconciliation).

A popular type of embezzlement is to hide the true receipt of negotiable documents, prepare a deposit slip, pre-sign a forgery of the owner's signature, and deposit the items with a "less cash" request.

Sole proprietorships and partnerships are most prone to these crimes. Refusing to allow "less cash" transactions for any of the company's commercial accounts removes the opportunity for employees to mix cash and negotiable documents and confusing an audit trail.

Summary:

Embezzlers prefer to commit crimes within companies that allow "less cash" deposits to commercial accounts, particularly involving documents containing un-witnessed signatures.

A policy restricting the negotiation of any payable instrument or document containing alterations or illegible information?

Documents are often intercepted, altered, and presented for payment or deposit. Allowing only witnessed alterations, and only with a supervisor's approval, indicates that the company is exercising reasonable care with its customers and documents.

Illegible signatures are often created by persons who sign their names frequently, as a matter of convenience. These are the same people who generally do not review the documents at statement processing time. Forgers know that it is much more difficult to compare a scrawled, illegible signature successfully than a clear, careful, legible signature.

Summary:

Embezzlers prefer to commit crimes within companies that allow the deposit or encashment of to altered or illegible documents; and which allow an illegible signature as the only one on the financial record.

A policy prohibiting the use or negotiation of any document written with a red, ball-point pen?

Documents written upon with a red, ball-point pen do not create a legible microfiche or photocopy. These types of documents are often used in "statement cycle" crimes, particularly internal property transfers, loan frauds and kites.

Summary:

Embezzlers prefer to commit crimes within companies that allow the negotiation of documents written with a red, ball-point pen, particularly financial documents.

A policy requiring that a personalized insert be placed in its check-imprinting machine, and that the reverse of all imprinted documents be examined for alterations?

Official checks and similar items created with a check-imprinting machine are often stolen, forged and altered. An insert containing the company's name, placed into the machine at time of manufacture, and used on all official checks and similar items, reduces the opportunity for negotiation of these items.

Imprinted documents are often "raised" or altered, with a pen. The alteration is often not evident upon the face of the document, but is often evident upon the document's reverse side.

Summary:

Embezzlers prefer to commit crimes within companies that use a check-imprinting machine without also using an identifying insert; that type information upon the document, rather than writing the information by hand or using a computer printer; and that do not routinely examine an imprinted document's reverse side for alterations.

7.3.4 Facilities

Has the company developed, implemented and provided a means to monitor and periodically update:

A policy requiring that at least two (2) employees must open and close a facility?

Not only is such a policy critical to addressing employee safety during robberies, burglaries and hostage events, but it limits access to the company's premises. Embezzlers frequently arrive for work early and leave the premises later than other employees, simply because they cannot conduct their embezzlement activities during normal hours without the risk of discovery.

Summary:

Embezzlers prefer to commit crimes within companies that allow employees to enter a facility alone, particularly during non-business hours.

A policy governing the issuance, control and collection of keys; security and alarm access codes and devices; cash vault security; cash-handling facility countdown after an unusual incident; and other security devices maintained as dual control techniques?

Employees frequently share keys, particularly both keys in a dual custody set, because it is more convenient than constantly locating the person who has custody of the other key. This also allows employees to manufacture unauthorized duplicate keys. Employees also share combinations in the same manner.

Key boxes often contain a set of "emergency keysets" containing unauthorized duplicates of dual custody keys. This may allow lost keys to be unreported, because an "extra" key is available.

Security and alarm codes and passwords are routinely shared for convenience, and are changed infrequently.

Companies are not always successful in retrieving keys and other access devices from employees who terminate employment. Keys, access codes and devices, and passwords are not always changed when an employee terminates employment. The decision is often made on a case-by-case basis.

Cash-handling employees often store and collect containers of cash and negotiable documents within their assigned cash vault areas without supervision or the presence of another control employee. Night drops are also often reconciled in single custody.

Upon the discovery of a significant out-of-balance count, a full reconcilement of a cash-handling facility is generally initiated.

Rarely is a second full reconcilement initiated when the cause of the out-of-balance condition is located. Embezzlers often use the time period immediately following a reconcilement to commit a theft.

Summary:

Embezzlers prefer to commit crimes within companies that practice ineffective or non-existent key and combination controls; which seldom change combinations, passwords and alarm codes; and which fail to control effectively necessary reconcilement tasks.

A policy governing the use and storage of employee identification stamps or other similar marking devices, and authorization forms?

Embezzlers rarely commit their crimes in an area where they maintain sole control or responsibility. They prefer to enter another employee's area of control and use documents, marking devices and other means to direct suspicion towards another employee. These means may include employee identification stamps, authorization forms, unattended keys, and unsecured access codes and combinations.

Summary

Embezzlers prefer to commit crimes within companies that allow certain critical functions to be under the control of a single person.

7.4 SUMMARY

This section addresses the development of an effective risk assessment model to use in determining your company's vulnerability to acts of embezzlement. The next section provides you with the Embezzlement Prevention Training Program as the final step in the prevention process.

8.0 EMBEZZLEMENT PREVENTION TRAINING PROGRAM

Companies are often wary of mentioning embezzlement to employees, believing that employees will begin thinking of and planning their own embezzlements. And rarely does a company create a formal training program to address the embezzlement issue, fearing that such a program will give employees "ideas". Companies hire what they believe to be the most promising or competent employees available: those persons who demonstrate an aptitude for the position, or are the most skilled in their particular area of expertise. If the employee is that skilled, or if the promising employee has passed his/her probationary period, the employee has developed sufficient working knowledge to embezzle.

An employee who is trained in loss prevention and security techniques is an asset to any company. This employee knows where the "windows of opportunity" lie within his/her position, and looks for techniques to stop potential losses. Developing and implementing a company-wide embezzlement prevention training program fulfills several goals:

- Developing the program causes senior management and board members to make clear the company's position regarding illegal and unethical conduct;
- By acknowledging that embezzlement exists, the company alerts employees that it is "on guard" against and prepared to deal with this type of crime;
- By teaching employees what to look for in their own and other's behavior, the company may prevent embezzlement by providing options if an employee is experiencing any of the commonly-accepted symptoms, and direction and support if the employee wants to report a suspicious incident or employee; and
- If an embezzlement does occur, the program makes investigation easier because employees will have been trained to help the investigator The program will also make prosecution easier by helping to establish that the company trained its employees appropriately; followed approved policies and procedures; and by helping the investigator to effectively document the investigation.

8.1 Embezzlement Prevention Training Program Handout

This company has always maintained the highest standards of business conduct. These standards were developed from a belief that a company must operate according to the basic principles of honesty, integrity, and concern for the community in order to gain and hold the public's trust.

It is critical to our success, and to your continued employment, that we conduct all of our business affairs according to these principles.

As an employee, you are responsible for making our commitment to honesty, integrity and concern for the community your commitment as well. We value each employee's positive contributions to the company. We recognize that working within a business offers many opportunities for personal and professional growth, as well as many temptations and opportunities to steal.

It is this company's policy to cooperate with law enforcement and regulatory agencies. We will also, whenever necessary, pursue both criminal and civil remedies against all employees who commit criminal acts against the company or its customers, or against other employees.

It is a simple fact that if an employee wants to commit a crime, he/she will commit that crime, regardless of any policies, procedures, laws or other regulations. The best that we can do is to design and implement effective policies and procedures to lessen the opportunity for, or impact of, criminal behavior. To this end, this company has developed comprehensive operations guidelines for you to follow.

The purpose of this material is to help you understand the very important issues associated with the crime of embezzlement. Because industry-wide losses caused by acts of embezzlement are more significant than losses caused by all other types of business crimes combined, we consider this topic appropriate for all employees. This material is to be discussed with each employee, regardless of position, and each member of the company's board of directors.

Embezzlement is the nation's most popular financial crime. The negative impact upon the nation's businesses and the public trust in those companies, has resulted primarily from either acts of embezzlement or self-serving transactions committed by employees. Yet, we have learned that embezzlement is the most predictable, rhythmic and cyclical of all crimes. And one of the easiest crimes to prevent.

8.2 What Is Embezzlement?

Embezzlement is defined as both misuse and theft. Embezzlement, or defalcation, is the intentional misuse or misappropriation of funds or property entrusted to an employee. The majority of embezzlements begin as a simple misuse of the company's funds for a short-term personal purpose.

Misuse is abuse of privilege or position, without a specific intent to steal. Examples of misuse are:

- Using the company's telephones, copy machines, and mail services for personal business;
- Using the company's equipment, machinery, vehicles, supplies, and computer programs for personal business; and
- Using the company's expense accounts and credit cards to pay for personal expenses.

Misappropriation is the taking of funds or property with a specific intent to steal. Examples of misappropriation are:

- Stealing cash or negotiable documents from another employee's area of control;

- Creating "cash loans" from one's own area of control to pay personal expenses on a "temporary" basis;
- Operating credit, interest and check kites;
- Short-changing customers during any transaction; and
- Arranging secret unsecured, personal loans from "favorite customers".

8.3 WHY ARE EMBEZZLEMENTS SO COSTLY?

Estimates are that for each $1.00 lost due to any crime, the company loses an additional $4.00. To put it another way, each loss caused by internal or external crime costs at least five times the original amount:

- One dollar in actual cash is lost;
- A second dollar is spent identifying how the crime was committed;
- A third dollar is spent in identifying who committed the crime;
- A fourth dollar is spent prosecuting the person who committed the crime; and
- A fifth dollar is spent in suing the person who committed the crime for the recovery of the money taken.

These calculations are conservative, and don't take into account the other losses the company will ultimately suffer. Remember that these losses affect our profit, and ultimately may affect your employment.

Embezzlements are emotional as well as financial crimes. Victims of embezzlement display the same progression and range of symptoms displayed by victims of sexual assault or catastrophic disasters: shock, disbelief, denial, rage, grief and recovery. This cycle generally peaks within six months of the crime, and it may take up to three years for the company to recover fully.

The actual monetary loss may be considerable, but it will be relatively minor compared to the losses caused by these factors that will become evident after an embezzlement has been discovered:

- Lowered employee morale due to increased security measures, and aggravated by distrust of other employees;
- Employees' disorientation and their accompanying mistakes, resulting in poor customer service;
- A reduction in actual tasks performed by employees, because of their pre-occupation with events related to the embezzlement;
- Disruption of normal operational activities as employees are re-allocated to perform investigative and security tasks;
- Adverse publicity due to management's inability to control the flow of information to the media; and

- The necessary interaction with the criminal justice system (law enforcement, courts and corrections).

8.4 Why Do Employees Embezzle?

All people have reasons for behaving as they do. All people have developed behavior patterns. No person changes an established behavior pattern without a significant reason. The principle of cause and effect applies to the relationship between a change in some aspect of a person's life, and an accompanying change in that person's behavior. There are three (3) primary motives for a person to embezzle:

- Need for money;
- Revenge; and
- Excitement.

8.5 What Symptoms Do Embezzlers Display?

While there is no such person as an "average" embezzler, most employees who embezzle consistently display universal crisis "symptoms". These symptoms are also known as "crisis signals" and serve as a warning that an employee is unbalanced mentally, physically, emotionally, spiritually or financially. These symptoms are clues that are often apparent to supervisors and coworkers, who are in daily contact with the employee.

Demonstrating any one of these symptoms does not mean that an employee is embezzling. It simply means that the employee is "at risk" of a breakdown of his/her morals, values, and ethics, and that intervention may prevent an escalation of the imbalance. As you review these symptoms, recognize that most people have demonstrated at least one such behavior or lifestyle event at some point in their lives.

The listed symptoms all involve a significant change in behavior, attitude, lifestyle or job performance. Active embezzlers generally display addictive behavior, and simultaneously demonstrate three (3) or more of these symptoms:

- Displaying a suddenly enriched, extravagant lifestyle, unsubstantiated by normal wages;
- Frequently requesting cash advances, or delaying repayment of prior loans;
- Receiving telephone calls at work from creditors;
- Having wages garnished;
- Borrowing constantly from fellow employees, and seldom repaying these loans;
- Displaying careless or sloppy work habits; failing to follow instructions or giving conflicting instructions; making unusual errors in judgment; being absent frequently from the work area; suffering repeated or unreasonable

accidents on or off the job; or displaying a significant change in behavior, attitude or performance;

- Failing to report for work or offering poorly explained absences from work; being chronically tardy and leaving work early; or taking excessive advantage of available sick time;
- Refusing to take time off, or passing vacation options;
- Constantly working overtime without sufficient reason, and often without pay;
- Gambling at the workplace, or excessive references to gambling activity;
- Making references to current excessive consumption of alcoholic beverages; consumption of alcoholic beverages during the work day; or evidence of frequent hangovers;
- Making references to substance abuse of a drug other than alcohol, either the overuse of prescription medication, or consumption of illegal drugs; substance abuse in any form during the work day; or evidence of the cumulative effects associated with substance abuse;
- Making references to significant domestic problems; telephone calls received at work from family members regarding domestic problems; or evidence of physical, mental or emotional spousal abuse and accompanying signals of distress;
- Meeting with questionable associates at the work place; and
- Creating disruptive or erratic behavior; displaying withdrawn or preoccupied manner; inappropriately displaying anger and frustration; suffering from extreme mood swings; and displaying a visible deterioration of physical appearance, and mental and emotional stability.

8.6 What Are My Responsibilities?

This company has developed a "Code of Conduct" statement, to define clearly what is, and is not, acceptable business behavior. This Code of Conduct is applicable to all employees, regardless of position, and to each member of the company's board of directors.

The Code of Conduct reflects the company's guiding philosophy, and describes our "company culture". Company culture is defined as the environment influenced by the prevalent morals, ethics, ideals, and standards for behavior, as developed, implemented and demonstrated by management. In other words, the company's conscience.

The Code of Conduct will be applied and enforced universally, not selectively. A complete Code of Conduct is included in your employee handbook. The sections of the Code of Conduct pertaining to your role in embezzlement prevention and investigation are as follows:

- The company operates based upon policies, procedures and techniques designed to provide a safe and secure working environment, and to minimize the opportunity for mistakes, misunderstandings, and inconvenience to employees and customers. You are expected to work within those policies and procedures, and your position description, at all times.
- You may not exceed the scope of your position description and level of authority without specific authorization from senior management, nor assume more responsibilities than you are authorized to exercise.
- All employees are required to provide handwriting and fingerprint samples, and a personal photograph at the request of the company. The company will conduct a credit check on all applicants, and may conduct a credit check at unspecified intervals during any employee's term of employment.
- Any incoming or outgoing telephone call on the company's telephone may be monitored or recorded, at any time and without prior notice.
- All employee accounts are subject to review by the company's audit department or internal investigators, at any time and without prior notice.
- All lockers, desks, cabinets, and similar places where things can be stored, belong to the company, and may be searched by its representatives at any time and without prior notice.
- You are not expected to act as a law enforcement officer, or a "cop". All employees are responsible for exercising "reasonable and prudent care" during each transaction or operation, while performing the tasks that they are employed to perform. While exercising reasonable and prudent care, you may uncover a crime in progress, but the primary goal is to minimize the risk inherent in all transactions. If you do suspect that a crime is being or has been committed, you must report your suspicions as discussed below.
- Employees' schedules and work assignments may be changed at unpredictable intervals. This is not designed to inconvenience you, but to promote effective internal controls.
- In addition to any statutory and regulatory required limitations on the solicitation and receipt of things of value and the use of privileged and confidential information, you must use extra caution to avoid any activity, investment, interest or association that could affect your business judgment. Even an appearance of conflict of interest could harm your reputation and the company's.
- No employee may make a statement concerning the company or its activities to the media without first obtaining the authorization to do so from the Security Officer or his/her designate.

  Reference **SUSPICIOUS ACTIVITY REPORT**, located after section 8.7.

- You have an obligation to report unusual or suspicious events caused by either internal or external sources. Report your suspicions concerning external events to your immediate supervisor. Report your suspicions concerning internal events to either the company's Security Officer or Auditor, and not to your immediate supervisor.

- Both the Security Officer and Auditor are aware that the person reporting the suspicion is acting upon his/her beliefs; that the reporting employee expects confidentiality; and that all employees have a reasonable right to that expectation. Confidentiality is limited – the Security Officer or Auditor may need to disclose your information to law enforcement agencies and/or senior management as part of internal investigation.
- You have an obligation to participate in any investigation involving the company's security, including any possible loss to the company, as long as your role in that investigation stems from your involvement as an employee. Any legal proceedings requiring your participation as an employee will be coordinated by the company.

8.7 Summary

This company strives to provide a work environment that is conducive to personal growth, accomplishment and satisfaction. We feel that all employees need to know where they stand if they are to be part of our service team. This company expects honesty, continuing competency and teamwork as part of the employee-employer relationship. You should expect to find those attributes displayed by all employees at all levels.

We ask that you participate in our crime prevention efforts, particularly with regard to the very real danger of embezzlement. If you have any questions about this material, contact the Security Officer or Auditor privately.

[This page intentionally left blank]

SUSPICIOUS ACTIVITY REPORT

Report # ____________________

Date:	Time:
Location:	
Branch/department:	
Persons involved:	
Employee #1	
Employee #2	
Employee #3	
Witness #1	
Address	
City/State/ZIP	
Home phone	
Work phone	
Describe activity:	

(continued on next page)

Notification:	
Officer notified:	
Date and time:	
In person or by phone:	
Agency notified:	
Date and time:	
In person or by phone	

Disposition:

Note: Completion of this preliminary report does not replace required reporting to regulatory agencies or the FBI.

9.0 LEADER'S GUIDE: EMBEZZLEMENT PREVENTION TRAINING PROGRAM

LEADER: Auditor, Security Officer, Department or Office Manager

DISCUSSION TIME: 60 minutes for presentation, 30 minutes for discussion.

9.1 OVERVIEW

This company has developed and implemented a strategic plan for preventing losses from internal sources. Training the company's personnel appropriately to implement the plan is critical to the plan's success.

9.2 OBJECTIVES

- To describe the company's policy regarding employee-employer relations, the Code of Conduct and any related regulatory issues, and criminal activities committed by employees.
- To inform all personnel about the company's loss prevention program, particularly regarding embezzlement, including the policies and procedures relating to the program's implementation on both a company and a department-wide basis.
- To train each employee to respond appropriately to suspicious events.

9.3 DISCUSSION MATERIALS

- Training handout: Embezzlement Prevention Training Program
- Employee Handbook containing Code of Conduct

9.4 MEETING PREPARATION: SECURITY OFFICER OR AUDITOR

1. Review or discuss the results of the latest operations audit to:
    - Determine the types and amounts of losses due to internal sources, if any;
    - Determine what controls, policies or procedures were violated that contributed to the losses, if any;
    - Determine what controls, policies or procedures are required to reduce future exposure to loss, if any, and recommend their implementation; and
    - Verify that appropriate controls, policies or procedures are now in place.
2. Review the company's Code of Conduct and Employee Handbook and the Embezzlement Prevention Training Program, and:
    - Determine if each is consistent with the other;
    - With a representative of the Personnel Department, draft any necessary changes to the Code of Conduct, Employee Handbook or Training Program to make them consistent with each other and to reflect the company's policy; and

- o Submit the completed Employee Handbook, including the Code of Conduct, and the Training Program for approval.

3. After receiving the necessary approval:
    - o Prepare information packets for each employee and board member;
    - o Prepare training rosters to document attendance at training events, and receipt forms for all personnel;
    - o Meet with the following groups separately:
        - ✓ Board of directors;
        - ✓ Executives and senior managers; and
        - ✓ Branch and department managers and supervisors.
4. Schedule staff training meetings, to be delivered by the appropriate managers;
5. Supply each manager with sufficient Employee Handbooks, Training Program handouts, rosters and receipt forms for all personnel and
    - o Have signed receipts returned to the Personnel Department for placement in the employee's file;
    - o Place the completed rosters in your security files; and
    - o Respond appropriately to the statements and suggestions forwarded to you by the manager delivering the training.

9.5 MEETING PREPARATION: MANAGERS AND SUPERVISORS

Prepare for the meeting by:

- Reading the Employee Handbook to familiarize yourself with the information, and to insure that you understand the key elements. Discuss questions or concerns with your supervisor.
- Reading the Training Program handout to familiarize yourself with the information, and to insure that you understand the key elements of embezzlement. Discuss questions or concerns with the Security Officer or Auditor.
- Distributing the Employee Handbook and Training Program handout and any related materials to each employee in your branch, office or department one (1) week before your meeting. Instruct employees to read all materials, note questions or comments directly on the copies, and to bring the materials to the meeting.
- Assembling all appropriate materials and displays to use as references during the meeting. Have extra copies of the materials available at the meeting.
    - ▪ Preparing a meeting outline on a flip chart to help guide your presentation, if appropriate.
    - ▪ Preparing a training roster. Reference the **Training Roster** form provided after Section 9.7.

9.6 CONDUCT THE MEETING

- Assign an employee to complete the **Training Roster** form and take notes during the meeting, and to deliver the signed roster and notes to you at the end of the meeting for your report. Reference the sample **Memo** located after Section 9.7.
- Introduce the purpose of the meeting, and the training program objectives. (Refer to your flip chart, if appropriate, throughout the presentation.)
- Refer to the Training Program handout and;
- Describe the company's:
  1. Business philosophy, duties and responsibilities to customers and employees;
  2. Efforts to develop and maintain a working environment that promotes honest and integrity for all employees;
  3. Recognition that opportunities for theft exist at the company; and
  4. Commitment to cooperate with law enforcement and regulatory agencies in all cases of suspected theft.
- Define embezzlement as a crime; discuss the differences and similarities between both misuse and misappropriation; discuss examples; and describe the potential impact of embezzlement upon the company.
- Describe the importance of following established policy and procedures, and practicing loss prevention techniques; describe the projected financial and emotional losses.
- Discuss the recognized motivations for embezzlement: the need for money, revenge and excitement.
- Describe the "crisis signals" that embezzlers display, and emphasize that demonstration of any one of these symptoms does not mean that an employee is embezzling.
  1. Acknowledge that most people have demonstrated at least one of the crisis signals at some point in their lives;
  2. Emphasize that active embezzlers generally display addictive behavior, and simultaneously demonstrate three (3) or more of the embezzlement symptoms; and
  3. Emphasize that the listed symptoms all involve a significant change in behavior, attitude, lifestyle or job performance.
- Refer to the Employee Handbook and Code of Conduct, and:
  1. Describe the terms "corporate culture" and "code of conduct";
  2. Discuss each employee's duties and responsibilities;
  3. Require each employee to sign and return the acknowledgment form contained in the Employee Handbook; and
  4. Open the meeting to questions and comments.

9.7 AFTER THE MEETING

- Retrieve the **Training Roster** form, the **Seminar Evaluation** form and notes from the note-taking employee.
- Using the notes and your personal observation, indicate in writing what issues need to be resolved and your suggestions for resolution.
- Complete the information requested on the attached sample **Memo**, and return the Memo, **Training Roster**, and your written report to the Security Officer or Auditor.

MEMO

To: Security Officer or Auditor

From: ____________________________

Date: ____________________________

Subject: Annual Embezzlement Prevention Training Meeting

I conducted an operational inspection for the _______________________________

Branch/Office/Department on _________________________.

I reviewed the appropriate branch/office/department's policies and procedures on _______________________.

I conducted a training meeting regarding the company's Embezzlement Prevention Training program on ____________________.

A copy of the training roster is attached.

Check one:

_______ The branch/office/department is in compliance with all policies and procedures relating to this program.

_______ The branch/office/department is not in compliance with all policies and procedures relating to this program. Please contact me immediately to discuss the indicated items:

_______ POLICY:

____

____

_______ PROCEDURE:

____

____

____________________________________ ____________________________

Name Title

[This page intentionally left blank]

Embezzlement Prevention Training Program

Training Roster

Date: ____________________

Branch/Office/Department: ____

Printed Name	Signature

[This page intentionally left blank]

Seminar Evaluation: Embezzlement Prevention Annual Training

Seminar name: ______________________

Seminar location:

Your name (optional):

Your title:

Seminar Content & Organization (1/Poor - 5/Excellent)	Rating
1. Will you be able to apply this information in your position?	
2. Was the seminar content well-organized?	
3. Were the handout materials useful and informative?	
4. Were the seminar topics adequately addressed?	
Seminar Instructor:	Rating
5. Were questions answered to your satisfaction?	
6. Was the instructor organized and well-prepared?	
7. Was the instructor knowledgeable and up-to-date in the subject matter?	
8. Did the instructor display enthusiasm for the topics and the class responses?	
9. Were you encouraged to ask questions and express opinions?	
10. Were the teaching aids, handout materials and techniques effective?	
Comments:	

[This page intentionally left blank]

bizmanualz®

Accounting Policies, Procedures & Forms

Section 600

Index

Section 600

Index

INDEX

SECTION Page or Heading

A

B

C

D

E

F

G

H

J

L

M

P

R

T

Y

[This page intentionally left blank]

Upgrade Today

Coupon Code: BMPB99

With this *Professional's Ready-to-Use Procedures Series* book, you've realized the benefits of pre-written procedures as a reference tool. Bizmanualz also publishes policies and procedures manuals in three-ring binder version that comes with a CD containing all contents in easily editable MS Word files.

Coupon code **BMPB99** allows you to deduct the price of this book from any editable manual or manual bundle that you purchase at www.bizmanualz.com. To view samples from any manual, visit **www.bizmanualz.com/samples**.

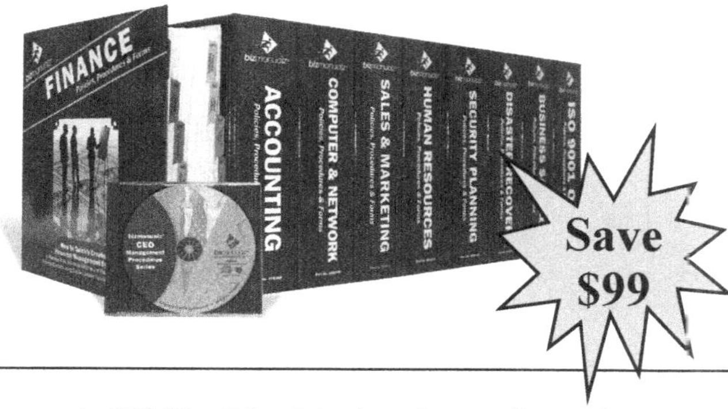

This coupon entitles you to **$99.00 off** the list price of any policy and procedure manual (with CD Rom) from Bizmanualz. That's right, we're offering you the entire purchase price of this book as a rebate toward your purchase of any Bizmanualz Policies, Procedures and Forms Manual.

You can place your order online or via phone or fax. Be sure to use coupon code **BMPB99** when you place your order.

www.bizmanualz.com

800-466-9953 (toll-free)

(314-863-5079 from outside the US)

314-863-6571 (fax)

One coupon per book. Coupon may not be used in conjunction with other promotional discounts or offers. Purchaser must use or reference coupon code listed above at the time of order. Coupon expires December 31, 2010

CPSIA information can be obtained at www.ICGtesting.com
Printed in the USA
LVOW03*2059240614

391557LV00002B/3/P

9 781931 591331